IMAGINING RELIGIOUS TOLERATION: A LITERARY HISTORY OF AN IDEA, 1600–1830

Imagining Religious Toleration: A Literary History of an Idea, 1600–1830

EDITED BY ALISON CONWAY AND DAVID ALVAREZ

UNIVERSITY OF TORONTO PRESS
Toronto Buffalo London

Library and Archives Canada Cataloguing in Publication

Title: Imagining religious toleration : a literary history of an idea, 1600–1830 / edited by Alison Conway and David Alvarez.
Names: Conway, Alison, editor. | Alvarez, David, 1966– editor.
Description: Includes bibliographical references and index.
Identifiers: Canadiana 20190098856 | ISBN 9781487501792 (hardcover)
Subjects: LCSH: English literature – Early modern, 1500–1700 – History and criticism. | LCSH: English literature – 19th century – History and criticism. | LCSH: Religious tolerance in literature.
Classification: LCC PR428.R46 I43 2019 | DDC 820.9/382—dc23

This book has been published with the assistance of the Social Science Research Council of Canada, DePauw University, and the University of Western Ontario.

University of Toronto Press acknowledges the financial assistance to its publishing program of the Canada Council for the Arts and the Ontario Arts Council, an agency of the Government of Ontario.

Contents

Acknowledgments

We would like to acknowledge, with thanks, the support provided by the University of Western Ontario and the Social Sciences Research Council of Canada for the symposium that allowed us to share the ideas presented in these essays. SSHRC and DePauw University also provided support for the research assistants who helped with the preparation of the manuscript for publication. We thank the contributors for their engagement, our editor, Mark Thompson, the readers for the University of Toronto Press, and our copy editor, Anne Laughlin.

IMAGINING RELIGIOUS TOLERATION: A LITERARY HISTORY
OF AN IDEA, 1600–1830

Introduction: Imagining Religious Toleration[1]

ALISON CONWAY

In the spring of 2018 I visited the University of York, where I was giving a talk on interfaith marriage, religious toleration, and the eighteenth-century novel. Before delivering my presentation, I met with Matt Matravers, the director of the Morrell Centre for Toleration, who observed that debates about religious toleration seemed to have become stuck, circling back to the same questions over and over again: Should crosses be displayed in government legislatures? Does free speech need to accommodate concerns about blasphemy? And so on. Positions within the toleration debate have hardened. On one side are those providing critiques of toleration discourse, such as Wendy Brown, Talal Asad, and Michael Sandel.; on the other are those who argue in defence of Western liberal traditions, such as John Rawls, Richard Rorty, and Joseph Raz. The irony of finding academia at an impasse in this particular historical moment was not lost on either of us: every day brings news of religious tensions fanning the flames of global conflict and widening partisan divisions within nations. The need to find compelling ways of speaking to these problems could not be more obvious. But how to breathe new life into this urgent, yet ossified, conversation?

Imagining Religious Toleration addresses this question by pursuing two lines of investigation. First, it studies representations of religious toleration in English literature before 1832 to show how imaginative writing casts light on subjects occluded by political and philosophical histories. We attend to a diverse group of literary texts that answer, in a variety of ways, the questions: What can literature say about toleration? How does literature produce and manage feelings of tolerance and intolerance? How was the "literary" understood to be connected to, or distinct from, political and religious discourses, in the advent of Western modernity? While we make no claims for the necessity or efficacy of literature as a means of promoting toleration, we do consider literary representations to be an insightful measure for a culture's understanding of the idea of coexistence in any given moment, precisely because they reveal what historical records and philosophical accounts do not show: the uneven development of modes of endurance and engagement among individuals and communities living in worlds riddled with conflict over religious differences.

The Whig narrative of progress that, in the nineteenth and twentieth centuries, shaped accounts of "the rise of toleration" in the West has been well studied.[2] Our intervention addresses the tendency of literary histories to underscore the secularization thesis advanced by this narrative. The reasons behind this rehearsal stem from interests in a range of subjects including the scientific revolution and its interest in the material world; modes of literary "politeness" that counter the force of religious affects in the eighteenth century; new literary forms like the realist novel and their interest in religious pluralism.[3] It seems clear that we are not yet "beyond" the secularization thesis despite a resurgence of critical interest in religious subjects. Peter Coviello convincingly argues that "we are only now beginning to grasp how deeply we remain in it: how shaped our conceptual frameworks are, down to their most elemental premises, by secularization."[4] What is required, Coviello claims, is a "different, broader kind of reimagining," one that acknowledges the extent to which "our very analytic tools and categories are built to produce the very secularization theses history has since disproven."[5] This study contributes to that reimagining.

Our second concern is to show how the methodologies of literary criticism and theory can open up a range of discourses to new findings. Thus "the literary," for our purposes, encompasses both works of literature and literary modes taken up by other textual practices. We ask: What literary techniques did philosophers, theologians, and political theorists use to frame the questions central to the idea and practice of religious toleration? The methodologies of literary analysis, we argue, reveal terrain as yet unexplored. By tracing the rhetoric employed by a wide range of authors, we see how tropes and figures we associate with literary texts – theatrical personae, for example, or narrative characters – shaped a variety of rhetorical practices and their hermeneutics over the course of two centuries.

Our investigation of religious toleration and the literary (broadly conceived) brings into sharp focus the social imaginary within which toleration's ethical quandaries appear. Instead of approaching the history of religious toleration either in relation to the development of tolerant individuals or to state sovereignty after Westphalia, these essays try to think the ethics and politics of toleration together. Our historical overview provides an understanding of religious toleration as a "complex and slippery historical phenomenon" in all of its modes – as imaginative fiction, philosophical principle, cultural practice, and state policy.[6] Further, our attention to what Jonathan Sheehan calls a "media-driven concept of the Enlightenment" allows us to tell a story of modernity that moves beyond the either/or accounts that have shaped traditional and revisionist narratives about religion: that either religion was "replaced" by humanist modes of thought or it proved resilient to, and critical of, the new science.[7] Instead of considering the rise of print culture as the rise of tolerance and secularization – in which the social bonds of religion find secular replacements – we explore how literary modes shape the formation of secularity: the historical background conditions that make modern religious toleration possible.[8] Such accounts of toleration insist neither on the triumph of scepticism over belief nor on the deepening of commitments to Christian charity to explain secularity's evolution after the Reformation. While we want to guard against the limits of Whig historiography, we also want to find some way to trace a path from the seventeenth-century's deep suspicion of toleration to the passing of the Catholic Relief Act in 1828, to tell a story that can account for the xenophobic violence of the Gordon Riots of 1780 and the new forms of global thinking in the Enlightenment and its aftermath. What links the essays in this volume is a commitment to a full account of the complexity of the texts that have grappled with the subject of religious toleration and the traditions to which they contribute. That is, we have tried to set aside what we think we know about toleration, to let these earlier texts speak to us, and to each other. A respect for the uncanny ability of the literary to put its finger on the pulse of history marks the critical disposition of the work collected here.

This study draws together literary periods from early modern to Romantic about which cultural historians have told very different stories of transformation and evolution. In the field of early modern studies, for instance, scholars have participated fully in the "religious turn" in literary history, taking up one strand of postsecularism – its commitment to re-weighting religious identities and practices in response to earlier humanist narratives of progress toward secularism.[9] In doing so, however, it has made few efforts to connect these histories to subsequent literary periods or to the present. By contrast, in the field of eighteenth-century studies relatively few literary critics have undertaken new histories of religion, as pointed out in a recent article by Corrinne Harol and Alison Conway: "For many years we assumed that Enlightenment essentially meant secularization, that while the Enlightenment project may have had nefarious consequences, secularity was perhaps the most longstanding and positive of the Enlightement's accomplishments."[10] Similar assumptions have led Romanticists to characterize early nineteenth-century literature as a response to the impasses of English Enlightenment thought, particularly its Anglican/deist hegemony; critics use the eighteenth century as a foil for what they consider to be a more fully realized aesthetic, secularized agenda, especially in Romantic poetry. Placed side by side, these accounts, as yet, say little to each other – scholars of the eighteenth century, for example, are unlikely to agree with the portrait of their literature drawn by Romanticists. In response to this impasse, the present collection of essays begins to sketch out what literary history from the early modern period to Romanticism might look like when not structured by the assumptions of the secularization thesis. Indeed, we have much to learn from one another. By drawing all three periods together here, we hope to revise literary history by thinking less about the "rise" of toleration and literature than their linked historical engagement.

Religious Tolerance in the Literary Imagination

In a 2013 essay, historian Alexandra Walsham argues that "we must place the imaginative world of literature at the centre of our investigations into the cultures of coexistence that emerged in early modern England."[11] Why? Because, as Walsham argues, sixteenth- and seventeenth-century authors put into words feelings that attended the experiences of both intolerance and tolerance. In their writing, she claims, they "circumnavigated the psychological thickets and negotiated the moral predicaments posed by pluralism."[12] This volume takes up Walsham's challenge, exploring in detail the questions she and others have raised in recent years about the contributions made by literary texts to the history of religious toleration in the West. How has literature fostered, or compromised, cultural practices of coexistence since the Reformation? What habits of mind did literature associate with the pain of difference, the pleasures of empathy at the advent of modernity? How do literary works reveal and rearticulate the historical conditions that shaped earlier understandings of tolerance as a lived experience?

Arguments for the efficacy of literary texts as tools for tolerance have been most famously advanced by Martha C. Nussbaum.[13] Nussbaum's thesis claims that literature encourages its readers to reach across cultural and historical divisions, that its affective power overcomes resistance to, or indifference toward, arguments for toleration.[14] Literature serves as a supplement to philosophy by generating feelings of empathy.[15] Using Lessing's *Nathan the Wise* (1749) as one example of a more general principle, Nussbaum argues that "the appealing portrayal of complex personalities and the power of poetry have been able to get under people's skins even when they are not terribly interested in philosophical first principles."[16] She goes on to suggest the idea of toleration promoted by such an aesthetic: "when we encounter people who differ in religion, we ought to focus on ethical virtues of generosity, kindness, and love, leaving the question of religious truth to one side in our civic interactions."[17] Here, literary texts train us to suspend our desire to convince others of their religious error in favour of peaceful coexistence fostered by fellow-feeling, introducing modernity's "buffered self" to the scene of reading and dramatic performance.[18] A call for an ethics based on benevolent affects and the polite navigation of religious opinions, Nussbaum's exhortations repeat those of Joseph Addison's *Spectator* essays and the sermons of numerous eighteenth-century latitudinarian preachers. Our ready understanding and investment in this form of religious toleration suggests more generally how indebted scholarly analyses are to frameworks put in place in the early modern period. As a result, we often reiterate rather than analyse the terms governing this tradition. Of course, both its historical and – given contemporary political urgencies – present desirability also pressure scholars not to simply study religious toleration but to promote it. This volume maintains that we cannot promote toleration without properly theorizing it, and we believe a reassessment of how literary texts engage the subject will provide scholars with more nuanced ways of talking about both past developments and present debates.

Nussbaum's arguments about literature are limited by the assumptions they make about what toleration requires and how the literary functions in relation to ideas and feelings. Further, Nussbaum's lack of historical specificity underestimates the extent to which literary representations of tolerance determine and are determined by social and political contexts. When confronted, for instance, with the example of *The Merchant of Venice*, Nussbaum claims that Shakespeare, in the absence of "real Jews," wrote "sheer fantasy."[19] By this account, the literary–in any instance–should function as a conduit of "true facts" gleaned from empirical observation, facts that, properly represented, align aesthetic consciousness with justice – a truth the best authors, Nussbaum argues, intuit.[20] In contrast, Stephen Greenblatt's reading of *The Merchant of Venice* argues that it is precisely the imaginative power of literary works – what he calls "Shakepeare's freedom" – that allows Shakespeare to draw a Jewish character that departs from early modern stereotypes even while *deepening* the sense of threat associated with not just one Jew, but all Jews. Shakespeare harnesses his talent to the creation of a "terrifying villain" whose hatred for Christians knows almost no limits.[21] For Greenblatt, the salient question is not how Shakespeare's play, in the final instance, fosters, or fails to foster, tolerance, but how it explores the psychological character of hatred and difference. Shakespeare's antidote to their corrosive effects is not mutual recognition, Greenblatt observes, but the Jew's assimilation, a conversion "to which the enemy finally consents because the alternative is to lose his life and his livelihood."[22] By this account, there is no reason to believe that Shakespeare would have written a different play had he encountered Jews in his daily life. Rather, the roots of anti-Semitism were deep enough in his Christian culture to provide a rich vein for Shakespeare to mine in his search for the truth of a particular feeling.

In a 2006 essay, "The Literary and the Ethical: Difference as Definition," Charles Altieri critiques Nussbaum's alignment of the literary with social justice. While acknowledging the power of Nussbaum's moral appeal, Altieri notes that "the very grandeur of her enterprise leads our attention away from those concrete processes by which literature does affect individual lives."[23] In the place of Nussbaum's pathos, Altieri advocates for ethos, describing the literary as a mode that leads us to "exemplary states" rather than any particular condition of ethical feeling or action:

> There is a deep connection between how we affirm our own relation to the states or actions we inhabit and how we ultimately come to affirm the sense of completeness and of intense participation afforded us by works of art. From the point of view of ethics the comparison to aesthetics foregrounds how closely our awareness of various exemplary states becomes fundamental to our own senses of identity.[24]

Altieri's account of the correspondence between our lives and the "intense participation" with "exemplary states" that literary texts invite provides a more expansive model than Nussbaum's for understanding what literature's engagement with toleration can look like. Altieri warns against requiring literary ethics to be overly dependent on one emotion, noting that the complexity of literary affect requires us to develop a more nuanced account of "the dangers attendant on what we [...] come to know in passionate ways."[25] An ethical self-consciousness results from our engagement with literary passions, but Altieri avoids inflecting this awareness with a positive moral content, as Nussbaum does, even as he underscores the intensity of the feelings, an awareness of how affect necessarily shapes our understanding of art – an awareness missing in the philosophical discourses that promote "pure" reason or scepticism as the grounds for toleration.

Altieri's understanding of the literary complements what Lars Tønder calls "sensorial reasoning" – "a reasoning that does not detach itself from the circumstances in which it is invoked but instead emphasizes the enabling power embedded in various lived experiences."[26] That is, the literary draws our attention to how, in Paul Yachnin's phrase, we "think feelingly" about ourselves and our relation to others, drawing on the experiential, rather than a purely cognitive, aspect of our reasoning. This attention to how literature can represent and transform affective intensities allows for a fuller description of tolerance than philosophers and historians have provided. The essays here show how broad the range of feelings associated with toleration can be, including what, according to Tønder, is most often left out: the experience of pain and its management. By attending to the modes of "agency and consciousness" instantiated by literature, we are able to measure the quality of endurance literary texts afford – the ability to put up with "the anxieties and hardship" that attend toleration.[27]

We begin with Shakespeare. Paul Yachnin places *The Merchant of Venice* in dialogue with early modern conversion narratives. Shakespeare's audience, he suggests, would have recognized in Shylock's forced conversion a version of their own encounters with state oppression, both Catholic and Protestant. Shakespeare's audience served as an interpretive community shaping the meaning of toleration in the space of the theatre, enacting a freedom unavailable elsewhere in early modern England. In turn, Shakespeare's dramatic text creates its own internal freedom by subverting anti-Semitic stereotypes in Shylock's canine language, which, Yachnin argues, transforms the "Jew-dog" figure into that of Diogenes, "the ancient philosopher known as the dog, notorious for his outrageous conduct in public and his savage denunciation of all forms of hypocrisy." Shakespeare's verbal play makes possible a counter-logic to emerge, one that marks Shylock's agency and humanity, a marking that is amplified by the audience's sympathetic identification with his suffering as fellow-victims of the state's cruel policies.

Sharon Achinstein's essay develops Yachnin's interest in state-sponsored violence, analysing how new understandings of cruelty and humanity made modern religious toleration possible. She begins by examining the transformation of Europe into a space of religious pluralism before showing how Aphra Behn navigates the new terrain of Anglo-European engagement in the global arena, "specifically in the context of interconfessional states." In her imaginative reconstruction of the colonial space of Surinam, Achinstein argues, Behn is able to move beyond the anti-toleration language that governs her critique of Protestant Dissent in Stuart England. In *Oroonoko*, Behn engages two different understandings of religious tolerance: that of Christian abolitionist discourse, intent on exposing "the hypocrisy of the enslaving English," and that of an emergent human rights language, whose indictment of cruelty puts ethical concerns first. Thus both religious and secular Enlightenments appear on the horizon of Behn's text. Within this frame of reference, we put the stress in different places in our analysis of the term, "religious toleration." Is it the religious principle of Christian charity, properly understood, that advances universal tolerance? Or is toleration required to manage claims to religious authority by subordinating them to a humanist ethical imperative committed to peaceful coexistence? Behn's narrative frames the questions taken up by Christian apologists and philosophers alike in the century that followed the publication of *Oroonoko*.

Colin Jager explores the potential of poetic form to move beyond the limits of both liberal and revolutionary accounts of toleration, to provide a "counter-factual" model capable of overcoming some of the impasses that came into view in the early nineteenth century. Translation, Jager claims, "provides a specifically romantic model of religious toleration." In his reading of *Prometheus Unbound*, the materiality of poetic language allows Percy Bysshe Shelley to "untranslate" the violence of the French Revolution, a product of the narrowness of its translation of Christian charity into the nationalist politics of fraternity. Drawing on Jürgen Habermas and M.H. Abrams, Jager delineates literary modes of incompletion and partiality that allow us "to name the possibility of a formal relation to otherness." Shelley's *Prometheus Unbound* represents humanity's belonging to an "earth" made inclusive through our participation in "familiar acts." The poem, Jager argues, invites the "radical multiplication of social bonds" that in turn foster tolerance. Toleration must be "enacted" rather than theorized, the poem maintains: there are no universal categories – either philosophical or political – that can properly "translate" the requirements toleration makes on us, as a species. Precisely because it goes beyond propositional knowledge, poetry best communicates these requirements to us.

The Tropes of Toleration

Reflections on "the agency of form"[28] what Paul Stevens calls its "illocutionary power" – move us beyond the arena of imaginative texts to consider the literary qualities of other kinds of writing that shaped the history of both ideas about, and practices of, toleration in the seventeenth and eighteenth centuries.[29] Our goal in this book is to interrogate what has become received wisdom concerning key authors and their contributions to the toleration debate. Here Mark Canuel challenges the familiar portrait of Joseph Priestley's thought as scientific and rationalist by attending to the "eccentric" literary modes that foster toleration in his writing. Attention to the literary qualities of the toleration debate not only allows us to see its different aspects, it also enables a closer examination of our own rhetorical modes and how they structure our assumptions about agency and autonomy. So, for example, Andrew McKendry's analysis of tropes of disability in seventeenth-century religious writing demonstrates what is historically particular to that moment's interest in compromised bodies and minds, but it also reveals what is particular to our own. If contemporary toleration debates have become rote, it may be because they routinely fall back on the same tropes. This volume shows how an attention to literary modes enables a better understanding of the presuppositions embedded in our figures and how they shape the arguments we make.

Elena Russo attends to one of the Enlightenment's key philosophers, Pierre Bayle, whose influence in Britain is now only beginning to receive the attention that it should. She analyses the dynamism of Bayle's rhetorical modes, revealing how his *argument à tiroirs* ("nested boxes argument") structures the radical content of his treatise on toleration, *A Philosophical Commentary*. Bayle uses irony, paradox, and chiasmus to de-familiarize his readers to themselves so they can better understand what it means both to persecute and to be persecuted. His anger and aggressive rhetorical moves encourage a visceral response in his readers, providing an early modern model of the sensorial reason Tønder has theorized in our own moment. Russo claims that Bayle's "emotionally charged" philosophical discourse situates religious toleration within a theological discourse, but this discourse occupies an uneasy relation with any kind of religious conformity, documenting time and again its tendency to harden into persecution. Russo's essay documents Bayle's delight in engaging, "sometimes obsessively," with the discourse of his adversaries and the enormous risks he takes by occupying the terrain of the taboo, shifting his rhetorical register between the high and the low in an effort to erode the girding that supported religious orthodoxies of the period. In the place of John Locke's "common sense" philosopher, a theatrical persona appears.

McKendry analyses how conceptions of blindness, and disability more broadly, shaped early modern understandings of religious difference and an emergent language of religious toleration. "[I]magining oneself as blind or 'lame,'" McKendry observes, could expose state intolerance as a kind of "embarrassingly ableist gaze – a secularizing ownership over our bodies (particularly our eyes) that was disabling in the most egregious sense." McKendry suggests that the "potentially conciliatory continuities of disability" that the period's writers sustained did not lay the foundation for liberal modernity, which instead reformulates religious identities in binaries of conformity and non-conformity, compulsion and freedom – a reformulation writ large in Milton's *Samson Agonistes*. Reading the tropes of disability and ableism as they were developed by seventeenth-century religious writers allows us to better understand, today, "how justice is distributed, how exceptions are defined, and where suffering takes place." By showing how seventeenth-century texts framed the nature and implications of disability, McKendry exposes the epistemological bedrock upon which our current conceptions of toleration and religious difference rest.

Mark Canuel's reading of Joseph Priestley attends to the literary "fictions" Priestley deploys in his theological texts and how they refuse the disciplinary regimes of political theory and philosophy. Priestley's model of toleration values, above all, the "tensions, overlaps, tentative resolutions" maintained by "artificial structures of felicitous social cooperation." What is unreal about the literary is precisely what enables the very real cultural practices of toleration. In the final instance, it is not the rationalism so often associated with Priestley's utilitarianism that makes possible a tolerant society, but rather the imaginative leaps that establish symbolic orders as placeholders for new social and political practices. Canuel closes his essay with reflections on the link between Priestley's interests and the imaginative world of the Gothic novel. Like Priestley's, Ann Radcliffe's fiction suggests that "proper character" results from "tolerant institutional and narrative strategies." *The Italian* further demonstrates its indebtedness to Priestley in its attention to a "spiritualized source of authority, reformed though it may be," an authority that counters, in its inclusiveness, the religious conformities insisted upon by the Inquisition abroad and Anglican hegemony at home. In Canuel's suggestive readings, we see how neither the Gothic novel nor the discourse of toleration proposed by Priestley require the rejection of the pain of religious difference from the literary and political spheres. Rather, both discourses teach us how to bear – even solicit – contention for the advancement of the common good.

Joanna Picciotto explores the literary hermeneutics of Methodism's language of toleration in the eighteenth century. In particular, she observes how Methodism's commitment to reading diverse spiritual testimonials fostered tolerance in an effort to identify, across a range of historical divides, "certain recurring features of Christian experience and the habits and behaviours associated with it." This commitment arose from an understanding of Christianity as both highly variegated and universal, an understanding fostered by close reading. This habit of close reading could inform daily acts of tolerance, Picciotto suggests, because early Methodists recognized "the continuity of aesthetic experience with everyday practice." Methodists proved not only avid readers, but also avid writers. For the kinds of testimonials that were produced, the emergent novel provided an important model for understandings of both character and of literary innovation. Against critics who have attempted to displace the centrality of character in our reading of the eighteenth-century novel, Picciotto argues for the significance of Methodist narratives that enhance "a sense of self as a person with potential for development," not tied "to any fixed narrative template." Rather than reading the novel form as a secular narrative mode that supplanted an earlier spiritual tradition, as is commonly argued, Picciotto looks at how Methodism's religious "novels" became, through their shared testimony, "common," material "through which one could exercise toleration remotely or at close range." Precisely because Methodist experiences proved multiple and volatile, their narrative representation helped to foster a tolerance of religious pluralism.

Toleration and Its Discontents

The essays summarized thus far positively value literature and literary modes for their capacity to imagine how toleration works and to reconfigure philosophical and theological discourses toward that end. But the literary does not always prove beneficent as a way to better practices or understandings of religious toleration. Corrinne Harol, David Alvarez, and Humberto Garcia examine the failure of tolerance in its early literary inceptions, providing salutary readings that counter the critical language of aesthetic triumphalism deployed by Nussbaum and others. We consider these "failures" key sources for the exploration of what it is that makes religious toleration such a difficult achievement both in the past and the present.

Harol's richly textured account of Margaret Cavendish's *The Blazing World* identifies the problem of 1660s England as central to the history of toleration debates: "Put broadly, the issue is that the more one embraces diversity as either a fact or an ideal of social or religious existence, the more difficult it becomes to imagine a form of government, other than absolutism, that can manage this diversity." Her reading of *The Blazing World* shows how the celebration of a fully vitalistic literary imagination and universe, one that recognizes the divisions of opinions as well as matter, does not necessarily lead us toward toleration. In fact, Cavendish's commitment to the freedom of that imagination and universe moves her in the opposite direction, toward the protection of liberty, for individuals and particular nations, in the face of hostility from those encountered outside the worlds created by both imaginations and states. "In the end," Harol notes, "Cavendish's text produces a very ambivalent attitude towards toleration: the literary imagination both understands the inevitability of diversity of opinion and fails to imagine a solution other than state violence" to the problem of dissent and conflict.

David Alvarez turns to Enlightenment satire and how it organizes religious affect so as to render its irrational powers less toxic in the public sphere: "we should approach Enlightenment satires of religion as, in some respect, social rituals through which the felt meaning of 'religion' in secular cultures is constructed." As part of the long tradition of Christian reform, such satires help to usher in the modern, Protestant understanding of religion that is amenable to liberal toleration. Alvarez analyses the legacy of this tradition in relation to recent debates surrounding the Danish cartoon controversy and the Charlie Hebdo murders. He argues that satire reveals the tenuousness of its claims to "disenchanting power" through its proximity to, and resemblance of, the object it criticizes. Insofar as the construction of a tolerant "buffered self" depends on the rhetorical force of satire, this self is also "punctured" since it is formed through and dependent on the cultural practice of Enlightenment satires of religion. On the one hand, such satires produce an understanding of tolerance that "disavows its implicit, culturally specific religious understandings and affect." On the other hand, because of its proximity to what it seeks to separate itself from, satire can also make these cultural elements explicit.

In his examination of Defoe's *Continuation of the Turkish Spy*, Humberto Garcia similarly reveals how the literary exposes toleration's fault lines. Defoe's recognition of toleration's geopolitical particularity and its potential for weaponization counters radical Enlightenment arguments for its universalism and pacifism. For Defoe, Garcia argues, it is precisely the universalist appeal of toleration that prevents English Dissenters from recognizing how it might be deployed as part of a political program aimed not at peace, but rather at the heightening of international conflict. The literary provides Defoe with a vantage point from which to engage in *realpolitik*, for his critique of toleration opens the way for the advancement of imperial ambition. By creating a space for phantasmatic identifications across East-West divides, Defoe is able to warn his readers of Ottoman aspirations to world domination while advancing English dreams of the same: "*A Continuation* hails the durable, unified confessional state Defoe wished Britain would flourish into in order to fulfil its imperial destiny." The literary, in this instance, structures a political manifesto for British expansion.

For those critical of the modern liberal state and its promotion of toleration, the failures here contribute to a larger political project, one that aims to challenge liberalism's account of its own success in securing the conditions for peaceful coexistence in the modern world. But while acknowledging the limits of liberal accounts of tolerance and the difficulty of putting it into practice, the essays of this volume seek to complicate the hermeneutics of suspicion that often attend critique.[30] Joanna Picciotto summarizes the critical dismissal this way: "A society can't be built on toleration – not only because its demands are too minimal (no one wants merely to be tolerated), but because toleration merely describes a special variety of rejection, a rejection without practical consequences. On this understanding, a society built on toleration is no longer a society at all." Picciotto responds to this critique as a historicist, suggesting that it reflects an "impoverished" understanding of the foundational practices and discourses it takes as its objects. For Canuel, the critique of toleration falters in its theorization of power: "Political theorists that range from Michael Sandel to Wendy Brown routinely find the logic of toleration to be flawed because toleration always implies a position of power from which persons and groups can be tolerated." But, as Canuel points out, we can never talk about government without talking about power. Our attention, then, should be directed not toward power "as such," "but rather about how power is configured." The essays gathered here claim that the literary provides a way of capturing the nuances of the social and political contexts so as to avoid the interpretive pitfalls of contemporary critique. Even those literary and philosophical texts that consider toleration a failed project provide subtle and illuminating ways of moving the project forward, we suggest. Finally, while we support the efforts to advance the politics of recognition so often promoted as the alternative, we also claim, with Alfred Stepan and Charles Taylor, that toleration remains "an essential asset" in the promotion of coexistence.[31] Without it, there is no middle ground between rejection and affirmation. "Absent toleration," Ira Katznelson observes, "unbridled conflict and coercion produce stark worlds of winners, who defeat pluralism, and losers, for whom the costs of engagement can be very high, even ultimate."[32]

To defend toleration, then, is not to merely rehearse the virtues of beleaguered Enlightenment discourses, again. Instead, it means, as these essays demonstrate, developing our understanding of tolerance beyond the models we have inherited from political philosophy and intellectual history. The essays that follow expand our understanding of religious affiliation, sociability, and coexistence in the two centuries under investigation. They identify, further, habits of mind that foster an alternative temporal frame to progress, a willingness to dwell with uncertainty and the fragility of religious and secular positions, not by moving toward scepticism, but by finding the intellectual and emotional resources to endure, enabling an openness to religious difference.

Analysing how the literary imagines – or fails to imagine – tolerant selves and communities in its representation of our cultural habitus helps us understand, we believe, how toleration's habits of minds might be fostered today and what forms of discourse and practice work best to promote them.

A two-day workshop in London, Ontario, served as the starting point for this volume. The generosity that found its way to that symposium colours the essays collected here. It is fitting that the volume concludes with Colin Jager's reflections on Shelley's "untranslatable love." Jager argues that Shelley's attempt to move the politics of love beyond national boundaries leads to another feeling, gratitude. Gratitude breaks the impasse of "a collective inability to imagine selves who could be loyal to more than [one thing]." In the place of boundaries rigidly maintained, gratitude fosters tolerance as "something developed internally" and shared. And so, in the interest of fostering conversation about the literary history of religious toleration, I note my gratitude for the fine scholarship in the pages that follow and my hope that the same generosity that marked their composition attends future work on this thorny subject.

NOTES

1 My thanks to David Alvarez for his contributions and editing.

2 The most often cited historians of the Whig narrative regarding toleration include A.A. Seeton, *The Theory of Toleration under the Later Stuarts* (Cambridge: Cambridge University Press, 1911); Richard Burgess Barlow, *Citizenship and Conscience: A Study of the Theory and Practice of Religious Toleration during the Eighteenth Century* (Philadelphia: University of Pennsylvania Press, 1962); W.K. Jordan, *The Development of Religious Toleration in England* (Gloucester: P. Smith, 1965). Critiques of this narrative can be found in *From Persecution to Toleration: The Glorious Revolution and Religion in England*, ed. Ole Grell, Jonathan Israel, Nicholas Tyacke Grell, Ole Peter, Jonathan I. Israel, and Nicholas Tyacke (Oxford: Clarendon Press, 1991). More recently, the "Enlightenment" thesis has been updated by what we might call neo-Whig historians; see, for example, Perez Zagorin, *How the Idea of Religious Toleration Came to the West* (Princeton: Princeton University Press, 2013). For an excellent summary of the toleration debate and its critical heritage, see the opening pages of Eliane Glaser's introduction to *Religious Tolerance in the Atlantic World: Early Modern and Contemporary Perspectives* (Houndsmills, Basingstoke: Palgrave Macmillan, 2014), 1–13.

3 For an explanation of this critical lacuna, see Corrinne Harol and Alison Conway, "Toward a Postsecular Eighteenth Century," *Literature Compass* 12, no. 11 (2015): 565–74.

4 Peter Coviello, "Introduction: After the Postsecular," *American Literature* 86 no. 4 (2014): 646.

5   Ibid., 647.

6   Judith Pollman, "Getting Along" (review essay), *History Workshop Journal* 64 no. 1 (2007): 421. Pollman's essay provides an excellent overview of the study of religious toleration.

7   Jonathan Sheehan, "Enlightenment, Religion, and the Enigma of Secularization: A Review Essay," *American Historical Review* 108, no. 4 (2003), 1076. This account establishes "a new constellation of formal and technical practices and institutions" as the reference point for our understanding of the Enlightenment, rather than focusing on philosophical or doctrinal principles (1075).

8   On the key distinction between secularization and secularity, see the "Editor's Introduction" in *Varieties of Secularism in a Secular Age,* ed. Michael Warner, Jonathan Van Antwerpen, and Craig Calhoun (Cambridge, MA: Harvard University Press, 2013), 3–31.

9   For an overview of recent early modern literary critics interested in religion, see Alexandra Walsham, "Cultures of Coexistence in Early Modern England: History, Literature, and Religious Toleration," *The Seventeenth Century* 28, no. 2 (2013): 119–22.

10   Harol and Conway, "Toward a Postsecular Eighteenth Century," 566.

11   Walsham, "Cultures of Coexistence," 128.

12   Ibid., 126.

13   Martha C. Nussbaum, *The New Religious Intolerance: Overcoming the Politics of Fear in an Anxious Age* (Cambridge, MA: Harvard University Press, 2012). In work by those engaging in literary criticism, we find similar ideas. For instance, in *Shakespeare and Tolerance* (Cambridge: Cambridge University Press, 2009), B.J. Sokol traces a pattern of recognitions that teach individuals how to value "otherness"; the presence of bigotry in plays such as *The Merchant of Venice*, he argues, "implies the existence of a counterbalancing frame of reference ... an early modern frame of reference allowing a place for racial and ethnic tolerance" (155). Ingrid Creppell claims that Daniel Defoe's novels turn the public mind towards "self reflection and an image or 'myth'" that advances toleration. *Toleration and Identity: Foundations in Early Modern Thought* (New York: Routledge, 2003), 152.

14   Sokol, *Shakespeare and Tolerance*, 148.

15   In her treatment of literary texts in *The New Religious Intolerance*, Nussbaum returns to the thesis she developed in *Love's Knowledge: Essays on Philosophy and Literature* (New York: Oxford University Press, 1990), in which the novel features, centrally, as a literary form crucial to "the shaping of sympathy" among readers (44).

16   Nussbaum, *New Religious Intolerance*, 165.

17   Ibid.

18   "As a bounded self I can see the boundary as a buffer, such that the things beyond don't need to "get to me," to use the contemporary expression." Charles Taylor,

"Buffered and Porous Selves," *The Immanent Frame*, 20 Sept. 2008. https://tif.ssrc.org/2008/09/02/buffered-and-porous-selves/.

19 Nussbaum, *New Religious Intolerance*, 166.

20 Ibid., 187. Historian David S. Katz draws the opposite conclusion from the dearth of Jews in early modern England: "The only Jews of most people's acquaintance were biblical figures, literary characters, and entirely imaginary, and it may be that this lack of personal contact with such an extraordinary people facilitated their readmission." *The Jews in the History of England, 1485–1850* (Oxford: Clarendon, 1994, 1996), 108.

21 Stephen Greenblatt, *Shakespeare's Freedom* (Chicago: University of Chicago Press, 2010), 71.

22 Ibid., 70.

23 Charles Altieri, "The Literary and the Ethical," in *The Question of Literature: The Place of the Literary in Contemporary Theory*, ed. Elizabeth Beaumont Bissell (Manchester: Manchester University Press, 2002), 34.

24 Ibid., 42–3.

25 Ibid., 39.

26 Lars Tønder, *Tolerance: A Sensorial Orientation to Politics* (Oxford: Oxford University Press, 2013), 5.

27 Ibid., 7.

28 Walsham, "Cultures of Coexistence," 118.

29 Paul Stevens, "Intolerance and the Virtues of Sacred Vehemence," in *Milton and Toleration* ed. Sharon Achinstein (Oxford: Oxford University Press, 2007), 253.

30 Wendy Brown, *Regulating Aversion: Tolerance in an Age of Identity and Empire* (Princeton: Princeton University Press, 2006). The suspicion with which Brown treats tolerance can be traced back to Thomas Paine's *Rights of Man* and to Herbert Marcuse's *A Critique of Pure Tolerance* (1965), and into the late twentieth century's poststructuralist political critiques.

31 Charles Taylor and Alfred Stepan, introduction to *Boundaries of Toleration* (New York: Columbia University Press, 2014), 10. Ira Katznelson, "A Form of Liberty and Indulgence: Toleration as a Layered Institution" in Taylor and Stepan, eds., *Boundaries of Toleration*, 39.

32 Katznelson, "A Form of Liberty and Indulgence," 39.

1 Shylock, Conversion, Toleration

PAUL YACHNIN

How *The Merchant of Venice* and We Grew Wise Together

On 26 January 1814, the essayist and philosopher William Hazlitt saw Edmund Kean's path-breaking performance of Shylock at Drury Lane. In a review of that first performance, which appeared in the *Morning Chronicle* on 27 January, Hazlitt applauded the intellectual, emotional, and physical vitality that Kean was famous for – "a lightness and vigour in his tread, a buoyancy and elasticity of spirit, a fire and animation ..." But he found fault with these qualities, ironically enough, precisely because they did not square with the character Kean was presenting: "In conveying a profound impression of this feeling, or in embodying the general conception of rigid and uncontrollable self-will, equally proof against every sentiment of humanity [...] we have seen actors more successful than Mr. KEAN [...] The fault of his acting was (if we may hazard the objection), an over-display of the resources of the art, which gave too much relief to the hard, impenetrable, dark groundwork of the character of Shylock."[1]

Two years later, after much thought and a thorough study of the text of the play, Hazlitt found that he had changed his mind about both Kean's performance and the character of Shylock. He allowed that he had formed "an overstrained ideal of the gloomy character of Shylock, probably more from seeing other players perform it than from the text of Shakespear":

> Mr. Kean's manner is much nearer the mark. Shakespear could not easily divest his characters of their entire humanity: his Jew is more than half a Christian. Certainly, our sympathies are more oftener with him than with his enemies. He is honest in his vices; they are hypocrites in their virtues. [...] Shylock (however some persons may suppose him bowed down by age, or deformed by malignity) never, that we can find, loses his elasticity and presence of mind. There is a wonderful grace and ease in all the speeches in this play. "I would not have parted with it (the jewel he gave to Leah) for a *wilderness* of monkeys!" What a fine Hebraism! The character

of Shylock is another instance of Shakespear's power of identifying himself with the thoughts of men, their prejudices, and almost instincts.[2]

I make the transformation of Hazlitt's judgment of Shylock my entry point for a number of reasons. For one thing, it, along with Kean's performance, represents one of the most important shifts towards a liberal understanding of the religious and racial politics of the play. By liberal, I mean the view that the political community and the category of the human itself are founded in private rights-bearing persons – all of them – rather than in persons designated as political actors and human beings by virtue of their high social status, White race, male gender, or Christian religion. Though never uncontested, the liberal view of the play has been dominant in criticism and in university classrooms for, say, the past seventy-five years. With the exception of anti-Semitic performances under the Nazis and in a few other places and at a few other times, a liberal interpretation of the play, though with some notable exceptions, has also been dominant in the theatre throughout the later nineteenth century, through the twentieth, and into the twenty-first centuries. While the grave genocidal crime of the Holocaust has made *Merchant* persistently difficult to stage and also set a tolerationist seal on the play, it did not cause the large-scale shift in how the play is generally viewed.

All this, of course, might sound more or less like a story about how Shakespeare planted the seed; how Kean, Hazlitt, and a few others nursed it; and how it grew into a handsome, spreading Shakespearean tree of freedom and toleration. And while I don't want to deny at all the progressive political value of Shakespeare's art over the long term, the story that I want to tell is more complex, more knotted, and far less teleological than my brief sketch so far might suggest. And though, as it will emerge, I disagree with his view, I nevertheless take to heart Harold Bloom's poignant reflection on the play. "As an old-fashioned bardolator," Bloom said, "I am hurt when I contemplate the real harm Shakespeare has done to the Jews for some four centuries now."[3]

So, to begin to think complexly about Shakespeare and toleration, consider Hazlitt's sentence about Shakespeare's ethics of characterization: "Shakespear could not easily divest his characters of their entire humanity: his Jew is more than half a Christian." We might think at first that the first clause is a kind of gracious understatement: "Shakespear could not easily divest his characters of their entire humanity" means really that all his characters are in fact fully human. But the second, parallel clause makes the meaning of the first clause more literal: In Shakespeare's artful hands, even a character like Shylock is partly human; in fact, he is more than 50 per cent human. It also requires us to take the whole sentence in more specific terms. If Shylock is, say, 55 per cent human, it is the Christian part of him that is human; it follows that the 45 per cent Jewish part of Shylock is not human.

If he is not fully human, the Jewish part might be demonic. Lancelot Gobbo comments that "the Jew my master [...] is a kind of devil" and "certainly the Jew is the very devil incarnation" (2.2.21–5).[4] Bassanio refers to Shylock as "this devil" (4.1.284). The identification of Shylock with the Devil is of a piece with the longstanding demonization of Jews in the Christian West. Chaucer's Prioress, to cite one example, recounts how "Our first foo, the serpent Sathanas, / [...] hath in Jues herte his waspes nest."[5] But given the dominant vocabulary of denigration in the play itself, especially the way Shylock is described by the Christian characters and by himself, it makes more sense to say that the Jewish part of Shylock, the part that is not human, is canine. As I have argued elsewhere, Shakespeare constructed Shylock's character in part in terms of caninity.[6] Shylock is battered by Christian claims about his currishness – "the dog Jew" (2.8.127), "impenetrable cur" (3.3.18), "inexecrable dog" (4.1.27), "this currish Jew" (4.1.127) – but he also increasingly becomes the dog he is said to be. "Thou call'd'st me dog before thou hadst a cause," he says to Antonio, "But since I am a dog, beware my fangs" (3.3.6–7). In the trial scene and the scene of his meeting with Antonio (3.3) leading up to the trial scene, his iterative use of the key word "bond" makes his conversation increasingly dogged:

> I'll have my bond; I will not hear thee speak.
> I'll have my bond; and therefore speak no more.
>
> ...
>
> I'll have no speaking; I will have my bond. (3.3.12–17)

The traditional posture of the role, which went back to the eighteenth century and which Kean adopted, had the actor bend at the waist and use a cane, so that he did not face the other characters directly but turned his head and looked upward at the others as a dog might look at a man standing over him.[7]

But even here, Shakespeare was not being original. In a remarkable book, *Jewish Dogs: An Image and Its Interpreters*, Kenneth Stow tracks the association between Jews and dogs through over one thousand years of Christian denigration of Jews back to the apparent founding text, Matthew 15.26: "But he answered and said, It is not meet to take the children's bread, and to cast *it* to dogs." "This verse," Stow comments, "was transmogrified into an image of Christian children hungering for the Eucharist, which 'Jewish dogs' incessantly plot to steal, consume, savage, or pollute."[8]

It might be said that I am making altogether too much of a single sentence, a little slip in the wording in what is in other respects a major forward-looking account of a controversial play. It is worth bearing in mind, however, how often leading liberal thinkers contradict their own general arguments for human community and for the concomitant toleration of difference. Voltaire provides an example close to Hazlitt's slip. In *The Philosophical Dictionary* (1764), he argues for tolerance as the primary virtue. "WHAT is tolerance?" he asks: he goes on to explain, "it is the consequence of humanity. We are all formed of frailty and error; let us pardon reciprocally each other's folly – that is the first law of nature."[9] In the same entry, he writes scathingly about social and political hierarchies that are built on intolerance. He speaks with great irony in the voice of "the men whom centuries of bigotry have made powerful [...] who [...] enrich themselves with the spoils of the poor, grow fat on their blood, and laugh at their stupidity." In the voice of this tyrant figure he says, "I possess a dignity and a power founded on ignorance and credulity; I walk on the heads of the men who lie prostrate at my feet; if they should rise and look me in the face, I am lost; I must bind them to the ground, therefore, with iron chains."[10]

But the irony is more layered than Voltaire realizes. As scholars such as Cornel West and others have argued, Voltaire was one of the leading exponents of pseudo-scientific racism.[11] "The Negro race," Voltaire wrote, "is a species of men as different from ours as the breed of spaniels is from that of greyhounds. [...] If their understanding is not of a different nature from ours, it is at least greatly inferior. They are not capable of any great application or association of ideas."[12] His advocacy of pseudo-scientific racism in the heyday of the slave trade means that his words speak not only in the voice of those whom centuries of bigotry have made powerful; they speak also and unwittingly in his own voice. He, too, cannot abide the idea that the oppressed could rise and look him in the face. He would be lost if he were compelled to recognize their common humanity with him, so he must bind them to the ground with chains. In this case, the chains are made not out of iron, but rather from widespread ideas about the natural inferiority of the non-White races. This second irony, an irony that emerges from the political and ideological situation of the text seen at a certain distance, is indeed so forceful that it seems almost to be part of, or we wish that it were part of, the meaning of the text that Voltaire intended his readers to understand.

The examples from Hazlitt and Voltaire illustrate a foundational claim that I want to make about the particular advantages of imaginative over discursive writing. Hazlitt and Voltaire formulate important forward-looking ideas about humanity and toleration, but their ideas are framed and constrained by ideology in ways that escape their attention and their intentionality. The ideology of religious and racial difference, which is sedimented in the vocabulary and forms of language with which Hazlitt and Voltaire must work, mines beneath their intended arguments in ways that, over time, have fractured and even rendered their texts obsolete. Their writings are admirable, but they have begun, we might say, to show their age. The meanings of literary texts are hardly unconstrained by ideology, but the constraints operate differently. Literary texts have different and more various modes of address, a less tightly bound relationship with the voice of the author, a less pronounced tendency to police the production of meaning, and indeed an ability to cultivate a multiplicity of voices.

The differences become evident when we consider, for example, Voltaire's own novella *Candide* (1759). It features a brief scene with a Black African slave who has suffered egregious mistreatment and even mutilation at the hands of his Dutch masters. In answer to Candide's horrified inquiry, the enslaved man tells his story and ends by putting in question precisely the polygenism that served to make respectable Voltaire's own racist views:

> This is the price you pay for the sugar you eat in Europe. [...] Dogs, monkeys, parrots, they're all a thousand times less wretched than we are. The Dutch fetishes who converted me tell me every Sunday that we are all the sons of Adam, Whites and Blacks alike. I'm no genealogist, but if these preachers are right, we are all cousins born of first-cousins. Well, you will grant me that you can't treat a relative much worse than this.[13]

On account of these formal features of address, voice, and meaning-making, literary texts are able to develop an orientation towards futurity and an enduring freshness born of their capacity to foster ongoing dialogue with readers and others over time. It follows from this claim about the character of literary writing and reading that the contribution a play like *Merchant of Venice* has made towards religious toleration does not belong to the play in its own time or to the meaning Shakespeare intended the play to have, however we construe that meaning. To call on an idea from Bakhtin, the play is an orchestrated structure of generative polyphony; it does not suppress the language of intolerance – anti-Semitism and other forms of hate speech speak volubly in the text – but its structured play of voices situates racial and religious intolerance dialogically with other ways of seeing and speaking.

All this is not to say that it is only literary texts (and other works of art) that do the real work of bringing to Western modernity the principles of enlightenment and equality and the recognition of other human beings as persons. Recognition of our common humanity is, after all, the grounding principle of toleration in a strong sense. By that, I mean something beyond the strict definition of the word "toleration," which the *Oxford English Dictionary* tells us means, "the action or practice of tolerating or allowing what is not actually approved; forbearance, sufferance."[14] Toleration in a strong sense lines up with what the *Stanford Encyclopedia of Philosophy* calls the "esteem conception" of toleration: The *Encyclopedia* offers the following explanation: "being tolerant does not just mean respecting members of other cultural life-forms or religions as moral and political equals, it also means having some kind of ethical esteem for their beliefs, that is, taking them to be ethically valuable conceptions that – even though different from one's own – are in some way ethically attractive and held with good reasons."[15]

We find these kinds of ideas in a range of non-literary texts from Shakespeare's time and from well before his time. The sixteenth-century Protestant hagiographer

John Foxe, to take only one example, invites his readers to follow the example of Christ by cultivating in themselves a fellow-feeling for the affliction of others and thereby awaking their own spirit of compassion:

> It is impossible for a man to know the afflictions of the miserable person, that never suffered himself affliction, that never had experience of pains, that never felte what payne mente. But [...] Christ had experience of our nature: how weake, how feble the nature of man is [...] He suffered and felte the infirmities and paynes of hys natural body. He hath therefore compassion upon man, when he doth see hym fall.[16]

Foxe's account of an affliction-based recognition of the personhood of the other is in some measure an inheritance from Pauline Christianity, which contributed, with many complications, towards a universalist idea of human community.[17] So it is not only works of the imagination that bring enlightenment and toleration to modernity. If Shylock had in hand John Locke's *Letter Concerning Toleration* (1689) when he went before the Court of Venice, he could have developed a powerful argument against the conversion to Christianity imposed upon him by the Duke and Antonio. It is rather that works of the imagination foster toleration differently from works of nonfiction. Voltaire's *Dictionary*, as we have seen, carries inside it a small, hidden ulcer of polygenist racism. It is an ulcer that can never heal because the authority of the author's voice keeps the text more or less just where it was when it started out in the world. And for all its evocation of the example of Christ's compassion for fallen humankind, Foxe's "Book of Martyrs" remains the greatest work of early modern English anti-Catholic propaganda. It does not matter that Foxe's book was the work of many hands; the stone walls of prejudice constructed within the text constitute a uniform anti-Catholic voice that impedes any movement towards an inclusive embrace of Christian compassion and the toleration of difference that such compassion would sponsor.

On the face of it, a literary text such as *The Merchant of Venice* is far less an argument for toleration than is Locke's *Letter*, but it is able to incite a movement towards toleration as a participatory, future-oriented process of dialogue and disagreement among readers, actors, essayists, and many others.[18] The dialogue and also the starkly divided opinions generated by *Merchant of Venice* do not remain in the penumbra of the play's meaning. They are folded back into what the play means since the meaning of literary and especially dramatic texts is not bound to a particular historical moment or to a particular authorial voice. The meaning of *Merchant* is dialogical and diachronic through and through. It contains, we might say, multitudes that it has gathered over the longue durée.

In a recent book, *Shakespeare's Individualism*, Peter Holbrook takes on a task similar to the one I have set for myself, but he approaches it very differently.

He allows the value of polyphony by affirming Coleridge's view of Shakespeare as "myriad-minded," but he points to what he sees as the severe limitations of such views.

> [E]mphasizing Shakespeare's intellectual openness can be overdone, with the plays and poems ending up a bland, self cancelling rendezvous of perspectives. [...] The claim of this book is that Shakespeare does have a point of view and that it is modern. [...] [M]ore than any other pre-Romantic writer, Shakespeare is committed to fundamentally modern values: freedom, individuality, self-realization, authenticity.[19]

While I admire much in Holbrook's book, I think he is wrong to ascribe a global authorial intentionality to Shakespeare's works. A play like *Merchant of Venice* is nothing like what a man, say someone like Hazlitt, might write in order to convey an organized or even a disorganized argument to a reader. A play is a made thing rather than an utterance – the creation of an artificer rather than an orator. Shakespeare's plays are assemblages of an extraordinary number and variety of literary, non-literary, and gestural languages. They are well-made artifices, designed in order to perform certain tasks. The production of discursive meaning or of philosophical or political argument is not one of those tasks.

Holbrook is also mistaken in his faith in Shakespeare's modern point of view on freedom, individuality, and so on. In order to grasp how Shakespeare has contributed to modern virtues, in as much as we can justly claim freedom or toleration as special virtues of modernity, we must first displace Shakespeare himself entirely from the centre of our thinking. Shakespeare crafted plays as entertaining, engaging works of art to be read in relatively cheap print editions and to be seen in a public playhouse, a venue that Steven Mullaney has characterized as "a complex cognitive space for playwrights, players, and audiences to occupy and experience – an inhabited affective technology."[20]

In the early modern playhouse and in the many places of reading, playgoing, playing, teaching, and writing that *Merchant of Venice* texts and performances have occupied since the late sixteenth century, the socially and politically creative work that the play has accomplished hardly belongs to Shakespeare alone. Because it speaks in so many different voices, the play has taken on meaning and purpose for people of all kinds and all views – from Charles Macklin's late eighteenth-century performance of a villainous Shylock ("slow, calm, in his impenetrable cunning [...] unflinching, even to the extreme of malice") to Henry Goodman's complex and even tortured Shylock (in the 1999 Trevor Nunn production); from Barbara Lewalski's learned defence of the Christians' treatment of Shylock, including the forced conversion, to Kenneth Gross's brilliant meditation on the identity of Shakespeare and Shylock ("This character I've made, this Shylock, is myself. He, like me, is a creature of strange commerce, breeding money through what others think of as contaminated, unholy means").[21]

In the company of these actors and scholars and very many others, the play has grown over time in the direction of modern wisdom, which is a wisdom that both embraces freedom and tolerance and that also participates in the remarkably durable forms of racial and religious hatred. This kind of wisdom does not belong to a single text or performance and it does not live in a single head (not even Shakespeare's). It is distributed across texts, performances, and people, and its growth has been centuries slow and very uneven. On account of its rich internal dialogism and the particular features Shakespeare built into his imaginative construction, many of which, as we will see, came from the time he lived in, *The Merchant of Venice* has served not only as a key inciting text of the contestatory interpretive work done by many different hands; it also has been and continues to be one of the most important gathering places of the distributed wisdom of modernity. To borrow another one of Bakhtin's insights, great literary works break through the boundaries of their own time; their lives in what he calls great time "are more intense and fuller than their lives within their own time."[22]

The Crisis of Conversion

The most important sources of the particular dialogical character of *Merchant of Venice* are the traditions of anti-Semitism, which included, as we have seen, the demonization and animalization of the Jews, and also what I will call the crisis of conversion. Conversion, in the period from the end of the fifteenth century until some time after Shakespeare's death, became the animating force of an age of intolerance, a period of appalling coercion and violence and one that also gave birth to new ideas and new practices of toleration. The play emerged from the confluence of traditional anti-Semitism, from the ever-rising religio-political tensions of the period, and from the expanding capacity to recognize the personhood of others, something driven, ironically enough, by state programs of conversion as well as by Shakespeare's theatre's artistic conversions of religious conversion.

In the period, conversion became a sublime instrument of power, a way for rulers to exercise control over the inward as well as the outward lives of their subjects and also a justification of wars of conquest that were said to be dedicated to converting whole new populations to Christian rule or, through the period of the Reformation, to the true form of Christian rule. The state exercise of conversional power extended from the Catholic Reconquista of the Iberian Peninsula from Islamic rule, to the European conquest of the Americas, to the wars of religion in France, to the extraordinary enterprise of the

Spanish Armada, to the social, political, and military struggles that swept across Northern Europe and the British archipelago.

The Armada in 1588 is a particularly important event for my purposes here because it incited widespread terror in England in the face of the threat of forced mass conversions of English Protestants back to Catholicism as well as a not illegitimate fear about the possibility of mass killings. Also important is the fact that Shakespeare began his career as a playwright in the wake of the destruction of the Armada, devoting most of his effort in that time of national celebration to writing plays about the history of England. On this account, English national identity came into being in large measure on the strength of its successful resistance against forced conversion.

Conversion as an instrument of state power was no less valuable when it came to ensuring the loyalty and tractability of the populations of European nations. To cite one example, the 1535 Henrician Oath of Supremacy in England, which led to the execution of Thomas More, required oath-takers to "utterly testifie and declare in my Conscience, that the Kings Highnesse is the onely Supreame Governour of this Realme and to promise that from henchforth I shall beare faith and true Allegiance to the Kings Highnesse, his Heires and lawful Successors: so help me God."[23]

The problem with conversion as an instrument of rule is twofold. It is very difficult to police the inward beliefs of people. Spanish Catholic authorities could never be sure that the conversions they had compelled their Muslim and Jewish subjects to undergo would stick over the long run. The same kinds of challenges dogged the conversional programs through the sixteenth century in England as the population, including Shakespeare's family, was harried back and forth by major shifts in the confessional identity, practices, and theology of the Church. The focus on inwardness also provided a strong foundation for conscientious resistance to state power, whether the resister was a public figure such as Thomas More or a private person like Shakespeare's daughter Susanna, a recusant Catholic who resisted having to choose between taking Communion at Easter 1606 or having to disclaim the authority of the Pope and to swear fealty to King James as ruler of the nation and head of the Church.[24] The Jacobean Oath of Allegiance was designed to penetrate to the hearts of oath-takers by requiring them to swear their allegiance "without any equivocation or mental evasion or secret reservation whatsoever."[25]

A secondary factor in the emergence of the crisis was the convergence of the policing of consciences and the growth of an activist press and a politicized theatre, a situation that made things hotter for individuals like Susanna Shakespeare and for the entire political community. Through the century, as the nation switched back and forth between the Church of Rome and the English Church, writers, printers, and government authorities, including the Elizabethan secret police, conducted a series of skirmishes around the printing and circulation of polemical tracts on both sides. Of course, the traditional Catholic Corpus Christi cycle drama was eradicated by the Protestant authorities. Perhaps more pertinent for the emergence of Shakespeare's conversional theatre was the Elizabethan state's suppression of the use of players by high-ranking aristocrats to promote their own religio-political views. In the first year of her reign, 1559, for example, Elizabeth moved to exclude the players from what people were just beginning to discern was a burgeoning public sphere:

> The Queen's majesty [doth] straightly forbid all manner interludes to be played either openly or privately, except the same be [...] licensed within any city or town corporate by the mayor or other chief officers of the same [... .] [H]er majesty doth likewise charge every of [her officers] [...] that they permit none to be played wherein either matters of religion or of the governance of the estate of the commonweal shall be handled or treated, being no meet matters to be [...] treated upon but by men of authority, learning, and wisdom, nor to be handled before any audience but of grave and discreet persons.[26]

Shakespeare's Theatre of Conversion

Shakespeare and his fellow theatrical practitioners set out to take advantage of the government's suppression of a politically purposeful theatre and the commercial opportunities available in a rapidly expanding metropolis. They were in any case not the players that the Queen had in mind in her 1559 Proclamation. They represented a new generation of artists who, while still in livery to high-ranking members of the Court, had nevertheless begun in the 1570s to cultivate a new collective identity by building permanent public playhouses in London and by developing an altogether new mode of theatrical entertainment that was able to repurpose and repackage what the Queen had called "matters of religion or of the governance of the estate of the commonweal." On account of these new conditions of theatrical production and new kinds of plays, Shakespeare and his fellows were able to address matters of urgent public concern without, for the most part, incurring the displeasure of the government.

The key matter of public concern was conversion. Confessional identity and the question of conversion were at the centre of early modern English social and political life. Conversion affected almost every man and woman in England from early in the sixteenth century until well after Shakespeare's death. In addition to his daughter and possibly his father, other people he was close to, like Ben Jonson and Christopher Marlowe, were also at times in danger because of their conversions against the state-sponsored religion or their resistance to conversion to Protestantism.[27]

Shakespeare modelled his innovative style of characterization on the problem of conversion. He mined the resources of problematized conversion across his whole canon, from *The Taming of the Shrew* to *The Tempest*, where characters such as Katherine and Caliban acquire more depth on account of the undecidability of their conversions. Katherine's father offers Petruchio "Another dowry to another daughter, / For she is chang'd, as she had never been" (5.2.114–15).[28] Her "submission" speech, however, is designed to raise questions about the authenticity of the change. Her character and her story translate to the domestic sphere the century-long religio-political program of changing people's inward beliefs, a program that itself fostered the inscrutable inwardness it then undertook to police. The question of conversion, we might say, grounds Shakespeare's portrayal of Katherine's inwardness, the quality that makes her not an open book and yet a book that we never tire of trying to read.

Shakespeare made theatre out of religious crisis. I suggest that his art also made it possible for his playgoers to think feelingly about conversion by re-locating it in stories that were almost emptied of religious doctrine but were nevertheless filled with religious language, thought, narrative features, and emotion. Bottom's Apuleian "translation" brings him close – seemingly only on account of his asininity – to a Pauline apprehension of the deep mysteries of God. In *Much Ado About Nothing*, Benedict quizzes himself about the possibility he might, like his fellow soldier, Claudio, become a lover: "May I be so converted and see with these eyes? I cannot tell; I think not: I will not be sworn, but love may transform me to an oyster; but I'll take my oath on it, till he have made an oyster of me, he shall never make me such a fool" (2.3.21–5). In the two *Henry IV* plays and *Henry V*, Hal stages the publicity around his drawn-out accession to the throne of England as a thought-out conversion narrative. In these and many other plays, the drama set the playgoers free to think about the question of conversion by attenuating its relationship with established doctrinal pathways of analysis and argument. Shakespeare did not untether conversion from religion, but he paid out so much line that conversion came to live and signify primarily in such characters as Katherine, Caliban, Bottom, Benedict, and Prince Hal, as well as in their particular stories.

Converting Shylock

Shylock's story is different from those in the catalogue just mentioned because he is to undergo an actual forced conversion while they are playing creatively and critically with neighbouring forms of conversion – human-animal transformation, the foolish and miraculous process of falling in love, and politicized conversional public relations. Bottom, of course, also engages in such play, but he does so with little or no critical consciousness. Shylock's singularity makes him seem slow-moving, unimaginative, incapable of conversional play. His stubborn resistance to transformation is set off by his daughter Jessica, who finds the freedom within herself to marry a Christian and to turn Christian.

She even initiates her Christianization by cross-dressing as what her future husband excitedly calls "a lovely boy," a transformation that takes place in a scene that resonates with the sexual convertibility of the beautiful protagonist Bassanio.[29] Portia and Nerissa go further still by dressing as men, taking on the juridical work of highly trained male professionals, and casting themselves as their own (male) lovers in order to arouse and to discipline their new husbands.

On this account, all the resources of this comedy of conversion as well as the various forms of anti-Semitism (mostly talk about Jews as devils or dogs) are arrayed against Shylock, whose hard-heartedness makes his forced conversion not only understandable but also justifiable, as if only compulsory transformation could serve to expand his rigid, limited cognitive and emotional repertoire. At the end of Act 4, Shylock is indeed the subject of a forced conversion, an action that has been at the centre of competing literary and theatrical interpretations of the play since at least the nineteenth century. It is important to insist at this late date that the play does not set itself against the rightness of Shylock's forced conversion to Christianity. But that, as I have been suggesting, is just the beginning of the story.

The evident wrongness of the forced conversion – wrong especially from a post-Enlightenment point of view – has incited countless theatrical and literary defences of Shylock. None of these is wrong; they are simply partial. They grow out of the ground that Shakespeare prepared by converting religious conversion into multiple new forms around characters such as Katherine Minola, Caliban, Bottom, Benedict, and Hal, among others. The inwardness effect that we noted in the case of "the shrew" Katherine is of a piece with Shylock's humanness, the sense of inward presence that was developed, as we have seen, by Edmund Kean, and subsequently by Henry Irving, whose long hesitation before knocking on the door of his house (the hesitation based on his intuition that his daughter had fled) caused late nineteenth-century audiences to weep copiously for the now childless father.[30] The text fosters this kind of engagement with Shylock by surprising us often with language that bears no trace of the stock villain. One example is his recollection of the turquoise ring given to him by his late wife Leah and traded for a monkey by his daughter Jessica. Another is his last moment in the play, where he has no speech of complaint or threat, but a flat, ordinary statement of compliance:

> I pray you, give me leave to go from hence;
> I am not well: send the deed after me,
> And I will sign it. (4.1.391–3)

I can also note that an Elizabethan audience might have had a native-born element of sympathy for Shylock on account of his very name. Stephen Orgel has argued that Shylock is not a Jewish name, but rather an English one. Orgel traces the name "Shylok" to Englishmen in Hoo and Sussex, as early as the fifteenth century.[31] Inasmuch as Orgel is right about Shylock's name, we can see how early modern audiences, seven years after the defeat of the Spanish Armada, might have developed a complex response to a character at once both an alien Jew and a native Englishman who finds himself surrounded and persecuted by an elite Catholic community.

The historical moment of Shakespeare's writing of *The Merchant of Venice*, especially with his playgoers' enhanced sensitivity to the brutality of forced conversion and their no doubt perdurable hatred of the Jews, joined with his drama's orchestration of social languages and its art of characterization to lay the groundwork for the debates that have lived inside the play for at least the past two centuries. The play's artistic and political value – its usefulness in the long, never-completed progress towards toleration in a strong sense – consists precisely in how it has been able to gather into itself and organize into a dynamic and even volatile mix a multitude of conflicting readings, arguments, and performances of the characters, the languages they speak, the actions they undertake, and their liberating or their devastating conversions.

Tailpiece

By way of adding one new thread to the complex fabric of the play, I want to end this chapter by suggesting that Shylock, before the court of Venice, is also the author of his own conversion. It is not the conversion visited upon him by the Christian court. His conversional agency brings yet another voice into the play, one that has been heard countless times, but has not been adequately recognized.[32] It is the voice of Diogenes, the "dog philosopher."

Shylock takes his mortal enemy to court. In the court case, he seeks to fulfil something akin to the ghastly cannibalistic desire that he mentioned first in soliloquy, when he said, "If I can catch him once upon the hip, / I will feed fat the ancient grudge I bear him" (1.3.43–4). Cannibalism is of a piece with the "blood libel," the widespread slander that Jews are always on the look-out to capture Christians, especially young males. These Christian victims are circumcised and then killed. Their blood is drained out and used in the preparation of Jewish foods, especially matzoh. Jews as dogs, in many versions of that slander, kill and then eat the flesh of Christians. In the medieval *Ovide Moralisée*, the character Actaeon becomes Christ himself. Upon his transformation into a stag, he is pulled down, killed, and torn to pieces by his own hounds. In the medieval *Ovide*, the hounds represent the Jews, cursed for their denial and killing of Christ.[33]

Open court, however, is a strange place in which to exact a bloody revenge. When Shylock's predecessor on the stage, Marlowe's Jewish villain Barabas, seeks revenge, he does it by poison and other forms of subterfuge. Shylock chooses open court so that his revenge will have the legitimacy of the law behind it and the visibility of the public sphere around it. But, I suggest, he is also mordantly playful in the court scene. He undertakes the conversion of his cannibal dog self into another breed altogether, that of Diogenes, the ancient philosopher known as the dog, notorious for his outrageous conduct in public and his savage denunciation of all forms of hypocrisy. It was Diogenes' habit, so tradition tells us, to do everything in public, the functions of Demeter and Aphrodite alike.[34] Shylock does not go that far, but his outlandish comments to the Duke and the officers of the state sitting in court come close to his Cynic forbear. The Duke asks him if he intends in fact to cut a pound of flesh from the merchant Antonio. "It is my humour," Shylock answers,

> Some men there are love not a gaping pig;
> Some that are mad if they behold a cat;
> And others when the bagpipe sings i' th' nose,
> Cannot contain their urine. (4.1.42, 46–9)

Shylock's strange and disgusting reference to uncontrolled urination in answer to the Duke's question about the possibility of forgiveness and mercy is tantamount to Shylock lifting his leg against the high bench of the Venetian court of law.

In a previous exchange with Antonio, Shylock says, "Thou called'st me dog before thou hadst a cause, / But since I am a dog, beware my fangs" (3.3.6–7). At court, Shylock bares his fangs in a double fashion – in the form of the knife he will use to cut a pound of Antonio's flesh from the place "nearest his heart" (4.1.251), and in the biting language that we will bring to bear against the moral corruption of the Venetian state. He emulates Diogenes' denunciation of hypocrisy when, in answer to the argument for mercy, he turns his attention to the Venetian slave trade and state's dependence on slave labour:

> What judgement shall I dread, doing no wrong?
> You have among you many a purchased slave
> Which, like your asses and your dogs and mules,
> You use in abject and in slavish parts,
> Because you bought them. Shall I say to you,
> "Let them be free, marry them to your heirs."
> ... You will answer
> "The slaves are ours." So do I answer you.
> The pound of flesh which I demand of him
> Is dearly bought: 'tis mine, and I will have it.
> If you deny me, fie upon your law!
> There is no force in the decrees of Venice. (4.1.87–101)

Could we say that Shylock has triumphed here, especially since it is the hypocrisy and amoral exercise of power that he has identified in the Venetian state that are brought to bear against him in the questionable judgment of the court? I offer this view of the court scene not, of course, because I think the play speaks for toleration as if with a single unified voice. I bring this dimension of the play forward because it is important for us to open our ears so that we are able to hear and attend to all the voices in the play, including the sounds of Shylock the currish Jew and Shylock the dog philosopher.

NOTES

1   William Hazlitt, *A View of the English Stage*, ed. John Warren (London: 1821), 1–2.

2   *The Merchant of Venice: Shakespeare: The Critical Tradition*, vol. 5, ed. William Baker and Brian Vickers (London: Continuum, 2005), 31.

3   Harold Bloom, "The Jewish Question: British Anti-Semitism," *New York Times Sunday Book Review*, 7 May 2010, accessed 15 April 2017, http://www.nytimes.com/2010/05/09/books/review/Bloom-t.html?mcubz=1.

4   All quotes from the play are from *The Merchant of Venice*, ed. Jay L. Halio (Oxford: Oxford University Press, 1993).

5   *The Complete Poetry and Prose of Geoffrey Chaucer*, ed. John H. Fisher (New York: Holt, Rinehart and Winston, 1989), 244.

6   Paul Yachnin, "Shakespeare's Public Animals," in *Humankinds: The Renaissance and Its Anthropologies*, ed. Andreas Höfele and Stephan Laqué (Berlin and New York: De Gruyter, 2011), 185–98.

7   For Kean's bent-over posture in performance, see Charles Edelman, *The Merchant of Venice: Shakespeare in Production* (Cambridge: Cambridge University Press, 2002), 109.

8   Kenneth Stow, *Jewish Dogs: An Image and Its Interpreters: Continuity in the Jewish-Catholic Encounter* (Stanford: Stanford University Press, 2005), xiv–xv.

9   Voltaire, *The Philosophical Dictionary*, trans. H.I. Woolf (New York: Knopf, 1924), https://history.hanover.edu/texts/voltaire/volindex.html, accessed 16 April 2017.

10   Ibid.

11   Cornel West, "Race and Modernity," in *The Cornel West Reader* (New York: Basic Books, 1999), 55–86. Also see Emmanuel Chukwudi Eze, ed., *Race and the Enlightenment: A Reader* (Cambridge, MA: Blackwell, 1997).

12   Quoted in Thomas F. Gossett, *Race: The History of an Idea in America* (Dallas: Southern Methodist University Press, 1963), 45.

13   Voltaire, *Candide and Other Stories*, trans. Roger Pearson (Oxford: Oxford University Press, 2006), 49.

14   "Toleration," *Oxford English Dictionary*, accessed 6 April 2018, https://en.oxforddictionaries.com/definition/toleration.

15 "Toleration," *Stanford Encyclopedia of Philosophy*, accessed 13 September 2017, https://plato.stanford.edu/entries/toleration/.

16 John Foxe, *The Acts and Monuments of the English Church* (1570), book 8, p. 1292, Acts and Monuments Online, accessed 10 September 2017, https://www.johnfoxe.org/.

17 See the wonderful discussion in Alain Badiou, *Saint Paul: The Foundation of Universalism*, trans. Ray Brassier (Stanford: Stanford University Press, 2003).

18 It is worth noting that even Locke's *Letter* has a significant tilt against toleration in a strong sense, since while Locke is clear and consistent about the requirement to allow non-Christians to practise their faith without hindrance, he does not go the next step towards allowing that non-Christian religions might have an equal share of the truth with Christianity.

19 Peter Holbrook, *Shakespeare's Individualism* (Cambridge and New York: Cambridge University Press, 2010), 22–3.

20 Steven Mullaney, "Affective Technologies: Toward an Emotional Logic of the Elizabethan Stage," in *Environment and Embodiment in Early Modern England*, ed. Mary Floyd-Wilson and Garrett Sullivan (London: Palgrave Macmillan, 2006), 71–89.

21 For Charles Macklin, see James Shapiro, *Shakespeare and the Jews* (New York: Columbia University Press, 1996), 89. For Henry Goodman, see "Introduction," *The Merchant of Venice*, ed. John Drakaki and Arden Shakespeare (London: Methuen, 2010), 152–6; Barbara Lewalski, "Biblical Allusion and Allegory in *The Merchant of Venice*," *Shakespeare Quarterly* 13 (1962): 327–43; and Kenneth Gross, *Shylock Is Shakespeare* (Chicago: University of Chicago Press, 2006), 15.

22 M.M. Bakhtin, "Response to a Question from the *Novy Mir* Editorial Staff," in *Speech Genres and Other Late Essays*, trans. Vern W. McGee, ed. Caryl Emerson and Michael Holquist (Austin: University of Texas Press, 1986), 4. Cf. 1–7.

23 State Papers Online, accessed 13 September 2017, http://gale.cengage.co.uk/state-papers-online-15091714.aspx.

24 James Shapiro, *The Year of Lear: Shakespeare in 1606* (New York: Simon and Schuster, 2015).

25 Quoted in Shapiro, *Year of Lear*, loc. 3322.

26 *Tudor Royal Proclamations*, ed. Paul L. Hughes and James F. Larkin, 3 vols. (New Haven, CT: Yale University Press, 1969), 2:115.

27 For Ben Jonson, see David Riggs, *Ben Jonson: A Life* (Cambridge, MA: Harvard University Press, 1989); for Marlowe's exciting and dangerous conversional history, see Charles Nicholl, *The Reckoning: The Murder of Christopher Marlowe* (New York: Harcourt Brace, 1992).

28 All Shakespeare quotations, except for those from *Merchant of Venice*, are from *The Riverside Shakespeare*, 2nd ed., G. Blakemore Evans, textual ed. (Boston: Houghton Mifflin, 1997).

29 The reading of the phrase in Halio's Oxford edition is "lowly boy," but it appears as "louely boy" in both the Quarto and Folio editions.

30 For Henry Irving's performance of Shylock, see "Introduction," *Merchant of Venice,*
    ed. Halio, 67–70.

31 Stephen Orgel, "Imagining Shylock," in *Imagining Shakespeare: A History of Texts
    and Visions* (Basingstoke: Palgrave Macmillan, 2003), 144–62.

32 For Diogenes in early modern thinking and in Shakespeare, see David Hershinow,
    "Diogenes the Cynic and Shakespeare's Bitter Fool: The Politics and Aesthetics of
    Free Speech," *Criticism* 56 (2014): 807–35.

33 I owe this observation about the *Ovide Moralisé* to Peggy McCracken's plenary talk,
    "Metamorphosis and Conversion: Becoming Stag in the *Ovide moralisé*," presented
    at the Transforming Bodies Conference, Cornell University, 21–22 April 2017.

34 See *The Cynic Philosophers: From Diogenes to Julian,* trans. Robert Dobbin (repr.
    Penguin Classics, 2012), 7–78; William Desmond, *Cynics* (Stocksfield: Acumen,
    2008), 19–24.

2 New World Behn: Toleration, Geography, and the Question of Humanity

SHARON ACHINSTEIN

Imagining European religious toleration in the early modern period demands the imagination of space: space as contained within national borders; spaces real and imagined of communities in communion (the parish, the graveyard); space outside borders for escape or inside them for refuge. It was long the practice of the English to move across borders in space to achieve freedom for the expression of unorthodox religious belief. Across national borders, voluntary flight – whether that of sixteenth-century reformers John Foxe or John Bale to Geneva, of the early modern recusants choosing safety in continental convents and religious houses, or of some 21,000 English Puritans setting sail across the Atlantic in the 1620s to 1640s – was a common response to religious persecution. Forced exile of minority communities through edict or war was also an outcome of early modern religious difference – as in the expulsions of Jews (1492) and Moriscos (1609) from Spain, the Piedmont Waldensians after the Massacre (1655) from Italy and France, and the Huguenots from France (1685). Where religious minority populations found refuge in both voluntary and involuntary migrations, freedom of worship and, sometimes, self-preservation, rather than toleration, was the aim.

The relationship of space to free exercise of religion in the European early modern period was profoundly shaped by the 1648 Peace of Westphalia, which not only put an end to one intense period of religious warfare, but created a new, international political order of sovereign states in the former Holy Roman Empire. It set a judicial framework for relations between the three main Christian denominations, and thus for religious coexistence. Many communities had found ways to live peaceably with one another despite religious diversity. However, these were practical arrangements that frequently broke down.[1] After Westphalia, states took up the mantle of legislating confession, although the mechanisms regulating and containing confessional conflict rarely resolved them. The religion of the ruler was to be the established religion of the territory, but liberty of assembly, worship, and education was granted for those of nonorthodox faiths. This was the foundation of a "new concept of international law based on state sovereignty."[2] In some localities, legislation was enacted allowing rights to religious minorities, including radical Christian sects, Mennonites, and Jews – none of whom had been mentioned in the Peace. Geography mattered, yet flare-ups of religious persecution recurred – atrocities such as the slaughter of the Waldensians in 1655, and, worst of all, the persecution that ensued after the 1685 revocation of the Edict of Nantes in France, which spelled disaster for the French Huguenots.[3] Huguenot refugees streamed into European countries, and renewed concepts of asylum, sanctuary, and refuge were developed. Indeed, the word "refugee" only entered the English language after Louis XIV's persecution of Protestants in Catholic France.[4] The concept of refuge was rooted in the medieval practice of sanctuary, which was intended to ensure that avengers did not kill fugitives before trial; it would increasingly come to be associated with political and humanitarian sympathy.

Refuge, exile, and emigration: these were to be understood as part of a vision of the world as separated by discrete places, places outside sovereign jurisdiction or impermeable to the persecution of state or church. As Ayesha Ramachandran reminds us, "global imagining" of a single "world" in early modern Europe was a project of modernity – the creation of a "concept, a category, a system of order."[5] A world-system model – as described by Immanuel Wallerstein – structured as core, periphery, and semi-periphery, emerged in the early modern period, one that separated core countries (associated with skilled labour and higher capital production) from the rest of the world (associated with low-skill labour, labour-intensive production, and extraction of raw materials). Wallerstein's scheme, developed in the 1970s, sees the early modern period as a transition from feudalism to capitalism, and although it has been questioned as to its universality and emphasis on the nation-state, its structures help us understand the ways that early modern religious uniformity as a state policy could not survive the new economic world-shaping order.

The focus here in this essay is how the English writer Aphra Behn reckons with the new conditions of political economy and sovereignty that accompanied England's transition into a European world power, specifically in the context of interconfessional states. This essay, in acknowledging the complications of sovereignty in regard to early modern colonial mapping, and in approaching the moral quandaries arising in the emergent slave system, looks at the question of toleration not simply as a political question, but as a moral one about the scope of Christianity as a framework for global living. Behn has long been associated with libertinism and unorthodox religious thought, two important strands for thinking about early modern toleration.[6] A human rights perspective, rather than a libertine one, is here applied to Behn, a writer who spares little in her depiction of the violence and inhumanity of those who torture and murder under the cloak of colonial power. Behn is an eyewitness to the early

Atlantic slave trade, her *Oroonoko* (1688) a work almost overdetermined in its relationship to discourses of rights, the human, and literature in early modernity. While the novella, as will be shown here, does not propose solutions, and though it offered sympathy for an age, a mode, and a heroism that it viewed as inevitably lost,[7] it also reflected a humanitarian Christianity that was divided itself between a colonialist civilizing project and its sceptical critique.

Written by the first female professional writer in England, and inaugurating the novel as a genre in England, *Oroonoko* tells the story of an African prince who, along with his wife, is enslaved and sent to Surinam to work on an English plantation. With its first-person narrator, the text purports to be an eyewitness account of the tragic demise of a noble hero who leads a slave rebellion, after the failure of which he murders his wife and is subjected to repeated torture before his martyr-like death. The book was published in England in 1688, around the time of the Glorious Revolution in Britain, in which a Dutch monarch, William of Orange, dethroned the Stuart line. The work recalled the period of civil wars and the "tragic martyrdom" of Charles I. Critics have noted the paradoxes of sovereignty in the novella as well as its full deployment of orientalizing tropes (the first section of the novella taking place in the kingdom of Coramantien), and especially the problematics of New World sovereignty; the menacing violence that is the sign of sovereign authority; the author's complicity in the acts of violence sustained in the name of preservation of property; the transformation of bodies, male and female, differently wrenched into commodities for reproduction and exchange;[8] and the language of liberty that is the slave's hope. There are thus many inroads to understanding human rights thinking in Behn.[9]

Geographical approaches to the novella have considered space as a register in which identities are produced as a function of periphery and core, native and European. The novella's main locations, Coramantien and Surinam, are emblematic of an eroticized and orientalized European colonial consciousness. And yet, insofar as she also partakes of the early modern inquiry into universal or humanitarian morality, Behn exhibits cutting-edge awareness of how early modern colonial enterprises could sharply challenge orthodox Christianity. As is well known, Behn expresses contrary attitudes towards political and religious dissent, Christianity and freethinking. What is suggested here is that, rather than being simply a vehicle for philosophical scepticism, the novella gives energy to representing the complex conditions under which territorial sovereigns sought, but could not maintain, authority – as was the case in the early modern Caribbean. Behn was most certainly an ambivalent supporter of the colonial order.[10] What follows below is a close exploration of the political context of the colony depicted in Behn's novella with the suggestion that the twin challenges of religiously diverse communities and the crisis of sovereignty in the Caribbean gave scope for thinking about toleration and the fundamentals of

Christian morality. Through a look at the historical conditions of Surinam, the setting of Behn's colonial slave society in *Oroonoko*, we will explore how her depictions participate in an emergent critique of the cruelties of the slave system as well as a challenge to Christianity. As will be shown, once the Caribbean setting, with its situated instabilities, is taken into account, her fiction produces an uneasy tension between Christian and moralist elements, opening up the space for two concurrent Enlightenments: the religious and the secular. In each of these, her novel endeavours to "put cruelty first."

For the great political theorist of liberalism, Judith Shklar, the charge of cruelty is a "purely human verdict upon human conduct," and in the early modern period, could be taken as a charge outside the sphere of revealed religion: "to put cruelty first [...] is to be at odds not only with religion but with normal politics as well."[11] In her analysis of Montaigne's reflections upon cruelty, Shklar observes how his emphasis on the actuality of pain and suffering produces a commitment to earthly morals. From the first principle of hating cruelty, she argues, emerges a discourse of secularity, one that, if it puts consideration of cruelty first, also condemns Christianity from a moral point of view. The desire to end cruelties has been, as Talal Asad puts it, "a major motive of secularism." Asad, in his anthropology of secularism, explores how "moral sensibilities about deliberately inflicted pain have been formed in modern secular society" and reveals that the "modern dedication to eliminating pain and suffering often conflicts with other commitments and values."[12] Taking Behn's novella as a site of movement within the discourses of religion and secularity, a movement produced by the colonial situation, and delivering both a religious and a secular mode of Enlightenment, we will see what happens as Behn puts cruelty first.

Behn's Worlds: Territories beyond the Nation

Behn, like other early modern utopian writers, was keen on exploring the ways that the globe was presenting new "worlds." The plurality of worlds took hold of her imagination, as evidenced by her translation of Fontenelle's *Entretiens sur la pluralité des mondes* (1686), which she entitled *Discovery of New Worlds* (1688). In her preface she comments that Fontenelle "ascribes all to Nature, and say[s] not a Word of God Almighty, from the Beginning to the End; so that one would almost take him to be a *Pagan*."[13] Behn suggests that the existence of non-Christian societies prompts the question of whether there were, indeed, alternatives to Christianity, and also whether there were laws of nature that could guide humanity. Early modern thinkers often used the trope of a fictional world to position themselves outside their own social constraints and, thus challenged norms, institutions, and culture; indeed that "outside" led to the development of an account of laws of nature in early modernity. Behn's works of fiction deploy the Americas to represent the barbarity and corruption of the English – as in *The Widow Ranter*, for instance – where the New World is figured at once as a place of libertine sensuality and political disorder. Elliott Visconsi has shown how Behn sees her colonial settings as "refractions of England's primitive history," highlighting the perils of popular rule, with her own writing as an instituting "project of civilization."[14] Yet, as Behn projects British worries onto foreign locales or indigenous peoples, she also refracts her understanding of sovereignty and religion through the experience of their crisis under colonial rule.

What might a consideration of Behn's spatiality in the factual worlds of her fiction contribute to an account of toleration? In *Oroonoko*, her speculation was not the same as that of Leibniz or Margaret Cavendish, who, in *Blazing World* (1666), imagines a "World of my own Creating" – picturing various worlds each having their own sun – and eventually reveals that there are an "infinite number of Worlds."[15] In the writing of Cavendish, as Corrinne Harol shows in her essay in this volume, the conceit of multiple worlds invites a "fictional thought experiment" that conveys the power of imagination to engage politics. Behn, instead, offers a description of arrangements actually existing, not a journalistic rendering to be sure, but an "eyewitness account" of the indigenes of Amazonia and of the forced workers on West Indian slave plantations. Her representations of these diverse populations focus on the question of social, not natural or species difference, and so her analysis of human variety does not take up the philosophical questions at the heart of Cavendish's fantasy. Behn's other worlds are not those of the imagination, but of the newly coordinated globe, those "distant worlds"[16] of the Caribbean. The Caribbean had acquired a newly appointed – and very real – governor, the heavy-drinking second Duke of Albemarle, to whom Behn had sent a panegyric, "To the Most Illustrious Prince, Christopher, Duke of Albemarle on his Voyage to his Government of Jamaica" (1687), in hopes of his patronage. Behn locates the challenge of diversity, then, in the questions of dominion and territorial sovereignty.

Behn's novella *Oroonoko* (1688) distributes its political imaginings across different spatial registers, with the territories of Coramantien and Surinam taken as separate "Worlds."[17] In Coramantien, the lovestruck Oroonoko, pining for Imoinda, longs to flee with his beloved to "an unknown world." The narrator refers to Oroonoko arriving in "our world," meaning Surinam, the "our" suggesting a shared colonial territoriality; as Oroonoko is led into slavery there, he exhorts his friends to hope for better treatment "in the next world we shall touch upon."[18] Yet the geography of "our" world slips around: it is not strictly a territorial marker, but a conceptual one. For instance, it is in this world called "ours" that Oroonoko is imprinted with an identity as "Caesar." As the narrator remarks, "For the future therefore, I must call Oroonoko, Caesar, since by that name only he was known in our western world" (108), a "western" designation that designates the Caribbean "world" as geographically coextensive with Western Europe.

The political thought of Behn has been aligned clearly with her British, anti-Whig, anti-Dissent writing. Political analysis of *Oroonoko*, focused on matters of sovereignty and slavery, has asked how the figure of Oroonoko is a response to British political crises of sovereign authority during and after the Restoration. The novella summons memories of the bloody civil war and regicide, with its discourse of anti-slavery co-opted from the Whigs but repurposed to bolster a Royalist vision of sovereign authority.[19] Yet political readings have illuminated how Behn uses "geographical difference to represent political difference" – Coramantien evoking a traditional absolutist society, and Surinam the emergent system of mercantile capitalism. Laura Rosenthal notes that in "both locations, love and liberty conflict with inept local authority."[20] Politics are thus to be understood as supranational as well as national.

Not only within Britain, but across Europe, sovereignty was the constitutive problem of political modernity, particularly as brought about through Europe's relationship with its others, "through its colonial project and the resistance of the colonized."[21] It was the Restoration monarchy, for instance, in establishing the Royal African Company, that made the triangular system of chattel slavery the official policy of England, heightening tensions with the Dutch over navigation and trade. After the founding of the Company of Royal Adventurers Trading to Africa in 1660, overseen by the Duke of York, its monopoly status granted by the Crown in 1672 as the Royal African Company, enslaved Africans were brought to English colonies in the Caribbean to work the expanding sugar plantations. The character of those colonies changed to one of harsh and violent suppression of its forced labour populations. This was the period during which Behn was allegedly a Royalist spy intended to report on Parliamentarian refugees in Surinam. Behn's novella takes place in the age of these plantations, the commodity of sugar mentioned prominently in her description of the manner of acquiring an enslaved labour force.[22]

Sovereignty over the colonial territories would come to involve struggle from within the fledgling European state system, with France, Spain, the Netherlands, Denmark, and England vying for power. But there was also struggle within European Christianity, which gave shape to a strand of Christian humanitarianism. The sovereign – and some would say, secular – principle of toleration that resides in the Westphalian model adheres to the view that states have an inviolable right to govern as they wish within territorial borders. Writing within the post-Westphalian order of states, a system constructed out of capitalist notions of the individual, property, sovereignty, jurisdiction, and religious non-interference, Aphra Behn is positioned within the cognitive mapping of early capitalism. To the long tradition of historical criticism of Behn that has focused on political questions of obedience and sovereignty must therefore be added facets of religious difference, economics, and change.[23] Behn's sojourn in colonial Surinam, during the period of its transformation to a racialized slave economy, produced a narrative that bears witness to and, as it exposes the fractures in Christian morality, seeks to mend them by evoking a discourse of humanity, and even of human rights.

However, Aphra Behn, as is well known, was no friend of toleration or religious dissent, and persistently sought to discredit religious dissenters by mocking their zeal and their lust. Her play *The Roundheads* has Lady Lambert explaining that the first thing learned by women attending conventicles (illegal forms of worship) is how to "jilt": "Kings are depos'd and Commonwealths are rul'd; / By Jilting all the Universe is fool'd."[24] If nonconformists come in for witty abuse, her depictions of Jews ("Monsters [...] of vast fortunes" in *The Rover*, part 2, which has two Jewish heiresses, described as a Giant and a Dwarf), non-Christians, and Muslims (the vengeful, lustful hero of *Abdelazer* rapes a European woman) are far worse examples of cultural narrowness. There, Behn shuttles between condescension and outright dehumanization. The association of social disorder with religious nonconformity in Restoration England is so commonplace, and reflected in her canon as to be hardly worth mentioning. Behn was not alone in her judgments. Slurs against the radical evils of schism and sedition abounded in the literature of the period as the Anglican theo-political religious order aligned itself to centralized concepts of sovereignty. The Anglican clergyman Richard Perrinchief stated baldly in his Restoration work, *A Discourse of Toleration*, that the state "cannot be safe while the Church is in a Tempest"; Archbishop Gilbert Sheldon declared nonconformity a "disease."[25] This movement against religious pluralism was a sharp backlash in response to twenty years of civil wars and revolution, a period that had seen the execution of the king and the exile of leading Royalists along with the sequestration of their lands and property.

Indeed, Behn has long been understood as something of a "gauge" of Royalist opinion regarding nonconformists. As Melinda Zook has outlined, Behn objects to their deceit and secrecy, that is, to their political manoeuvring.[26] Her Tory-partisan Exclusion Crisis plays – *Sir Patient Fancy* (1678), *The Feign'd Courtizans* (1679), and especially *The Roundheads* (1682) – all show the threat Dissent posed to order, peace, and stability, in short, to the sovereignty in the state.[27] In the pitched battle during the Exclusion Crisis, which produced propaganda on both sides of toleration, Behn repeatedly mocked Whigs and Puritans through an attack on canting religion seen as a challenge to sovereign authority, for instance in *The Roundheads* (performed 1681), which depicts Whig "canting" preachers, epitomized by the lay preacher Ananias. In her only tragedy, *Abdelazer* (performed 1676), the titular character laments, "The giddy Rout are guided by Religion / More than by Justice, Reason, or Allegiance."[28]

Although this account helps us see how Behn's views on Dissent are a stand-in for her critique of Whig political ideology, nonetheless, once the factor of the slave economies in the New World is figured in, the critique of Dissent looks a little different. Republicans and Royalists, Whigs and Tories, shared a common interest in the colonial enterprise, and with it, chattel slavery, and this makes Behn's portrait rather complex. Indeed, her narrator crosses ideological lines in her evident respect for, and close alliance with, George Martin, brother to the "great Oliverian" Henry Martin (*Oroonoko*, 117), against the governor Byam. These facts suggest a more nuanced approach is needed to take into account the realities of opportunistic alliance and indeed common cause across ideologically and religious diverse identities in the new economic orders of the colonies.

In terms of Behn's ideas about freedom of religion, scholars have debated the extent to which she was a Christian thinker at all. Behn has been seen as hostile to religion and as a "sceptical freethinker,"[29] with *Oroonoko* actively critical of Christianity, from the vantage point of a "virtuous atheist."[30] Behn's translation of the freethinking work Fontenelle's *History of Oracles* shows her deep engagement with sceptical thought,[31] the translation revealing her "uneasiness with the prejudices of her time."[32] Behn's poem "The Golden Age" (1684) imagines time before religion, where "every Vow inviolably true; / Not kept in fear of Gods, no fond Religious cause."[33] All religion, not simply Dissenting nonconformity, seems her enemy, as seen in her repeated attacks on priestcraft and religious hypocrisy, applied equally to radical religious leaders, as in *The Roundheads*, but also to the salacious (Anglican) chaplain Mr. Prayfast in *The Wandering Beauty* (1687). Once the larger international religious geography is taken into perspective, Behn's topical attacks on religion may be understood in a new light, with a larger question about toleration and the morality of Christianity coming into view from the experiences of colonial domination and enslavement.

Territory, Sovereignty and Religion: "Cuius regio, eius religio"

"Whose realm, his religion": The Latin phrase produced by the Peace of Augsberg (1555) emerged out of the period of conflict between Roman Catholic and Protestant forces within the Holy Roman Empire. Matters of religion would be settled by individual states, as later enshrined more widely in the Peace of Westphalia (1648) to end the terrible European wars of religion. "Cuius regio, eius religio" meant that the question of religious difference would be resolved on the principle of territory. Yet in the midst of European states' scramble for trade and settlement, territorial disputes, and conquest and reconquest, along with denominational plurality from the start, it was impossible to effect a state church in many of these spaces of conquest. Territorial definitions of religion evaporated, especially in the Caribbean. Indeed, when it came to many of the North American colonies, religious liberty had been an essential part of their foundation.

Toleration, in practice and in policy, abounded in the Caribbean colonies held by the English from the 1640s.[34] In the 1640s Barbados flourished as a place where religious toleration worked in practice; Protestants, Jews, and Roman Catholics were made welcome in this first period of the "Sugar Revolution."[35] The management of religion in Surinam under Parliamentarian rule allowed for "liberty of conscience" in 1652.[36] Promises of liberty of worship, extended to the Jews, were offered in the Caribbean, and the first synagogue in the region was built in 1654 in English-controlled Surinam, where a thriving Jewish community survives to this day.[37] Those coming to Surinam from England were a diverse religious lot, and included the likes of Henry Adis, a London General Baptist leader, and John Oxenbridge, a university-trained Independent minister.[38] While in 1655, Cromwell's "Western Design," his military campaign to wrest power from the Spanish in the Caribbean, early on took an avid Protestant cast, it was also nonetheless driven by a pragmatic and commercial spirit that allowed for tolerance on the ground. Although Cromwell's expedition in Hispaniola was a disaster, his fleet did take Jamaica, which soon became a refuge for Quakers from Barbados as well as for Sephardic Jews expelled from Brazil after the defeat of the Dutch by the Portuguese in 1654.

The British Crown had been actively involved in Caribbean settlement, more so than in the New England or Chesapeake colonies; it was in the Caribbean that continual wars were going on between Britain, Spain, the United Netherlands, and France over nominal sovereignty. It was a lucrative spot to control; in 1666, it was reported, Barbados, the Leeward Islands, and Surinam had sent yearly "value" of more than £800,000 to England.[39] In the Caribbean, religious liberty was granted even after the Restoration as a means of transporting unwanted religious minorities, who were put to use as a brace against foreign powers. Settling the Caribbean colonies required inducements, and religious liberty was one of them. Allowing migration removed Dissenters from the centre, and after the passage of the Coventicles Acts in 1664, they could be punished for repeated offences by transportation to the colonies.[40] Their toleration in these colonial spaces was a by-product of this voluntary or coerced movement in space.

If religious uniformity was impracticable and even unwanted in the Caribbean colonies, however, the forms of sovereignty practised there were often in excess of those at home. The governorship of Surinam, for instance, was a proprietorship, where Francis Willoughby, 5th Baron Lord Willoughby of Parham, was a colonial ruler with disproportionate power. As Sarah Barber has shown, Willoughby's career divides into two, the first part taking place in Lincolnshire, where he was a Presbyterian with anti-court sympathies; he was also involved in the civil war heading the Lincolnshire parliamentary forces and rose to become Speaker of the House of Lords. However, Willoughby's second career was in his making common cause with the Royalists after his impeachment. With his estates sequestered, the Duke of York named him vice-admiral of the Royalist fleet, whereby he sought his fortunes in the Caribbean. He was reconfirmed proprietor of Surinam following the Restoration.[41] Willoughby had wide latitude to run the place as he wished, and it was rumoured that his Surinamese estate at Parham, according to Behn's fictional *Oroonoko*, "was as much exempt from the law as Whitehall," a judgment confirmed by the recent historical work of Barber.[42]

Surinam, not an island but part of the mainland, was seen as a means to expand English holdings in the western hemisphere with unbounded horizons. Absolute sovereignty and all forms of petty tyranny ruled there. *Surinam Justice* (1662) was the title of a long pamphlet protesting Willoughby's autocracy and his maltreatment of settlers, his "arbitrary and tyrannical way of proceedings."[43] Willoughby, also as governor of Barbados, brought in legislation that created the categories of "slaves as real estate" and not as "chattels," that is, real, as opposed to leased or personal, property, a distinction that allowed inheritance by the slaveholder's heirs.[44] In the 1650s, while Willoughby was away from the colony, arguing his case for his legal right to it, an elected assembly was established, with a governor elected on an annual basis and a six-man council acting as executive. But it was a time and place of rapid political change; with the restoration of the monarchy in 1660, Willoughby took up the governorship of the Caribbean and his title to Surinam was confirmed. While, during the mid-seventeenth century, Willoughby was part of the centralization and brutality of authority produced by the new regimes of slavery, he did nonetheless promote a policy of religious liberty, one that, for example, had motivated the Baptist Henry Adis, along with six other families, to settle there and pledge allegiance to him.[45] These tensions between sovereignty and toleration were felt all over the Caribbean and give energy to Behn's novella, as we shall see.

Colonial sovereignty in the seventeenth-century Caribbean was amazingly unstable during this period, as Alison Games's rich historical studies have shown, with colonies changing "hands with breath-taking rapidity and with considerable, if small-scale, violence during the frequent wars of the second half of the seventeenth century."[46] In this period, the Spanish lost Jamaica and the lesser Antilles to England, France, and the Netherlands; the English took Dutch Tobago in 1666, but quickly lost it to the French. On the northern coast of South America, called the "Wild Coast," settlements at Surinam, Pomeroon, Cayenne, and Essequibo flipped dramatically among French, Dutch, and English claimants. Unlike other inhabitants who fled or rebelled against new sovereigns, in Surinam, the English – who were almost the only European population living there – stayed put under Dutch rule after 1667. The colony had changed its political affiliation and, thus, a new situation arose in the Caribbean: English men and women now found themselves living under a foreign colonial power.

Rules governing the handling of religious difference in the English Protestant colonies differed from those in England itself. England's policy was to transport prisoners of war and religious nonconformists, and promises of religious liberty made under the Commonwealth and Protectorate were continued in Restoration period in the Caribbean.[47] Henry Adis, in a letter posted from Surinam to Lord Willoughby in 1663 (published in London in 1664), praised the liberty of conscience that ruled in the place. He also complained that lawlessness, drunkenness, and violence were endemic. As Adis saw it, the English in Surinam "who call themselves Christians, yet by their debauched Atheistical Actions, evidence themselves more brutish by far, than the very Heathens themselves, to the shame and stink of Christianity amongst them."[48] Willoughby was an autocrat and would have taken no reassurance from the recent experience of Barbados in the 1650s, where a religiously diverse population, fractious with civil unrest, required a military intervention by the Commonwealth fleet.[49] The colony had been ruled by an elective and representative assembly in the 1650s, with which Willoughby's autocratic tendencies, and the rule of his deputy William Byam, were at odds.

The handover of Surinam to the Dutch in the Treaty of Breda (1667) was another sign that the Dutch had won the war known as the Second Dutch War; a small part of the resulting agreement asked for the revocation of English claims to dominion over the seas, a revision of the British Navigation Acts. Following the Medway disaster, England had agreed to cede Surinam to the Dutch. When England lost that war they also lost control over the English religious and political exiles, and the next decade saw a further series of hostilities.[50] After the handover, instability in the sovereignty of the colony laid the conditions for numerous slave rebellions, news of which made its way into the English press. Alison Games has described the English remaining in Surinam, subject to Dutch sovereignty, as "an uneasy yet optimistic integration of a subject people": in effect the English were mistrusted or held under house arrest during times of renewed European conflict.[51]

The implications of this complex setting for an understanding of Behn's colonial location for her story cannot be overestimated. As her narrator recounts, the place has so little history because the Dutch "killed, banished and dispersed all those that were capable of giving the world" (108) the colony's story.[52] In the changed conditions of political sovereignty in England in 1688, there were many who were deeply anxious about what a Dutch invasion might feel like. Calling this simply a "Tory" perspective leaves out the facts of global geographies essential to the understanding of *Oroonoko*'s political thinking on toleration and sovereignty. We have long seen the various ways that fictions of sovereignty haunt *Oroonoko*. The forms of sovereign authority are noticeably absent or unstable in her New World works, whether in *The Widow Ranter* (set in colonial Virginia) or in *Oroonoko* (set in colonial Surinam), which show inhabitants as subjected to the violence of the powerful. In her sojourn in Surinam in 1663–4, Aphra Behn was aware of these political dissonances.

Under the absent Lord Willoughby, William Byam, deputy governor of Surinam, becomes the treacherous coward; Banister, the "wild Irishman" (139), another enemy, is deemed "a fellow of absolute barbarity" (140), only to later become governor of Surinam. Indeed, the entire novella exists in a kind of suspension of time: Surinam is awaiting its absent governor's return. A strong plea for the arrival of the governor, the novella is also a call for a justice yet to come.

Who Is Converting Whom? Christianity vs Humanity

With these wider contexts in mind, it is time now to turn our focus to Behn's *Oroonoko*. In the remainder of this essay, it will be shown how Behn adopts a humanitarian Christian discourse – not a scepticism about morality, but rather a new awareness of how slavery violates the dictates of humanity. In the novella, there are two distinct discourses through which the morality of slavery is interrogated, the Christian and the humanitarian. These are not mutually exclusive, but indeed lead to two different Enlightenments: the religious and the secular. Within a humanitarian Christianity, Behn may be aligned with the London merchant Thomas Tryon (1634–1703), who presented "the Complaints of the Negro-Slaves against the hard Usages and barbarous Cruelties inflicted upon them" after sojourning in the Caribbean during the period 1663 to 1669, and seeing the place in need of total reform.[53] Tryon was a mystic, a sometime Anabaptist, and a vegetarian, his views not far from those reflected in the many writings from different denominations supporting a benevolent Christianity highly critical of current slavers' practice. The accounts of his colonial experiences beginning in 1682 were published by the Quaker printing house of Andrew Sowle and his daughter Tace Sowle. A moral rebuke to contemporary practitioners of the slave system, his two tracts on slavery, "The Negro's Complaint of their Hard Servitude, and the Cruelties Practised upon them" and "A Discourse in the Way of Dialogue, Between an Ethiopean or Negro-Slave and a Christian, That was his Master in America," appeared in a publication entitled *Friendly Advice to Gentleman-Planters of the East and West Indies* (1684). A further work, his *Dialogue between an East-Indian Brackmanny or Heathen Philosopher, and a French Gentleman concerning the Present Affairs of Europe* (1683), also discussed the topic of slavery. In the last, a peace-loving, vegetarian, natural philosopher Indian discusses faith with a Catholic Frenchman. It turns out that they mutually enlighten each other. The Frenchman says, "You have not only gratified my Curiosity, but in several things informed my Understanding. And I heartily wish that your Virtue and Morality were crowned with true Christianity, and our Christianity embellisht with the real practice of your Virtue, Temperance and Moderation."[54] The attack on colonialism was not structural but ethical, a personal reform of morals through the discourse of temperance.[55] As Susan Dwyer Amussen has shown in *Caribbean Exchanges: Slavery and the*

Transformation of English Society, 1640–1700 (2007), the novelty of English slavery "had to be assimilated at home," and evidence of this is that such debate over the treatment of enslaved people began to take place in England across religious, economic, and political divides.[56]

In the final part of Tryon's *Friendly Advice*, the Ethiopian, or "Negro-Slave," is in "Dialogue" with the American slaveholder, who tries to explain the tenets and duties of Christianity. The Christian fails abysmally. The Ethiopian's speech takes up more than twice the space of the "Master's." His claims are well-ordered and voluminous. Upon hearing the principles of Christianity, the Ethiopian charges its propounder with hypocrisy.

> I cannot but also much wonder and admire that you *Christians* live and walk so wide from, and *contrary* unto all those undeniable Truths and holy Rules, so that what you preach with your *Tongues*, you pull down with your *Hands*, and your daily Conversation gives the Lye to your Profession.[57]

By enumerating examples of Christians' burdensome and violent actions – not only their physical abuse of enslaved workers, but abuses against their own bodies, the natural world, and its beings – the Ethiopian explains that the "extravagancy" of the so-called Christians "*cannot be maintained* but chiefly by *great Oppression* of Men and Beasts" (166). Amassing his facts, he summarizes that "the generality of your *Christians* do act the clean contrary" (183) to the professed faith. Imploring, "will you make us believe, that those men have *any Religion*, who have *no God*? Or have they indeed *a God*, who prefer their *Lusts*, or *Wealth*, or *Honour*, or any thing in the World before him, and his holy Commands" (184). The slave's logic is impeccable and the "Master," after a brave attempt to counter the reasoning, finally succumbs to it. Out of rejoinders, he at last promises to "*amend* our Practices," rather than to "study Arguments to *cloak* and *defend* them" (215). While startling in its representation of the enslaved speaker besting his Christian oppressor's argument, a genre with which Behn engages in *Oroonoko*, this pamphlet nonetheless does not seek to abolish slavery, or to deny Christianity's truths. Its aim is to make slaveholding more humane and its practitioners more virtuous, thus adhering to Christian principles. It is, in the end, "Friendly Advice."

I spend time with these ideas and methods of the pamphleteer Tryon because he was in Behn's circle of colonial experience. Behn herself wrote an encomiastic poem on one of Tryon's tracts, *The Way to Health, Long Life, and Happiness* (1683), a work promoting a vegetarian diet, and this poem was prefixed to another of Tryon's works in 1685.[58] *The Way to Health* recommended a regimen and diet intended to overcome physical ailments and a more general moral reform, as she put it in her poem, "how to eat, and live." Her sales pitch? Easy: "I've tri'd thy Method, and adore thy Theme."[59] Behn's commendatory poem recalls a former "State of Innocence" that recalls "that blest golden Age, when Man was young,"

> When the whole race was Vigorous and Strong;
> When Nature did her wond'rous dictates give,
> And taught the Noble Savage how to live;
> When Christal Streams, and every plenteous Wood
> Afforded harmless drink, and wholsom food;
> ....
> When every Sense to innocent delight
> Th'agreeing Elements unforc'd invite;
> When Earth was gay, and Heaven was kind and bright. (lines 4–8; 13–15)

In its evocation of a state of pristine nature, these words may also reflect something of the colonial vision of a land and people unencumbered by the dual corruptions of society and religion, such as are presented in the first pages and elsewhere in *Oroonoko* describing the land and its native inhabitants: "these people represented to me an absolute idea of the first state of innocence, before man knew how to sin; and 'tis most evident and plain, that simple Nature is the most harmless, inoffensive and virtuous mistress" (77). Arcadian fantasy, yes, but given a particular locale in the New World. Behn's novella represents a natural virtue, with the character Oroonoko exemplifying in his debate with the perfidious captain that one can swear an oath on "honour" rather than "upon the word of a Christian" (104).

Tryon does not simply exhort the Western Planters to reform their ways; he presents a voice of one oppressed, speaking back. Likewise, Behn's approach to the matter of slavery, to represent the bodies and voices of the enslaved, is a means of recognizing a common humanity. The dialogue between the Ethiopian and his enslaver presumes equal participation in debate, a common rationality, and shared protocols for persuasive discourse, rather than the imposition of silence, fear or force.[60] It shares common elements with the cross-confessional commentary by the outspoken Muslim Mehmet in the "Turkish Spy" series in the early eighteenth-century, which is at once a product of the Enlightenment but also a satire aimed at Christian persecution, as Humberto Garcia shows in his essay in this volume. Behn launches a critique of Christian hypocrisy while still upholding the premise of its universality. It is striking that in Behn's novella, the narrator has made an effort to convert Imoinda to Christianity, "telling her stories of nuns, and endeavouring to bring her to the knowledge of the true God" (113). Conversion of an enslaved person seems desirable; Behn places her Imoinda within the frame of Christian salvation, one of rational persuasion and "friendly" discourse.

Oroonoko's experience, however, speaks otherwise. His education in Christian behaviour is won from experience, not doctrine. Oroonoko will have none of this Christianity, and finds the narrator's talk of the "true God" not to his liking. He "would never be reconciled to our notions of the Trinity of which he ever made a jest; it was a riddle, he said, would turn his brain to conceive, and one could not make him understand what faith was" (113). His education into the meaning of Christianity is through the perfidy of his oppressors, after his betrayal by the ship's captain into slavery: "'Tis worth my suffering to gain so true a knowledge both of you and of your gods by whom you swear" (106). The clear implication is that the Christian's word is worth nothing. Like the facts enumerated by Tryon's Ethiopian, Behn's hero gives a rousing speech to his fellow rebels and counts up "all their toils and sufferings, under such loads, burdens, and drudgeries, as were fitter for beasts than men, senseless brutes, than human souls" (125–6). He concludes his rebellious speech with a comment on the hypocrisy of the Christians: "there was no faith in the white men, or the gods they adored, who instructed them in principles so false, that honest men could not live amongst them; though no people professed so much, none performed so little" (130). Indeed, the Christians have become the enemies of mankind, "with them a man ought to be eternally on his guard," and one ought "never to eat and drink with Christians without his weapon of defence in his hand, and, for his own security, never to credit one word thy spoke" (130). If self-preservation is the bedrock on which the concept of natural right was to be founded in this period, it is clear here that Christians' perfidy excludes them from the conditions enabling any moral society. As Tryon's "The Negro's Complaint" not only protests the conditions of servitude, it also charges the "Master" with religious hypocrisy. The "Negro" objects, "though they boast, and speak excellent things of the *Christian Religion*, and contemn us for being ignorant of it; yet 'tis plain they never design that we should know and embrace it; for why else do they make it loathsome in our Eyes, by acting so contrary to its *Genuine* Nature and Principles?" (138). Here, as in *Oroonoko*, a discourse of natural right or law creeps in as a challenge to Christianity. This is a whisper of secular Enlightenment.

In the late seventeenth century, writers from various Christian denominations sought to amend, though not abolish, slavery. Aimed to reform the slave-holders and ameliorate the conditions of the forced labourers, their writings took a humanitarian approach, with authority of their own testimony as eyewitness. This was the approach of Anglican priest Morgan Godwyn, author of *The Negro's and Indians Advocate, Suing for their Admission into the Church* (1680), who visited Barbados and Virginia in the mid to late 1670s. On his title page he quotes from Acts 4:20: "We cannot but speak the things which we have seen and heard."[61] In another slavery-reform pamphlet, *Trade Preferr'd before Religion* (1685), Godwyn warned that in their slave-holding, the English were losing their own Christianity, and he protested against the "degenerated English" for whom, through "want of Discipline, Christianity doth seem to be wholly lost, and nothing but Infidelity to have come in its place." Godwyn exposes that the settlers do "Brutifie" their enslaved workers, "to unman and unsoul" them, and thereby do sin against God.[62]

Early humanitarian Christianity was not always a high road to secularity; however, the twin projects of converting enslaved workers to Christianity and of improving the morals of their enslavers, to adhere to the principles of a humanitarian Christianity, were efforts common to Anglicans and Dissenters alike. The nonconformist minister Richard Baxter urged slave holders to exhibit mercy towards their enslaved workers, and not to deny them the light of Christ, and he pressed an ideal of moral trusteeship that became embodied into colonial law.[63] In his *Christian Directory* (1673), Baxter gave "Direction to those Masters in foreign Plantations who have Negro's and other Slaves." Baxter, like Behn, exhorted his readers to "Sufficiently difference between *Men* and *Bruits*. Remember that they are of as good a kind as you; that is, They are reasonable Creatures, as well as you; and born to as much natural liberty [...] Remember that they and you are equally under the Government and Laws of God." Baxter saw the perfidy of those who kidnapped Africans into slavery, likening them to "Pirats," committing "one of the worst kinds of Thievery in the world [...] such persons are to be taken for the common enemies of mankind." So, too, are those who buy and sell men. Baxter, like Behn's characters in *Oroonoko*, reversed the ordinary hierarchy of European/barbarian: "Is not he the basest wretch and the most barbarous savage, who committeth the greatest and most inhumane wickedness? And are theirs comparable to these of yours?" Baxter does not indeed seek to overturn the system of slavery, but rather to bring it into a more humane shape: "remember that even a slave may be one of those Neighbours that you are bound to love as your selves."[64]

Antislavery discourse in the seventeenth century was developed along these Christianizing lines where the institution of slavery was seen to degrade not only the enslaved but also, and especially, the enslavers: as Godwyn put it, "Both Freemen and Slaves being there equally involved in the *same* Calamity" (61). Godwyn denies that the slaveholders are true Christians:

> [I]f none of all these *Considerations* will prevail, the last thing I shall propose, is, That you will now at length remove that *Vizard,* and undeceive the World, who have been apt hitherto, because *going by that Name,* to believe you *Christians:* Which Name with what face Men can thus usurp, whose practices do prove them not so much as *tollerable Heathens,* is in truth my great wonder and astonishment [...] so your *Inhumanity, Avarice,* and *Irreligion,* may no longer be a Stain and Reproach to that *Profession.* (163–4)

The critique, as yet, is not of Christianity itself, but of the slavers. To preserve true Christianity, in this view, the unchristian degenerates who practise cruelty upon slaves must be reformed along Christian lines.

Putting Cruelty First

Surinam was only in English hands for sixteen years (1651–67), traded to the Dutch for the island of Manhattan. Coincidentally, in 1674, it was John Locke, serving as secretary to the council of trade and the government of the West Indies and American colonies, who oversaw the voluminous correspondence concerning the handover and resettlement of the English settlers in Surinam at this time. Over time, in the hands of the Dutch, the colony would become a "byword for European cruelty and excess."[65] In Voltaire's *Candide*, the hero loses his own faith as he enters Surinam and observes the "abomination" of enslaved men and women there.[66]

Indeed, in the works of all these humanitarian writers from Behn to Voltaire, cruelty is taken to be true Christianity's opposite. There is thus a double legacy of Christianity: that Christianizing the enslaved people was an effect of power and subjugation, as it would be for the character Imoinda in Behn's *Oroonoko*, but also that the slave world prompted the emergence of a discourse of humanity in the critique of slavery's cruelty, albeit along Christian lines. It is too easy to dismiss Christianity as simply a means to impose colonial subjugation. Christianity was also an exit strategy from racialized hierarchy, a recognition and a warrant to recognize universal personhood, with a potential for neighbourliness and mutuality. In *Oroonoko*, the narrator's attempt to convert Imoinda, and her remarks concerning the need for milder treatment towards enslaved workers, fall in line with this Christian humanitarianism.

What does this mean for Behn? Exploring the multi-denominational colonial setting of Surinam in light of the political instability of its sovereign forms of government and its weak territorial claims, we see that Behn is engaging forcefully with a critique of the Christian hypocrisy of the enslaving English, as well as with a founding of a new moral order on the grounds of humanity. Her work – like that of nonconformists Tryon, Godwyn, Baxter, and others – turns a mirror on the European enslavers. The "devilish Wrath"[67] slavers exhibit is not Christian, these works make plain, and the voices of those who are victimized in the exercise of that cruelty are embodied and given voice. Her appeal to humanity accompanies a full-scale exposure of the weakness of Christianity in its inability to restrain both political overreach and excesses of cruelty, and through it, the novella opens the way for a more vigorous critique. The frail yet powerful account is not only a form of commemoration or testimony that almost attains a quality of "ethical responsibility," as Mallipeddi has put it,[68] but is also a statement of a humanitarianism that insists upon a natural equality.

To return to liberal theorist Shklar, who, in her essay "Putting Cruelty First," powerfully explains that although hating cruelty is compatible with biblical religiosity, "to put it *first* does place one unalterably outside the sphere of revealed religion. For it is a purely human verdict upon human conduct, and so puts religion at a certain distance."[69] Like Voltaire's *Candide*, Behn's novella observes the failure of Christianity under the slave system from a moral point of view; it is a system made visible by the cruelty and dishonesty of the colonial rulers. Behn did not go so far as to question the system of sovereignty and economy that gave rise to this failure, but her narrator holds out hope that political institutions, the restoration of proper authority, and proper diet and health could bring humanity back to a better course. As such, *Oroonoko* shares with *The Merchant of Venice* an ability, in the words of Paul Yachnin in this volume, to "incite a movement towards toleration as a participatory, future-oriented process of dialogue and disagreement," two of the prime features of a specifically literary mode of tolerationist thought (23). Behn's novella does provide a utopian moment, the instance of wishing that the king had not "parted so easily with [Surinam] to the Dutch" (115), a Surinam that has "there eternal Spring, always the very months of April, May and June. The shades are perpetual, the trees, bearing at once all degrees of leaves and fruit, from blooming buds to ripe Autumn" (115). The depiction of this Edenic land, out of joint with time, is one whose enjoyment depends upon the hidden labour of slavery: St John's Hill, where the "best house" was set was "fit to entertain people in, at all the hottest hours of the day" (116), the cool repose afforded by that residence in silent opposition to the heat and sweat of overburdened, but barely visible toilers. Behn recalls how at that place, "the sweet blossoms [...] made it always sweet and charming, and sure the whole globe of the world cannot show so delightful a place as this grove was" (117). Yet despite this nostalgia, this longing, her own narrative leaves her readers with a repugnant physical landscape: one that is hot, sweaty, stinking, oppressed by the stench of the decaying corpse of Imoinda, the smoke and smoulder of Oroonoko's mutilated flesh. The public enormity of the crime of slavery felt in these final moments makes us wonder if Behn shows it is impossible to be a good human and a good slaveholder. *Oroonoko* does put cruelty first in its refusal to separate a lived, shared, human experience from an awareness of the shared bonds of morality.

The theory of toleration in *Oroonoko*, then, engages with the literary but in a different way than as a kind of feeling for or recognition of others unlike ourselves. It is neither a form of rhetoric nor a form of empathy. Indeed, one is repelled by the violence and stink of the final sections of *Oroonoko*. One recoils in horror at the hero's murder of his beloved, his self-mutilations. One very much wishes, like the narrator, to be out of that place. It is however, a testament to the necessity of witness, not only to the hypocrisy of a universalizing but arrogant Christianity and to a fully secular, sceptical critique, but to a life undone by cruelty: these contradictions take place in the narrative construction of a life. The story forms a life, gives narrative form to an experience, an outlook, an outlandish vision, pausing again and again on moments of cruelty. The story as modest witness pushes the reader from the familiar and the comfortable towards a recognition of the incoherence of values as well as of the conditional edifices of authority, and thus towards an avowal of complicity.

NOTES

1 Benjamin J. Kaplan, *Divided by Faith: Religious Conflict and the Practice of Toleration in Early Modern Europe* (Cambridge: Harvard University Press, 2007), 336, 346.

2 Harold J. Berman, *Law and Revolution, II: The Impact of the Protestant Reformations on the Western Legal Tradition* (Cambridge: Harvard University Press, 2003), 62.

3 Ole Peter Grell and Roy Porter, "Introduction," in *Toleration in Enlightenment Europe*, ed. Ole Peter Grell and Roy Porter (Cambridge: Cambridge University Press, 2000), 1–22.

4 Caroline Shaw, *Britannia's Embrace: Modern Humanitarianism and the Imperial Origins of Refugee Relief* (Oxford: Oxford University Press, 2015), 18.

5 Ayesha Ramachandran, *The Worldmakers: Global Imagining in Early Modern Europe* (Chicago: University of Chicago Press, 2015), 7.

6 See Sarah Ellenzweig, *The Fringes of Belief: English Literature, Ancient Heresy, and the Politics of Freethinking, 1660–1760* (Stanford: Stanford University Press, 2008), 53–82.

7 Ramesh Mallipeddi, *Spectacular Suffering: Witnessing Slavery in the Eighteenth-Century British Atlantic* (Charlottesville: University of Virginia Press, 2016); Laura J. Rosenthal, "*Oroonoko*: Reception, Ideology, and Narrative Strategy," in *The Cambridge Companion to Aphra Behn*, ed. Derek Hughes and Janet Todd (Cambridge: Cambridge University Press, 2004), 151–65; Jonathan Elmer, *On Lingering and Being Last: Race and Sovereignty in the New World* (New York: Fordham University Press, 2008).

8 Ros Ballaster, "Seizing the Means of Seduction: Fiction and Feminine Identity in Aphra Behn and Delarivier Manley," in *Women, Writing, History, 1640–1740*, ed. Isobel Grundy and Susan Wiseman (Athens: University of Georgia Press, 1992), 93–108; Charlotte Sussman, "The Other Problem with Woman: Reproduction and Slave Culture in Aphra Behn's *Oroonoko*," in *Rereading Aphra Behn: History, Theory and Criticism*, ed. Heidi Hutner (Charlottesville: University of Virginia Press, 1993), 212–33.

9 See Albert J. Rivero, "Aphra Behn's *Oroonoko* and the 'Blank Spaces of Colonial Fictions," *SEL* 39, no. 3 (1999): 447–8; Christopher Loar, *Political Magic: British Fictions of Savagery and Sovereignty, 1650–1750* (New York: Fordham University Press, 2014); Ros Ballaster, "Taking Liberties: Revisiting Behn's Libertinism," *Women's Writing* 19, no. 2 (2012): 165–76; Ros Ballaster, "Rochester, Behn and Enlightenment Liberty," in *Lord Rochester in the Restoration World*, ed. Matthew C. Augustine

and Steven N. Zwicker (Cambridge: Cambridge University Press, 2015), 207–30; Michael L. Stapleton, *Admired and Understood: The Poetry of Aphra Behn* (Newark, DE: University of Delaware Press, 2004); Richard Frohock, "Violence and Awe: The Foundations of Government in Aphra Behn's New World Settings," *Eighteenth-Century Fiction* 8, no. 4 (1996): 437–52; Alvin Snider, "Atoms and Seeds: Aphra Behn's Lucretius," *Clio* 33, no. 1 (2003): 1–24; Sophie Tomlinson, "'A Woman's Reason': Aphra Behn Reads Lucretius," *Intellectual History Review* 22, no. 3 (2012): 355–72; Sarah Ellenzweig, *The Fringes of Belief: English Literature, Ancient Heresy and the Politics of Freethinking, 1660–1760* (Stanford: Stanford University Press, 2008).

10 Susan Z. Andrade, "White Skin, Black Masks: Colonialism and the Sexual Politics of *Oronooko*," *Cultural Critique* 27 (1994): 189–214.

11 Judith N. Shklar, "Putting Cruelty First," in *Ordinary Vices* (Cambridge, MA: Harvard University Press, 1984), 7–44, at 9.

12 Talal Asad, *Formations of the Secular: Christianity, Islam, Modernity* (Stanford: Stanford University Press, 2003), 100–1.

13 Aphra Behn, "The Translator's Preface," in [M. de Fontenelle], *A Discovery of New Worlds. From the French* (London, 1688), [Sig. A8v].

14 Elliott Visconsi, "A Degenerate Race: English Barbarism in Aphra Behn's *Oroonoko* and *The Widow Ranter*," *ELH* 69, no. 3 (2002): 673–701, at 674, 680.

15 Margaret Cavendish, *The Blazing World, in Paper Bodies: A Margaret Cavendish Reader*, ed. Sylvia Bowerbank and Sara Mendelson (Peterborough, ON: Broadview Press, 2000), 153, 156, 212.

16 Aphra Behn, "To the Most Illustrious Prince Christopher Duke of Albemarle, on his Voyage to his Government of Jamaica," in *The Works of Aphra Behn*, 7 vols., ed. Janet Todd (Columbus, OH: Ohio State University Press, 1992) (henceforth *WAB*), 1.224.

17 On Behn's *Oroonoko* and place in relation to memory, see Laura Runge, "Constructing Place in *Oroonoko*," in *Gender and Space in British Literature, 1660–1820*, ed. Mona Narain and Karen Gevirtz (London: Routledge, 2016), 19–33.

18 Aphra Behn, *Oroonoko, The Rover and Other Works*, ed. Janet Todd (London: Penguin, 1992), 86, 79, 106. All citations to *Oroonoko* are to this edition.

19 Melinda Zook, "Contextualizing Aphra Behn," in *Women Writers and the Early Modern British Political Tradition*, ed. Hilda L. Smith (Cambridge: Cambridge University Press, 1998), 75–93; Laura Brown, *Ends of Empire: Women and Ideology in the Early-Eighteenth Century* (Ithaca: Cornell University Press, 1993); Laura Doyle, *Freedom's Empire: Race and the Rise of the Novel in Atlantic Modernity, 1640–1940* (Durham: Duke University Press, 2008).

20 Rosenthal, "*Oroonoko*: Reception, Ideology," 152, 160.

21 Michael Hardt and Antonio Negri, *Empire* (Cambridge: Harvard University Press, 2000), 70; and compare with Elmer, *On Lingering*, 3.

22 Behn, *Oroonoko*, 78: "Those then whom we make use of to work in our plantations of sugar are negroes, black slaves altogether, which are transported thither in this manner."

23 Corrinne Harol, "The Passion of *Oroonoko*: Passive Obedience, the Royal Slave, and Aphra Behn's Baroque Realism," *ELH* 7, no. 2 (2012): 447–75; Victoria Kahn, *Wayward Contracts* (Princeton: Princeton University Press, 2004).

24 Behn, *The Roundheads*, *WAB*, 2.409.

25 John Marshall, *John Locke, Toleration and Early Enlightenment Culture* (Cambridge: Cambridge University Press, 2006), 440, 450.

26 Melinda Zook, "Religious Nonconformity and the Problem of Dissent in the Works of Aphra Behn and Mary Astell," in *Mary Astell: Reason, Gender, Faith*, ed. William Kolbrener and Michal Michelson (Aldershot: Ashgate, 2007), 99–113. See also Alison Conway, *The Protestant Whore: Courtesan Narrative and Religious Controversy in England, 1680–1750* (Toronto: University of Toronto Press, 2010).

27 Melinda Zook, *Protestantism, Politics, and Women in Britain, 1660–1714* (London: Palgrave Macmillan, 2013), 114.

28 Behn, *Abdelazer*, Act IV, lines 342–3, *WAB*, 5: 293.

29 Janet Todd, *Gender, Art and Death* (Oxford: Polity Press, 1993), 44–8; Christopher Hill, "Freethinking and Libertinism: The Legacy of the English Revolution," in *The Margins of Orthodoxy: Heterodox Writing and Cultural Response, 1660–1750*, ed. Roger D. Lund (Cambridge: Cambridge University Press, 1995), 54–72, at 66.

30 Anita Pacheo, "Royalism and Honor in Aphra Behn's Oroonoko," *SEL* 34 (1994): 491–506.

31 Ellenzweig, *Fringes*; Arlen Feldwick and Cary J. Nederman, "'Religion Set the World at Odds': Deism and the Climate of Religious Tolerance in the Works of Aphra Behn," in *Beyond the Persecuting Society: Religious Toleration before the Enlightenment*, ed. John Christian Laursen and Cary J. Nederman (Philadelphia: University of Pennsylvania Press, 1998), 216–31; contrast with Alison Shell, "Popish Plots: *The Feign'd Curtizans* in Context," in *Aphra Behn Studies*, ed. Janet Todd (Cambridge: Cambridge University Press, 1996), 30–49, which argues for Behn's sympathy towards Catholicism.

32 Line Cottignies, "The Translator as Critic: Aphra Behn's Translation of Fontenelle's 'Discovery of New Worlds' (1688)," *Restoration* 27, no. 1 (2003): 23–38, at 32.

33 Behn, "The Golden Age," lines 108–9, in Behn, *WAB*, vol. 1, p. 33.

34 Carla Gardina Pestana, *The English Atlantic in the Age of Revolution, 1640–1661* (Cambridge: Harvard University Press, 2007), 128–31.

35 Matthew Parker, *The Sugar Barons: Family, Corruption, Empire, and War in the West Indies* (London: Bloomsbury, 2011), 65.

36 *Calendar of State Papers*, Colonial Series, 371 (7 Jan. 1652).

37 Sarah Barber, *The Disputatious Caribbean: The West Indies in the Seventeenth Century* (New York: Palgrave, 2014), 204; Aviva Ben-Ur, "Peripheral Inclusion: Communal Belonging in Suriname's Sephardic Community," in *Religion, Gender, and Culture in the Pre-Modern World*, ed. Alexandra Cuffel and Brian Britt (New York: Palgrave Macmillan, 2007), 185–210, at 185; in 1684, Jews comprised 28.6 per cent of Surinam's European population, owning 30.3 per cent of the slaves (Ben-Ur, 187).

38   Carla Gardina Pestana, *Protestant Empire: Religion and the Making of the British Atlantic World* (Philadelphia: University of Pennsylvania Press, 2009), 119.

39   Barber, *Disputatious*, 78.

40   Pestana, *English Atlantic*, 223.

41   Barber, *Disputatious*, 191–2.

42   Behn, *Oroonoko*, 134; Barber, *Disputatious*, 203.

43   Robert Sanford, *Surinam Justice* (London, 1662), A3r.

44   Barber, *Disputatious*, 172.

45   Henry Adis: "as for the freedom of our Liberties in the service of our God, according to what was promised by your Lordship, and also by the Act of Council of this Colony, manifested," in Henry Adis, *A Letter sent from Syrranam to his Excellency, the Lord Willoughby or Parham* (London, 1664), 3.

46   This history is indebted to the excellent work of Alison Games, "Cohabitation, Surnamese-Style: English Inhabitants in Dutch Suriname after 1667," *William and Mary Quarterly* 72, no. 2 (2015): 195–242, at 200; and see also Barber *Disputatious*.

47   Barber, *Disputatious*, 204.

48   Adis, *A Letter*, 4.

49   Barber, *Disputatious*, 71, 181.

50   See Steven C.A. Pincus, *Protestantism and Patriotism: Ideologies and the Making of English Foreign Policy, 1650–1668* (Cambridge: Cambridge University Press, 1996), 401, 406.

51   Games, "Cohabitation, Suriname-Style," 198 n. 4, 201, 202.

52   On the urgency of commemoration and the politics of space, see Runge, "Constructing Place."

53   Thomas Tryon, *Friendly Advice to Gentleman-Planters of the East and West Indies* (London, 1684), title page.

54   Thomas Tryon, *A Dialogue between an East-Indian Brackmanny or Heathen Philosopher* (London, 1683), 20.

55   Kasey Evans, *Colonial Virtue: The Mobility of Temperance in Renaissance England* (Toronto: University of Toronto Press, 2012), 203–7.

56   Amussen, *Caribbean Exchanges*, 180.

57   Tryon, *Friendly Advice*, 160.

58   Philotheus Physiologus [Thomas Tryon], *The Way to make All People Rich: or Wisdom's Call to Temperance and Frugality* (London, 1685).

59   Behn, "On the Author of that Excellent Book Intituled The way to Health, Long Life, and Happiness," *WAB* vol. 1, p. 180, lines 50, 64–5. Ruthe T. Sheffey was the first to discover this relationship; see "Some Evidence for a New Source of Aphra Behn's *Oroonoko*," *Studies in Philology* 59, no.1 (1962): 52–63. On Tryon, see Phillipe Rosenberg, "Thomas Tryon and the Seventeenth Century Dimensions of Antislavery," *William and Mary Quarterly* 61, no. 4 (2004): 609–42; Nigel Smith, "Enthusiasm and Enlightenment: Of Food, Filth and Slavery," in *The Country and the City Revisited: England and the Politics of Culture*, ed. Gerald MacLean, Donna

Landry, and Joseph P. Ward (Cambridge: Cambridge University Press, 1999), 106–18; Timothy Morton, "The Plantation of Wrath," in *Radicalism in British Literary Culture, 1650–1830*, ed. Nigel Smith and Timothy Morton (Cambridge: Cambridge University Press, 2002), 64–85.

60 Sheffey, "Some Evidence," has pointed out the significant parallels between this interchange and that of Oroonoko and his enslavers when she unearthed the connection between Behn and Tryon.

61 Morgan Godwyn, *The Negro's & Indians Advocate, suing for their admission to the church* (London, 1680), title page.

62 Godwyn, *The Negro's & Indians Advocate*, 4, 20–1, 24.

63 David Bryon Davis, *The Problem of Slavery in Western Culture* (Oxford: Oxford University Press, 1966), 338; Amussen, *Caribbean Exchanges*, 180–2; Richard Baxter, *Christian Directory* (London, 1673).

64 Baxter, *Christian Directory*, 557, 559, 558, 560.

65 David Wallace, *Premodern Places: Calais to Surinam, Chaucer to Aphra Behn* (London: Wiley, 2006).

66 Voltaire, *Candide*, ch. 19 (par. 5): "thou hadst not guessed at this abomination; it is the end. I must at last renounce thy optimism." Paul Yachnin, in chapter 1 of this volume, also reads this moment as a touchstone for toleration questions.

67 Tryon, *Friendly Advice*, 145.

68 Ramesh Mallipeddi, "Spectacle, Spectatorship, and Sympathy in Aphra Behn's Oroonoko," *Eighteenth-Century Studies* 45, no. 4 (2012): 475–96, at 489.

69 Shklar, *Ordinary Vices*, 9.

3 Blind or Blindfolded? Disability, Religious Difference, and Milton's *Samson Agonistes*

ANDREW MCKENDRY

A man with impaired vision falls to his death because his poorly made glasses distort his view of a narrow bridge. Who is at fault: the government, the engineer, the lens-maker, or the man himself? Our answer to this question can reveal a lot about our attitudes towards disability, liability, and justice, but perhaps it can also reflect our approach to religious difference. The Yorkshire minister Richard Chapman certainly thought so; this is the scenario he formulates, in his 1635 *Hallelu-jah: or, King David's Shrill Trumpet*, as a way of grappling with that most troubling perplexity of Christian salvation: How can it be considered just to damn those who never received grace? As Chapman explains it,

> even as a halfe blind man passing over a narrow bridge using spectacles, which make the bridge seeme broader then it is, the blind man being thus deceived falls headlong into the water; So by the spectacles of corrupt naturall reason and presumption which the wicked man looks through, the mercy of God which is the bridge is made too broad & his justice shrunk too narrow, leaning upon the one & forgetting the other till he tumble downe into the brimstone Gulfe of perdition.[1]

It may be no *Paradise Lost*, but for Chapman the tale demonstrates that as God "*is mercifull so is he just*, and of most exact integrity" (145). More pointedly, the story illustrates how it can be that Anglicans, Catholics, Muslims, Jews, and Pagans are substantially responsible for their own damnation – even if they are, in an important sense, disabled. But we may have some misgivings concerning this parallel, and perhaps not because we disagree on the extent and operations of salvation; is it really fair to blame a man with impaired vision (with bad glasses, at that) for this fatal error? Can disability really be considered a culpable condition? It may sound like I am bringing an anachronistically modern sensibility to Chapman's crudely ableist analogy, but such questions – posed in the same terms but with different stakes – were at the heart of early modern theological debates. Immersing ourselves in these debates can help unsettle those "elemental premises" – about autonomy, identity, and difference – that secularization has insensibly naturalized.

The linking of disability and religious difference would have been familiar to seventeenth-century readers, but this pairing is somewhat unusual in modern scholarship. Even as theorizations of tolerance and toleration have extended far beyond matters of religious belief, disability has been surprisingly marginal in such scholarship – just past the imaginable "subjects of tolerance," and just out of frame of critical confrontations with "differences" that cause discomfort. "Skin colour, religion, language, dietary custom, dress and behaviour" are the signs that Michael Ignatieff recognizes in his expanded conception of tolerance.[2] Wendy Brown demonstrates how tolerance entails a regulation not only of religious but of ethnic, racial, and even sexual identity;[3] it consistently feels like (as Tobin Siebers pithily put it) "disability is the other other that helps make otherness imaginable."[4] Though disability studies, for its part, has hardly eschewed the historical significance of religion,[5] the thick complexities of religious difference often figure negligibly alongside those of disability; religious experience (not to mention specific confessional identities) is regularly treated as context or "background," far less constitutive of subjecthood than disability.[6] In the most penetrating accounts from both fields, the latent filiations between the two areas of study are palpable; the sensorial approach to tolerance recently proposed by Lars Tønder, which resituates pain and embodiment at the centre of political theory, skirts the boundaries of disability without ever engaging the topic,[7] while the recent collection entitled *Disability and Political Theory* (2016) exposes the shortcomings of liberal ideology but eschews any substantial discussion of religious difference or toleration.[8] Even the most conscientiously intersectional accounts of disability, such as *The Biopolitics of Disability* (2015), find no place for religious identity alongside the diverse frameworks of "critical race studies, queer studies, political economy, sociology, cultural studies, literary theory, visual anthropology, and social history, among others."[9] This methodological disjunction is all the more unpropitious considering how regularly scholarship on disability and toleration converge over the same priorities: probing the limits of liberal autonomy and rational personhood,[10] exposing the deficiency of "neutrality" and privileged indifference,[11] and interrogating our definitions of citizenship.[12] If disability has marked the troubled edges of liberalism, in part because our foundational conceptions of freedom and personhood – from John Locke to Amartya Sen – have been defined against disabled bodies,[13] then attempts to critique, revise, or challenge established modes of liberal tolerance must engage more fully with the reorientations of identity and reconfigurations of knowledge that disability studies has pursued.

This chapter seeks to contribute to such a shift, though I should admit that my motivations are historiographic as much as methodological; it is difficult, perhaps even distortive, to study seventeenth-century ideas of tolerance without attending to disability. Disability studies scholars can ignore the extensive discussions of legal and civil "disability," just as historians of toleration can discount the unruly inflections of the term. The "disabilities" of Catholics and Dissenters were, one is required to suppose, purely legal in character and experience, this form of the term bearing no relationship to questions of embodiment or labour. But when we turn to writing from the period, these disciplinary horizons blur, not only because the meaning of "disability" was amorphous and fluid, often conflating the forces of law and physiology, but also because religious identity and difference were so regularly conceived in terms of blindness, deafness, and "lameness." In many cases, estimations of difference and error, and thus the justice and feasibility of tolerance or "charity" (particularly towards the "blindness" of popery), came to hinge substantially on how an author conceptualized disability. Roger Lund has shown that many seventeenth-century writers represented deformity as an unnatural deviation from universal order,[14] and Corrinne Harol demonstrates, in her piece in this volume, how broader conceptions of "variety" and diversity could undergird attitudes towards religious difference. But the dynamic could operate in the other direction as well; precisely because "metaphors of disability serve to extrapolate the meaning of a bodily flaw into cosmological significance,"[15] responses to bodily impairment could be the foundation for competing conceptions of how religious difference should be treated. If from one perspective Catholic transubstantiation must not be suffered since "error is dangerous to the soul, because it is its blindness,"[16] from another the imperative to integrate weak members into the Christian community was a corollary of corporeal variety – for even a man with palsy, gout, blindness, or deafness was surely "a true man still."[17] If we cannot dismiss these as dead metaphors, nor read them as legibly secular treatments of the body, we must investigate the historically specific confluence of these fields.

Blindness seems like such a familiar disability that we can easily forget how fraught the condition was before the hegemony of secularization and medical discourse.[18] Perhaps because our own period is so concerned with classification, the relationship between disability and sin during the early modern period has often been oversimplified, historians assuming that disability (particularly visible deformity) served as a readily accepted sign of spiritual abjection.[19] Yet, seventeenth-century readers were primed with a long-standing and nuanced discourse on impairment and illness, one which was arguably more attentive to the ambiguities of disability than exists today. As this chapter aims to demonstrate, the theological uncertainties that surrounded blindness both furnished and problematized distinctive forms of "liberality" and forbearance[20] – imperatives that exceeded the pragmatism traditionally associated with early modern modes of toleration.[21] Though corporeal affliction was regularly understood as a distinctive occasion for longanimity and charity, these stances were always unstable, but not always unproductively so; schemas of atonement, marking out who could be saved and how, frequently turned on what blindness entailed, and thus reframing the nature of blindness – and "disability" more broadly – could shift the boundaries of salvation and accommodation. The theological and social possibilities of this destabilization were articulated most pointedly in the regular denunciations of what we might call soteriological ableism:[22] the tendency to treat disability as a legible mark of spiritual depravity. Recounted in John 9, the story of the man born blind served as one of the most culturally prominent subtexts for these debates, in part because it provocatively pushed the limits of who might be considered blind or sighted. Situating John Milton's writing, particularly *Samson Agonistes* (1671), in the context of this paradigmatic uncertainty, I argue that his most enigmatic poem turns to blindness as a way of exploring the adulteration of choice that attended the Clarendon Code, the set of reactionary laws that recast heterodoxy as Dissent. At a moment when Dissenters were understood as "disabled," *Samson Agonistes* imagines their limitations in material terms in order to probe the political ramifications of imposing belief. What the "literary" offers us here, then, is not exactly a new mode of tolerance but rather a staging of the way that such possibilities are preceded, and potentially precluded, by paradigms of ability and autonomy. The forms of interfaith relations that emerge (both directly and adversely) from these figurations of blindness cannot be readily endorsed, since they obtained before integral elements of liberalism – secular autonomy, individual "rights," physiological "normalcy"[23] – were firmly established. But foregrounding these unsettling encounters does suggest how a productive engagement with the most intractable paradoxes of toleration will demand a shift in our foundational ideas of ability and disability.

The regularity with which sin was conceptualized as a corporeal impairment during the seventeenth century made religious difference amenable to forms of forbearance that offered alternatives to a dubious "toleration" (which, we should remember, was a far more morally suspect principle than it is today). Imagining Catholic idolatry or Jewish ignorance, for example, as an unfortunate "blindness," rather than a purposive stance, made it subject to distinctive modes of pity and charity (in the seventeenth-century sense of the term). Viewed optimistically, this approach to difference mollified the culpability of error and even heresy, allowing Christian writers to assert the primacy of their beliefs without irrevocably condemning others; though in the strictest sense God could distribute punishment as He saw fit, most writers suggested that "he that sinneth out of ignorance, more easily findeth favour, then hee that sinneth against knowledge."[24] But viewed more critically, this framing of difference functioned to evacuate these competing beliefs of rational and theological legitimacy, frequently so that they could serve more instrumentally in formulating the rhetorical and political power of the forbearing party. These manoeuvres provide the foundational infrastructure that, as Brown and Tønder point out, theorists of "superior tolerance" have typically effaced,[25] and in this sense the essential privilege toleration avails might be considered able-bodiedness, the tolerating party demonstrating, above all, their capacity for intellectual and corporeal continence. Modern critics have been struck by the exclusionary rhetoric of the Old Testament (particularly Leviticus and Deuteronomy),[26] but such proscriptions were most significant to contemporaries for the way they distinguished the duties of charitable treatment. Matthew 15:14 ("Leave them; they are blind guides. If the blind lead the blind, both will fall into a pit") was cited in the most "negative" forms of tolerance, calling for Protestants to let Catholics damn themselves.[27] However, far more sophisticated modes of interpersonal charity could be furnished by biblical injunctions to accommodate and even welcome the halt, blind, and lame. If one form of toleration entails the renunciation of other attitudes and modalities, it is not surprising that, at a moment when anxieties about popery and the Antichrist were uppermost, disabled persons were invoked as a means of regulating religious identities. The seventeenth-century emergence of toleration as a "normative" discourse, as Ingrid Creppell charts it,[28] depended quite substantially on the boundary-marking characteristics of disabled persons – both as objects of disavowal and accommodation. Readers were often asked to "consider whether amongst the papistes" injunctions to such charity were best observed; for the papists such inclusiveness was "but a marke to know Heretikes which will not receave the Popes Ceremonies."[29] Protestant writers regularly censured papists for their persecution of the lame and crippled,[30] a practice imputed to their facile equation of disability with sin. As a testament to the cruel "spirit of Popery," for instance, a 1689 tract urging Protestant union against popery alleges that Bishop Bonner persecuted "a poor pitiful blind harper"; "*such blind abjects as thou,*" the notorious blackguard proclaimed, "*will be following Heretical Preachers; but when they come once to feel the Fire, will be the first that fly from it.*"[31] Shaming such uncivilized cruelty need not be so dramatic, of course, and in many situations a subtle flourish of magnanimous (and distinctively Protestant) restraint could serve just as well. Offering some "charitable advice" to the hateful Catholics, who see Protestants as "Reprobates, Hereticks, Schismaticks," the Scottish physician David Abercromby (himself a Protestant convert) bids his readers to "pardon [him] the freedom" of his analogy: "you are not unlike [...] those that are blind from their birth," he remarks, "more to be pitied for this gross mistake, than blam'd."[32] The pity that disabled persons evoked (or least were supposed to evoke), then, functioned to delegitimize the religious other, to preclude or neuter recognition – for pagan beliefs, for Catholic doctrines, or for sectarian tenets.

But while tolerating disability could thus serve as a means of performing a legitimating forbearance, such a tactic could not function as reliably when blindness was simultaneously understood as the defining characteristic of post-lapsarian existence. Like a blind man who cannot know colour, humankind was considered "blinde by nature, and ignorant of God and goodnesse, and of our selves uncapable of right judgment in matters of faith: for flesh and bloud cannot attaine unto it."[33] "Our minds being blind," John Downe explained, "we cannot our selves see the way" to salvation.[34] Christian (especially Protestant) readers were called to reflect daily on their "natural blindness."[35] We should not assume this was derogatory in any unalloyed sense; disability (and specifically blindness) was commonly the starting-point for salvation, and as historians such as Margaret Aston and Stuart Clark have shown, impugning established regimes of visuality was an important mode of repudiating Catholicism.[36] Being blind to sinful sights, particularly idolatrous ones, could be a blessing.[37] Nor did the prevalence and "naturalness" of disability mean simply that "we are all disabled," but rather that difference was conceptualized and contested within these parameters – as different degrees, states, and modes of disability or incapacity. Most Christian writers agreed that since the Fall humans were born "blind" to some degree, and many suggested that this blindness could variously be mitigated, prosthetically managed, or cured through Christ, often with reference to Mark 10:46, Matthew 9:27–30, John 9, or Acts 9. Some writers certainly hoped to deploy the trope "without discussing every minute particular Analogy,"[38] but disagreements abounded about the accessibility and mechanics of this process, blindness serving as a battleground in debates over the workings of salvation and the implications of religious difference. Conceiving of the Church as a hospital, for instance, John Donne asserted that even "men borne in *Paganisme*, or *Superstition*" could be mended.[39] Thomas Draxe, however, marked a physiological difference between the elect and the reprobate as a way of explaining how the latter were biologically responsible for their fatal blindness, "for even as the Owle by the brightness of the Sunne is blinded, albeit all other birds are enlightened by it [...] so by the same holy Scripture and glorious Gospell, whereby the Elect are enlightened and converted, the reprobate are blinded and hardened, and that onely through their owne default and impotency."[40] Since they concerned above all the nature and extent of human abilities, epochal controversies on atonement and election often involved elaborate reformulations of blindness – of how blindness occurred, of how substantially it hampered ambulation,[41] of how it could be managed or remedied.[42] Whereas William Charke, for instance, extended the potential of redemption by blasting the idea that "God hath left some in their blindenesse,"[43] others like William Allen and Henry Dodwell marshalled the persistent materiality of the disabled body to dispute the doctrine of justification by faith alone (with reference specifically to Dissenters); the blind and the lame healed by Christ, they insisted, were saved only *after* their corporeal afflictions were materially cured.[44]

This is what the traditionally posited equation of sin and disability oversimplifies: disability (particularly blindness) was inseparable from sin, but the precise character and extent of this alterity was a matter of profound and far-reaching disagreement. How much did human "disability" divide humankind from God,[45] and how much were men differentiated from each other (and from women) by different forms and degrees of disability? The intracta-bility of these questions made imputations of blindness, both disparaging and magnanimous, at once needful and precarious. If tolerance "is generally con-ferred by those who do not require it on those who do,"[46] then even charitable Christians were in a conflicted position; they were called to tolerate the "blind-ness" of "Jewes, Turks, Infidels, and Hereticks,"[47] but in doing so one might as readily be a subject of God's unparalleled tolerance, which was often conceived as a sufferance of our "naturall blindnesse."[48] Shifts in philosophical and soteri-ological paradigms actuated the possibilities of repairing the damage of the Fall, as Joanna Picciotto has demonstrated,[49] such that as the century progressed religious writers were impelled to awkwardly qualify this blindness, usually as a means of both asserting the significance of human capacities and regu-lating the parameters of salvation. Robert Abbot, for instance, argues that sin occurs "*naturally*, by some defect in natural generation. So there being a natural defect now in mans propagation, through sin he brings forth blind Whelps. Though more or lesse," he explains, "for *natural excellency* man bee not borne blinde ..."[50] As reason came to play an increasingly substantial role in salvation, contemporaries considering it a "privilege of mankind not to be led blindfold; but to be governed by their Reason,"[51] a panoply of variations – "voluntary blindness,"[52] "wilful blindness,"[53] "Cimmerian blindness"[54] – provided a means of apportioning agency and guilt, and many writers managed these classifica-tions dexterously as a way to broker tolerance and moral status. Though ac-knowledging that papists "live in a state of damnation," for instance, George Downame assigned their culpability primarily to the clergy by representing the laypeople as "blindfolded" by their leaders.[55] Strategically restrained, the Catholic controversialist Anthony Champney characterized his Protestant opponent Richard Pilkinton as either "blind or blinde foulded" ("verie shorte sighted or rather starke blind"),[56] inviting Pilkinton to consent to his de-author-ization by accepting an exonerating disability. But as these examples suggest, such manoeuvres were always hazardous, built as they were on a theologically volatile, fragile constellation of contested subtexts that reliably "abled" no fallen man. As Lennard Davis demonstrates, before the ascendency of the "normal" body, human embodiment was measured against an unreachable "ideal."[57] Theological discourse was the bedrock of this worldview; not only was there an ever-present danger of relapsing almost imperceptibly into a "natural" state of blindness (even for most Calvinistically inclined writers), but there was an equally terrifying possibility of mistaking one's capabilities – of thinking one can see while one remains blind.

Surveying these seemingly muddled negotiations of sight, spirit, and sal-vation, it feels like we are seeing seventeenth-century divines stumble over a shifting lexicographic landscape; the conceptual unruliness of blindness was, in part, an outcropping of the semantic fluidity of the term "disability," which was being negotiated across a number of fields. Before the nineteenth century, "disability" and its cognates were most often used to describe a general state of incapacity, applying "to people and things who are unable to perform the tasks such people and things usually perform."[58] Critics are divided on whether we can consider disability an "operative category" during the seventeenth century,[59] though it is certainly true that no "simple binary opposition between able-bodied and disabled" existed in early modern England.[60] Precisely because its meaning and role had not yet been so codified by medical science, however, the term was a significant confrontation point in contemporary thought. It sparked questions we might recognize: does "disability" refer to the common incapacities of all humankind, or does the term more narrowly refer to the exceptional limitations that could arise by birth or accident? Is "disability" absolute or relative, irrevocable or provisional?

Seventeenth-century writers were asking and answering these questions, in some cases as an attempt to delineate disability as an "operative category" – but not for the same reasons and ends that we might. For us, the political and economic ramifications of such a distinction are foremost, but for seventeenth-century Christians the most pressing stakes were soteriological since the extent and justice of salvation could turn on what "disability" meant. Thus when his perennial opponent Thomas Blake argued that faith was entirely "disabled" from effecting salvation, Richard Baxter retorted that "thats not fitly called disability."[61] His fine-grained articulation of the term in his response to Blake demonstrates how crucially such definitions might partition culpability and accommodation: "the disability which I speak of," he explains,

> is not such as in a Godly man, to do any good without Christ and the Spirit, as in the second cause to act without the first: or in a partial cause, to act without its compartial: but such as is in an unregenerate man to do the work of the Regenerate; or in any broken instrument, or disabled agent, to do its own part of the work till it be altered, and made another thing, as it were.[62]

Such skirmishes over who and what could be fitly called "disabled" might be regarded as part of the prehistory of the modern concept, since they impelled many divines to carve out a form of soteriologically exceptional "disability." This was a process essential to the naturalization of disability under capitalism, which theorists have argued effectively created the category of modern "disability" by devaluing and excluding unprofitably formed bodies.[63] David Turner has observed that "how a society defines disability and whom it identifies as deformed or disabled may reveal much about the society's attitudes and values concerning the body, what stigmatises it, and what it considers 'normal' in physical appearance and competence."[64] These debates remind us that even the stakes of "normalcy" and competence are historically contextual. Not just "state benefits, medical care and supportive technological assistance"[65] – for writers like Blake and Baxter, these debates were most immediately an important site for negotiating the boundaries of salvation and accommodation, since they could exempt and absolve (or condemn) those who could properly be considered "disabled" from certain rites or demands. In other words, definitions of disability inflected opinions on how much diversity a given community (Christian, Protestant, Anglican, Presbyterian, etc.) could tolerate.

We are now in a position to understand how blindness, conceived before "disability" was a stable operative category, could signify at once alterity and identity with others, and thus how blindness might have been an important threshold in conceptualizations of religious difference. Writers turned to impairment as a naturalized "similitude" for spiritual brokenness and impotence,[66] but the disability it entailed could never be confidently disavowed. Or rather, disavowing this disability was a theological matter, one in which the position of the "able-bodied" or "normal" viewer was highly suspect – at the margins or beyond the ambit of orthodoxy.[67] This context makes these moments particularly germane to our attempts to interrogate the hegemony of liberal tolerance, which critics have connected with "the power to define people, cultures, languages, or practices as 'different.'"[68] For their part, many seventeenth-century polemicists recognized, albeit within the parameters of their own political and theological concerns, that laying claim to such a privileged position (a posture imputed to Dissenting "fanatics")[69] was a strategy of power – a way to "judge, condemn, and sentence" those with different beliefs.[70] Doubts about corporeal faculties did not mean, of course, that at a practical level contemporaries actively identified or even sympathized with the blind, "lame," or "crippled," and indeed we must be careful not to eclipse the real suffering, both bodily and social, attendant to impairment. Injunctions against haughty "scoffing and derision," in fact, were often presented as a corrective to the "grand excellence of the Age": tripping up the blind and mocking the lame.[71] But the tropological ubiquity of blindness (and "disability" more broadly) did allow encounters with such impairment, in religious writing at least, to serve more readily and meaningfully as an occasion for a decentring misprision – the kind of "dis-orientation from one's normative frame" that has been associated with more robust modes of interpersonal tolerance.[72] Indeed, it is remarkable how frequently the signs of sensory ability and knowledge capsize in homiletic discourse. In his 1622 sermon on John 1:8 ("He was not that light, but was sent to beare witnesse of that light"), for instance, Donne warns that even the most "wakened man" may be effectively blind, for if he resists both sleeping and "winking," he might still fall into a negligent seeing; "how often may you surprise and deprehend a man," he remarks, "whom you thinke directly to look upon such an object, yet if you aske him the quality or colour of it, he will tell you, he saw it not? That man sees as little with *staring*, as the other with *winking*." Such negligent looking,

Donne warns, "shall but aggravate our condemnation, and it shall be easier at the day of Judgment, for the *deaf* and the *blinde* that never saw *Sacrament*, never heard *Sermon*, then for *us*."[73]

Returning habitually to instances of impairment, contemporary sermons demonstrate how such a disruption of spiritual privilege could turn most sharply on the hermeneutic treachery of the disabled body. An astonishingly wide range of writers argued that outward defects, even of the most obnoxious or debilitating kind, *did not* reliably reflect internal corruption. "The things that defile a man," divines regularly asserted, "are from within, in himself [...] not [in] any outward deformitie, ill cloathes, natural foulenesse, &c."[74] "Bodily deformity," Thomas Draxe affirmed, "doth nothing prejudice the estate of Gods Saints before God, (as the examples of *Job, David, Mephibosheth, Ezechias, Aza, Lazarus,* &c. and of innumerable besides demonstrate)."[75] The case of Job, most frequently invoked, established that corporeal afflictions could equally serve as a trial, and in this sense might be the proofs of an upright Christian. As Calvin had remarked, "god doth punish those that be his for divers causes [...] As wee see that holy Job was oppressed with miserie above all other men, and yet was hee not urged with his sinnes: but God had respect unto another thing: namely, that his godlines may be the better declared even in adversitie."[76] Early modern scriptural interpretation was rife with intense disagreement and profound ambiguity, but there were few sites more intractably and disruptively indeterminate than the afflicted body.

Such a discourse was certainly significant at a time when impairment was perhaps more visible than today,[77] though the primary aim of such admonitions was to repudiate soteriological presumption. "Presumptuous sins" were the bugbear of Christian divines,[78] who advanced that even if there is a fateful distinction between the saved and the damned, between the elect and the reprobate, "presumption" about our estate "is to be avoided as well as despaire. For as none more complaine that they want this assurance, than they that have it; so none more boast of it then they that have it not. The fond hypocrite takes his owne presumption for this assurance: he lives after the flesh, yet brags of the Spirit."[79] "We blind sinners," Draxe argued, "must not take upon us to judge of the guilt, and to determine the circumstances of mens sinnes, and of their estate before God."[80] Though there were many ways in which a presumptuous Christian might be humbled, the encounter with impairment was uniquely efficacious, as it ostensibly compelled even the most circumspect viewer to pass judgment and thus to expose their own deficiency. The most culturally prominent and unsettling scene of such error was the story of the man born blind recounted in John 9. Coming across a blind man as he passes from the temple, Jesus heals the afflicted man by spreading spit-imbued clay on his eyes. The bulk of the narrative concerns the incredulous Pharisees (to whom we will return momentarily), but the encounter is framed by the misguided question of the apostles: "who did sin," they ask, "this man, or his parents, that he was born blind?" Jesus explains that "neither hath this man sinned, nor his parents: but that the works of God should be made manifest in him."[81] The exchange was often read as a warning against assuming too much about the spiritual capacities of others: "by which example," Calvin averred, "we are taught to take good heed, least that if we enquire after the judgements of God beyond the meane of sobrietie, the wandering errour of the minde doe carry vs away, and throwe us headlong into most horrible dungeons."[82] Yet, as Jesus himself suggests, this transgression seems unavoidable, since the blind man is a sign (of Christ's status), one that all are called to read for spiritual meaning. Disability studies scholars have noted how impairment generates an "interpretive occasion."[83] David T. Mitchell argues that disability invariably "inaugurates the need to interpret human differences both biological and imagined."[84] In response to John 9, seventeenth-century commentators described a similar dynamic, the sight of impairment producing an inexorable impulse to (mis)read the body. In his own interpretation of the passage, Calvin reckons that this impulse is built into our cognitive makeup:

> First of all, seeing the scripture doth testifie that all afflictions whereunto mankinde is subiect doe proceede from sinne: so often as we see any man in miserie, it cannot be, but that this cogitation must needes come into our minde, that the discommodities wherewith he is oppressed, are punishments laid upon him by the hand of God. But here we are wont to erre.[85]

The difficulty, as Calvin demonstrates, is that this discomfiting misapprehension emerges from a theologically sound foundation; suffering *does* come from sin (i.e., the Fall), so one naturally (though wrongly) concludes that the cripple must be a punished sinner (which they are, albeit in the same sense that all are). Thus the encounter with a visibly impaired body elicits a kind of heuristic stumble, a reprisal of the Fall that reminds the viewer of their fatal short-sightedness.

Milton's Sonnet XIX ("When I consider how my light is spent") might be said to dramatize such a disorienting blunder, the speaker misinterpreting earthly disability as a legible form of spiritual disability:

> When I consider how my light is spent,
> Ere half my days, in this dark world and wide,
> And that one talent which is death to hide,
> Lodged with me useless, though my soul more bent
> To serve therewith my maker, and present
> My true account, lest he returning chide,
> Doth God exact day-labour, light denied,

> I fondly ask; but Patience to prevent
> That murmur, soon replies, God doth not need
> Either man's work or His own gifts, who best
> Bear his mild yoke, they serve him best, his state
> Is kingly. Thousands at his bidding speed
> And post o'er land and ocean without rest:
> They also serve who only stand and wait.[86]

Whether we treat the poem as a "personal" engagement with his own blindness,[87] or whether we approach it as a reflection on "disability" in the more abstract sense we have been exploring, Sonnet XIX is clearly situated in this discursive context; the foundational error of the speaker is to treat a disabled body (disabled most patently to productive labour) as an intelligible index of the (disabled) spirit, and the reference to "day-labour" invokes John 9:4: "I must work the works of him that sent me, while it is day," Jesus explains, for "the night cometh, when no man can work." This subtext, in fact, helps explain the turn away from the parable of the talents, and from financial metaphors altogether, in the sestet; only Jesus may be considered sufficiently "abled" to do productive work for God, while man must be contented with a monarchical system in which the dynamics of salvation are less perceptibly codified. Indeed, though the elevation of "waiting" has sometimes been seen as a reassuring turn (not only for the speaker but for the disabled Milton),[88] it closes the poem on a somewhat indeterminate note.[89] Like much of the sermonic discourse on disability, which neither disavowed nor certified the spiritual state of disabled persons, the poem distinguishes a form of salvific waiting without confirming that the waiting of the speaker is so efficacious. In other words, the aim here is not to comfort the speaker but to stabilize the theological frame at the expense of epistemological stability, leaving us rather less certain about the spiritual status of the speaker, or even ourselves. All we know, in fact, is that bodily motion – at least that visible to us – is no reliable measure of spiritual aptitude. In this sense, the poem might be seen as employing disability in a recognizably instrumental sense as a way of decentring the presumptuous Christian from their ableist perspective.

Seeing the sonnet as a dramatization of this paradigmatic moment aligns it productively with a number of other such sites of mistaken disability throughout Milton's writing – ranging from Satan to Samson. The very origins of sin are rooted in such a misperception, Satan becoming first "fraught / With envy" because he "thought himself impaired."[90] His fatal malice emerges "*through* pride" (emphasis added), but its immediate cause is the faculty of vision itself, for he cannot "bear ... that sight" of the Son's honour (664–5). If we conceive of toleration in terms of bearing pain,[91] an approach consistent with Milton's monist leanings,[92] then the filiation with the speaker of Sonnet XIX appears as a matter of different capacities for and strategies of tolerance; whereas the speaker is able to save himself by refiguring the crushing weight of the talents as "waiting," Satan is crippled by this sight. We might object (quite fairly) that the sonnet speaker is only empowered to effect such a transformation thanks to an accommodating intervention (the interceding voice of "Patience"), but contemporary conceptions of salvation often imagined the power of the Holy Spirit (or Christ) as an assistive prosthetic (a staff, a set of spectacles, a guide for the blind). To interrogate the uneven distribution of such prosthetics is to ask those theodical questions that so troubled seventeenth-century writers.

Our modern sensibilities might incline us to imagine such fateful slips as a failure to see the inward character of disabled persons, but within the monist framework that Milton generally privileges this error might be said to arise from our tendency to delimit corporeal ability to distinct organs. As John Rogers has shown, Milton was drawn to the idea of an uncompounded body, one in which sense and vitality are distributed to every part.[93] While this does not mean that Milton endorses an entirely de-organized human body, *Paradise Lost* suggests how our inclination to conceptualize disability so clumsily emerges from a fallen organ-centric ocularity. Roused with dangerous arrogance by the news of the redemption, Adam is warned by Michael not to assume that Satan is "disabled" in any legibly material way – an assumption that would leave him vulnerable to his deceptions. "Now clear I understand," Adam gushes, "needs must the Serpent now his capital bruise / Expect with mortal paine: say where and when / thir fight, what Stroke shall bruise the Victors heel" (376, 383–5). Against his impulse to envision this spectacular combat, Michael advises Adam not to dream "of thir fight, / As of a Duel, or the local wounds / Of head or heel":

> Not therefore joins the Son
> Manhood to Godhead, with more strength to foil
> Thy enemy; nor so is overcome
> Satan, whose fall from Heaven, a deadlier bruise,
> Disabled, not to give thee thy death's wound: (386–92)

Adam is partly right that Christ will disable Satan, but his focus on "local wounds" – a heel injury, a crippling concussion – leads to a gross misunderstanding of how this process will work. This is not, to be sure, a purely metaphorical battle, nor is it one in which disability is moored to specific organs. Michael explains that the fall will result in a "deadlier bruise," but it seems like any accommodation to Adam's organ-centric vision is difficult and imperfect; Michael condescends to describe Satan in terms of "armes," "head[s]," and "heel[s]," but tries to explain that this "God-like act" will disable Satan in a "far deeper" manner than these idioms express (432).

Though contemporary mistrust of ocularity sometimes implied an endorsement of blindness, John 9 was often invoked as a repudiation of such a simple inversion. The story is one in which performances, signs, and embodiments of blindness (not to mention deafness) circle dizzyingly. Since congenital blindness is known to be incurable, the Pharisees refuse to believe that the man had been born blind (an attitude that would have strangely appealed to readers chronically suspicious about fraudulent performances of disability).[94] Indeed, the economic forces that undergirded such anxieties are a factor in the misgivings of the man's neighbours, those who "before had seen him that he was blind" wondering if this is "he that sat and begged?" Some say it is he, while others say he only resembles the former indigent – a confusion the man resolves (and thus complicates) by affirming his identity. When Jesus articulates the implication of this miraculous transformation, explaining that he is come "for judgment ... that they which see not might see; and that they which see might be made blind," the Pharisees take up his discourse facetiously: "are we blind also?" they scoff. Jesus rebukes these counterfeit cripples, admonishing them that if they were actually blind, they would have no sin "but now ye say, we see; therefore your sin remaineth."

It was easy to repudiate the contemptuous ableism of the Pharisees ("we see" was a byword for sinful presumptuousness),[95] but Christ's concluding remarks troubled seventeenth-century commentators; does this mean that the blind are without sin? Was the blind man the one who could see all along? Are the blind, after all, tolerating our infirmities? Contemporary commentators generally rejected such facile readings, explaining that "though all punishment be for sin, and this man had such a common cause, yet no sin was the reason why he was singled out for this suffering."[96] But the account of the man born blind, besides – or rather by – putting pressure on broader conceptions of disability and defect, presented one of the most challenging scenes of interfaith encounter. The miraculous regeneration of the blind man, effected seemingly without personal impulse and *before* spiritual regeneration, represented a persistent exception to the "ordinary" workings of faith, one that many schemas had to carefully downplay.[97] Such a precedent not only authorized the most antinomian claims to privilege within the Christian community, but it also underscored the possibility that even the most extreme boundaries of salvation – the alterity of Jews, Muslims, pagans – were provisional.[98] Equally complicated was the behaviour of the blind man, which served simultaneously as a model for Christian comportment and a challenge to Christian identity. Because he had been blind since birth, he was often imagined as an embodiment of cultural decontextualization, a framing amplified by the rise of the "Molyneux Question": if cured, would a man blind his entire life be able to distinguish and name by sight the objects that he had previously known through the sense of touch?[99] In interpretations of the biblical story, this detachment from visual phenomena begets a hermeneutic austerity that was widely considered exemplary; when the Pharisees declare that Jesus is a known sinner, and thus disabled to such miracles, the man responds that "whether he be a sinner or no, I know not: one thing I know, that, whereas I was blind, now I see."[100] Against the presumptuousness of the apostles, the arrogance of the Pharisees, and even the strategic recalcitrance of his parents, the blind man's response was distinctively poised between precarious scepticism and fatal "self-conceitedness"[101] – a means of asserting a secure faith while repudiating divisive certainty about its dynamics.[102]

Yet, this hermeneutic restraint – this refusal to assign soteriological meaning to disability or able-bodiedness – was also the occasion for a more controversial response, one that pushed at the limits of contemporary attitudes towards tolerance and religious difference. Exasperated by the relentless prodding of the Pharisees, the once-blind man strikes back with a (surprisingly ableist) rebuke. When they ask *again* how Jesus "opened [his] eyes," he answers "roundly":[103] "I have told you already, and ye did not hear: wherefore would ye hear it again? Will ye also be his disciples?" For many readers, the response marked the radical boundaries of Christian salvation, abjuring those who could never be cured of their deafness to God. The "blun[t]" response demarcated the alterity of Satan (and Bishop Bonner!), who could not be saved by even the most compelling signs.[104] Henry Hammond paraphrased the questions (as did many commentators) as a plain admonition, the failure to hear as a culpable refusal: "I have told you, and you did not heed it; or else, I have told you plainly and distinctly enough already."[105] "Since they had no purpose to become scholars of Christ," George Hutcheson explained, "there was no reason that his glorious works should be so much revealed to them."[106] As many saw it, the query of the cured man demonstrated that sufficient effort had been made to save these deaf sinners.

But are these questions, perhaps, in earnest? Is it possible that the once-blind man is genuinely inviting these inveterate sinners to Christian fellowship? Some readers thought so, affirming that the man "heartily wished they would" become disciples. John Lightfoot argued that the man "speaketh it seriously and from a good heart."[107] Such a response seems almost implausibly charitable, but the phrase could intrude a moment of charity into otherwise severe denunciations of "wicked men": against his revilers, David "might have asked them one question, Will ye also be his disciples? Had they intended to have taken his yoke upon them, David would willingly have instructed them in the way, yea hee would have beene their guide."[108] The tension surrounding this passage was apparently so common that in his influential *Annotations* (1685), Matthew Poole acknowledged that "some think the form of speech, implieth a hearty wishing and desiring that they would be so; but others think, he speaks Ironically."[109] If irony is integral to liberal modes of tolerance (including that pursued by Pierre Bayle, as Elena Russo demonstrates elsewhere in this volume),[110] then this unusually tone-deaf response might be considered an eccentric alternative to both disavowal and tolerance, both of which depend on initially identifying "wrong" beliefs. In other words, this misrecognition of the religious other enables a distinctive form of recognition, one that exhibits some of the characteristics that theorists have sought in substitutes for the reigning liberal model. This is far from a facile scepticism, the man firmly asserting an epistemological judgment (that he has irrefutably gone from blindness to sight) in the face of social and legal intimidation. Hermeneutic misconstruction cannot be called "mutual respect"[111] or "recognition"[112] in any straightforward sense, to be sure, because it forestalls or sidesteps conflict. But this response nonetheless presents a stimulating moment of solicitation, presenting the basic rudiments of toleration – at least a "disposition or outlook that encourages" peaceful co-existence,[113] a "will to relationship" that seeks continued engagement.[114] After all, in failing (or refusing?) to properly contextualize their speech, the man sees the Pharisees as spiritually "abled" in provocative ways; this *felix culpa* imputes to them the volition and the capacity to be saved in a manner that ruffled many Christians. Interpreting their behaviour in this way seems admittedly imperial, situating the Pharisees within Christian models of salvation, but the man himself, we should remember, is outside such imperatives, for he learns that Jesus is the Lord only subsequently; he is not inviting them into his own system of beliefs, but asking how they position themselves in relation to this new community. This response came from a distinctively exceptional situation, yet divines regularly enjoined their readers to adopt such detachment, and the cured vision of the once-blind man was often represented as the ideal of regenerate sight. Even as theorists of toleration have demonstrated that the practice of tolerance need not be undergirded by a uniform virtue or principle, they have typically considered "misrecognition" as fundamentally disabling. Charles Taylor, for instance, observes that "nonrecognition of misrecognition [...] can inflict a grievous wound," while Axel Honneth conceives of misrecognition as "injurious" and "impair[ing]."[115] Within a framework that grants or even privileges such wounds as needfully mortifying, indeed the foundation of well-being, such a charitable misrecognition presented an appealing alternative to a dangerously knowing forbearance.

The story of the man born blind provides a productive counterpoint to *Samson Agonistes* in that it illuminates the potential proximity between the fatal errors of the Philistines and the blindness of Samson himself. The poem turns dramatically on this paradigmatic misreading of the lamed body, the Philistines bereft of (or "deaf" to) the prosthetic interventions that save the sonnet speaker and Adam. Responding to the boasting Harapha, who assumes that his affliction is a stable manifestation of personal transgression, Samson explains that his disability is an element in a larger schema beyond their view: "I was to do my part from Heav'n assign'd, / And had perform'd it if my known offence / Had not disabl'd me, not all your force."[116] Yet, in opening up this vista (the prerogative of Christ in John 9), Samson refuses to diminish his own exemplary role, repeatedly situating himself at the centre of the various texts he imagines. "Tell me Friends," he asks the Chorus anxiously, "Am I not sung and proverb'd for a Fool / In every street, do they not say, how well / Are come upon him his deserts?" (202–5). As we have seen, Samson's view of his blindness as a coherent mark of special abjection would have struck seventeenth-century readers as misguided, and many of Samson's descriptions of his disability (particularly "half dead"[117] and "living death"[118]) underscore the continuity of his condition with the "natural blindness" of all humankind (79, 100). Manoa invokes the curing of the blind man, in fact, to remind Samson that even in the most apparently exceptional case, the possibility of further exceptions is neither foreclosed nor assured: "But God who caus'd a fountain at thy prayer / From the dry ground to spring, thy thirst to allay / After the brunt of battle, can as easie / Cause light again within thy eies to spring, / Wherewith to serve him better than thou hast" (581–5). Manoa narrowly turns this possibility to Samson's benefit, but it is also part of the drama's larger tendency, examined by critics such as Elizabeth Sauer and Susannah Mintz, to present potentialities of interfaith recognition between Israelite and Philistine;[119] the curing of the blind Philistines is never a foregone conclusion, a fact emphasized by the troubles of sight that attend virtually every character in the play. If, as Tønder has recently proposed, suffering might serve as a foundation for more robust modes of interpersonal tolerance,[120] we might ask why Samson cannot experience his blindness as a source of potential connectedness, or at least of charity towards the "blind" Philistines. Such an attitude was certainly available to contemporary readers, and its presence is signalled most sharply in the play by Dalila, who begs Samson to "let weakness then with weakness come to parl / So near related, or the same of kind" (785–6).[121]

Samson's hostile response suggests why he must characterize this gesture as a calculated show – and perhaps more fundamentally why the potentially conciliatory continuities of disability are inhibited under the regulatory frameworks of liberalism. "How cunningly," he announces, "the sorceress displays / Her own transgressions, to upbraid mine?" (819–20). Samson hears Dalila's harangue as a performance denatured by concerns with law and punishment – and with good reason. When she sees that Samson will broach no substantial propinquity, Dalila admits what Samson never can: that her choice was inexorably mediated by state compulsion. "It was not gold, as to my charge thou lay'st, / That wrought with me: thou know'st the magistrates," she explains,

> And Princes of my countrey came in person,
> Sollicited, commanded, threatn'd, urg'd,
> Adjur'd by all the bonds of civil Duty
> And of Religion, press'd how just it was,
> How honourable, how glorious to entrap
> A common enemy, who had destroy'd

> Such numbers of our Nation: and the Priest
> Was not behind, but ever at my ear
> Preaching how meritorious with the gods
> It would be to ensnare an irreligious
> Dishonourer of *Dagon*: what had I
> To oppose against such powerful arguments? (849–62)

Soliciting, commanding, threatening, urging, adjuring, pressing, preaching: Dalila exposes the manifold arsenal of state power, as well as the manner in which violence is housed between outwardly pacific civil and religious discourses. The initial enjambment – "thou know'st the Magistrates" – underscores how substantially this view of agency inflects Samson's later encounter with the magistrate, and thus why he must reject it. Dalila argues that even the "constantest" men could have "yielded without blame" to such versatile compulsion, but Samson forcefully rejects a model that figures agency as an accommodation to the law (848). He sets her betrayal in the context of "*Philistian* gold," narrowing the struggle as an internal one of will against greed, and he promptly elevates the discussion away from the civil law to the "law of nature" (890). From the outset of the poem, however, Samson has been described as "yielding," and his subsequent compliance with the civil magistrate is all the more dubious after he has condemned it as "vile, contemptable, ridiculous ... execrably unclean, prophane" ("Argument," 407, 593, 1361–2). Everyone is allowed to change their mind, of course, but for those interested in legitimizing these fateful "motions" (as a mark of spiritual regeneration and divine sanction), Samson's timing could not be worse; the manifestation of his volition coincides so closely with the sharp edge of coercion that it is nearly impossible to tell which is efficacious. These "motions" may indeed be beyond human law and rationality, but in their junction with the regulation of human choice they are dramatically adulterated.

As Sharon Achinstein has demonstrated, *Samson Agonistes* grapples with the questions of consent, conscience, and "public proof" that were raised by the Clarendon Code, and her account of the contextual resonances of the play is judicious.[122] Yet she passes over perhaps too nimbly the difficulties presented by Samson's blindness, underestimating how the poem might be staging a struggle with how contemporary political theory (particularly that of Hobbes) positioned disability as "the limiting condition of freedom."[123] In couching his contests with state coercion within the more restrictive parameters of his blindness, Samson calls attention to the bind in which the penal laws placed the "disabled" subject, whose power of choice was occluded by an "artificiall" choice between conformity and nonconformity. We should remember that the spiritual welfare of Dissenters depended on properly parsing the nature and effect of their "disability" – on deciding what demands it exempted them from.

As Baxter put it, for instance, Dissenters were called to serve "till bonds or disability constrain us to forbear it."[124] In the ways that it puts pressure on this threshold, Samson's blindness serves less to express the despair or disillusionment of Restoration Dissent than to materialize the delusive adumbration of independent choice that the Clarendon Code entailed. When the Public Officer arrives to compel the blind Samson to attend the idolatrous festival, a scene which would have struck Restoration Dissenters as quite familiar, he concludes that he "cannot come," but eventually reverses his decision: "I with this Messenger will go along, / Nothing to do, be sure, that may dishonor / Our Law, or stain my vow of *Nazarite*" (1385–6). Considering how fundamentally liberal modes of agency are premised on paradigms of able-bodiedness,[125] I am inclined to take his initial assertion seriously – as a (however ironically charged and perhaps erroneous) conception of freedom as "the absence of ... externall Impediments to motion," as described by Hobbes.[126] Indeed, the officer's warning that they will come drag Samson "though [he] wert firmlier fastn'd then a rock" (1398) echoes the most sharply ableist element of Hobbes's schema of autonomy: "when the impediment of motion," Hobbes explains, "is in the constitution of the thing it selfe, we use not to say, it wants the Liberty; but the Power to move; as when a stone lyeth still, or a man is fastned to his bed by sicknesse."[127] By dragging Samson like a stone, the Philistines will publicly expose his powerlessness – not by binding him, but rather by showing that walking to the temple independently is beyond his capacity. Seeing Samson's initial refusal to come as a recognition of this "powerlessness" entails reading his later justifications as dissimulations that serve to submerge the troubling implications of this realization: ability and consent are grounded not on independence but on dependence[128] – and perhaps, for a "disabled" subject, more insidiously on the support of state-controlled prosthetics (a submersion integral to liberal personhood).[129] As the opening scene of the play demonstrates, Samson can only ambulate with the assistance of his guide, a decisive dependence considering that Christ was often imagined as the guide for the blind. And while his trepidation about approaching interlocutors reminds us how disabled persons are subject to increased levels and distinctive forms of violence ("fraud, contempt, abuse and wrong," as Samson describes it [76]),[130] it is his pretensions to strength that ironically underscore how much his agency is determined by the structure of the environment itself. When Harapha boasts that he would have thwarted Samson on the battlefield, for instance, Samson challenges him to single combat – as long as they fight in a narrow chamber (1116–18). Samson amplifies the imaginative resonances of the duel by juxtaposing the giant's dazzling armaments with his singular oaken staff, but this appeal to generic signals serves to obfuscate the stakes of this request; Samson is asking for a reconfiguration of space, one that alters how "safety" and precarity are distributed not only for disabled persons, but equally for the able-bodied. Before any other ramifications – political, historical, theomachic – of such an encounter can be determined, its parameters must be imposed (a process Samson imagines passively as "let[ting] be assign'd" [1116]). Harapha's shift to the "safety" of glorious arms, then, might be considered not just a refusal of this reconfiguration, but an attempt to efface the way that power inheres in the ability to organize space – to determine where one might be safely "aloof" (135) and where one may be "at one spears length" (348).

With the systemic infrastructure of his disability in mind, we can appreciate how the most seemingly pointed manifestations of state violence that Samson can defy conceal a more puissant form of compulsion – a threat to deny the prosthetics that make agency possible. The opening line of the poem marks Samson's dependence upon the assistance of a prosthetic, but it remains briefly possible that this dependence is not enervating but auspicious. As we have seen, Christians regularly imagined themselves as blind men led by God, and the absence of the Guide from not only the "Argument" and the "Persons," but from the dialogue of the drama as well, animates the prospect that Samson is being led directly by the Holy Spirit: "a little onwards lend thy guiding hand / To these dark steps, a little further on" (1–2). Samson choosing to be guided to the temple by the Public Officer, then, might be seen as a concession to a form of autonomy that, even as it permits him to smash their idols, represents a shameful perversion of this most godly relationship (underscored perhaps by the Chorus's hope that "Holy One / Of *Israel*" will be his "guide" [1426–7]). Indeed, when Samson agrees to go to the temple so that "they shall not trail [him] through thir streets" like a beast, his abiding strength and his attraction to their "advantages" and "art" suggest he consents not because he fears their "engines," but because he relies on them (1402, 1401, 1399). It is notable, then, that he describes the Public Officer so artfully as a "messenger" (to conflate him, perhaps, with the less problematically *Hebrew* "Messenger" who appears later in the play) when he is in fact the drama's most material agent of coercion. The type of agency Samson does achieve, then, is conditioned on his acceptance of what Lucas Pinheiro describes as the "ableist contract";[131] Samson consents to the effacement of his most fundamental dependence so that he can pretend to those forms of autonomy recognized by the reigning regime. The sense that Samson becomes a "free moral agent" or a "'fit'" adult man as the play progresses, in other words, is a ruse that he is compelled to devise.[132] His various claims to "Sole Author[ship]" formulate a false dichotomy – between "constraint" and unfettered choice – that equips him to adopt a spiritually and politically denaturing form of personal autonomy (an "internalized ableism") (376).[133] If we see Samson as a representation of Restoration Nonconformists, his blindness marks the insidious effect of their "disabilities," for he is forced into a discursively obfuscated position in which the only way he can articulate his faith, even those "inward" motions that Milton had sometimes imagined insulated from compulsion, is through a reductive secularization of dependence. This might be why (especially alongside the reams dedicated to the complexities of conscientious action in contemporary writing) his assertion of a hermetic autonomy, one that may freely reject conformity even after strategically "passing," is at once self-assured and hollow. "Masters commands come with a power resistless," he decides:

> To such as owe them absolute subjection;
> And for a life who will not change his purpose?
> (So mutable are all the ways of men)
> Yet this be sure, in nothing to comply
> Scandalous or forbidden in our Law. (1404–9)

As critics have observed, the passage is drenched in ambiguity and equivocation, and for present purposes we might consider the concession to the "mutability" of man not as a recognition of earthly contingency, but as an ownership of our capacity to live prosthetically (here a recognition Samson perverts). Martin Dzelzainis is partly right that this moment is presented as an exchange of earthly slavery for divine slavery,[134] but it seems rather to stage the profanation of this process, Samson laying claim to an unattainable continence. The knowing eye roll of the Public Officer –"I praise thy resolution, doff these links" – might be more ironic than we think, then, marking the way that Samson's production of autonomy is an acceptance of external impediments that conceal his fundamental powerlessness (1410). Indeed, when the "guide" returns briefly later on to help Samson to the pillars, it seems more certain that Samson is now assisted by Philistines: "At length for intermission sake they led him / Between the pillars; he his guide requested / (For so from such as nearer stood we heard) / As over-tir'd to let him lean a while / With both his arms on those two massie Pillars" (1629–33).[135] To be sure, relying on Philistine assistance does not necessarily abolish his political or spiritual authority, and it is hard to criticize Samson for failing to develop a social model of disability that indicts the Philistine built environment. But it is hard to deny that his oddly effaced dependence on Philistine guidance complicates his claims to autonomy: is Samson really obeying the motions of the Lord, or merely complying with the "normal background conditions" such as they are arranged by the Philistines?[136]

Without sanctioning either explanatory framework, we can appreciate how such difficulties are substantially a consequence of religious compulsion itself, which by privileging particular "displays" of faith positions able-bodied performance as the foremost locus of soteriological meaning. As Paul Yachnin argues in this volume, the policies of forced conversion that prevailed throughout the early modern period fostered a realm of inwardness that challenged coercion, and many contemporary proponents of toleration condemned religious compulsion as an attempt to influence "inward" belief through "outward" means. For Milton, "the care of souls cannot belong to the civil magistrate, because his power consists only in outward force; but true saving religion consists in the inward persuasion of the mind, without which nothing can be acceptable to God."[137] But the problem with such a policy was not only that it was (ostensibly) irrational. Privileging outward performance – making public display the index of virtue – would confuse, perhaps entirely obscure, the workings of authentic belief. As Milton puts it in *The Reason of Church-Government* (1642), "if the form of the ministry be grounded in the worldly degrees of authority, honour, temporal jurisdiction, we see with our eyes it will turn the inward power and purity of the gospel into the outward carnality of the law; evaporating and exhaling the internal worship into empty conformities, and gay shews."[138] To the extent that such a policy constrained the motions of faith, it could be considered more fundamentally a conditioning of "ableistnormativity" – an internalized compulsion to pass based on those codes of behaviour that are publically recognized.[139] In the face of the epistemological treachery of the body, penal laws reified and enforced our transgressive ocularity. Fears that such a policy (so focused on visual performance) would contribute to papist idolatry were common, but in *Areopagitica* (1644) Milton suggests that codifying such performances might even alter our perception and experience of corporeality itself; an Adam without free will, like a subject under "prescription, and compulsion," he contends, would be "a meer artificiall *Adam*, such an *Adam* as he is in the motions."[140] "The motions" here refers to puppet shows, the term occasioning a telling slip that demonstrates how under such impositions spiritual "motion" is reduced to a set of culturally measurable forms of bodily performances, ones that we can distinguish only by their framing (because this is presented as "the" motions, not "his" motions). This is why, at its most profound level, regulating belief entails "licencing dancers, that no gesture, motion, or deportment be taught our youth but what by their [the state's] allowance shall be thought honest."[141] If such a trope presents a critique of theatricality,[142] it also exposes the paradigms of able-bodiedness that subtend such a regulatory regime, marking how the law defines what forms of expression, activity, and labour are assigned value (considered "honest" or "profitable"). For a poet who posits a substantial continuity between inward and outward motions,[143] this is more than a mere metaphor; controlling the actions of the body will modify the way we express and perceive faith.

In *Areopagitica* the reader is positioned such ("outside the box," so to speak) that they can distinguish "artificiall" shows from the true exertions of a vigorous spirit, but in *Samson Agonistes* this same convergence of forces is embedded so thoroughly in legal proscription that it becomes impossible to judge the "rouzing motions" upon which so much depends.[144] The entire action of the play, of course, takes place as part of the festival day for Dagon, a mandatory holy day that culminates with Samson's spectacular show. From the outset, Samson marks how his most intimate motions – ambulation, respiration, inspiration (the "breath of Heav'n") – are a consequence of this occasion, and from the perspective of the Philistines as much as the viewer there is no question about his coming to the temple (10). Taking place at the theatre, alongside "Gymnic Artists, Wrestlers, Riders, Runners, / Juglers and Dancers, Antics, Mummers, Mimics" (1323–5), Samson's fatal performance is hard to distinguish from these "gay shews," especially when he prefaces it with such a crowd-pleasing advertisement:

> Hitherto, Lords, what your commands impos'd
> I have perform'd, as reason was, obeying,
> Not without wonder or delight beheld.
> Now of my own accord such other trial
> I mean to shew you of my strength, yet greater;
> As with amaze shall strike all who behold. (1640–5)

Is Samson manifesting motions, or putting on the very puppet show (suitable for an intermission) that he has been called to the theatre to put on? In some sense, Samson ironically inverts the theatricality of the regime, taking the invitation to sacrifice to its most violently submissive extreme. But such a shift nonetheless dramatically reduces the parameters of choice. As Wittreich demonstrates, the phrase "of my own accord" was traditionally presented as the antithesis to divine inspiration,[145] so while it might mark Samson's persistent reprobation, it is also significant here for the way it maps out the diminished stakes of this encounter; the staging is now between personal agency and state compulsion (rather than divine impulsion). To the extent that such a reading seems like a crude reduction of the epistemological and theological possibilities raised by this heroic event, it is not inconsistent with the legal environment of post-Restoration Dissent; to equate *this* Samson with his other (more pellucidly antinomian) manifestations, whether in Milton's earlier writings or in the preceding tradition, is to neglect how expressions of faith were mediated by the imposition of uniformity under the Restoration regime. In other words, we might see the play as maintaining the theoretical possibility of antinomian action while staging its epistemological adulteration by state regulation; this is a play about the coerced concessions by which motions become "motions." Though this reduction might be relegated to the setting of Hebraic law, it extends significantly beyond the setting of the play. The preface, promising to "temper and reduce" deviant impulses "to a just measure" using medical techniques, participates in this regulation, the poet positioning himself (like Samson) legibly in relation to established prescriptions for the body; by prescribing sour for sour, salt for salt, the speaker aims to generate uniformity at the most elemental level. Preceding the title page, the unusually conspicuous invocation of licensing noted by Wittreich signals the continuity between Samson's situation and that of the play itself; for both "author[s]" the precondition of their appearance is that they perform those "gesture[s], motion[s], [and] deportment[s]" that are intelligible in the eyes of the law (376).[146]

While this approach to the poem may not decisively resolve the most pressing questions surrounding the poem (Is Samson's brutality just? Is he a terrorist?),[147] it does suggest that these questions might depend on conceptions of disability and impairment before they do on ideas of belief and ethics. As we have seen, the depth and significance of religious difference was partly a function of the agency and constraints disability entailed. When the semi-chorus stumbles over the possible capacities of the Philistines in their final moments – "insensate left, or to sense reprobate, / And with blindness internal struck" – we are reminded of how much the justice (and painfulness) of this final act depends on the nature and culpability of their disabilities (1685–6). And we also notice, more disconcertingly, how these modes of disability are consolidated retroactively, perhaps not only to sanction punishment but to palliate it; as modern readers, we probably hope that the Philistines were senseless when they were crushed by the temple stones. If such a reading of the poem seems a capitulation to modern concerns about ableist ideology, we should remember that seventeenth-century religious writing was hostile to ableism in its own way – for reasons partly antithetical to those driving current struggles for disability rights. And religious compulsion was indeed contested in these terms, its opponents arguing not only that it made specious claims to a mode of divine sight, but also that so demanding a legible performance of belief from the body might engender illegible fissures in the body political. In his animadversions on the Clarendon Code, for instance, John Corbet disavowed active resistance (as did most Dissenters), but in doing so he noted that a body apparently "free from violent or convulsive motions ... may fall into a Paralytick, or Hectick Distemper, or an Atrophy. There be sullen Mutinies," he warned, "that make no noise, but may loosen all the Joynts and Ligaments of Policy."[148] At the site of Samson's awful finale it must certainly have been loud, but from our position – acquainted with the disaster third-hand (from a printed messenger) – this is indeed a muted mutiny, taking place at precisely that distance that Samson is enabled to walk. It is a distance we might consider a measure of how much spiritual expression was reconstituted by the regulation of belief under the Restoration regime.

One of the abiding priorities of disability studies has been to foreground the voices of disabled persons themselves,[149] but *Samson Agonistes* suggests how problematically such voices might be mediated by the law even as they appear. What possibilities inhere, then, for a form of expression that effectively transcends or foils regulated conventions of gesture, motion, and deportment – that furnishes a contentious agency for the disabled subject? Here political theory is markedly deficient, as Barbara Arneil has recently argued,[150] but for guidance seventeenth-century writers might have turned to John 9, a text concerned with how to frustrate state coercion. Vexed by the unsatisfactory responses of the cured man, the Pharisees turn on his parents, asking them if their son (if he really *is* their son) was indeed blind from birth. Recognizing that any answer to this "captious"[151] interrogation will be subject to legal reconstruction, the parents yield up their son – but not before they publicly accentuate the precondition for his autonomy:

> But by what means he now seeth, we know not; or who hath opened his eyes, we know not; he is of age; ask him: he shall speak for himself. These words spake his parents, because they feared the Jews: for the Jews had agreed already, that if any man did confess that he was Christ, he should be put out of the synagogue. Therefore said his parents, He is of age; ask him.[152]

Though not always considered a model of Christian fortitude, this strategically "prudential" evasion could be used as a means of qualifying or compromising statements made under duress (particularly from ecclesiastical authorities).[153] At his execution in 1662, for instance, the regicide John Okey, caught between the proscription against justifying his crimes and the imperative to obey his conscience, decided to answer as "the Parents of him that was born blind, being asked by the *Pharisees* how he came to sight?... *He is of Age, let him speak for himself*: and so the Cause is sufficiently able to speak for it self."[154] In *Samson Agonistes*, Milton allows his hero to speak for himself, but not without marking the conditions that make Samson of age.

In exploring the limitations of liberal tolerance, then, we might weigh who is considered "of age" – designated as an autonomous subject – in contemporary models of personhood. Even as more recent scholarship on toleration has sought to challenge Enlightenment models of rational subjectivity, it has been difficult to conceive of tolerance outside the context of "choice," "belief," or "practice." These categories are decidedly problematized, however, by the persistent and widespread existence of disability. What level of cognitive capacity does "choice" require? What degrees and forms of motion are treated as meaningful? What levels of dependence preclude autonomous action? If secular forms of sovereignty and personhood are subtended by a theological infrastructure as postsecular theory has suggested, then seventeenth-century debates about justification, punishment, and conformity might contribute to more robust inquiries about how justice is distributed, how exceptions are defined, and where suffering takes place. At their best, theorizations of tolerance endeavour to admit these difficulties, refusing to say "we see." But when even the apostles stumble, we should take care.

NOTES

1 Richard Chapman, *Hallelu-jah: or, King David's Shrill Trumpet* (London, 1635), 144–5.

2 Michael Ignatieff, "Nationalism and Toleration," in Susan Mendus, ed., *The Politics of Toleration in Modern Life* (Durham: Duke University Press, 2000), 85.

3 Wendy Brown, *Regulating Aversion: Tolerance in the Age of Identity and Empire* (Princeton: Princeton University Press, 2006).

4 Tobin Siebers, "Tender Organs, Narcissism, and Identity Politics," in Sharon L. Snyder, Brenda Jo Brueggemann, and Rosemarie Garland-Thomson, eds., *Disability Studies: Enabling the Humanities* (New York: Modern Language Association, 2002), 51.

5 See, for instance, Brian Brock and John Swinton, eds., *Disability and the Christian Tradition: A Reader* (Grand Rapids: William B. Eerdmans Publishing, 2012); C.F. Goodey, *A History of Intelligence and "Intellectual Disability": The Shaping of Psychology in Early Modern Europe* (New York: Routledge, 2011); Irina Metzler, *Disability in Medieval Europe: Thinking about Physical Impairment in the High Middle Ages, c. 1100–1400* (New York: Routledge, 2010); Candida R. Moss and Jeremy Schipper, eds., *Disability Studies and Biblical Literature* (New York: Palgrave, 2011).

6 Notable exceptions to this tendency are Amos Young, *Theology and Down Syndrome: Reimagining Disability in Late Modernity* (Waco: Baylor University Press, 2007); Andrew Picard and Myk Habets, eds., *Theology and the Experience of Disability: Interdisciplinary Perspectives from Voices Down Under* (New York: Routledge, 2016); Darla Yvonne Schumm and Michael Stoltzfus, eds., *Disability and World Religions: An Introduction* (Waco: Baylor University Press, 2016); Johann-Christian Põder, "Theology, Disability, and Human Rights: Difficult Past, Promising Futures," in John-Stewart Gordon, Johann-Christian Põder, and Holger Burckhart, eds., *Human Rights and Disability: Interdisciplinary Perspectives* (New York: Routledge, 2017); Jason Reimer Greig, *Reconsidering Intellectual Disability: L'Arche, Medical Ethics, and Christian Friendship* (Washington, DC: Georgetown University Press, 2015); Wayne Morris, *Theology without Words: Theology in the Deaf Community* (New York: Routledge, 2016); Nick J. Watson and Andrew Parker, eds., *Sports, Religion and Disability* (New York: Routledge, 2015).

7 Lars Tønder, *Tolerance: A Sensorial Orientation to Politics* (Oxford: Oxford University Press, 2013).

8 Barbara Arneil and Nancy J. Hirschmann, eds., *Disability and Political Theory* (Cambridge: Cambridge University Press, 2016).

9 David T. Michell and Sharon Snyder, eds., *The Biopolitics of Disability: Neoliberalism, Ablenationalism, and Peripheral Embodiment* (Ann Arbor: University of Michigan Press, 2015), 20.

10 See, for instance, Susan Mendus, *Toleration and the Limits of Liberalism* (Atlantic Highlands: Humanities Press International, 1989); Bernard Williams, "Toleration:

An Impossible Virtue?" in David Heyd, ed., *Toleration: An Elusive Virtue* (Princeton: Princeton University Press, 1996); Will Kymlicka, "Two Models of Pluralism and Tolerance," *Analyse & Kritik* 13 (1992): 33–56; Moshe Halbertal, "Autonomy, Toleration, and Group Rights: A Response to Will Kymlicka," in Heyd, *Elusive*; Matthew Festenstein, "Toleration and Deliberative Politics," in John Horton and Susan Mendus, eds., *Toleration, Identity and Difference* (London: Palgrave Macmillan, 1999); Elizabeth Purcell, "Disability, Narrative, and Moral Status," *Disability Studies Quarterly* 36, no. 1 (2016); Lawrence Becker, "Reciprocity, Justice, Disability," *Ethics* 116, no. 1 (2005): 9–39; Tobin Siebers, *Disability Theory* (Ann Arbor: University of Michigan Press, 2008), 176–86.

11 See Barbara Herman, "Pluralism and the Community of Moral Judgment," in Heyd, *Elusive*; George Carey, "Tolerating Religion," in Mendus, *Modern*; I.M. Young, *Justice and the Politics of Difference* (Princeton: Princeton University Press, 1990); Karl-Otto Apel, "Plurality of the Good? The Problem of Affirmative Tolerance in a Multicultural Society from an Ethical Point of View," *Ratio Juris* 10, no. 2 (1997): 199–212; Anna Galeotti, "The Range of Toleration: From Toleration as Recognition Back to Disrespectful Tolerance," *Philosophy and Social Criticism* 41, no. 2 (2015): 93–110; Melissa S. Williams and Jeremy Waldron, eds., *Toleration and Its Limits* (New York: New York University Press, 2008); Charles Taylor, *Multiculturalism: Examining the Politics of Recognition*, Amy Gutmann, ed. (Princeton: Princeton University Press, 1994); Alasdair MacIntyre, "Toleration and the Goods of Conflict," in Mendus, *Modern*; Dario Castiglione and Catriona McKinnon, eds., *Toleration, Neutrality and Democracy* (Dordrecht: Springer Science + Business Media, 2003).

12 See Rayna Rapp and Faye Ginsberg, "Enabling Disability: Rewriting Kinship, Reimagining Citizenship," *Public Culture* 13, no. 3 (2001): 533–56; Andrea T. Baumeister, "Multicultural Citizenship, Identity and Conflict," in Horton and Mendus, *Difference*; Will Kymlicka, *Multicultural Citizenship: A Liberal Theory of Minority Rights* (Oxford: Oxford University Press, 1996); Jürgen Habermas, "Religion in the Public Sphere," *European Journal of Philosophy* 14, no. 1 (2006): 1–25; Douglas C. Baynton, *Defectives in the Land: Disability and Immigration in the Age of Eugenics* (Chicago: University of Chicago Press, 2016); Nancy J. Hirschmann and Beth Linker, eds., *Civil Disabilities: Citizenship, Membership, and Belonging* (Philadelphia: University of Pennsylvania Press, 2015); Sue Donaldson and Will Kymlicka, "Rethinking Membership and Participation in an Inclusive Democracy: Cognitive Disability, Children, Animals," in Barbara Arneil and Nancy J. Hirschmann, eds., *Disability and Political Theory* (Cambridge: Cambridge University Press, 2016).

13 In conceptualizing the "learning processes" requisite to the constitutional state, for instance, the most disquieting consequence that Jürgen Habermas encounters is the possibility that the "collision of fundamentalist and secularist camps" can be traced back to "learning deficits" – a difficulty that demands a "self-limitation of political theory" (18–19). On the problems disability poses for political theory,

see Eva Feder Kittay, "At the Margins of Moral Personhood," *Ethics* 116, no. 1 (2005): 100–31; Barbara Arneil and Nancy J. Hirschmann, eds., *Disability and Political Theory* (Cambridge: Cambridge University Press, 2016); Barbara Arneil, "Disability, Self Image, and Modern Political Theory," *Political Theory* 37, no. 2 (2009): 218–42; Carol A. Breckenridge and Candace Vogler, "The Critical Limits of Embodiment: Disability's Criticism," *Public Culture* 13, no. 3 (2001): 349–57; Eva Feder Kittay, "When Caring Is Just and Justice Is Caring: Justice and Mental Retardation," *Public Culture* 13, no. 3 (2001): 557–79; Lennard J. Davis, "Bodies of Difference: Politics, Disability, and Representation," in Snyder, Brueggemann, and Garland-Thomson, *Enabling*; Nancy J. Hirschmann, "Disability Rights, Social Rights, and Freedom," *Journal of International Political Theory* 12, no. 1 (2016): 42–57; Stacy Clifford, "Making Disability Public in Deliberative Democracy," *Contemporary Political Theory* 11, no. 2 (2012): 211–28.

14 Roger Lund, "Laughing at Cripples: Ridicule, Deformity, and the Argument from Design," *Eighteenth-Century Studies* 39, no. 1 (2005): 91–114.

15 David T. Mitchell, "Narrative Prosthesis and the Materiality of Metaphor," in Snyder, Brueggemann, and Garland-Thomson, *Enabling*, 25.

16 *A Disuasive from Popery* (Dublin, 1681), 19.

17 Robert Abbot, *A Triall of Our Church-Forsakers* (1639), 98.

18 On the history of blindness as a concept, see Moshe Barasch, *Blindness: The History of a Mental Image in Western Thought* (New York: Routledge, 2001); Edward Wheatley, *Stumbling Blocks before the Blind: Medieval Constructions of a Disability* (Ann Arbor: University of Michigan Press, 2010); Nicholas Wade, *Natural History of Vision* (Boston: MIT Press, 1998); Susannah Biernoff, *Sight and Embodiment in the Middle Ages* (New York: Palgrave Macmillan, 2002).

19 Contemporary writers often conflated blindness with other defects and deformities, but the fact that the condition was not as visually conspicuous certainly altered its meaning and effects. Though we should also recognize (as Milton perhaps marks in his "Sonnet: To Cyriack Skinner") that the lower visibility of such a disability could present its own challenges, among them the demand for "proof." On the complexities of invisible disability, see N. Ann Davis, "Invisible Disability," *Ethics* 116, no. 1 (2005): 153–213.

20 Richard Allestree, *The Gentleman's Calling* (London, 1660), 101.

21 This view is largely associated with John Rawls, *Political Liberalism* (New York: Columbia University Press, 1993), though it can be found in numerous accounts of the topic. For studies that problematize or dispute this view, see Perez Zagorin, *How the Idea of Religious Toleration Came to the West* (Princeton: Princeton University Press, 2003); Ingrid Creppell, "Toleration, Politics, and the Role of Mutuality," in M. Williams and Waldron, *Limits*; Noah Feldman, "Morality, Self-Interest, and the Politics of Toleration," in M. Williams and Waldron, *Limits*; Ingrid Creppell, *Toleration and Identity: Foundations in Early Modern Thought* (New York: Routledge, 2003).

22 For accounts of ableism, generally conceived as a systemic presumption of able-bodiedness that denigrates disability, see Fiona Campbell, *Contours of Ableism: The Production of Disability and Abledness* (New York: Palgrave, 2009); Gregor Wolbring, "The Politics of Ableism," *Development* 51 (2008): 252–58; Thomas Hehir, "Confronting Ableism," *Educational Leadership* 64, no. 5 (2007): 8–14; Carli Friedman, "Defining Disability: Understanding of and Attitudes towards Ableism and Disability," *Disability Studies Quarterly* 37, no. 1 (2017).

23 On the construction of the category of "normalcy," see Lennard Davis, *Enforcing Normalcy: Disability, Deafness, and the Body* (New York: Verso, 1995).

24 John Hayward, *The Strong Helper* (London, 1614), 196.

25 Tønder, *Tolerance*, 32–3; W. Brown, *Aversion*, 176–205.

26 Proscriptions against blind and lame sacrifices were invoked during the period, but usually metaphorically. See Henry Anderson, *A Loyal Tear Dropt on the Vault of the High and Mighty Prince, Charles II* (London, 1685), 5; William Harrison, *A Plaine and Profitable Exposition, of the Parable of the Sower* (London, 1625), 27; John Hayward, *Hell's Everlasting Flames Avoided* (London, 1696), 44.

27 George Downame, *The Christians Freedome* (Oxford, [1635]), 48–9; Edward Chaloner, *Credo ecclesiam sanctam Catholicam* (London, 1623), 52; Roger Williams, *The Bloudy Tenant, of Persecution, for Cause of Conscience* (London, 1644), 53–4.

28 Creppell, *Identity*, 2.

29 *An Answere in Action to a Portingale Pearle* (London, [1570]), B[v].

30 See, for instance, Francis Hastings, *An Apologie or Defence of the Watch-Word* (London, 1600), 21.

31 *The Absolute Necessity of Standing by the Present Government* (London, 1689), 10.

32 David Abercromby, *Protestancy to be Embrac'd* (London, 1682), 145–7.

33 John Golburne, "The Translator to the Reader," in *Acts of the Dispute and Conference Holden at Paris* (London, 1602), *4[r].

34 John Downe, *Certaine Treatises of the Late Reverend and Learned Divine, Mr John Downe* (Oxford, 1633), 26. See also Adam Harsnett, *A Cordiall for the Afflicted* (London, 1638), 522–3; Richard Alison, *The Psalmes of David in Meter* (London, 1599), Aii[r].

35 William Attersoll, *The Badges of Christianity* ([London], 1606), 345. See also Thomas Morton of Berwick, *Two Treatises Concerning Regeneration* (London, 1597), 5–6; Thomas Adams, *The Happines of the Church* (London, 1619), 285; Roger Williams, *George Fox Digg'd Out of his Burrowes* (Boston, 1676), 198; Matthew Poole, *A Seasonable Apology for Religion* (London, [1673]), 58; John Owen, *The Reason of Faith* (London, 1677), 89.

36 Margaret Aston, *England's Iconoclasts: Laws Against Images*, vol. 1 (Oxford: Oxford University Press, 1988); Stuart Clark, *Vanities of the Eye: Vision in Early Modern European Culture* (Oxford: Oxford University Press, 2007).

37 See, for instance, Thomas Draxe, *The Christian Armorie* (London, 1611), 143–50.

38 Richard Allestree, *Forty Sermons* (London, 1684), 261.

39 John Donne, *Fifty Sermons* (London, [1649]), 37. See also Thomas Morton of Berwick, *A Treatise of the Nature of God* (London, 1599), 25.

40 Thomas Draxe, *The Worldes Resurrection* (London, 1608), 25. See also John Yates, *God's Arraignment of Hypocrites* (Cambridge, 1615), 163–4.

41 See Disney Gervase, *Some Remarkable Passages in the Holy Life and Death of Gervase Disney* (London, [1692]), 244.

42 Walter Charleton, *The Darkness of Atheism Dispelled* (London, 1652), 263; Henry Harrison, *The Weary Traveller* (London, 1681), 134.

43 William Charke, *An Answeare for This Time* (London, 1583), 84.

44 William Allen, *A Discourse of the Nature, Ends, and Difference of the Two Covenants* (London, 1673), 201–2; Henry Dodwell, *Separation of Churches From Episcopal Government* (London, 1679), 85, 186. See also George Downame, *A Treatise of Justification* (London, 1633), 427.

45 As Barbara Arneil puts it, before the nineteenth century human beings are seen as "lacking in different degrees in relation to God," rather than as "bifurcated into two categories of humanity: normal and abnormal." Arneil, "Disability, Self Image," 219–20.

46 W. Brown, *Aversion*, 186.

47 Richard Allestree, *The Practice of Christian Graces* (London, 1658), 623.

48 John Chapman, *A Most True Report of the Myraculous Moving and Sinking of a Plot of Ground* ([London], [1596]), A3v.

49 Joanna Picciotto, *Labors of Innocence in Early Modern England* (Cambridge: Harvard University Press, 2010).

50 Robert Abbot, *The Young-Mans Warning-Peece* (1639), 30. See also John Williams, *The Characters of Divine Revelation* (London, 1695), 8–9; Jacques Abbadie, *The Art of Knowing One-Self* (1695), 99.

51 John Williams, *Scripture the Rule of Faith* (London, [1696]), 17. See also John Wilson, *The Scriptures Genuine Interpreter Asserted* (London, 1678), 1–21.

52 Giovanni Diodati, *Pious Annotations, Upon the Holy Bible* (London, [1643]), 26; John Howe, *A Discourse of an Unconverted Man's Enmity* (London, 1700), 12–13; William Sherlock, *A Discourse Concerning the Divine Providence* (London, 1694), 198.

53 See Joseph Alleine, *Christian Letters* (London, 1673), 101; William Allen, *An Admonition to the Nobility and People of England and Ireland* ([Antwerp, 1588]), xxxv; Attersoll, *Badges*, 17; Samuel Doolittle, *A Sermon Occasioned by the Late Earthquake* (London, 1692); Thomas Hayne, *The Equall Wayes of God* (London, 1632), 13; William Thomas, *Scriptures Opened and Sundry Cases of Conscience Resolved* (London, 1675), 367; Edward Stillingfleet, *Twelve Sermons Preached on Several Occasions* (London, 1696), 309; William Sherlock, *A Discourse Concerning the Divine Providence* (London, 1694), 198–9.

54 Chapman, *Hallelu-Jah*, 111; Jack Dawd, *Vox Graculi* (London, 1622), 42.

55 Downame, *Justification*, 326. See also Sir Francis Hastings, *A Watch-Word to all Religious, and True Hearted English-Men* (London, 1598), 12; Berwick, *Nature*, 21. Alternatively, see Simon Harward, *The Solace for the Souldier and Saylour* (London, 1592), F3^{v}.

56 Anthony Champney, *Mr. Pilkinton his Parallela Disparalled* (Saint-Omer, 1620), 142.

57 Davis, *Normalcy*, 105.

58 Jeffrey Wilson, "The Trouble with Disability in Shakespeare Studies," *Disability Studies Quarterly* 37, no. 2 (2017).

59 On this debate, see "Disabled Shakespeares." Special Issue, *Disability Studies Quarterly* 29, no. 4 (2009); Wilson, "Trouble."

60 Nicholas Mirzoeff, "Blindness and Art," in Lennard J. Davis, ed., *The Disability Studies Reader* (New York: Routledge, 1997), 384.

61 Richard Baxter, *Richard Baxters Apology Against the Modest Exceptions of Mr. T. Blake and the Digressions of Mr. G. Kendall* (1654), 29.

62 Ibid., 103.

63 On "disability" as a consequence of industrial capitalism, see Marta Russell and Ravi Malhorta, "Capitalism and Disability," *Socialist Register* 38 (2002): 211–28; Marta Russell, "Disablement, Oppression, and the Political Economy," *Journal of Disability Policy Studies* 12, no. 2 (2001): 87–95; Nirmana Erevelles, "Disability and the Dialectics of Difference," *Disability & Society* 11, no. 4 (1996): 519–38; Nirmana Erevelles, *Disability and Difference in Global Contexts: Enabling a Transformative Body Politic* (New York: Palgrave MacMillan, 2011).

64 David M. Turner, "Introduction: Approaching Anomalous Bodies," in David M. Turner and Kevin Stagg, eds., *Social Histories of Disability and Deformity* (New York: Routledge, 2006), 2.

65 Ibid.

66 John Bunyan, *The Acceptable Sacrifice* (1689), 47.

67 See, for instance, Draxe, *Resurrection*, 30–1. Such a view was also supported by early modern medical discourse, in which the body was imagined as naturally porous and volatile. On this, see Hobgood and Wood, "Introduction: Ethical Staring," in *Recovering*, 11–13.

68 Anna Galeotti, *Toleration as Recognition* (Cambridge University Press, 2002), 8.

69 Thus the possibility of absolutely disavowing blindness was not impossible, but rather theologically radical. See, for instance, Edward Haughton, *The Rise, Growth, and Fall of Antichrist* (London, 1652), 31. For a typically jocular contemporary treatment, see *The Quakers Art of Courtship* (London, 1689), 70–1, in which a crafty Quaker pawns off a blind horse on an unsuspecting citizen because he "imagined a blind Horse to be suitable for one that was without Light."

70 Richard Alison, *A Plaine Confutation of a Treatise of Brownisme* (London, 1590), 2.

71 Richard Allestree captures this cultural tension in his animadversions on "scoffing and derision"; "alas," he laments, "many of us would rather put a stumbling block in the way of the Blind, pull away the Crutch from the Lame, that we may

sport our selves to see them tumble: such a sensuality we have in observing and improving the imperfections of others, that it is become the grand excellence of the Age to be Dextrous at it": *The Government of the Tongue* (Oxford, 1677), 119. On the abiding (albeit complex) cruelty to disabled persons, see David M. Turner, "Disability Humor and the Meanings of Impairment in Early Modern England," in Hobgood and Wood, *Recovering*; Simon Dickie, *Cruelty and Laughter: Forgotten Comic Literature and the Unsentimental Eighteenth Century* (Chicago: University of Chicago Press, 2011); Lund, "Laughing."

72 Kathryn Abrams, "Forbearant and Engaged Toleration: A Comment on David Heyd," in M. Williams and Waldron, *Limits*, 212.

73 Donne, *Sermons*, 344–5.

74 Nicholas Byfield, *The Paterne of Wholsome Words* (London, 1618), 104–5.

75 Draxe, *Armorie*, 144.

76 John Calvin, *A Harmonie Upon the Three Evangelists* (London, 1584), 220.

77 There is some debate about how prevalent disabilities were during the early modern period; while the deficiencies of medical treatment may have left more individuals with visible signs of impairment (such as smallpox), they would also have ensured a higher mortality rate for others (such as military injuries).

78 John Dod, *Foure Godlie and Fruitful Sermons* (London, 1611), 7–8.

79 Adams, *Happines*, 330–1.

80 Draxe, *Armorie*, 79.

81 John 9:2–3.

82 Calvin, *Harmonie*, 220. See also William Burkitt, *Expository Notes with Practical Observations on the Four Holy Evangelists* (London, 1700), Kkkk2^r; George Hutcheston, *An Exposition of the Gospel of Jesus Christ, according to John* (London, 1657), 177; Augustin Marlorat, *A Catholike and Ecclesiasticall Exposition Of the Holy Gospell After S. Iohn* (London, 1575), 334; John Williams, *A Sermons Preach'd Before the King at Whitehall, on January 30, 1696* (London, 1697), 27.

83 Rosemarie Garland-Thomson, *Freakery: Cultural Spectacles of the Extrordinary Body* (New York: New York University Press, 1996), 1. Sharon L. Snyder and David T. Mitchell conceive of disability as "that which exceeds a culture's predictive capacities or effective interventions." *Narrative Prosthesis: Disability and the Dependencies of Discourse* (Ann Arbor: University of Michigan Press, 2000), 3.

84 Mitchell, "Narrative" in *Enabling*, 17.

85 Calvin, *Harmonie*, 219.

86 John Milton, "Sonnet XVI," in John Carey and Alastair Fowler, eds., *The Poems of John Milton* (London: Longmans, 1968).

87 For biographical readings, see Eleanor Gertrude Brown, *Milton's Blindness* (New York: Columbia University Press, 1934), 51–6; David Urban, "Milton's Identification with the Unworthy Servant in Sonnet 19: A Response to Margaret Thickstun," *Connotations* 22, no. 2 (2012): 260–3; Carol Barton, "'They Also Perform the Duties of a Servant Who Only Remain Erect on Their Feet in a Specified Place

in Readiness to Receive Orders': The Dynamics of Stasis in Sonnet XIX ("When I Consider How My Light Is Spent")," *Milton Quarterly* 32, no. 4 (1998): 109–22. The most influential challenge to the tendency to read the poem as a reflection on Milton's own blindness is Dayton Haskin, *Milton's Burden of Interpretation* (Philadelphia: University of Pennsylvania Press, 1994); but see also Margaret Thickstun, "Resisting Patience in Milton's Sonnet 19," *Milton Quarterly* 44 (2010): 168–80; Joseph Pequigney, "Milton's Sonnet XIX Reconsidered," *Texas Studies in Literature and Language* 8, no. 4 (1967): 485–98.

88 See, for instance, Harry F. Robins, "Milton's First Sonnet on his Blindness," *Review of English Studies* 7 (1956): 360–6; Fitzroy Pyle, "Milton's First Sonnet on His Blindness," *The Review of English Studies* 9 (1958): 376–7; Angelica Duran, "The Blind Bard, According to John Milton and his Contemporaries," *Mosaic: An Interdisciplinary Critical Journal* 46, no. 3 (2013): 143–4; David Urban, "The Talented Mr. Milton: A Parabolic Laborer and His Identity," *Milton Studies* 43 (2004): 1-18; Russell M. Hillier, "The Patience to Prevent That Murmur: The Theodicy of John Milton's Nineteenth Sonnet," *Renascence* 22, no. 4 (2007): 247–73.

89 For those who emphasize the uncertainty that remains, see Ann Gossman and George W. Whiting, "Milton's First Sonnet on His Blindness," *Review of English Studies* 12, no. 48 (1961): 364–72; Tobias Gregory, "Murmur and Reply: Rereading Milton's Sonnet 19," *Milton Studies* 51 (2010): 21–43.

90 John Milton, "Paradise Lost," in Carey and Fowler, *Poems*, V:665.

91 On the potential role of pain in reconceptualizing tolerance, see G. Carey, "Tolerating Religion," in Mendus, *Modern*; Tønder, *Tolerance*; Mary Warnock, "The Limits of Toleration," in Susan Mendus and David Edwards, eds., *On Toleration* (Oxford: Oxford University Press, 1987).

92 On the complexities of Milton's monism, see Stephen Fallon, *Milton among the Philosophers* (Ithaca: Cornell University Press, 1991); John Rogers, *The Matter of Revolution* (Ithaca: Cornell University Press, 1996); William Walker, "Milton's Dualistic Theory of Religious Toleration in *A Treatise of Civil Power*, *Of Christian Doctrine*, and *Paradise Lost*," *Modern Philology* 99, no. 2 (2001): 201–30; Raymond B. Waddington, "'All in All': Shakespeare, Milton, Donne and the Soul-in-Body Topos," *English Literary Renaissance* 20, no. 1 (2009): 40–68; Philip Donnelly, "'Matter' versus Body: The Character of Milton's Monism," *Milton Quarterly* 33, no. 3 (1999): 79–85; Stephen Hequembourg, "Monism and Metaphor in *Paradise Lost*," *Milton Studies* 52 (2011): 139–67; Rachel J. Trubowitz, "Body Politics in *Paradise Lost*," *PMLA* 121, no. 2 (2006): 388–404.

93 John Rogers, "The Secret of Samson Agonistes," *Milton Studies* 33 (1996): 111–32.

94 See Kevin Stagg, "Representing Physical Difference: The Materiality of the Monstrous," in Turner and Stagg, *Social Histories*; Simone Chess, "Performing Blindness: Representing Disability in Early Modern Popular Performance and Print," in Hobgood and Wood, *Recovering*.

95 See Draxe, *Resurrection*, 36.

96 Richard Baxter, *A Paraphrase on the New Testament* (London, 1695), R3[r]. See also, Hutcheson, *Exposition*, 177; Marlorat, *Catholike*, 331–2.

97 John Downe, *Certaine Treatises of the Late and Learned Divine, Mr. John Downe* (Oxford, 1633), 23–4. See also Thomas Taylor, *Moses and Aaron* (London: 1653), 288.

98 This was not a problem, of course, for writers who endorsed toleration. See William Rogers, *The Bloudy Tenent* (London: 1644), 2.

99 In many cases these two traditions seem to converge, often with strange results. On the Molyneux Question, see Mark Paterson, *Seeing with the Hands: Blindness, Vision and Touch after Descartes* (Edinburgh: Edinburgh University Press, 2016).

100 John 9:25.

101 Richard Baxter, *A Treatise of Self-Denial* (London, 1675), 97.

102 On the excellence of this response, see Jeremiah Burroughs, *Gospel Remission* (London, 1668), 78; Joseph Alleine, *Divers Practical Cases of Conscience* (London, 1672), 67; John Beadle, *The Journal or Diary of a Thankful Christian* (London, 1656), 48; Arthur Hildersam, *CLII Lectures Upon Psalme LI* (London, [1635]), 342; Matthew Henry, *An Account of the Life and Death of Mr. Philip Henry* (London, 1698), 10; Thomas Manton, *One Hundred and Ninety Sermons on the Hundred and Nineteenth Psalm* (London, 1681), 605; John Owen, *Phronēma tou Pneumatou* (London, 1681), 155; Samuel Rutherford, *Influences of the Life of Grace* (London, 1659), A1[v].

103 Hutcheson, *Exposition*, 187.

104 Thomas Fuller, *A Comment on the Eleven First Verses of the Fourth Chapter of S. Matthew's Gospel* (London, 1652), 53; John Trapp, *A Brief Commentary of Exposition Upon the Gospel According to St. John* (London, 1646), 50.

105 Henry Hammond, A Paraphrase and Annotations upon all the Books of the New Testament (London, 1659), 297. See also Diodati, *Pious Annotations*, 73–4.

106 Hutcheson, *Exposition*, 188. See also Marlorat, *Catholike*, 349–50.

107 John Lightfoot, *The Harmony, Chronicle and Order of the New Testament* (1655), 48.

108 William Bloys, *Meditations Upon the XLII Psalme* (London, 1632), 341.

109 Matthew Poole, *Annotations Upon the Holy Bible*, vol. 2 (London, [1696]), gg[v].

110 See Richard Rorty, *Contingency, Irony, and Solidarity* (Cambridge: Cambridge University Press, 1989).

111 On the "mutual respect" or "mutuality" model of tolerance, see Amy Gutmann and Dennis Thompson, *Democracy and Disagreement* (Cambridge: Belknap Press of Harvard University Press, 1996); Michael Walzer, *On Toleration* (New Haven: Yale University Press, 1997); Creppell, "Mutuality," in M. Williams and Waldron, *Limits*.

112 On the "recognition" model of tolerance, see Charles Taylor, "The Politics of Recognition," in *Multiculturalism* (Princeton: Princeton University Press, 1994); Galeotti, *Recognition*; Cillian McBride, *Recognition* (Cambridge: Polity Press, 2013); Rainer Forst, "'To Tolerate Means to Insult': Toleration, Recognition, and Emancipation," in Bert van den Brink and David Owen, eds., *Recognition and*

Power: Axel Honneth and the Tradition of Critical Social Theory (Cambridge: Cambridge University Press, 2007); Axel Honneth, *The I in We: Studies in the Theory of Recognition* (Cambridge: Polity Press, 2012).

113   B. Williams, "Impossible," in Heyd, *Elusive*, 19.

114   Creppell, "Mutuality," in M. Williams and Waldon, *Limits*.

115   Charles Taylor, "Recognition," in *Multiculturalism*, 26; Axel Honneth, "Integrity and Disrespect: Principles of a Conception of Morality Based on the Theory of Recognition," *Political Theory* 20, no. 2 (1992): 188–9.

116   John Milton, "Samson Agonistes," in Carey and Fowler, *Poems*, lines 1217–19.

117   See Richard Holland, *The Good Samaritane* (London, 1700), 10; Thomas De Laune, *Tropologia, or, A Key to Open Scripture Metaphors* (London, 1681), 256.

118   See, for instance, *Thēnoikos the House of Mourning* (London, 1660), 43; Manton, *One Hundred and Ninety Sermons*, 897; Milton, *Paradise Lost*, X:788.

119   Susannah Mintz, *Threshold Poetics: Milton and Intersubjectivity* (Newark: University of Delaware Press, 2003), 175–212; Susannah Mintz, "Dalila's Touch: Disability and Recognition in Samson Agonistes," *Milton Studies* 40 (2002): 38–60; Elizabeth Sauer, *Milton, Toleration, and Nationhood* (Cambridge University Press, 2014), 136–58. See also Victoria Kahn, "Disappointed Nationalism: Milton in the Context of Seventeenth-Century Debates about the Nation-State," in Paul Stevens and David Loewnstein, eds., *Early Modern Nationalism and Milton's England* (Toronto: University of Toronto Press, 2008); Angela Balla, "Wars of Evidence and Religious Toleration in Milton's Samson Agonistes," *Milton Quarterly* 46, no. 2 (2012): 65–85.

120   Tønder, *Tolerance*.

121   An analysis of the filiations between "disability" and gender during the seventeenth century is beyond the scope of this essay, but newly developed theoretical alliances between feminist and disability studies (not to mention queer studies) might substantially open up the complexities of *Samson Agonistes*. See Kim Hall, *Feminist Disability Studies* (Bloomington: Indiana University Press, 2011); Alison Kafer, *Feminist, Queer, Crip* (Bloomington: Indiana University Press, 2013); Helen Deutsch and Felicity Nussbaum, eds., *"Defects": Engendering the Modern Body* (Ann Arbor: University of Michigan Press, 2000).

122   See Sharon Achinstein, "'Samson Agonistes' and the Drama of Dissent," *Milton Studies* 33 (1997): 133–58; Achinstein, *Literature and Dissent in Milton's England* (Cambridge: Cambridge University Press, 2003), 115–53. On the context of Restoration Dissent, see Nicholas Jose, "Samson Agonistes: The Play Turned Upside Down," in Nicholas Jose, ed., *Ideas of the Restoration in English Literature, 1660–71* (Cambridge: Harvard University Press, 1984), 142–63; Laura Knoppers, *Historicizing Milton: Spectacle, Power, and Poetry in Restoration England* (Athens: University of Georgia Press, 42–66); Achinstein, "Samson Agonistes and the Politics of Memory," in Mark R. Kelley and Joseph Wittreich, eds., *Altering Eyes: New Perspectives on "Samson Agonistes"* (Newark: University of Delaware Press, 2002); John Coffey, "Pacifist, Quietist, or Patient Militant? John Milton and the

Restoration," *Milton Studies* 42 (2002): 149–74; Blair Worden, "Milton, Samson Agonistes, and the Restoration," in Gerald Maclean, ed., *Culture and Society in the Stuart Restoration: Literature, Drama, History* (Cambridge: Cambridge University Press, 1995); David Norbrook, 'Republican Occasions in Paradise Regained and Samson Agonistes," *Milton Studies* 42 (2002): 122–48; Barbara Lewalsi, "Milton's Samson and the 'New Acquist of True (Political) Experience," *Milton Studies* 24 (1988): 233–51; Janel Mueller, "The Figure and the Ground: Samson as a Hero of London Nonconformity, 1662–1667," in Graham Perry and Joad Raymond, eds., *Milton and the Terms of Liberty* (Cambridge: Brewer, 2002).

123 Nancy J. Hirschmann, "Disabling Barriers, Enabling Freedom," in Arneil and Hirschmann, *Political Theory*, 106.

124 Richard Baxter, *An Apology for the Nonconformists Ministry* (London, 1681), 20.

125 On the essential ableism of liberal theory, from Hobbes to Rawls, see Lucas G. Pinheiro, "The Ableist Contract: Intellectual Disability and the Limits of Justice in Kant's Political Thought," in Arneil and Hirschmann, *Political Theory*; Anita Silvers, "Formal Justice," in Anita Silvers, David Wasserman, and Mary B. Mahowald, eds., *Disability, Difference Discrimination: Perspectives on Justice in Bioethics and Public Policy* (New York: Rowman & Littlefield, 1998); Martha Nussbaum, *Frontiers of Justice: Disability, Nationality, Species Membership* (Cambridge: Harvard University Press, 2006); Clifford, "Deliberative Democracy."

126 Thomas Hobbes, *Leviathan* (London, 1651), 107.

127 Ibid.

128 On the problems that the dependence associated with disability poses for traditional models of liberal autonomy, see Eva Kittay, *Love's Labor: Essays on Women, Equality, and Dependency* (New York: Routledge, 1999); Eva Kittay, "The Ethics of Care, Dependence, and Disability," *Ratio Juris* 24, no. 1 (2011): 49–58.

129 For the broader conception of prosthetics on which this reading draws, see David Wills, *Prosthesis* (Palo Alto: Stanford University Press, 1995); Jay Timothy Dolmage, *Disability Rhetoric* (Syracuse: Syracuse University Press, 2014), 106–24.

130 On this, see Joan Tronto, "Disability and Violence: Another Call for Democratic Inclusion and Pluralism," in Arneil and Hirschmann, *Political Theory*; Andy J. Johnson, J. Ruth Nelson, and Emily M. Lund, eds., *Religion, Disability, and Interpersonal Violence* (New York: Springer, 2017); Karen Hughes et al., "Prevalence and Risk of Violence against Adults with Disabilities: A Systematic Review and Meta-Analysis of Observational Studies," *Lancet* 379 (2012): 1621–9; J.R. Petersilia, "Crime Victims with Developmental Disabilities: A Review Essay," *Criminal Justice and Behavior* 28, no. 6 (2001): 655–94.

131 Pinheiro, "Ableist Contract."

132 Warren Chernaik, "Tragic Freedom in *Samson Agonistes*," *The European Legacy* 17, no. 2 (2012): 201. See also Rosanna Cox, "Neo-Roman Terms of Slavery in Samson Agonistes," *Milton Quarterly* 44, no. 1 (2010): 17–19.

133 Campbell, *Contours*, 16–29.

134 Martin Dzelzainis, "'In Power of Others, Never in My Own,'" in Blair Hoxby and Ann Baynes Coiro, eds., *Milton in the Long Restoration* (Oxford: Oxford University Press, 2016), 300.

135 Though considering this is still only second-hand, it is possible that this "guide" is associated with the Holy Spirit; much of the ambiguity of the poem inheres not only in the "motions" but in how the blind Samson is "guided."

136 Hirschmann, "Barriers," 101.

137 John Locke, *A Letter Concerning Toleration* (London, 1689), 7.

138 John Milton, "The Reason of church-Government Urg'd Against Prelaty," in Don Wolfe, ed., *Complete Prose Works of John Milton, Volume 1: 1624–1642* (New Haven: Yale University Press, 1953), 766.

139 See Campbell, *Contours*; Tobin Siebers, *Disability Theory* (Ann Arbor: University of Michigan Press, 2008), 102–19.

140 John Milton, *Areopagitica*, in Ernest Sirluck, ed., *Complete Prose Works of John Milton, Volume II: 1643–1948* (New Haven: Yale University Press, 1959), 527.

141 Milton, "Areopagitica," 523. If we see Milton as endorsing a theatrical or even *theatrum mundi* view of earthly existence, then this might be considered instead an arrogation of God's role as spectator or puppet-master. See David Loewnstein, *Milton and the Drama of History: Historical Vision, Iconoclasm, and the Literary Imagination* (Cambridge: Cambridge University Press, 1990); Knoppers, *Historicizing*; Vanita Neelakanta, "'Theatrum Mundi' and Milton's Theater of the Blind in 'Samson Agonistes,'" *Journal for Early Modern Cultural Studies* 11, no. 1 (2011): 30–58.

142 On Milton's vexed attitudes towards theatre, see Victoria Kahn, "Aesthetics as Critique: Tragedy and Trauerspiel in *Samson Agonistes*," in Marshall Grossman, ed., *Reading Renaissance Ethics* (New York: Routledge, 2007); Linda Gregerson, "Milton and the Tragedy of Nations," *PMLA* 129, no. 4 (2014): 672–87; Elizabeth Sauer, "The Politics of Performance in the Inner Theater: 'Samson Agonistes' as Closet Drama," in Stephen B. Dobranski and John P. Rumrich, eds., *Milton and Heresy* (Cambridge: Cambridge University Press, 1998); Dennis Kezar, "Samson's Death by Theater and Milton's Art of Dying," *ELH* 66, no. 2 (1999): 295–336.

143 On this topic, see Marshall Grossman, "Poetry and Belief in 'Paradise Regained, to which is added, Samson Agonistes,'" *Studies in Philology* 110, no. 2 (2013): 382–401.

144 The divisive ambiguity of Samson Agonistes "rouzing motions" and his consequent destruction of the Philistines has been a topic of extensive scholarship. For summaries of the debate, see Alan Rudrum, "Milton Scholarship and the Agon over Samson Agonistes," *Huntington Library Quarterly* 65 (2002): 465–88; Elizabeth Sauer, "Discontents with the Drama of Regeneration," in Peter C. Herman and Elizabeth Sauer, eds., *The New Milton Criticism* (Cambridge: Cambridge University Press, 2012).

    For those who suggest variously that these rousing motions are from God, that he is regenerated, and that his final act is justified, see Radzinowicz,

Toward "Samson Agonistes": The Growth of Milton's Mind (Princeton: Princeton University Press, 1978); John S. Bennett, *Reviving Liberty: Radical Christian Humanism in Milton's Great Poems* (Cambridge: Harvard University Press, 1989); Joseph Summers, "The Movements of the Drama," in Joseph Summers, ed., *Lyric and Dramatic Milton* (New York: Columbia University Press, 1965), 153–75; Arnold Stein, *Heroic Knowledge: An Interpretation of "Paradise Regained" and "Samson Agonistes"* (Minneapolis: University of Minneapolis Press, 1957); Anthony Low, *The Blaze of Noon: A Reading of "Samson Agonistes"* (New York: Columbia University Press, 1974); Norman T. Burns, "'Then Stood Up Phinehas': Milton's Antinomianism, and Samson's," *Milton Studies* 33 (1996): 27–46; David Loewenstein, "The Revenge of the Saint: Radical Religion and Politics in Samson Agonistes," *Milton Studies* 33 (1996): 159–80; David Loewenstein, *Representing Revolution in Milton and His Contemporaries: Religion, Politics, and Polemics in Radical Puritanism* (Cambridge: Cambridge University Press, 2001), 269–91; Louis Schwartz, "The Nightmare of History: *Samson Agonistes*," in Angelica Duran, ed., *A Concise Companion to Milton* (Oxford: Blackwell, 2006); Christopher Hill, *The Experience of Defeat: Milton and Some Contemporaries* (New York: Viking, 1984); Regina Schwartz, "*Samson Agonistes*: The Force of Justice and the Violence of Idolatry," in Nicholas McDowell and Nigel Smith, eds., *The Oxford Handbook of Milton* (Oxford: Oxford University Press, 2009); David Urban, "'Intimate Impulses,' 'Rousing Motions,' and the Written Law: Internal and External Scripture in *Samson Agonistes*," in Durham and Pruitt, *Uncircumscribed*; William Kerrigan, "The Irrational Coherence of *Samson Agonistes*," *Milton Studies* 22 (1986): 216–32; Jose, "Upside Down."

For those who argue (the "antiregenerationist" reading) that Samson remains fallen or merely human and that his final act is meant to be rejected, see Joseph Wittreich, *Shifting Contexts: Reinterpreting "Samson Agonistes"* (Pittsburgh: Dusquesne University Press, 2002); Irene Samuel, "*Samson Agonistes* as Tragedy," in Joseph Wittreich, ed., *Calm of Mind: Tercentenary Essays on Paradise Regained and Samson Agonistes in Honor of John S. Dieckhoff* (Cleveland: Press of Case Western Reserve University, 1971); Kenneth Burke, "The 'Use' of *Samson Agonistes*," *Hudson Review* 1 (1948): 151–67; R.W. Serjeantson, "*Samson Agonistes* and 'Single Rebellion,'" in McDowell and Smith, *Oxford Handbook*, 613–31; and Tobias Gregory, "The Political Message of *Samson Agonistes*," *SEL* 50 (2010): 175–203.

For those who conclude, in diverse ways, that the play leaves the meaning of his violence indeterminate, see Stanley Fish, "Spectacle and Evidence in 'Samson Agonistes,'" *Critical Inquiry* 15, no. 3 (1989): 556–86; Sauer, "Performance"; Marshall Grossman, "Textual Ethics: Reading Transference in *Samson Agonistes*," in Grossman, *Renaissance Ethics*; John T. Shawcross, "Misreading Milton," *Milton Studies* 33 (1996): 181–203; Shawcross, *The Uncertain World of "Samson Agonistes"* (Cambridge: Brewer, 2001); Russ Leo, "Milton's Aristotelian Experiments: Tragedy, Lustratio, and 'Secret Refreshings' in Samson Agonistes," *Milton Studies*

52 (2011): 221–305; Holly M. Spyniewski and Anne McMaster, "Double Motivations and the Ambiguity of 'Ungodly Deeds': Euripides 'Medea' and Milton's 'Samson Agonistes,'" *Milton Quarterly* 44, no. 3 (2010): 145–6.

145 Wittreich, *Reinterpreting*, 223–6.

146 Ibid., 15–18.

147 On Samson as potential terrorist, see John Carey, "A Work in Praise of Terrorism?" *Times Literary Supplement* (6 September 2006): 15–16; Feisal G. Mohamed, "Confronting Religious Violence: Milton's Samson Agonistes," *PMLA* 120 (2005): 327–40; Feisal G. Mohamed, *Milton and the Post-Secular Present: Ethics, Politics, Terrorism* (Palo Alto: Stanford University Press, 2011); Feisal G. Mohamed, "Reading Samson in the New American Century," *Milton Studies* 46 (2006): 149–64; Stanley Fish, "'There Is Nothing He Cannot Ask': Milton, Liberalism, and Terrorism," in Michael Lieb and Albert C. Labriola, eds., *Milton in the Age of Fish: Essays on Authorship, Text, and Terrorism* (Pittsburgh: Dusquesne University Press, 2006); David Loewenstein, "Samson Agonistes and the Culture of Religious Terror," in Lieb and Labriola, *Age of Fish*; Joseph Wittreich, *Why Milton Matters: A New Preface to His Writings* (New York: Palgrave, 2006), 141–94; Gregory, "Political Message."

148 John Corbet, *A Discourse of the Religion of England* (London, 1667), 28.

149 See, in particular, James Charlton, *Nothing About Us Without Us* (Berkeley: University of California Press, 2000).

150 Barbara Arneil, "Disability and Political Theory: An Introduction," in Arneil and Hirschmann, *Political Theory*.

151 Marlorat, *Catholike*, 346.

152 John 9:21–3.

153 Poole, *Annotations*, Fff2.

154 John Barkstead, *The Speeches, Discourses, and Prayers, of Col. John Barkstead, Col. John Okey, and Mr. Miles Corbet* (London, 1662), 50–1. See also John Foxe, *Acts and Monuments of Matters Most Speciall and Memorable, Happenyng in the Church* [vol. 2, part 2] ([London], 1583]), 2015.

4 Imagining Worlds and Figuring Toleration: Freedom, Diversity, and Violence in *A Description of a New World, Called The Blazing-World*

CORRINNE HAROL

The title of Margaret Cavendish Newcastle's most famous work of prose fiction, *A Description of a New World, Called the Blazing-World* (1666), suggests several things about the way I want to read its investigation into toleration and the literary imagination.[1] The title gestures to the "New World," that destination, in the Restoration period, of pilgrims fleeing religious persecution in England, as well as the locus of indigenous pagan cultures that shadow Europe's Protestant/Catholic sectarianism. The title also invokes seventeenth-century philosophical debates about the nature of "worlds," which revolved around how the particularity of the material world relates to the larger whole. Although the two "worlds" in the title reference the same world (the "Blazing" one), the repetition suggests both the text's doubling techniques and its fictional thought experiment, which implies a Galilean universe wherein the earth, shaped like a globe, is just one of many such worlds in the universe. I am suggesting that Cavendish's emphasis on "world" gestures to the extent that the understanding of our world, earth, as a globe in a universe, allows for both the reality and the imagination of other worlds and the connections among them.[2] This conception of worlds within a universe is a phenomenon that turns out to have scientific, political, and aesthetic implications and applications. *The Blazing World* was appended to Cavendish's *Observations on Experimental Philosophy,* a configuration that indicates that together the texts will investigate the relationship between the literary imagination and philosophical or scientific truth, expressed in the titles as the difference between description and observation.[3] Cavendish describes the two texts as having "Sympathy and Coherence with each other," and she uses a simile to express this relation: the two texts "were joyned together as Two several Worlds, at their Two Poles."[4] The textual configuration is thus analogous to the thought experiment, and it suggests that Cavendish is engaged in thinking about the relationship between science and literature as a way of thinking about the nature of worlds, including new worlds, real worlds, and fictional worlds. I will be arguing that in *The Blazing World* the literary imagination, as a world-creating faculty that shares attributes with politics and science, necessitates an engagement with questions about toleration – and the state-sanctioned violence that toleration seeks to manage.[5]

The connection between literary imagination and political power is a prominent theme of *The Blazing World*. Though Cavendish announces (in her preface "To the Reader") that she "cannot be Henry the Fifth, or Charles the Second," she will, via her literary imagination, "endeavour to be, Margaret the First," and because she has "neither Power, Time nor Occasion, to be a great Conqueror" rather than "not be Mistress of a World" she has made "One of [her] own" (*BW*, 124). Later in the text, the immaterial creatures of the Blazing World suggest that everyone has such power: "every human Creature can create an Immaterial World fully inhabited by Immaterial Creatures, and populous of Immaterial subjects [...] all this within the compass of the head or scull" (*BW*, 185). The epilogue continues this theme, inviting readers to imagine themselves as subjects of the Blazing World "in their minds, fancies or imaginations" or, if they prefer, to "create worlds of their own, and govern them as they please" (*BW*, 225). These testimonies to the world-creating powers of the literary imagination have been read by critics as an assertion of the sovereignty of the individual artistic subject, incidentally female, a paean to the potency of the imagination to promote both female empowerment and peace.[6] In such readings, the text's reactionary and violent elements, along with Cavendish's own well-known conservative politics, must be explained away or segregated from her literary and intellectual accomplishments.[7] This essay instead sees these aspects of Cavendish's project as inherently connected.

The Blazing World was written in a crucial time for the history of toleration, a history that reveals the close connection between toleration and state violence. The Restoration began and ended with crises about how peace and freedom of conscience may coexist. The Declaration of Breda (1660) promised to replace the "distraction," "confusion," "bleeding," and "wounds" that characterized the Civil Wars and interregnum with "quiet and peaceable" rule.[8] Its logic was that political peace depends upon religious toleration. But still, it prioritized peace, and therefore the state, over religious freedom, with Charles promising that under his rule "no man shall be disquieted or called in question for differences of opinion in matter of religion, *which do not disturb the peace of the kingdom* (emphasis mine).[9] This declaration – and especially the religious freedom that it promised – proved to be one of the most contentious aspects of Charles's rule. During the 1660s, while Cavendish was writing and publishing *The Blazing World*, Charles's efforts to instantiate religious freedom in the name of political peace were stymied by Parliament.[10] At this time, Cavendish and Charles were grappling with a problem that has been central to the question of toleration throughout its history: put broadly, this is the issue that the more one embraces diversity, as either a fact or an ideal of social or religious existence, the more difficult it becomes to imagine a form of government, other than absolutism, that can manage this diversity. A central paradox in the history of toleration is that it is a liberal and secular ideal that, at least when Cavendish was writing, seemed more compatible with (and was advocated for on behalf of) Catholic monarchists.[11] Liberal theorists of the generation after Cavendish continued to struggle, as liberal theorists still do, to resolve this problem.[12] As Elena Russo's essay in this volume demonstrates, John Locke can imagine common ground in religion and politics only by becoming more normative around forms of sociability and morality. Pierre Bayle is more inclusive of religious difference than Locke, but he does not seem to be able to imagine a form of government that can formally manage this diversity. As Russo puts it, in the "beauty contest" (that is, in the contest to be more liberal and modern) between Bayle and Locke, Bayle is credited with being more "far-reaching and robust" but also with being both more "ambiguous" and less hopeful about the possibility of toleration outside of a "strong state" that is "willing to assume the responsibility of enforcing the peace" (120, 126). This question of civil peace extends further into international politics, and theorists of toleration posed the related question of whether toleration *within* a nation could be a model for peace *between* nations. The Restoration problem of the violence of sectarian conflict and civil war – and the role of sovereignty in managing it – was thus analogous to questions about violence between sovereign nations.

One prominent way that theories of the Enlightenment, and indeed of the long arc of modernity more broadly, attempted to resolve such dilemmas in political philosophy was to turn to the natural sciences, to ground political ideas in theories of nature, a topic that Mark Canuel's essay in this volume pursues with respect to Joseph Priestley, writing later in the eighteenth century.[13] Materialist philosophy was revived and renovated in the seventeenth century in tandem with the emergence of new political theories and realities. Enlightenment thinkers – Thomas Hobbes and Locke exemplify this trend in England – posited that humans are entities that are subject, like atoms, to the physical laws of matter and motion, a move that makes possible a science of politics that can (theoretically) manage humans just as a science of nature can (theoretically) manage the natural world.[14] In other words, political science was founded in natural science, with many thinkers believing that if they could just formulate or understand the laws of the natural world adequately, then they could solve problems of human political organization, which include those of diversity, freedom, and violence.[15] When grounded as such in science, questions of politics and toleration can be approached in a variety of registers – from atoms, to humans, to the world, to worlds, and to the universe or the divine cosmos – with each point a possible analogy for the other. This strain of thinking ran into much theological controversy, with the charge of atheism inevitably invoked against such theories, because they could be seen as threatening to both human exceptionality and divine creation.

Margaret Cavendish occupied a singular position in seventeenth-century England, one that set the stage for her entry into these debates. As a young member of the court in exile with her influential husband, William Cavendish, the Duke of Newcastle, Cavendish was exposed to the leading-edge political, philosophical, scientific and aesthetic theories of day; she was conversant with controversies between rationalist and empiricist epistemologies as well as among monistic, dualistic, and pluralist theories of matter. Cavendish's husband was a patron of Hobbes – her marriage took place a few months after a dinner party her husband hosted at which Hobbes and John Bramhall famously debated liberty of conscience – and Hobbes is generally considered to be a major intellectual influence on her long writing career. Certainly, they ruminated on the same topics, including materialism, political power and violence, the nature of political and cultural systems, and the faculty of the imagination. While her intellectual affinities with Hobbes are complex, her relation to the Royal Society is more straightforward: having satirized the new science in *The Blazing World*, she was in turn mocked when she visited the academy the following year, an event memorialized in an account in Samuel Pepys's diary.[16] Known in her day for dressing up in outlandish clothes, including male ones, and for refusing the rules of spelling and grammar in the service of literary invention and originality, Cavendish is most commonly modified by the adjective "singular." And it is a word that captures how her legacy has been explored: she is remembered both as a unique figure – one specifically important to women's literary history – and as someone, who, for better and for worse, was committed to ideals of singularity.[17] On the negative side, her royalism, monotheism, and theocracy have proved (in, for example, Catherine Gallagher's influential reading as well as in Rachel Trubowitz's account of the "female monarchical self") a stumbling block for critics who do not share her political orientation – though, in a move whereby the critical problem becomes its own solution, her feminism is often considered inextricable from her monarchism.[18] On the positive side, perhaps, stand both the way her singularity is seen as related to her literary invention and accomplishment and the way her commitment to singularity informs her vitalism. In the literary realm, being singular means being original and unique, and thereby generating variety – and modernity, in the sense of pluralism – in literary forms and genres, while from a vitalist standpoint, singularity challenges both mind/body and subject/object dualism and human exceptionalism; thus it is amenable to critical trends in anti-humanist thinking.[19] Cavendish's "singularity" thus stands politically on the side of a conservative traditional view, while philosophically, scientifically, and aesthetically it is on the side of originality and therefore multiplicity and difference – in short, modernity. I start with Cavendish's singularity (or its flip side: what Alexandra Bennet calls her "often contradictory self representation") and her position in relation to Hobbes and the Royal Society as a way into thinking about how her self-presentation and her scholarly reception are related to her political and philosophical positions.[20]

In order to explore how Cavendish connects science, the literary imagination, and the politics of toleration in *The Blazing World*, I analyse the text's engagement with the problem of "parts," "particulars," "variety," and "division" in natural philosophy as offering a corollary to religio-political questions about difference of opinion. I read *The Blazing World* as a thought experiment in whether a fully vitalistic universe can peacefully support "division" of opinions as well as matter – and thus in how "opinion" in science is related to opinion in religion and to the governmental structures that manage both. Through this approach I endeavour to reconcile what seem to be two opposing aspects of Cavendish's thought: her thoroughgoing vitalism, which sees substance (including rational thought) as both self-moving and infinitely various, and her commitment to absolute monarchy and state-sponsored violence in the political realm. Unfortunately, I do not find that Cavendish offers any particularly useful – to our twenty-first-century perspective – solutions, for *The Blazing World* ends with a revocation of the sovereign's decree of toleration and with the invasion and conquest of another sovereign world. *The Blazing World* tries to imagine how freedom of conscience, academic freedom, and biological diversity can peacefully coexist. It suggests that they can and do coexist in the individual but not in what Cavendish calls the world, which is at once a product of human (sometimes literary) culture; a self-enclosed totality that must be managed by power and violence; and just one such world among many in a universe. Thus, I read *The Blazing World* as an engagement with the failure of both the literary imagination and the liberal project of toleration, precisely because of their relation to each other.

The world that Cavendish's imagination creates, the Blazing World, is notable, in so far as it is different from seventeenth-century England, both for its diversity and for its peacefulness. The Blazing World is full of a variety of what we call species – bear men, lice men, fox-like men and so on – as well as a variety of what could be seen as races: in the Imperial City, the creatures are not morphologically distinct but they are of different colours, some "azure, some of a deep purple, some of a grass-green, some of a scarlet, some of an orange-colour, &c." (*BW*, 133). An ethos of "neighbours" informs relations among these different populations. The bear and fox men, for example, treat each other with "civility and courtship" (*BW*, 127). The narrator and the inhabitants of the Blazing World attribute this peaceful coexistence of difference to the fact that they have but one language, one Emperor, one religion, and "one opinion concerning the worship and adoration of God" (*BW*, 135).

The geography of the Blazing World supports both this diversity and this peacefulness – the topography is dominated by islands, which demarcate the lands of the different species and which are accessible only by long passages over water. As island communities, the hybrid animal men of the Blazing World have "no other enemies but the winds" (*BW*, 129).[21] The seat of the Blazing World is called Paradise, and its geography affords even more protection; with only one entry via a barely visible cleft in a wall of high rocks, it is then approached via a labyrinth "so winding and turning" that only small boats could pass (*BW*, 131). The Imperial City itself is like an island within an island within this natural fortress: it appears "in form like several islands; for rivers did flow betwixt every street," with a series of gates, so artfully placed that "a stranger would lose himself" (*BW*, 131). So the geography and architecture of the Blazing World exclude the category of strangers and thereby make the category of enemies impossible. The Blazing World is a "world" because its diverse parts are unified culturally and politically and perhaps because physical difference, and therefore difference of opinion, is mediated by geography: it is configured for peace. Following the travelogue of the Blazing World that brings the protagonist to the Imperial City, she is made Empress of this Blazing World, and she must consider how to govern it, a question that the text pursues, obliquely, via the question of parts and wholes in nature.

This philosophical question of the relationship of parts and wholes is the central concern of the *Observations on Experimental Philosophy* – the textual world attached to *The Blazing World*. The *Observations'* critique of experimental science rests largely on the analytic method of the Royal Society, which assumes a discoverable relation between parts and wholes. "Nature cannot be known by any of her parts," Cavendish asserts repeatedly (*OEP*, 200). For example, the five human senses, she argues, each provide a "perfect knowledge in each part" and yet are "ignorant of each other" (*OEP*, 46). This example of the human senses is a microcosm of the way all of nature works. All matter is "self-moving" and "self-knowing," but – or because of this – there can be no extrapolation from parts to wholes (*OEP*, 30). If this is true for bodies, it is even more true for Nature: "Now if there be such variety of several knowledges, not only in one creature [...] what may there be in all the parts of nature?" (*OEP*, 47). As Deborah Boyle explains, an observer cannot know matter as well as the matter knows itself, and thus Cavendish's vitalism and her critique of experimentalism rest on the fact that difference of opinion is derived from the nature of matter as self-knowing.[22] Whereas Descartes distinguishes truth (*sciencia*) from opinion, Cavendish thinks all knowledge is opinion, derived from one's situation in a particular body, place, and time. Peter Dear has argued that the experimentalist community focused on description rather than causation, as a means to avoid "socially disruptive disagreements."[23] Cavendish's vitalism, by contrast, finds disagreements inevitable, fundamental to the nature of matter, a proposition that the "description" of the Blazing World, which occupies most of the first half of the text, supports.

This diversity in nature raises the problem of how these self-knowing and self-moving parts can be unified into a whole, natural or political. Many critics want to see in vitalism a liberatory, tolerationist vision that science might offer to politics, a model for managing difference or for balancing freedom and restrictions on freedom: if self-knowing and self-moving entities can coexist in nature then why not in society? (This of course begs the question of how peaceful nature is.) Critics have tended to read a liberal/feminist strain in Cavendish and in vitalism more generally.[24] But the corollaries between nature and politics in Cavendish are quite complicated. She will argue, in the *Observations,* and demonstrate, in *The Blazing World,* that parts can be "figured" into wholes, but these figures are not stable, they are not based on mutually accepted truths, and they do not supersede the nature of the parts from which they are formed.

The inherent divisiveness of knowledge, for Cavendish, cannot be rectified by "Art" (by which Cavendish means science). As she explains, "Art, which is but a particular creature, cannot inform us of the truth of the infinite parts of nature, being but finite itself" (*OEP,* 48). There is thus no possible knowledge of wholes. What there is, instead, is "figuration" – the unification or reconfiguration of parts into new holistic formations: nature is "infinitely various in her works – and subject to infinite changes" (*BW,* 148). The question is not whether there can be universal knowledge – Cavendish dismisses this possibility – but rather how parts "ignorant of each other" can "agree in the production of a figure" (*OEP,* 159). This is a question for both scientific knowledge and governance. In an analogy between science and religion that is telling for my argument about how her natural philosophy relates to her politics of toleration – and thus how figuration relates to parts – Cavendish explains,

> Although every part hath its own knowledge and perception; yet, when many parts are conjoined into one figure, then, by reason of that twofold relation of their actions and near neighbourhood, they become better acquainted. And, as many men assembled in a church, make but one congregation, and all agree to worship one God, in one and the same manner or way; so, many parts conjoined in one figure, are, as it were, so many communicants, all agreeing, and being united in one body. (*OEP,* 159)

This passage suggests that vitalistic nature and religious communion work by a similar process of figuration, whereby participation in the figure promotes peaceful relations – not knowledge but neighbourly acquaintance based on proximity.[25] Thus, the two worlds of Cavendish's text – the scientific and the literary – explore the relations between particular knowledge and unifying figuration in the related spheres of science and religion (or culture more broadly).

The analogies between these two spheres – explicit and implied – transmute across the two texts as Cavendish explores what diversity of opinion means in each sphere. For example, at the level of nature as well as, implicitly, geopolitics, there are "factions and quarrels" that produce "mixed species," which then have the effect of driving other species out of their habitation. Cavendish sees such struggle as inevitable and morally neutral, a function of the self-moving, self-knowing nature of matter. Of hybrid invasive species, for example, the Empress learns from the worm men: "their life [...] is their own, and not their Parents; for no part or creature of Nature can either give or take away life, but parts do onely assist and join with parts, either in dissolution or production of other Parts and Creatures" (*BW*, 153).

Cavendish's solution to how a body politic can be unified out of such diversity of form, opinion, and intention is in conversation with both Hobbes and the Royal Society, as Anna Battigelli has argued.[26] Hobbes's famous solution to this problem, the Leviathan, is a process of amalgamation whereby the unruly multitude is unified into a singular sovereign. It is an artificial process that produces an artificial, that is cultural, entity; unity is produced *ex nihilo*, sharing no substance with that which it unifies.[27] The Royal Society's analytic method works differently, by producing difference or disfiguration out of unity and purpose: the louse that the Empress sees as a pest to humans while recognizing its own incontrovertible destiny to be louse-like, is disarticulated from its nature – made "strangely shaped" – by the analytical machine of the microscope, which produces information so "tedious" that the narrator forebears relation of it (*BW*, 144). Cavendish's thought process, by contrast, is synthetic and figurative rather than analytical or accretive: from parts and divisions she conceptualizes a singularity that is of the same substance, though a different figuration, as the parts, and she imagines that by nature of participating in the same figure, parts develop affinities.[28] Cavendish does not take the natural world as a metaphor, cause, or measuring stick for politics. Instead, when it comes to representing how science relates to politics and how parts unify into wholes, Cavendish relies on simile. A literary figure that resists abstraction, simile expresses both the relationship between science and culture and the fundamental way that each works on its own; simile is used by Cavendish to explore how entities in nature and politics are configured and thus can be reconfigured. In short, Cavendish's philosophical commitments explain the inevitability of division of opinion, locating it at the most basic level of matter. Opinion, as function of matter, cannot be unified or a force of unification, but it can, over time, be figured and reconfigured. The role of governance is a similar process of figuration, which should seek not to rectify or exacerbate divisions but rather to shape them into a connected whole: a world.

When the protagonist is made Empress of the Blazing World, she bases her theory, as well as her initial practice, of political rule on vitalism (all substance is self-moving), monism (one religion, one sovereign, one substance), and what we might now call a very liberal approach to difference: the Empress at first allows her subjects – who are variously coloured, diversely speciated, and differently abled – the liberty to pursue erroneous beliefs and specialized experience. In other words, the Empress shares philosophical positions about nature that reflect the *Observations*, and she tries to base a politics and a government – like so many seventeenth-century thinkers did – on these scientific principles. The first sovereign action of the Empress is to create schools, which are the means whereby difference, inherent in the material reality (which is in turn connected to the geographical arrangement) of her subjects, becomes manifest in opinion. The bear men take the position of the Royal Society regarding the world-uniting potential of scientific knowledge: without microscopes, they say, "the world ... would be but blind" (*BW*, 143). But the telescopes and microscopes so beloved by the bear men do nothing to settle the "differences and divisions" over cosmology (*BW*, 140); rather, they fracture their users' opinion even more. The Empress's proposed solution – the dissolution of the schools and the instruments that multiply opinion – is countered by the bear men's argument that arguing is their "only delight" and "dear to [them] as [their] lives" (*BW*, 142); in response the Empress agrees to let them have their debates in their school as a long as they do not cause "factions or disturbances in state, or government" (*BW*, 142). The problem the Empress is addressing – as was Charles II at the same time – is explicitly the one of what "the world" believes and what kind of belief can be tolerated or indulged by a government committed to peace (*BW*, 145).[29]

While there is no difference of opinion about religion in the Blazing World before the Empress arrives, she, finding its inhabitants ignorant of religious truth, introduces the potential of such difference by converting her subjects to her own religion. Although conversion is easy enough (apparently one just needs to utter the religious truth to make people believe), maintaining religious conformity requires a spectacular display, one that is managed by the Empress's scientific knowledge, which she has gained by her travels and inquiries. There may be only one religious truth, but Cavendish knows full well that there is more than one way to worship, just as there are multiple possible sovereignties, languages, and worlds. To manage this, the Empress builds two chapels: one for preaching sermons of terror and one for preaching sermons of comfort. These chapels are separate from the religious truth she, and now her subjects, believe. They are not about truth or salvation but rather the management of her subjects as a community; these places of religious practice function as a kind of figuration or world-remaking made possible by the Empress's sovereignty and her scientific knowledge. The key to the Empress's problem – that is, what causes the need for a management strategy – is that she transports the truth of God to a different world, that her notion of religious truth transcends worlds and thus threatens them. Not so for organized religion, which is for Cavendish something very different from religious truth and is related to the sovereign's role in maintaining peace. This is why the Empress's preaching and her religious rituals bear almost no relation (except causal) to each other, with the former a matter of simple truth and the latter reliant on conjuring the power and the protection of a god-like figure in the form of the Empress's sovereignty. Truth is one thing, and the figuring and reconfiguring power of religion, politics, and culture another. The Blazing World is peaceful when it has only one language, one religion, and one sovereign, a configuration that is restored via the Empress's spectacular religious practices.

And this is all well and good for the majority of the first part of *The Blazing World*: the introduction of divisive scientific opinion, religious truth, and religious ritual and conformity seem to have no political or cultural ramifications that cannot be reversed (as in the case of her schools) or managed (as in the case of her religious practices). Well, except that the Empress is lonely and a bit bored, which results in her inviting a "scribe" in the form of a fictional Margaret Cavendish, to join her in the Blazing World. So now in addition to an imaginary world having been paired with a "real" one and a philosophical text with a literary one, we have a fictional character, based on a real one, who provides a double for the imaginary character. This imaginative process is repeated – doubled again – when Margaret Cavendish, who is envious of the Empress's sovereignty and her world, desires to learn how to make her own world. Even before she begins to practise this world-imagining skill, the initially doubled world has proliferated – first by the revelation that the fictional Cavendish hails neither from the same world as the Empress nor from the world of the readers but from yet a third world and, second, by the immaterial spirits' revelation that there are "infinite" worlds already existing (*BW*, 184).[30] Alas, none of these infinite worlds are available to the characters' imaginative desire for sovereignty because, the spirits inform us, "none [...] is without government" (*BW*, 185). This suggests that worlds and governments are synonymous or at least coexistent. Indeed, this seems to be one of the points that the characters learn by their imaginative world-making. The character Margaret Cavendish tries to formulate a world based on the "opinions" of a variety of philosophers, both ancient and modern: Thales, Pythagoras, Plato, Epicurus, Aristotle, Descartes, and Hobbes, but all these worlds are unsatisfactory because they torment her mind with monsters, puzzles, puppets, and other unpleasant mental experiences (*BW*, 189–90). The two women discover that neither "opinion" nor "pattern" can provide the basis for a world – or a government (*BW*, 189). Instead, they allow the "rational matter" in their minds to "move to the creation" of imaginary worlds, which turn out to be so "full of variety" and "so [...] wisely governed" that they are beyond the capacity of human language to describe (*BW*, 188). In other words, the rational matter of the mind, via its capacity for figuration, produces at once the variety and the coherence characteristic of worlds, at least of peaceful ones.

The text's doublings and its world-imagining exercise are a kind of allegory for how the literary imagination works. By reformulating materials and ideas already existing, the literary imagination is a kind of figuration that proliferates versions (new configurations) of reality.[31] This is why the figure of two worlds is both the text's thought experiment and form and why simile is its fundamental trope: the fictional Blazing World, indeed, any fictional world, will be produced out of the matter already existing – in this case, the philosophical truths explicated in the *Observations* and the life experience of Margaret Cavendish. Along similar lines, just as worlds cannot be successfully figured from opinion, art should not be formed "methodically and artificially" from rules. For example, theatrical plays in the world of Margaret Cavendish are properly "composed of old stories, either Greek or Roman or some new-found world" (*BW*, 192). The literary imagination, like singular models of sovereignty, offers a method of synthesis via figuration; it produces similitude and unity from experience rather than from theorization or analysis. For Cavendish, the literary imagination is world-creating, not a means of understanding or creating *ex nihilo* but rather a process of figuring and synthesizing various parts.[32]

These processes of figuration and refiguration, of doubling and simile, mean that worlds are not isolated. We see this in the ways that the imaginary world-creating exercises of the Empress and the fictional Margaret Cavendish redound to the political situations of the worlds of both. First the Empress decides, based on her imaginative world-creation, that the differences of opinion produced by her schools threaten the Blazing World with "rebellion," and hence she dissolves them (*BW*, 201). And so goes the world of academic freedom monitored by a sovereign who cares about the pleasures and honours the differences of her subjects. With its mandated and manipulated religious conformity and its restriction on intellectual debate, the Empress's Blazing World turns out to be rather intolerant. To the extent that this revocation of liberty of conscience represents a change of mind, it is fully consistent with Cavendish's philosophical commitments – the mind as matter is subject to reconfiguring change just as all matter is – as well as with her literary method. One of Cavendish's most common literary strategies involves arguing with herself – changing her mind and changing it again.[33] It is another of her techniques for doubling and a way in particular of figuring – as well as addressing directly – questions of toleration in literary forms. In her *Orations of Divers Sorts* (1662), for example, she writes three orations about liberty of conscience. One oration argues for such liberty under the conditions where subjects already have a religion, because trying to change their religion will threaten peace; the second oration argues against liberty of conscience because it leads to liberty in the state, which threatens peace and safety; and the third – where she attempts to find a mean between a "furious" and a "factious" people – argues that liberty of conscience is acceptable with respect to private devotion as long as it does not impact the public (in other words, she makes an argument for toleration based on secularization).[34] The *Orations*, and indeed the rest of Cavendish's oeuvre, is replete with such internal difference of opinion – she sometimes takes six or seven positions on the same topic. This plastic ability of the mind is ultimately what allows it to be world-figuring and reconfiguring, because minds, like worlds, are united not by opinion but by form and figuration. And so, we seem to have two opposing aspects to Cavendish's thought: on one hand, a commitment to the contingency of all opinion and the power of the individual imagination, and on the other hand, a commitment to peace that may trump this philosophical belief in the inevitability of diverse opinions. So we have not quite resolved this problem and neither has the Empress. Let me turn briefly to some recent ways of thinking about some of these issues in order to set up my reading of the text's efforts to address this problem.

The question of the politics of the concept of "the world" has a long philosophical tradition, one that sees critics split on whether worlds are inherently violent or peaceful and tolerationist (or better). Martin Heidegger's conception of a world rests on its relation to protection and to how a world's inhabitants imagine themselves in relation to God: "in a world's worlding," Heidegger writes, "is gathered that spaciousness out of which the protective grace of the god is granted or withheld."[35] So once one imagines a world, protection is imperative and is imagined as proceeding from a power outside the world, from a god whom the world's inhabitants must share if they are to be considered as inhabiting the same world. The etymology of toleration is derived from toll, which is a tax to be paid at the polity's boundary, and is also related to telos, a tax for the gods and also a limit of the polity.[36] For Heidegger, the telos must be established in order for a world to world – that is, to protect. This is why governments, religions, and worlds are coterminous, why worlds need gods, and why acts of imagination or worlding necessarily invoke the instinct to protect. Emmanuel Levinas's critique of Heidegger's philosophy of the world rests on the fact that this need to protect permits the universalizing tyranny of the state.[37] But this critique of Heidegger leads also to a sense that in the conception of the "world," in the ways that "world" necessitates encounters with others and other worlds, lies the possibility of encounters that are hospitable rather than violent – that is, encounters between others that go even beyond mere peace and tolerance. In Jacques Derrida's reading of Levinas, the protectionism and violence fundamental to worlds is centred on the decisionism that founds both politics and religion. When a community recognizes that it must make a decision (e.g., to protect itself), it recognizes the prior decision that founded their community, a decision inevitably authorizing violence and ascribed to an entity that transcends the world. For Derrida, this means that "the world" is that in which the "absence-presence of God *plays*" – a play that allows us to "think the essence *of God*."[38] If God plays at the borders of worlds, this explains why religious difference is a fundamental issue for worlds: at the borders of worlds, the encounter with the essence of God (or with other religions) may authorize violence or may soften the world's boundaries. Gilles Deleuze and Felix Guattari are sanguine about the positive (tolerationist, at a minimum) possibilities of encounters between worlds, arguing that in the encounter with the other lies the possibility of peace via the dissolution of the boundaries of the self and world. The other appears, in their account, as "neither subject nor object but as something that is very different, a possible *world*" (emphasis mine); an encounter with such an other / world can redistribute "subject and object [...] figure and ground, margins and center."[39] For Deleuze and Guattari, the encounter with the possibility of another world is both frightening and hopeful, ultimately salutary if one opens up to the experience – it can be a way of destabilizing the self and the world, or making the "world go by."[40] Philosophers thus differ on the centrality of violence to worlds, but they pose the central question – will an encounter with others and other worlds be violent or peaceful? – that *The Blazing World* ends by asking. Its answer is less hopeful than Deleuze and Guattari's.

The importance of this philosophical debate to literature has been taken up by a number of literary critics.[41] Eric Hayot argues for literature as a place where such conflicts between "the world" and other worlds (or the universe) are mediated at the level of form. For Hayot, there exists an inherent affinity between literature and the world, because literature involves always toggling between parts and wholes and because the idea of "the world" is bounded and embedded in an idea of the universe. "The world" necessitates the development of a concept of wholeness in relation to greater wholeness. For Hayot, modernity is defined by the arrival of "the universal" as a history-making event and the literary as a process whereby that world view is formalized. So when Descartes says "the matter of the heavens and the earth is one and the same, and there cannot be a plurality of worlds," and Spinoza concurs with "life is always the same and everywhere one," we, according to Hayot, "recognize the seemingly paradoxical combination of universalism and multiplicity as central to the entire modern world view."[42] In modernity, we assume that everyone lives in the same world. For Hayot, this means that the world is "whatever one has a good theory of," and literature is a means of formalizing one's world view. Pheng Cheah comes at these questions differently from Hayot, arguing that literature can "world" because of its receptivity and because of its temporality, factors that allow it to contest the hegemony of one world – global capitalism – and through this contestation to bring about new worlds.[43] For Cheah, because literature's temporality underlies its world-remaking power, its possibilities go beyond the mediation of conflict that Hayot imagines. I have been arguing that Cavendish might be up to something similar to what both Hayot and Cheah claim as literature's special role, in so far as she uses the literary imagination to address questions of worlding. Cavendish, however, sides with form and figuration against theory, and thereby is more materialist and formalist than Hayot. She also seems much more resolutely committed to the material and the formal connections between imagined and real worlds than Cheah is, a commitment that limits the political imaginary of such form and figuration.[44] Cavendish's philosophical positions on the nature of the literary imagination (contra Hayot and Cheah) help to explain, I argue, why the Blazing World, which can seem rather utopian (or at least peaceful) when it is the only world, turns quite violent when worlds encounter each other.

After the Empress and Margaret Cavendish engage in their world-creating exercise, in which they experience the figuring power of the mind as productive of peace and harmony, they endeavour to influence other worlds, ones that seem at once more real and more difficult to govern. The central conflict in the "real" Margaret Cavendish's life was the loss of her husband's lands and fortune during the interregnum. Cavendish devoted a great deal of effort to right what she considered this political wrong. In *The Blazing World,* this real aspect of Cavendish's life has an analogue: the fictional Cavendish and the Empress travel "as lightly as two thoughts" to Cavendish's home in order to try to resolve a similar conflict that Cavendish's husband is having (*BW*, 190). The problem is figured via personification: Prudence and Honesty are aligned with the Cavendishes' cause, while Fortune is the Cavendishes' antagonist, with Folly and Rashness on its side. The Empress and Margaret Cavendish convene a trial to mediate the conflict, but the judge, Truth, proves ineffectual at resolving the conflict between these personifications. This experience – of reflecting upon the nature of conflict and the impossibility of changing opinions that are fundamentally connected to identity and/or to other worlds (and personification is the trope for this, an antagonist to simile) – offers a counterpoint to the elation of the world-imaginings of these two characters. This is because the liberating potential of the imagination is also the threat to the security and protection of the world. If Margaret Cavendish can enter the Blazing World and if the two of them can travel "as lightly as two thoughts" from one world to another, the security of each individual world is at stake (*BW*, 190). The glorious power of the literary imagination gives each individual the power to construct a world and, thus, to threaten others' worlds. If every individual – or even every sovereign nation – can construct a world, each world in fact becomes part of another larger world.[45] The text asks this question directly: is "man a little world?" it wonders (*BW*, 169). We more commonly hear its cousin, also relevant given the topography of the Blazing World: whether every man is (or no man is) an island. In this collapsing of the individual and the world, the text's central conflict can be seen, whereby the freedom inherent in matter, and therefore in minds, comes into conflict with the protection that worlds demand.

The Blazing World, like all worlds, is made up of "parts." On a textual level, this partitioning relates not only to the philosophical and literary texts but also to the two highly unequal parts of the literary text. The first part, by far the longest (making up about 80 per cent of the whole), fulfils the promise of the title by being mainly description; the governing actions, such as they are, of the Empress are revoked by the end, and the imaginary worlds are easily dissolved, leaving the Blazing World – as well as the worlds of Margaret Cavendish (fictional and real) – more or less as it was when the protagonist arrived. The much shorter second part, by contrast, is a fast-paced tale of massive military innovation and destruction. Elaborate planning allows the Empress to travel to her original world, where the nation of her nativity is besieged by enemies. The problem in this world is precisely that it is partitioned into "several sovereign governments" (*BW*, 189). The Empress solves this problem by exploiting the physical realities and the knowledge of her Blazing World: the firestone that allows water to burn (in the Blazing World) proves militarily as well as spectacularly useful when transported to this other world, and the telescopes of the bear men that were divisive in the singular Blazing World prove unifying in military affairs. In a relentless series of sieges, which rely on equal parts science, spectacle, and the Empress's command of her diverse troops, she routs all the enemies – actual and potential – of her native land, bringing all other inhabitants of that world into submission, that is into one world, which is monitored and symbolized by the tribute they must all pay to the King.

Thus, the text's celebrated exploration of literary world-creation offers a view of the literary imagination as producing the experience of the world not as parts but as a whole and at the same time as producing a recognition of the limits of the human imagination: as self-moving rational matter itself, the literary imagination can only produce vitalistic worlds that resemble our own – worlds that are close to it and that, therefore, threaten it. This is how Cavendish refutes political solutions – such as those of Hobbes – that rely on *ex nihilo* creation of a body politic, because they violate the laws of nature that are discoverable in the literary imagination. The literary imagination can experience the unity and the thoroughgoing materiality of the world that we experience as diverse, and thus it can manage – via figuration – the "opinions" that are produced by these natural laws but that create religio-political strife. But this same world-creation process that allows for the literary imagination also produces unlimited worlds because matter is inherently diverse and subject to refiguration. In the end, Cavendish's text produces a very ambivalent attitude towards toleration: the literary imagination both understands the inevitability of diversity of opinion and fails to imagine a solution other than state violence.[46]

NOTES

1 Margaret Cavendish Newcastle, *The Blazing World and Other Writings*, ed. Kate Lilley (London: Penguin, 1992). Hereafter abbreviated to *BW*. All further references

will be to this edition, unless otherwise stated. Following current scholarly convention, I will use her married name, Cavendish, throughout.

2   On the seventeenth-century conception of worlds and universes, and its impact on the literary imagination, see Mary Baine Campbell, *Wonder and Science: Imagining Worlds in Early Modern Europe* (Ithaca: Cornell University Press, 2004). Campbell situates Cavendish within the early modern "impulse to bring a world into imagined being" and the literary tradition that this impulse spurred (*Wonder*, 185). Compared with Robert Hooke, whose microscope figures the internal, domestic world, Cavendish is exploring the larger political dimensions of this literary tradition. See Robert Hooke, *Micrographia, or, Some physiological descriptions of minute bodies made by magnifying glasses: with observations and inquiries thereupon* (London: Printed by J. Martyn and J. Allestry, 1665).

3   Cavendish, *Observations upon Experimental Philosophy: Cambridge Texts in the History of Philosophy* (Cambridge: Cambridge University Press, 2001). Hereafter abbreviated *OEP* for the purposes of citation. On the significance of description to eighteenth-century epistemology, see Joanna Stalnaker, "Description and the Nonhuman View of Nature," *Representations* 135, no. 1 (2016): 72–88, and Cynthia Wall, *The Prose of Things* (Chicago: University of Chicago Press, 2014). Stalnaker's analysis of Georges Cuvier gets at my point about Cavendish, for whom "Description" in the title suggests a "broad sweeping view" of the world, which does not privilege human perspective ("Description and the Nonhuman View of Nature," 75).

4   From the dedication "To All Worthy and Noble Readers" in the 1668 edition of *The Blazing World*, when *The Blazing World* was published separately (Boston: Northeastern University Women Writers Project, 2002).

5   Eric Hayot, *On Literary Worlds* (Oxford: Oxford University Press, 2012); Martin Heidegger, "The Origin of the Work of Art," in *Poetry, Language, Thought*, trans. Albert Hofstader (New York: Harper & Row, 1971), 15–76.

6   For feminist readings of Cavendish that celebrate these world-creating gestures, See Sylvia Bowerbank, "The Spider's Delight," *English Literary Renaissance* 14, no. 3 (1984): 392–408; Catherine Gallagher, "Embracing the Absolute," *Genders* 1 (March 1988): 24–9; Elaine Hobby, *Virtue of Necessity* (Ann Arbor: University of Michigan Press, 1989); Rosemary Kegl, "'The World I Have Made,'" in *Feminist Readings of Early Modern Culture: Emerging Subjects*, ed. Valerie Traub et al. (Cambridge: Cambridge University Press, 1996); Lisa Sarasohn, *The Natural Philosophy of Margaret Cavendish: Reason and Fancy during the Scientific Revolution* (Baltimore: Johns Hopkins University Press, 2010); and Rachel Trubowitz, "The Reenchantment of Utopia and the Female Monarchical Self," *Tulsa Studies in Women's Literature* 11, no. 2 (1992): 229–45. I diverge from this tendency in Cavendish studies to read her as protofeminist – not because I question the validity of her early feminist perspective, but because I think it obscures the more conservative aspects of her writing.

7   "Conservative" is anachronistic – there would be no full-blown ideology of conservatism until the nineteenth century (on this history see Karl Mannheim, "On

Conservative Thought," in *From Karl Mannheim*, ed. Kurt H. Wolff (Piscataway, NJ: Transaction Publishers, 1993), 260–350). I use this term here colloquially to indicate what it is that critics, typically liberal, find distasteful about Cavendish's politics: monarchism, Catholicism, and, in the case of the *Blazing World,* intolerance. But Mannheim's larger points about conservative thought are consonant with my argument about Cavendish. For Mannheim, conservative thought is marked by "intuitive, qualitative, concrete forms of thought" ("Conservative," 273), which oppose the kind of rationalizations and generalizations that mark liberal thinking and that are generally consistent with the idea of a "world" view.

8 Charles, England and Wales, Sovereign, *His Majesties Gracious Letter and Declaration Sent to the House of Peers: By Sir John Greenvill, Kt. from Breda, and Read in the House the First of May, 1660* (London: Printed by John Macock and Francis Tyton, 1660), 9–10. Its discussion of the elimination of "discord, separation and difference of parties" promotes political unity, not the toleration of political and social diversity that we have come to know as toleration, but it was an important step in defining the state's key stake in what we now call toleration and also secularization: difference of opinion in religion was to be separated from politics (ibid., 12).

9 Charles, *His Majesties Gracious Letter,* 12. Similar language, but with an important difference in which freedom of religion is just example and not exception, appears in the Declaration of the Rights of Man and the Citizen adopted by the French assembly during the French revolution: "No-one shall be interfered with for his opinions, even religious ones, provided that their practice does not disturb public order as established by the law" (26 August 1789).

10 Charles issued the Royal Declaration of Indulgence in 1672 but was forced to withdraw it in 1673. James II's move in 1687 to issue an even more capacious indulgence precipitated his downfall in 1688, as well as the passage of the Act of Toleration in 1689. Parallel events took place with the Hugenots in France. Charles's motives for promoting religious tolerance have always been suspect. I speak here more to his rhetoric than his motives.

11 Scott Sowerby, *Making Toleration: The Repealers and the Glorious Revolution* (Cambridge, MA: Harvard University Press, 2013), 59. Sowerby observes that granting freedom of conscience was perhaps even a way that the Stuarts endeavoured to strengthen the monarchy.

12 I am grateful to Alison Conway for helping me to understand this problem and this history in these terms.

13 For a sense of the long history of this problem in philosophy, see the essays in Ann Ward, *Matter and Form: From Natural Science to Political Philosophy* (Rowman & Littlefield, 2009).

14 The obverse of this movement, and synergistic with it, is the imagining of nature as matter that, once its rules were understood, could be managed and manipulated. Francis Bacon is credited with the strong articulation of this idea, which has been the subject of much scholarly critique. Cavendish, and my argument about her take

on worlds, can also be seen as in conversation with Spinoza and Leibnitz. As Garth Kemmerly puts it, "Spinoza saw the world as a single comprehensive substance like Descartes's extended matter, while Leibniz supposed that the world is composed of many discrete particles, each of which is simple, active, and independent of every other, like Descartes's minds or souls" ("Philosophy Pages," accessed 11 August 2017, http://www.philosophypages.com/). My argument about Cavendish positions her between these two views, though the philosophical and political nuances of this possible connection are beyond the scope of this essay.

15   This assumption persists in the twenty-first century, as exemplified by trends in new materialism and object-oriented ontology. See, for example, Jane Bennett, *Vibrant Matter: A Political Ecology of Things* (Durham: Duke University Press, 2009); Karen Barad, *Meeting the Universe Halfway: Quantum Physics and the Entanglement of Matter and Meaning* (Durham: Duke University Press, 2007); Graham Harmon, "The Well-Wrought Broken Hammer: Object-Oriented Literary Criticism," *New Literary History* 43, no. 2 (2012): 183–203; and the essays in Diana Coole and Samantha Frost, *New Materialisms: Ontology, Agency, and Politics* (Durham: Duke University Press, 2010). We might ask why and when thinkers take this approach and what its limitations are (a question Colin Jager posed to me when I presented an earlier version of this paper). Answering it is beyond the scope of this essay, but I do think my argument here counters such critical trends that assume natural science and politics can be solved together, by showing the dead end of Cavendish's approach to this problem.

16   Samuel Pepys, *The Diary of Samuel Pepys,* ed. Robert Latham and William Mathews, vol. 9 (London: G. Bell & Sons, 1970), 123. For context on this event, see Samuel I. Mintz, "The Duchess of Newcastle's Visit to the Royal Society," *Journal of English and Germanic Philology* 51 (1952): 168–76.

17   On Cavendish's self-representation as a solitary genius, see James Fitzmaurice, "Fancy and the Family: Self-Characterizations of Margaret Cavendish," *The Huntington Library Quarterly* (1990): 199–209.

18   Gallagher accounts for Cavendish's commitment to absolutism as a means of imagining autonomous subjectivity for a woman ("Embracing the Absolute"). Trubowitz builds on this argument by arguing that the "competing demands of radical feminism and social conservatism" account for Cavendish's generic innovations ("The Reenchantment of Utopia and the Female Monarchical Self: Margaret Cavendish's Blazing World," *Tulsa Studies in Women's Literature* 11, no. 2 (1992): 229–45, at 229.

19   For a post-humanist reading of *The Blazing World,* see Aaron R. Hanlon, "Margaret Cavendish's Anthropocene Worlds," *New Literary History* 47, no. 1 (2016): 49–66. For Cavendish's critique of subject/object relations see Eve Keller, "Producing Petty Gods: Margaret Cavendish's Critique of Experimental Science," *ELH* 64, no. 2 (1997): 447–71. For her general critique of the Royal Society, see Anna Battigelli, *Margaret Cavendish and the Exiles of the Mind* (Lexington: University Press of

Kentucky, 2015). On her vitalism see John Rogers, *The Matter of Revolution: Science, Poetry, and Politics in the Age of Milton* (Ithaca: Cornell University Press, 1998).

20 Alexandra Bennett, "Margaret Cavendish and the Theatre of War," *Margaret Cavendish*, ed. Sara Heller Mendelson (Farnham: Ashgate, 2009), 103–13, at 103.

21 Cavendish reflects on the implications of England being an island nation in "An Oration concerning Shipping" in *Orations of Divers Sorts, Accommodated to Divers Places*; Margaret Cavendish. *Political Writings*, ed. Susan James (Cambridge: Cambridge University Press, 2003), 111–293.

22 Deborah Boyle, "Margaret Cavendish on Perception, Self-Knowledge, and Probable Opinion," *Philosophy Compass* 10, no. 7 (2015): 438–50. In Boyle's account, Cavendish's philosophy does not equate all opinions (some are more probable than others), but I think Cavendish, especially in *The Blazing World* is engaged in thinking about the political problem, not just the epistemological one, of difference of opinion.

23 Peter Dear, "A Philosophical Duchess: Understanding Margaret Cavendish and the Royal Society," in *Science, Literature and Rhetoric in Early Modern England*, ed. Juliet Cummins and David Burchell (Aldershot: Ashgate, 2007), 130.

24 For examples of the way that critics locate a feminist politics in her vitalist science, see Lisa Sarasohn, who takes Cavendish as describing "the freedom that inheres in matter" (*The Natural Philosophy of Margaret Cavendish*, 91–2); John Rogers, who argues that seventeenth-century vitalism "necessitated feminism" (*The Matter of Revolution*, 15); and Gabrielle Starr, who links Cavendish's vitalism to her anti-Platonic aesthetics, grounding both in her situation as a woman ("Cavendish, Aesthetics, and the Anti-Platonic Line," *Eighteenth-Century Studies* 39, no. 3 [Spring 2006], 295–308). The liberatory potential of vitalism is once again, in the twenty-first century, something of a critical darling – see, for example, Jane Bennett (*Vibrant Matter*). Speculating about this longer tradition is beyond the scope of this essay, but I can suggest that, then and now, vitalism offers a means to measure the success or failure of liberal politics, including toleration, or to leverage its yet unrealized possibilities. But more to my point, vitalism has been a way to redeem the more unseemly aspects of Cavendish's politics – her monarchism or even absolutism.

25 Benjamin Kaplan, *Divided by Faith: Religious Conflict and the Practice of Toleration in Early Modern Europe* (Cambridge, MA: Harvard University Press, 2007), 8. Benjamin Kaplan's approach to toleration comes close to how I am reading Cavendish here: toleration is typically seen as philosophical (as in enlightenment theory) or political (as related to government action) but he takes it up as a practice – a habit of peaceful coexistence.

26 Battigelli, *Margaret Cavendish and Exiles of the Mind*, 61–5.

27 Alan Ryan, "Hobbes, Toleration, and the Inner Life," in *The Nature of Political Theory*, ed. David Miller and Larry Siendentop (Oxford and New York: Clarendon Press, 1983), 197–218, at 215–17. Alan Ryan argues that while Hobbes does not seem to have much to say about the "inner life" he nonetheless offers an argument

for toleration – one based on epistemological not moral reasons: the sovereign is bound by expediency, and it is impossible to get people to agree on everything – to completely control what they think. Therefore, there is no point in trying. Though Hobbes argues for "real Unitie" there is "no submergence of individual substances in some superior whole."

28 For important contemporary accounts of the relationship between analysis and synthesis, see John Locke, *An Essay Concerning Human Understanding*, 4th ed., ed. P.H. Nidditch (Oxford: Oxford University Press, 1975), xxii, 9; Gottfried Wilhelm Leibniz, *New Essays on Human Understanding*, 1703–5, 1st ed. 1765, trans. and ed. P. Remnant and J. Bennett (Cambridge: Cambridge University Press, 1981); and Immanuel Kant, "Analysis," *Critique of Pure Reason*, 1st ed. 1781, 2nd ed. 1787, trans. Paul Guyer and Allen W. Wood (Cambridge: Cambridge University Press, 1997). If we take John Locke as exemplary of the tradition of British empiricism, he defines what we know as analysis thusly: "all our complex Ideas are ultimately resolvable into simple Ideas, of which they are compounded, and originally made up, though perhaps their immediate Ingredients, as I may so say, are also complex Ideas." So analysis is the reverse of amalgamation – but both are processes that in Locke's terms involve "combining" or "composing" (or their reverse). Leibnitz is also interesting here. In trying to explain how a subject/predicate can be reduced to an "identity," he explains the "great value" of algebra (i.e., the "art of symbols") consists in the way it "unburdens the imagination." Kant defines synthesis as unification of a concept with another not contained in it – he distinguishes analysis from synthesis on the basis that synthesis produces new knowledge. While these enlightenment definitions are revealing, a full consideration of their relevance to Cavendish is beyond the scope of this essay. Here I am taking synthesis as a general concept of knowledge that exceeds analysis or amalgamation, that includes the more specific concept of figuration, and that also in Cavendish's case, contra Leibnitz, involves the imagination.

29 Although they are often conflated, I am contrasting indulgence with toleration, based on the fact that Stuart monarchs' efforts to instantiate religious liberty, especially the Declarations of Indulgence issued by James II, figure liberty of conscience as an indulgence granted from the love of a monarch for his people. The 1689 Act of Toleration, by contrast, begins to figure toleration as a right. This is a point I argue at more length in my current book project, tentatively entitled *Conservative Forms: 1688 and the Literary Field*.

30 These other worlds, those that are not the Blazing World, are called "E" and "ESFI." Both are imagined doubles of England. The Duchess calls her world the "Blinking world of Wit" (*BW*, 220).

31 Anne Thell, "'[A]s lightly as two thoughts': Motion, Materialism, and Cavendish's Blazing World," *Configurations* 23, no. 1 (2015): 1–33, at 17. Thell argues in a related line that for Cavendish the imagination "is a potent generative force that supersedes sense perception yet also remains material."

32 Oddvar Holmesland, *Utopian Negotiation: Aphra Behn and Margaret Cavendish* (Syracuse: Syracuse University Press, 2013), 97. For Oddvar Holmesland, Cavendish's idea of unity is based in nature (not in worlds). For him, the phrase "nature tends to Unity" means that the imagination, being composed of natural motions, is capable of communing with nature.

33 For an incisive reading of Cavendish's narrative strategies and their relation to diversity of opinion, see Battagelli, *Margaret Cavendish*, 73–80.

34 *Orations of Divers Sorts, Accommodated to Divers Places*; Margaret Cavendish, *Political Writings*, ed. Susan James (Cambridge: Cambridge University Press, 2003), 168.

35 Heidegger, "The Origin of the Work of Art," 144. I recognize that the theories of Heidegger – along with Cavendish – are problematic to a liberal perspective. Heidegger's politics – and its relation to the world-domination aspirations of Nazi Germany – has been the subject of no small amount of criticism, so I will not rehearse that argument here, except to say that in so far as my reading of "worlds" in Cavendish relates to Heidegger, then I side with those who cannot separate his aesthetic, philosophical, and political theories and activities, just as I cannot separate Cavendish's conservatism and her literary innovation.

36 For these multiple denotations, see the *Oxford English Dictionary*. For a discussion of the critical tradition, see Wade Sikorski, "Toleration and Shamanism," *New Political Science* 13, no. 1 (1993): 3–20.

37 Emmanuel Levinas, *Totality and Infinity: An Essay on Exteriority*, trans. Alphonso Lingis (Dordrecht: Kluwer, 1991); see especially 130–5. In comparing Levinas and Heidegger on the question of totality, Graham Harmon invokes the idea, relevant for my point about the geography of the Blazing World, of islands as spaces where the totalizing force of worlds can be escaped. For Levinas (unlike Heidegger), Harmon claims, "the tool-system is riddled with gaps and tropical islands where individual things take shape for our enjoyment" ("Levinas and the Triple Critique of Heidegger," *Philosophy Today* 53 [2009]: 407–13, at 409).

38 Jacques Derrida, "Violence and Metaphysics," in *Writing and Difference*, trans. Alan Bass (London: Routledge, 1978), 97–192, at 133.

39 Gilles Deleuze and Félix Guattari, *What Is Philosophy?* (New York: Columbia University Press, 2014), 17.

40 Ibid., 18.

41 The larger scholarly conversations about "world literature" and the critiques of universal cosmopolitanism (as, in Kant's words, the means to perpetual peace) would be avenues to take these questions further, though it is beyond the scope of this essay. On world literature see Emily Apter, *Against World Literature: On the Politics of Untranslatability* (London: Verso Books, 2014); Amir Mufti, *Forget English!: Orientalisms and World Literature* (Cambridge, MA: Harvard University Press, 2016); and Gaytri Spivak, "Rethinking-Comparativism," *New Literary History*, 40, no. 3 (2009): 609–26. On cosmopolitanism, see Kwame Anthony Appiah, *Cosmopolitanism: Ethics in a World of Strangers (Issues of Our Time)* (New York: W.W. Norton &

Company, 2010); Seyla Benhabib, *Another Cosmopolitanism* (Oxford: Oxford University Press, 2008); Jacques Derrida, *On Cosmopolitanism and Forgiveness*, trans. Mark Dooley and Michael Hughes (London: Routledge, 2001); Eddy Kent and Terri Tomsky, *Negative Cosmopolitanism* (Montreal and Kingston: McGill-Queen's University Press, 2017).

42 Hayot, *On Literary Worlds,* 108.

43 Pheng Cheah, *What Is a World?: On Postcolonial Literature as World Literature* (Durham: Duke University Press, 2016).

44 I am not taking a position on the feasibility of any of these positions. I will say that my concern about Hayot's argument is that it relies on a limited notion of literary "worlds" (with its centrality of the concepts of realism, romanticism, and modernism) in ways that seem unlikely to be able to address the problems of diversity of opinion and worlds in either the seventeenth century or the twenty-first. Cheah's argument, with its championing of postcolonial literature as the site of reimagining the "world" of "global" capitalism, offers a more politically appealing locus of literary world reimagining, but I, like Cavendish, tend to be more sceptical about claiming such wholesale powers for the literary imagination.

45 Susan Mendus, "Introduction," in *Justifying Toleration: Conceptual and Historical Perspectives* (Cambridge: Cambridge University Press, 2009); Kobi Assoulin, "Beyond 'Good': Richard Rorty's Private Sphere and Toleration," עיון /*Jerusalem Philosophical Quartery* 60 (2011): 53–71, at 63, emphasis mine. Susan Mendus identifies the roots of toleration as respect for the other person, as it is supported by the Kantian imperative. Kobi Assoulin glosses this imperative as the demand for subjects to "Recogniz[e] the other as an autonomous entity, who is entitled to shape her *private world.*" So this world-creating faculty that *The Blazing World* celebrates is also the fundamental problem of toleration.

46 Geraldine Wagner, "*Romancing Multiplicity*: Female Subjectivity and the Body Divisible in Margaret Cavendish's *Blazing World,*" *Early Modern Literary Studies,* 9, no. 1 (2003): 1–59; B.R. Siegfried, "The City of Chance, or, Margaret Cavendish's Theory of Radical Symmetry," *Early Modern Literary Studies,* Special Issue 14 (2004). Critical solutions to the violence at the end of the text have been, to my mind, unsatisfactory and based on a desire to preserve Cavendish as an avatar of female modernity. Wagner, for example, argues "although Margaret and her characters have trouble escaping this oppressive dialectic of domination and submission (they repeatedly assume the roles of conquerors and rulers), the text shows a way out by constructing the self as multiple" (59). According to John Rogers, Cavendish engages "the science of animist materialism with the unembarrassed intention of exploring the revolutionary potential of its antipatriarchal logic" (*The Matter of Revolution,* 181). For B.R. Siegfried, "Singularity makes good on the promise of liberty and Cavendish's seeming autocracy is precisely because people have agency" (para. 29).

5 How to Handle the Intolerant: The Education of Pierre Bayle

ELENA RUSSO

Pierre Bayle's entire life was shaped by the experience of violence, both political and theological, and by the search for new modes of spiritual resistance against it. He was born in 1647 to a Calvinist minister in a small Protestant stronghold sixty miles south of Toulouse, and came of age during the contentious, traumatic decade that preceded the Revocation of the Edict of Nantes.[1] Separated from his family since 1670, Pierre Bayle had been writing critically about French policies on dissent from the safety of his residence in Rotterdam. The French authorities couldn't get their hands on him, so they arrested his brother Jacob instead. Jacob died in prison in 1685 as a consequence of torture and mistreatment. Bayle had ended up in Rotterdam following a chain of events triggered by a youthful error: while studying at Toulouse, in his early twenties, he had converted to Catholicism. A year and a half later, a new spiritual crisis led him to abjure Catholicism, reconcile with his family, and thus become, under French law, a "relapsed heretic." To avoid incarceration, he fled the country and never saw his family again.

After two years in Geneva, where he witnessed with dismay a great deal of animosity between Calvinist factions, Bayle returned to France under an assumed name and won the chair of philosophy at the Academy of Sedan, a Protestant enclave. There he met Pierre Jurieu, a professor of theology and Hebrew. Six years later, in 1681, the Academy of Sedan was shut down by Louis XIV, and Bayle and Jurieu moved to Rotterdam. Bayle took up the chair of philosophy and history at a small, newly founded academic institution, the Schola Illustris, a kind of preparatory school for the university. Jurieu was granted a chair of theology, probably owing to the help of Bayle's influential friend and patron Adrian Van Paets. Twelve years later, Jurieu used the considerable influence he had garnered to have Bayle fired from his job. By then, Jurieu had become the advocate of a holy war against France, an ardent Orangist, and a fierce polemicist who did not baulk at tampering with the scriptures in order to serve his political ends.[2]

Jurieu had been in Bayle's cross-hairs for years. In Bayle's lifelong battle for freedom of conscience, Jurieu was a constant target, the underlying figure behind historical "fanatics," fraudulent diviners, "little prophets,"[3] theocrats, millenarists, and visionaries, such as the Dominican friar and theocratic leader Girolamo Savonarola, and all the theologians who, like Augustine, argued that forced conversions were legitimate.

This is, briefly put, the context of Bayle's contribution to the debate on toleration. It's important to keep in mind that Bayle had far more skin in the game than other advocates of toleration. Of course I am thinking of Locke, for a comparison between the two is all but inevitable. Scholars have a tendency to sponsor their own beauty contest: who got there first, who did it better, who was the more "modern" of the two. Scholars of Bayle point out that the latter's position is more far-reaching and robust than Locke's; that Bayle, unlike Locke, is willing to extend tolerance to Catholics and atheists. Conversely, scholars of Locke note that sometimes Bayle's writings are ambiguous and subject to multiple readings, and that Locke in the end softened his stance towards papists.[4] Not to mention that Bayle, though witty and incisive, was scarcely sensitive to the virtues of brevity. Raymond Klibansky suggested that the reason why Locke received so much more attention is that he wrote a short work.[5] Bayle's manner was to write and rewrite, correcting himself, constantly refining his arguments in light of the objections he had gotten, or was trying to pre-empt. He engaged with his adversaries on their terrain, using precedent and examples from history, building his case dialogically. This style, as historian John Christian Laursen says, "can be read as a deliberate strategy. The medium is part of the message: toleration of many viewpoints is justified from many viewpoints."[6] As I am going to show, the form and the style in which the argument for toleration is being made (the rhetorical strategies, the persona of the speaker and the authority he claims, the things he withholds, the feigned naïveté, the use of paradox, and more) are at least as significant as any summary we can make of the propositions the argument lays out.

Bayle approached religion as a comprehensive social, human and political phenomenon, and in a manner very unlike Locke's. Bayle is unique in his willingness to explore the dark side of religious passions, his scant regard for rhetorical restraint and philosophical gravitas. His life and thought were deeply marked by the painful experience of the *odium theologicum* that he endured both in absolutist France and in the partially tolerant Dutch Republic. Bayle remained on the receiving end of sectarian strife throughout his life, including during his stay in Rotterdam, a city divided by quarrels between orthodox Calvinists and Dissenters.[7] That did not prevent him from butting his head against powerful institutions and individuals and from writing things that shocked and troubled not only his adversaries, but also his friends. His major work in defence of toleration drew the sharpest criticism not from the likes of Jurieu, but from moderate Calvinists like Jean Le Clerc and Elie Saurin. In the Republic of Letters, the virtual community that he founded – the first and perhaps the most remarkable of the networks of the Enlightenment – Baylean debate prevailed. As a form of debate it did not resemble the conversational Lockean model, which stressed civility and politeness and sought to tone down disputes, especially theological ones, when they became too animated.[8] Bayle was an exemplary practitioner of the kind of *parrhesia* Foucault has analysed: telling the truth at the risk of losing everything, including one's life or, as was the case for Bayle, one's own identity and standing within the community.[9]

However, Bayle did make an effort to lay down the epistemological foundations for a broad-based ethics of religious toleration. He did so in the influential book *A Philosophical commentary on these Words of the Gospel "Compel Them to Come in,"* published in October 1686. The title is a citation from Luke 14:23, which, via Augustine's commentary, was being used by Catholic proselytizers who wanted to ground forced conversion in the Gospel's teachings.[10] Augustine had endorsed the persecution of dissenters and heretics, provided it was done by "Christ's Church" (that is, by his own) and for the "right" reasons. "There is an unjust persecution: it is that done by the impious against Christ's Church," Augustine wrote, and "there is a righteous persecution: it is that done by Christ's Church against the impious. The Church persecutes out of love; the impious out of cruelty."[11]

France's hegemonic Catholic Church could afford such arrogance. However, as members of a minority religion, one barely tolerated by their countrymen, seventeenth-century French Huguenots had invoked, with far greater conviction than other Calvinist communities, the principles of reciprocity and toleration. Had that been a merely opportunistic move? Had Calvinists turned the other cheek because they couldn't afford to do otherwise? These are questions Bayle now asked. For the thing that made him a stranger to his own people and fuelled his indignation was seeing that the Augustinian mindset was now being embraced in Protestant countries, such as England; that it triumphed at the heart of his own community – in Rotterdam, among his former friends; that Jurieu, who had once been his close ally, was now a shrill advocate of invading France, deposing the king, and forcing his own faith on the entire country. The roles were now being reversed, and it was Catholics and Calvinist dissenters who suffered. The Rotterdam Consistory now invoked the same trite arguments in order to repress the Arminians; the Arminians invoked them against the Socinians and antitrinitarians. But the Socinians and antitrinitarians did none of that, because they stood at the lowest ranks of the pecking order and were thus forced to be tolerant for lack of other options.

Doctrinal self-righteousness, Bayle wrote in the *Commentary*, bolstered by secular power, fuels intolerance and hatred. Each sect is convinced that it alone is the *one true church*, and since there is no impartial, other-worldly referee to settle the dispute, the result is the reciprocity of mutual hate.[12] In the name of God, the strong oppress the weak, who will do the same when they are a little less weak, for today's victims are tomorrow's persecutors. That's a point that Bayle never stops pressing on his own community (which goes some way towards explaining why he ends up losing his job). To those who follow these principles, there is no crime that can't be legitimated, as long as it is done in the name of religion: the most atrocious behaviour seems just because God orders it; moral values, civic duty, and penal laws are turned upside down, and wrong becomes right.

It's in light of this stance that we must read the famous article "David," published in the first edition of the *Dictionnaire historique et critique* of 1697 (and bowdlerized by Bayle in the edition of 1702, following the censure of the Consistory of the Walloon Church of Rotterdam).[13] Here, Bayle comes down sharply on the crimes committed by King David, who nonetheless was, as the Bible says, "a man after [God's] own heart."[14] The article is a not-so-veiled allusion to King William III, who, at the onset of the Glorious Revolution had been called "the New David," and whose politics Bayle disapproved of. But that's only part of the story. The ultimate target of Bayle's barbs in "David" is Jurieu's political use of the David figure in some of his sermons. Jurieu had argued, biblical text at hand, that a monarch chosen by God may transgress Christian morality for the sake of defending religion: therefore a religious end justifies all means, including usurpation, rebellion, war, and unconditional hatred of "God's enemies."[15] Bayle's closely argued analysis of David's emblematic role engages intimately with Jurieu's account of the relationship between faith and political power.

As for the Augustinian argument that one may *force* people to embrace "truth" when the salvation of their soul is at stake, Bayle rejects it in the *Commentary* with a two-pronged strategy grounded both in Calvinist theology and in natural rights. All that God wants, Bayle argues, is sincerity of belief and loving dedication. There is ultimately no difference between those who worship in the correct way and those who do it incorrectly, as long as each person follows the voice of God that speaks to her conscience, the reason being that the individual conscience is sovereign and responds only to God, not to any church.[16]

Embedded in Bayle's defence of the right of the individual to decide for herself is the radical argument that no institutionalized religion has a pre-eminent access to truth and that no church may suppress others for doing it "wrong." It would be much better, Bayle suggests, if they all lowered their pretensions and came to terms with one another, for the playing field is a very crowded one.[17]

In considering religion as a set of claims that are impossible to prove rationally, Bayle makes a distinction between theological and scientific disputation, a distinction that becomes the ground for toleration. While in the Republic of

Letters no-holds barred argument is the rule, until people come to some agreement (or they don't, and the debate rolls on) in matters of faith, mutual tolerance is necessary because we don't have the means to reach certainty through rational discussion, the clash of ideas, or experimental means:

> As faith affords us no other criterion of orthodoxy than the inward sentiment and conviction of conscience, a criterion common to all, even the most heretical souls; it follows that all our belief, whether orthodox or heterodox, is finally resolved into this, that we feel it, and it seems to us that this or that is true. Whence I conclude that God does not expect, from either orthodox or heretic, a certainty grounded on scientific search or discussion, but accepts from each that they love what appears true to them.[18]

Tolerance is an ethical and political virtue: it's the precondition for any form of justice. At this point, let us make it clear that Bayle's understanding of tolerance is not rooted primarily, as Jonathan Israel has argued, in a "secular conception of individual freedom."[19] To be sure, Bayle's theological framing of conscience as the voice of God may be translated in secular terms as a defence of natural rights (or of what we today would call human rights): forcing a person to act against her conscience means alienating her from reason and will and depriving her of any autonomy. Nobody can decide for others what they should believe: each person must be free to decide for herself. Thus, the state ought not to interfere with how its citizens practise or do not practise their faith, whether they are Jews, Muslims, Catholics (as long as they do not conspire against the state), Protestants, Arminians, Socinians, or antitrinitarians; everybody ought to be free to worship as they think best. Or, for that matter, *not* to worship: atheists should be free to be who they are, like everyone else. (I will return to the issue of atheism, for it is crucial to Bayle.)

But Bayle's argument for tolerance is also very much a spiritual one. It is grounded in the same notion of a hidden God, *Deus absconditus*, that was elaborated by Blaise Pascal, who also insisted on the primacy of love above reason.[20] Because humans can never attain a true understanding of divine nature, they are forced to accept the humbling fact that any form of worship is necessarily going to be imperfect. Thus, the originality of Bayle's position consists in his speaking both from inside the faith and outside of it, in his in-betweenness, and in never settling on a theological position or on a secular one. Such a carefully constructed cognitive dissonance is indeed the reason why his writing is so thought-provoking.

However, having made the individual conscience sovereign in matters of belief, the problem remains of who, or what, should regulate individual behaviour. How should we deal with the good-faith intolerant individual who claims to speak in the name of God, such as the assassin of Henri IV, who firmly believed murdering the king was an act of piety?[21] How can we know that what speaks to our conscience is the voice of God and not that of prejudice and indoctrination?[22] In other words, is there a self-regulating mechanism embedded in our conscience? When he wrote the *Commentary*, Bayle was inclined to answer affirmatively. God, he argued, has given the human mind a disposition to seek the truth and be guided by reason and by the principles of justice and natural equity. Thus, whenever the scriptures seem to contradict those principles, as when they order people to commit a crime or to be drawn into a course of action leading to crime (as in Luke 14:23, "compel them to enter"), such meaning ought to be rejected as false, or requiring further interpretation. There is a "surest key for understanding scripture," Bayle writes:

> if by taking it in the literal sense we oblige men to commit crimes, [...] we oblige them to commit Actions which the Light of Nature [*lumière naturelle*], the precepts of the Decalogue, or the Gospel morality forbid; then it's to be taken for granted that the sense we give it is false, and that instead of a Divine Revelation, we impose our own visions, prejudices, and passions on the people.[23]

The issue here is one of theological coherence: obvious contradictions ought to be ruled out when they nullify the Gospel's imperatives of charity and moderation. But Bayle goes further:

> There are axioms against which the clearest and most express Letter of the Scriptures can avail nothing: as that the whole is greater than the part; that if from equal things we take things equal, the remainder will be equal; that it is impossible that contradictories should be true; or that the essence of a subject should subsist after the destruction of the subject. Should the contrary be shown a hundred times over from Scripture, should a thousand times as many Miracles as those of Moses and the Apostles be wrought in confirmation of a Doctrine repugnant to these universal principles of common sense; man, such as he is, could not believe a shred of it and would sooner persuade himself that the Scriptures spoke only Metaphors, or that these miracles were Devil-made, than that the light of reason were false in these instances.[24]

God has given all humans, regardless of their creed, a guide, a touchstone for finding their way among the intricacies of dogmas and moral choices: this is a "hardwired" feature of the mind which pre-exists and pre-empts all revealed creeds. Much as the body knows, through the faculty of taste, which foods are good for it and which are damaging (a Cartesian notion), conscience also knows by intuition what is good for it spiritually. Bayle is invoking here the Cartesian and Malebranchian distinction between conscience as the site of natural morality (akin to a kind of natural law, though he does not use that term), and conscience as the site of individual belief, which might be subject to prejudice and error.[25] Thus, a universal, God-given principle of reason is available to all human beings, regardless of creed, culture, and nationality.

In the *Commentary*, Bayle confronts intolerant theologians (in this specific case, the Augustinians) on their own ground and he defends the necessity of toleration using theological parameters. Guiding the believer through the steps of a tight-knit argument, Bayle intends to demonstrate rationally that tolerance is embedded in spiritual practice, that it is a theological and ontological necessity. But it's a battle with no end in sight, and though Bayle has no warm feelings for prophets in general, he is himself very much a *vox clamantis in deserto* who never stops clamouring and arguing, and pressing his point with his own community.

In the years that followed the publication of the *Commentary*, Bayle kept up his struggle with religious zeal, which he saw increasingly as an overweening, divisive passion unwilling to coexist with other similar passions, and unable to regulate itself. In 1706, the year he died, Bayle expressed his fears again: "Can we ever trust," he asked in his last work, "people who are convinced that they don't need to respect oaths and promises, or follow the laws of justice and equity in their dealings with heretics?" And how should we judge an individual who trusts his divine inspiration so much that "if his conscience told him to kill you, he would kill you without hesitation, trusting that the Holy Ghost has ordered him to do so?"[26] Seeing his former friend and companion of exile Pierre Jurieu become increasingly "radicalized," seeing him adopt against "heretics" the same kind of intolerance they had once been the target of, might have contributed to Bayle's despair: "We find them [the objections against intolerance] good provided that we use them against others; but they seem bad to us when they are used against us."[27]

Throughout his life, a profound mistrust of religion as a political, revolutionary agent put Bayle at odds with the mainstream of the Rotterdam Dutch Reformed Consistory, which strove to contain the various forms of dissidence that threatened its hegemony, both doctrinal and political. It is likely that Bayle's unflinching commitment to a non-political view of religion, to pacifism and toleration, had its roots in his life in France before the Revocation, under a strand of Calvinism that had embraced its identity as a minority religion; pacifism, endurance, and persuasion of a pedagogical kind were the only weapons that Calvinist writers advocated. Theirs had been a sincere conviction, but also a defensive stance, a strategy for survival. Walter Rex points out that as persecutions increased in the years leading to the Revocation, arguments defending the peaceful nature of the Gospels and the non-violent nature of true Christianity became more and more frequent in Calvinist writings.[28] As Bayle's early biographer Pierre des Maizeaux wrote, Bayle's own brother, the pastor Jacob Bayle, had died as a martyr to the concept of *Craignez Dieu; honorez le roi* (Fear God; Respect the King). Jacob had refused to convert under pressure in prison, thus honouring God; and even when he knew that he would die as a result of his unjust imprisonment, he continued to speak of the Christian's duty to oppose nothing to his persecutors but with "prayers and tears."[29]

Thus, we may well say that Bayle's embattled cry for divesting religion of any weapon other than perseverance, endurance, and rhetorical persuasion was a result not only of the traumatic experience of the Revocation, the loss of his country and his family, but also of the religious values he had grown up with. Jurieu's radical departure from the moderate positions he had shared with him, when both had been teaching at the Academy of Sedan, was for Bayle a betrayal of everything that he, his family, and his community had stood for. The example of Jurieu led Bayle to be wary of all individuals imbued with a strong sectarian passion. Bayle had moved from a country in which his religion was repressed to another in which it was triumphant, but he still found himself on the receiving end of persecution: before becoming the rhetorical figures most prevalent in his writings, irony, paradox, and chiasmic antithesis had been the very structure of his life.

We can see that irony distinctly in a letter that Bayle wrote in 1693, shortly after his expulsion from his teaching job, to his cousin and long-time friend Jean Bruguière de Naudis, who was living in France: "You'll be a hundred times a better Protestant if you only see our religion where it is being persecuted: you'd be outraged to see what it looks like where it is dominant."[30] In Bayle's view, religion becomes ethically corrupt when it becomes politically hegemonic, or when it strives to play a political role. (His critique is still valid today, when various Evangelical currents are courting state power, however irreconcilable with the principles of their faith, in an effort to advance their own interests.)[31]

In this respect, Bayle differed from Locke, who, as a member of the dominant sect, confronted toleration from a position of strength. Where Bayle and Locke converged was in their common advocacy of a strong state, neutral in its stance towards all religions, and willing to assume the responsibility of enforcing the peace, protecting minorities, and repressing sectarian violence. The way Bayle saw it, only people's behaviour – not their religious convictions – would fall under the jurisdiction of the law. Bayle addressed the need for *civil* toleration, that is, "the right of all religions, both heretical and orthodox, to remain separate and distinct from one another within the secular framework of the state."[32] He called for a kind of *laïcité*: both philosophers saw the role of the state as neutral with respect to spiritual matters.[33] But Bayle's thoughts on the role of the state are not especially developed or innovative, for that is not where he primarily focuses his attention.

The originality of Bayle's thought does not reside in the propositional content of his arguments alone. The form of those arguments is at least as important: his use of irony, paradox, and implicature; the way he engages insistently, sometimes obsessively, with the discourse of his adversary, quoting from it, exposing its contradictions, hoisting it on its own petard; his fearless discussions of sexuality;[34] his willingness to tread on ground so slippery that scholars still can't figure out whether Bayle spoke from within the faith or outside of it.[35] All these features make for an emotionally charged style of philosophy that highlights the emotions of the speaker and foregrounds his persona in an eminently theatrical way, with his irreverent claims or his simulated naïveté. Bayle was unquestionably a precursor of Diderot, who, of course, read him, but not of Voltaire, who stole from Bayle but was anything but dialogical. It would be appropriate to look back at Bayle's Renaissance predecessors, for Bayle never fit into the confines of French classicism. Notable among these forebears was one who was, like him, a polemicist and debunker of ecclesiastical myths: the great scholar Lorenzo Valla, who impugned, with a feisty theatricality and a wicked erudition akin to Bayle's, the authenticity of the Donation of Constantine.[36]

Bayle's scarce regard for hierarchies drives him to tread over the divide between high and low. In the *Commentary*, he does not hesitate to introduce theologico-sexual analogies into serious arguments: "It is as impossible for a Protestant to discover the truth of Transubstantiation, as for a man to discover that his mother's husband did not beget him."[37] Indeed, many of the analogies of good-faith, innocent error that support the rights of the "errant conscience" are provocatively drawn from such transgressive realms as adultery, sexual violence, or parricide, either from mythology or from some famous judicial case. Thus the wife of Martin Guerre was not guilty of adultery because she sincerely believed that the impostor who impersonated her husband was the real thing. The legendary Alcmena, who had sex with Jupiter while he impersonated her husband, was equally innocent of the same sin.[38] A man who has killed his father, not knowing it was his father, is guilty, but not as much as one who has killed his father in full knowledge of what he was doing.[39] Or consider the case of a general who has ordered his pillaging troops not to harass and rape the women of a captured town: the general had expected his orders to be obeyed, even if it turned out that some of these women were not women at all, but boys dressed as women.[40] All these examples are of such a nature as to cast a troubling light on the proximity of belief and desire.

Let us now consider two passages that illustrate how Bayle's ethical vision is reflected in the very shape of his argument. The first is about the social identity of atheists. As we know, Locke declared that atheists were inherently antisocial, for individuals who feared no punishment in the afterlife would not be sufficiently motivated to maintain oaths, promises and compacts that would run against their immediate interest. "Promises, covenants, and oaths, which are the bonds of human society, can have no hold upon an Atheist. The taking away of God, though but even in thought, dissolves all," he wrote in the *Letter on Toleration*.[41] Voltaire thought just the same. Without fear of divine retribution, how could he be sure that his valet would not murder him in his sleep and steal his silverware?[42]

Bayle thought otherwise. In his first important work, *Various Thoughts on the Occasion of a Comet* (1682), he discussed at length the social psychology, so to speak, of atheists and believers: in particular the question of "whether one can have a conception of morals without believing that there is a God."[43] It is a false prejudice, Bayle writes, to say that fear of divine retribution is what drives people to curb their interests and pleasures, and that those who have no such fears do exactly as they please and are more dangerous than feral animals (§133). "It is all well and good to say this [...] when one makes metaphysical abstractions," Bayle remarks (§134). But experience, he explains, tells us differently. Various proofs follow, drawn from recent and ancient history. He offers the contemporary example of pious, Christian soldiers (obviously he had in mind the French king's *dragonnades)* who live by blood and carnage: just let them loose against people of a different faith, and they will commit all kinds of atrocities with perfect peace of mind (§139). And what about the Crusaders? No one will deny that they were extremely pious, and that the Crusades represented the finest hour in the history of Christianity. Yet both Eastern and Western Christians acted in vicious and disloyal ways so that they came to hate each other more than they hated their enemies (§140).

Bayle's inference is that human beings don't act according to their principles (§136). Even though they know in their conscience what natural equity is, they follow their own turbulent desires. Human beings do not decide on a course of action based on their general knowledge of right and wrong, but according to contingent circumstances and immediate interests. In other words, they compartmentalize. Therefore, if belief in a system of rewards and punishments is insufficient motivation for people's actions, it follows that both atheists and Christians are driven by the same things: that is, by their own temperament, by the weight of their habits, by education and past actions. And, above all, by fear of the law. Religion, therefore, would seem to have little or no influence on people's behaviour. A society of atheists, Bayle concludes, would be just as viable as a society of believers (§161; §172; §178).

Bayle organizes his argument as a series of a chiastic parallels, or mirror structures, that, as we are going to see below, relentlessly emphasize the existence of reciprocities and equivalences between a sect and its adversaries (or the discrepancies between the sect's scriptures and its practices). Basically his method harks back to the parable in Matthew 7:3, in which the hypocrite is outraged by the speck in someone else's eye, but unaware of the log that is stuck into his own.

But there is more to Bayle's reasoning than a simple reminder that we ought to do unto others and so on, although the Gospel's advocacy of charity, equity, and reciprocity is a major inspiration behind his notion of toleration. Bayle's conclusions are more far-reaching, and it is anyone's guess whether he wants to be a reformer or a demolisher of his faith. If non-believers are capable of acting ethically, whereas Christian believers commit horrible crimes in the name of their doctrines, then how can anyone say that there is a necessary relationship between faith and morality? Do institutionalized religions play a positive role in society? Readers are invited to ask these questions and draw their own conclusions. Although his personal experience is present in every page, the inner Bayle remains deeply private and beyond our reach.

The way Bayle satirizes Christianity's attempt to establish its theological superiority over Islam in his article "Mahomet (Mahomet AA, Remarks L-P)" in the *Dictionnaire critique et historique* further elucidates how his system of argument works. Many Christian apologists (Jurieu in particular – he is always in Bayle's mind) argued that the rapid expansion of Christianity, which they claimed happened without the use of force, was proof positive of the fact that God favoured the Christians. Islam, on the other hand, spread rapidly only because it used military force. Ergo, God was not on the side of Islam. Bayle attacks this biased historiography: the claim of peaceful expansion may only apply to the first three centuries of Christianity; after that, Christians made extensive use of force against other peoples. Christian theodicies are predicated upon fallacious historiographies that always give Christians the starring role. Christianity has no claim whatsoever to having a monopoly on the truth or to marching in lockstep with Providence.

Bayle then proceeds to examine tolerant and intolerant passages in the Qur'an and concludes that neither Christians nor Muslims really live by the principles established in their holy books: the former because they preach peace but practise war; the latter because, although their book calls for violence, they tolerate other religions in their midst:

> The Mahometans, following the principles of their faith, are obliged to employ violence to destroy other religions; and yet they tolerate them now, and have done so for many ages. The Christians have no order but to preach and instruct; and yet, since time immemorial, they destroy with fire and sword those who are not of their religion. [...] The conclusion which I would draw from all this is that men are little governed by their principles. The Turks, we see, tolerate all sorts of religions, though the Alcoran enjoins them to persecute the Infidels: and the Christians, we see, do nothing but persecute, though the Gospel forbids them to do it.[44]

In praising Islam's practice of toleration, Bayle casts doubt on the moral superiority that Christians assert over every other faith, a superiority that is the very foundation of their intolerance of others and their internecine strife.

Both examples demonstrate Bayle's use of what the French call *argument à tiroirs*, or "nested-boxes argument."[45] The reader opens one box, accepts a premise, only to find that it opens onto to a whole series of interconnected claims that are articulated around each other, but not in a linear way (i.e., not as a syllogism), and which involve ethical, political, and theological consequences. Thus, a seemingly innocent statement turns out to contain, by inference or implicature, a number of more radical ones. Bayle's statements branch out, sometimes a little wildly, in unexpected directions and apparent digressions. The example of virtuous atheists – as well as that of Muslims, whose scriptures talk tough, but whose behaviour is moderate – demonstrate that if people do not live according to the principles they advocate, it is because religious creeds are not the sole foundation of ethical behaviour. In fact, they often are antithetical to it.

But there is more. The point that Bayle is trying to drive home is not that religion may negatively impact our social behaviour, as the reign of terror the French unleashed on their Calvinist fellow citizens demonstrated (Locke too had plenty of examples of misplaced zealotry in the *Letter*). It is that, most of the time, religion is socially irrelevant to our decision making and habit formation. If individual and social morality are independent of our other-worldly beliefs and theologies, then religion has no role in policing society: far from being indispensable to it, as its devotees allege, it is irrelevant to society's foundations and welfare. Fear of damnation, Bayle argues, is not sufficient to deter people from acting badly. And, moreover, it is not even necessary.

Is this Bayle's way of driving home the point that the secular and the spiritual jurisdictions ought to be separate and distinct? That religion may play a role in the life of individuals, but not in that of the state? Certainly, but not solely.

Locke would have replied to Bayle that the violence and prevarication that people impute to religion are due in reality to those who "mix[ed] together and confound[ed] two things that are in themselves most different, the Church and the Commonwealth," and who let themselves be "moved by Avarice and insatiable Desire of Dominion."[46] The remedy is to "contain each of them within its own bounds" and to distinguish the priest's sphere of influence from that of the magistrate.[47] But Locke also believes, unlike Bayle, that both powers, the secular and the spiritual, must coexist within the individual in order to make a citizen whole. A "*Good Life*" ("morum rectitudo" in the Latin original: decent or upright customs and manners) consisted in the "safety both of Mens Souls and of the Commonwealth. Moral Actions belong therefore to the Jurisdiction both of the outward and inward Court:" that is, to the public jurisdiction of state law and to the privacy of individual conscience (which may or may not fall under the purview of one's own Church – this point remains open).[48]

In the *Letter Concerning Toleration*, Locke's main concern is with laying down the conditions that make such reconciliation possible: he is proposing a course of action and speaking as a legislator. Bayle, on the other hand, speaks from the margins; he sees himself as an outsider.[49] He circles around other people's writings, exposes the fault lines, the contradictions and the spurious arguments; he sets the historical record straight; he provides the reader with a heuristic method and with tools for asking the right questions; he reprograms the intolerant mindset and proposes an education.

No one has better described the spirit of Bayle's method than Foucault when he explains his own. Neither Bayle nor Foucault intend to build a philosophical *system*: what they offer is a *critique*. Theirs is an activity "condemned to dispersion, dependency and pure heteronomy," working to bring forth "a future or a truth that it will not know nor happen to be," choosing to work at the margins of other disciplines (philosophy, science, politics, ethics), seeking not only to eradicate errors, but pursuing "something which is akin to virtue."[50]

NOTES

1 By the 1660s, the Catholic clergy had been pressuring King Louis XIV to close the Huguenots' colleges and hospitals and exclude them from public office. In 1670, the clergy requested that children seven years of age or older be converted to Catholicism and taken from their parents. Mixed marriages were to be annulled and the children of those unions would be considered illegitimate. Schools and churches were gradually destroyed, people lost their jobs, and, in the last months, the army was called in, as recalcitrant Protestant families were forced to quarter the king's soldiers, the notorious *dragons,* in their homes. Harassment, pillage, and even rape were used by the soldiers as tools for pressuring people to convert. Finally, all civil privileges and religious freedoms were revoked by Louis XIV's Edict of Fontainebleau of 1685. The Protestant religion was criminalized throughout the kingdom, people were forced to convert or be deprived of their property and children; at the same time, routes to emigration were closed (though some 200,000 people managed to emigrate to Switzerland, Germany, Holland, and England). For a fine-grained, myth-busting account of the experience of the Revocation, as lived by one aristocratic migrant family, see Carolyn Chappell Lougee, *Facing the Revocation. Huguenot Families, Faith, and the King's Will* (New York: Oxford University Press, 2017).

2 See Hubert Bost's biography of Bayle, *Pierre Bayle* (Paris: Fayard, 2006).

3 When in 1686 an illiterate shepherdess from Dauphiné started prophesying and experiencing ecstasies, to be followed by several other such cases, Jurieu embraced these "miracles" as signs of a soon-to-come invasion of France by the king's enemies, in order to restore the Protestant faith. This claim appeared in his writings in 1689, after the Glorious Revolution. See Walter Rex, "Pierre Bayle: The Theology and Politics of the Article on David," (Part II), *Bibliothèque d'Humanisme et Renaissance* 25, no. 2 (1963): 370.

4 John Marshall, *John Locke, Toleration and Early Enlightenment Culture* (Cambridge: Cambridge University Press, 2006), 688.

5 Raymond Klibansky, preface to *Epistola de Tolerantia / A Letter on Toleration*, by John Locke. Latin text edited by Raymond Klibansky; English translation with an introduction and notes by J.W. Gough (Oxford: Clarendon Press, 1968), xxxv.

6 John Christian Laursen, "Baylean Liberalism: Tolerance Requires Nontolerance," in *Beyond the Persecuting Society: Religious Toleration before the Enlightenment*, ed. John Christian Laursen and Cary J. Nederman (Philadelphia: University of Pennsylvania Press, 1998), 198. See also Sally Jenkinson, "Two Concepts of Tolerance: Or Why Bayle Is Not Locke," *Journal of Political Philosophy* 4, no. 4 (1996): 302–22. Locke and Bayle of course knew each other's work and might have met (on this point, see Bost, *Pierre Bayle*, 176). Locke resided in Rotterdam between 1687 and 1689, and returned to England upon the accession of William and Mary. He lived for one year in the house of the learned merchant Benjamin Furly, a Quaker, a proprietor of an extraordinarily rich library, and the host of the Circle of the Lantern, a gathering of intellectuals which Bayle, who lived nearby, attended occasionally. What we know for sure is that Locke became acquainted with Bayle's work as early as 1682, when Bayle published his first important book, the popular *Various Thoughts on the Occasion of a Comet*; Locke had a copy of this book in his library and made various extracts from it in 1684. He probably read Bayle's *Critique of Maimbourg's History of Calvinism*, also published in 1682, before Locke drafted his own *Epistola de tolerantia* in the winter of 1685–6. Bayle on his part read Locke's *Epistola* sometime before 1702, as is evidenced by a reference to an "anonymous Latin letter" written by "an Englishman" (the margin says "Locke") in the second edition of the *Dictionnaire historique et critique*, under the article "Sainctes."

7 See Jonathan Israel, "The Intellectual Debate about Toleration in the Dutch Republic," in *The Emergence of Tolerance in the Dutch Republic*, ed. C. Berkvens-Stevelinck, J. Israel and G.H.M. Posthumus Meyjes (Leiden: Brill, 1997), 3–36.

8 On Locke's and Bayle's different conversational rules and values, see Marshall's *John Locke, Toleration and Early Enlightenment Culture*, 517–21.

9 Michel Foucault, *The Government of Self and Others II: The Courage of Truth. Lectures at the Collège de France 1983–1984*, ed. Frédéric Gros., trans. Graham Burchell (New York: Picador, 2012).

10 Augustine, *De la tolérance: Commentaire philosophique*, ed. Jean-Michel Gros (Paris: Honoré Champion, 2013), 60. In 1685, a French translation of two of Augustine's letters against the Donatists (letters 93 and 185) was published under the auspices of the Archbishop of Paris and became an official tool of Catholic propaganda. It was entitled *Conformité de la conduite de l'Église de France pour ramener les protestants avec celle de l'Église d'Afrique pour ramener les Donatistes à l'Église catholique*. For a modern translation see *The Works of Saint Augustine: A Translation for the 21st Century*, translation and notes by Roland Teske (Hyde Park, NY: New City Press, 2001–5).

11 I am translating from the 1685 French translation of Augustine (the one that Bayle read), cited in the introduction to Bayle's *De la tolérance: Commentaire philosophique*, 20.

12 Pierre Bayle, *A Philosophical Commentary on These Words of the Gospel, Luke 14. 23, "Compel them to Come In, That My House may be full,"* ed. John Kilcullen and Chandran Kukathas (Indianapolis: Liberty Fund, 2005), part 1, ch. 4, p. 89.

13 The full, uncensored version was published in the appendix. Bayle blamed the editor for that, for the book would not sell without the article restored.

14 Samuel, 13:14. Bayle drew his material from the first three books of Kings.

15 For an in-depth analysis of the theological and political stakes at play in the "David" article (in particular regarding the Calvinist doctrines of justification and sanctification) see the luminous readings by Walter Rex in "Pierre Bayle: The Theology and Politics of the Article on David" (Part I), *Bibliothèque d'Humanisme et Renaissance* 24, no. 1 (1962): 168–89, and "Pierre Bayle: The Theology and Politics of the Article on David" (Part II), *Bibliothèque d'Humanisme et Renaissance* 25, no. 2 (1963): 366–403. See Part II, 396–8, for a discussion of William as the "new David."

16 "If we examine this matter ever so little, we shall find that conscience with regard to each particular man is the voice and the law of God in him, known and acknowledged as such by him who carries this conscience about him: so that to violate this conscience is essentially believing that he violates the law of God." Pierre Bayle, *A Philosophical Commentary*, pt. 1, ch. 6, p. 113. Freedom of conscience is of course also central to Locke's theory of toleration: "No Man can, if he would, conform his Faith to the Dictates of another. All the Life and Power of true Religion consists in the inward and full persuasion of the Mind." John Locke, *A Letter Concerning Toleration* (1689) in *A Letter Concerning Toleration and Other Writings*, ed. Mark Goldie, trans. William Popple, (Indianapolis: Liberty Fund, 2010), 13.

17 See Joanna Picciotto's "Methodist Toleration" in this volume for an example of radical acceptance of religious pluralism that would have been very congenial to Bayle.

18 *A Philosophical Commentary*, pt. 2, ch. 10, p. 265.

19 "Bayle, Enlightenment, Toleration and Modern Western Society" *The Pierre Bayle Lecture*, 2004; http://eamelje.net/texts/israel_pierre_bayle_lecture_2004.pdf.

20 See *Pensées* (1670), article IV. *Des moyens de croire*, Brunschvicg edition (Paris: Garnier, 1964).

21 The question of whether we should tolerate intolerant behaviour and risk the survival of the tolerant society is of course a much-debated paradox. See Karl Popper, *The Open Society and Its Enemies*, vol. 1, 1945; John Rawls, *A Theory of Justice*, 1971; Michael Walzer, *On Toleration*, 1995.

22 "Should people agree in making all the children of a city believe that it was the will of God they should kill all the inhabitants of another city, they would firmly believe it, and never come off of this belief, unless they went through a new course of instruction." *A Philosophical Commentary*, pt. 2, ch. 10, p. 275.

23 *A Philosophical Commentary*, pt. 1, ch. 1, p. 66.

24 *A Philosophical Commentary*, pt. 1, ch. 1, pp. 66–7. Translation modified.

25 See Gianluca Mori, "Conscience et tolérance," in Gianluca Mori, *Bayle Philosophe* (Paris: Honoré Champion, 1999), 273–321.

26 *Réponse aux questions d'un provincial*, 4 vols. (Rotterdam: Reinier Leers, 1704–7), vol. 3, ch. 29, p. 986.

27 Bayle, *Nouvelles lettres de l'auteur de la Critique Générale de l'Histoire du Calvinisme, 1685*, in Bayle, *Oeuvres diverses* (The Hague, 1727–31). Quoted in Gianluca Mori, "Pierre Bayle, the Rights of Conscience, the 'Remedy' of Toleration," *Ratio Juris* 10, no. 1 (March 1997): 46.

28 Rex quotes the influential *La Défense de la Reformation contre le livre intitulé Préjugez légitimes contre les Calvinistes*, by Jean Claude (Rouen: Jean Lucas, 1673), p. 22): "As soon as we try to usher faith in by force, rather than convince, we close the heart to it. Such method may be good, perhaps, in those worldly Empires and Religions that don't care to conquer the spirit, as long as they rule over the body. But it's not the one chosen by Jesus Christ, whose throne is in our consciences." See "Pierre Bayle: The Theology and Politics of the Article on David," pt. 1, p. 182.

29 Rex, "Pierre Bayle: The Theology and Politics of the Article on David," pt. 1, p. 181.

30 Letter of 28 December 1693 in *Dictionnaire historique et critique, La vie de M. Bayle* [by Pierre des Maizeaux], vol. 16 (Paris: Desoer, 1820), 165.

31 Lest we think that the struggle for political power is no longer a concern of modern Churches, see the striking critique that the Catholic priest Antonio Spadaro and the Presbyterian pastor Marcelo Figueroa, two authors close to Pope Francis, have made of American Catholic ultraconservatives for entering into an "alliance of hate" with Evangelical Christians to back President Trump. Spadaro and Figueroa defend the secular state and the peaceful, pastoral role of religion. "Evangelical Fundamentalism and Catholic Integralism: A Surprising Ecumenism," July 2017, *La Civiltà Cattolica* (an online, multilingual journal), July 2017: http://www.laciviltacattolica.it/articolo/evangelical-fundamentalism-and-catholic-integralism-in-the-usa-a-surprising-ecumenism/.

32 Walter Rex, *Essays on Pierre Bayle and Religious Controversy* (The Hague: Martinus Nijhoff, 1965), 79.

33 Marlies Galenkamp, "Locke and Bayle on Religious Toleration," *Erasmus Law Review* 5, no. 1 (2012): 92; and Gianluca Mori, *Bayle Philosophe*, 319.

34 See the *Fourth Clarification on Obscenities*, published in the second edition of the *Dictionnaire Historique et Critique* (1702), as an answer to the criticism the first edition had received. Selections from this text have been published in Pierre Bayle, *Historical and Critical Dictionary, Selections*. Trans. Richard H. Popkin (Indianapolis: Hackett Publishing, 1991), 436–44.

35 Mara Van der Lugt provides a brief but informative discussion of the state of the field in Bayle studies (especially regarding the vexed question of his personal faith or lack thereof) in the introduction to her *Bayle, Jurieu, and the "Dictionnaire Historique et Critique"* (Oxford: Oxford University Press, 2016), 2–14. For a summary

of the "Bayle enigma" (was he an atheist, a deist, a sceptic, a fideist, a Socinian, a liberal Calvinist, a libertine, a Judaizing Christian, a secret Jew, a Manichean?) see https://plato.stanford.edu/entries/bayle/.

36 Lorenzo Valla, *On the Donation of Constantine* (1440), trans. G.W. Bowersock (Cambridge, MA: Harvard University Press, 2008). Carlo Ginzburg sees Valla as an exemplary author uniting successfully rhetoric, the art of the emotions, with reason-driven, erudite proofs. The same could be said of Bayle. See "Lorenzo Valla on the "Donation of Constantine," in Carlo Ginzburg, *History, Rhetoric and Proof* (Hanover: University Press of New England, 1999), 54–70.

37 *A Philosophical Commentary*, pt. 2, ch. 10, p. 273.

38 *A Philosophical Commentary*, pt. 2, ch. 10, p. 273.

39 *A Philosophical Commentary*, pt. 2, ch. 8, p. 221.

40 *A Philosophical Commentary*, pt. 2, ch. 10, p. 256.

41 Locke, *A Letter Concerning Toleration*, 52.

42 See Voltaire's *Dictionnaire philosophique*, s.v. "Athéisme."

43 *Various Thoughts on the Occasion of a Comet*, trans. Robert C. Bartlett (Albany: State University of New York Press, 2000), 221, §178. (The book is divided into paragraphs; I'll be subsequently referring to the paragraphs.)

44 "Mahomet," remark AA. I am quoting from the reliable English translation of the *Dictionnaire* (2nd edition) in 5 volumes (1734–38): *The Dictionary Historical and Critical of Mr. Peter Bayle. Second Edition Carefully collated with the several Editions of the Original; in which many Pages are restored* (London: Printed for J.J. and P. Knapton, D. Midwinter, J. Brotherton [and others] 1737), vol. 4 (M–R), 39.

45 The point is made by Jean-Michel Gros in "L'art d'écrire dans les 'éclaircissements' du *Dictionnaire historique et critique* de Pierre Bayle," *Revue philosophique de la France et de l'étranger* 130 no. 1 (2005): 21–37.

46 *A Letter Concerning Toleration*, 60.

47 *A Letter Concerning Toleration*, 61.

48 *A Letter Concerning Toleration*, 45. "Forum externum" and "forum internum." In French, "for intérieur" is in current use to indicate the judgment of conscience.

49 Bayle often borrows someone else's persona in his works, speaking for instance to his own community in the voice of a Catholic.

50 Michel Foucault, "What Is Critique?" in *The Politics of Truth*, ed. Sylvain Lotringer, trans. Lysa Hochroth and Catherine Porter (New York: Semiotext(e), 2007), 42–3.

6 The Difference Enlightenment Satire Makes to Religion: *Hudibras* to Hebdo

DAVID ALVAREZ

What difference has Enlightenment satire made to religion? And how might this difference both limit and enable our ability to imagine toleration? Juxtaposing the following two quotations opens up some new ways to think about these questions. The first is from Fredric Bogel's book on satiric form, in which he argues that satire works as "a literary mechanism for the production of differences."[1]

> The "first" satiric gesture [...] is not to expose the satiric object in all its alien difference but to *define* it as different, as other. [...] Satire, then, is a rhetorical means to the production of difference in the face of a potentially compromising similarity, not the articulation of differences already securely in place.[2]

The second quotation is from the anthropologist Saba Mahmood, whose work on secularism contends that it is not "natural bedrock" but "a historical product" which cannot be understood simply as "the modern state's retreat from religion":[3]

> secularism has sought not so much to banish religion from the public domain but to reshape the form it takes, the subjectivities it endorses, and the epistemological claims it can make.[4]

The first quotation insists on the productive power of satire to create difference and produce boundaries. The second argues that secularism does not remove but instead reshapes religion. Taken together, they invite us to think about how Enlightenment satires of religion work to produce a secular conception of the felt meaning of "religion." Instead of approaching religious satires as "the articulation of differences already securely in place" between good and bad forms of religion, or between the religious and the secular, we might consider how such works "reshape the form" of religion to construct such differences.

Satire would thus be an important site not only for analysing the "mutual trans-formation and historical emergence" of the religious and the secular but also for thinking about how the contemporary practice of religious satire works to reproduce a modern conception of religion.[5] This would be to consider Enlightenment religious satire not as part of secularization (e.g., the emancipation of humanity from religion) but in relation to the formation of secularity, the historical conditions of possibility that make possible forms of political secularism.[6]

In line with several of the essays in this volume, I am exploring the relationship between the roles that literary works play in promoting religious toleration as an ethical practice and toleration as a form of secular governance and statecraft.[7] How might religious satires in the Enlightenment work to remake religion into forms amenable to secular governance? Pursuing this question can illuminate how the practice of this tradition conditions recent debates, particulary those surrounding the Danish cartoon controversy and the Charlie Hebdo murders. As anyone who has read about these events soon discovered, the analysis of these controversies usually boils down to a rather predictable clash between Muslim objections to blasphemy and the liberal right to freedom of speech – especially the right to satirize religion. What might the study of eighteenth-century satire – especially its analyses of satiric form – contribute to this debate?

Scholarship on Enlightenment religious satire has done little to trouble how these debates are framed in terms of blasphemy vs. free speech. Mahmood's work offers an opportunity to try to think outside of this framework insofar as she argues that to approach the question of the Danish cartoons in such terms is "to accept a set of prior judgments about what kind of injury or offence the cartoons caused and how such an injury might be addressed in a liberal democratic society." For Mahmood, the legal discourses of freedom of speech and religion contain "normative conceptions enfolded" within an unexamined understanding of "what constitutes religion and proper religious subjectivity in the modern world."[8] Defined in terms of belief in creeds, personal choice, interiority, and the symbolic value of images, icons, and signs, this "modern" conception of religion "owes its emergence to the rise of Protestant Christianity and its subsequent globalization."[9]

Mahmood argues that this modern, Protestant definition of religion is presupposed by secular legal discourses, which put in place a kind of cryptonormativity that creates an "inability to understand the sense of injury expressed by so many Muslims" in response to the publication of the Danish cartoons. Indeed, such liberal-secular legal discourses render "religious pain," at best, a contradiction in terms and, at worst, a hypocritical cover for the assertion of power. Tracing this definition of religion back to John Locke's *Letter Concerning Toleration* (1689), Mahmood highlights how Locke's separation of church and state relies upon a conception of "worldly harm" in which legally recognized pain is restricted to harm to one's body or private property. Contending that "for many Muslims, the offense the cartoons committed was not against a moral interdiction ('Thou shalt not make images of Muhammad') but against a structure of affect, a habitus, that feels wounded," the main point of Mahmood's analysis of the Danish cartoon controversy is that the felt meaning of "religion" for Muslims cannot be articulated within the legal framework of blasphemy and freedom of speech in liberal-secular cultures.[10]

The conception of religion that supports this legal framework can be usefully linked to the larger historical development of what Charles Taylor has described as the "buffered self."[11] For Taylor, the disenchanted world of modernity has "important Christian motives" and is achieved largely through a changed understanding of ourselves as beings with a stronger sense of self-possession, a sharper divide between mind and body, and a growing confidence in our power to order the world and ourselves as disciplined, instrumental agents.[12] Instead of being vulnerable to external forces that can invade or possess us, the buffered self has the capacity to take a distance from our feelings, to disengage from outside forces. It is "invulnerable, as master of the meanings of things for it."[13] Proper religious subjectivity is able to distance itself from "religion," which poses no threat to self-possession and is instead, in Locke's words, "the voluntary and secret choice of the mind."[14] For the buffered self, any religion – and religiosity, more generally – is a choice. Linking Taylor's buffered self to Mahmood's conception of a modern, Protestant conception of religion highlights the ethical and other attractions of such a self-understanding as well as the historical formation of modernity's relation to "religion."[15]

What role does Enlightenment satire play in the production and maintenance of such an understanding of religion and the self? Misty Anderson argues that the vitality of graphic satires of religion in the eighteenth-century owes much to the tension between publically circulating images of religion and "the ethos of an increasingly privatized, Protestant spirituality."[16] Her work also suggests that we can bring into better focus the Enlightenment lens through which we see ourselves and others, particularly religious others, by analysing how satire has helped to shape that lens. The focus of my essay is not to explain, as Mahmood does, how Muslims experience religious satire, or to argue that Muslims need to have their own Reformation or Enlightenment. Instead, I am arguing that Enlightenment religious satire contributes to redefining "religion" along modern, Protestant lines. Such an understanding of religion enables liberal forms of secular governance, including religious toleration. Yet in so far as political liberalism relies on a generalized Protestant conception of religion, its ability to do justice to those who do not share this Western tradition seems limited. Mahmood thus urges that "for anyone interested in fostering greater understanding across lines of religious difference it would be important to turn not so much to the law as to the thick texture and traditions of ethical and intersubjective norms that provide the substrate for legal argument."[17] She holds out modest hope for a revision of cultural understandings that would contest the normativity of "religion" as expressed through the power of the law.

One element of the "thick texture and traditions of ethical and intersubjective norms" in modern secular cultures is the tradition of Enlightenment religious satire. From the time of John Dryden's "Discourse Concerning the Original and Progress of Satire" (1693) to the present, the usual answer to the question of what satire is good for is that it aims to make us better people. By exposing and condemning evil, satire reforms its readers. As Alexander Pope explains, "Vice is a monster of so frightful mien, / As, to be hated, needs but to be seen."[18] This understanding of satire as an instrument of moral improvement informs not only scholarly books with limited readership but also more popular accounts. For example, Tim Parks, in a column entitled "The Limits of Satire" published in the *The New York Review of Books* shortly after the Hebdo attacks, explains that satire has a "noble motive: the desire to bring shame on some person or party behaving wrongly or ignorantly."[19] Indeed, according to Parks, satire fails when it "doesn't point toward positive change, or encourage people to think in a more enlightened way." Satire exposes the truth of vice, or, in the case of Enlightenment satires of religion from Voltaire to Hebdo, the truth about religious oppression and violence. Such an understanding of satire obviously champions freedom of speech, since it insists that no matter how ugly or offensive, the truth about the relationship between violence, terrorism, and religion must be stated to advance the emancipation of humanity.

But if reform is the goal of satire, Parks argues that the Hebdo cartoons are clearly satirical failures. They arguably did not work to reform their satiric targets. This failure leads Parks to fall back on another standard way of thinking about the Hebdo cartoons. He distinguishes between "the right to free expression and the sensible use of it." If satire fails to reform, then it's not a "sensible use of it."[20] Perhaps your own experience has been different, but the end result of reading satires in my eighteenth-century courses has, according to Parks's understanding of satire, not been "a sensible use of it." I am sceptical that at the end of my courses on satire my students – I refrain from speculations about my own ethical improvement – have been reformed by the satires we have read. The experience is better captured by Jonathan Swift, who observes in the preface to *The Battle of the Books* (1704) that "[s]atyr is a sort of *Glass*, wherein Beholders do generally discover every body's Face but their Own; which is the chief Reason for that kind Reception it meets in the World, and that so very few are offended with it."[21] And, similarly, in the preface to *A Tale of a Tub* (1704), he comments about satire that "'[t]is but a *Ball* bandied to and fro, and every man carries a *Racket* about Him to strike it from himself among the rest of the Company."[22] Bogel builds upon how Swift theorizes satire in these passages to argue that it is at least as much about the production and policing of identity as it is about making us into better people. Readers of satire usually seek a "self-flattering portrait," and so they identify the object of satire not with themselves but with others.[23] The rhetorical action of satire is thus to move the reader to identify with the satirist and against the object of satiric attack. In so far as the form of satire works to make this difference between the satiric object and the reader, it does not simply denote reality but helps to shape it, both conceptually and affectively. As Bogel argues, satire "is better understood as a literary mechanism for the production of differences in the face of anxiety about replication, identity, sameness, and undifferentiation." Seen in this light, "satire [...] reimpose[s] [...] classifications [...] [It] is a ritual of separation" that creates "powerful acts of rejection and exclusion."[24] In the context of the historical formation of the "secular" and of "religion," Bogel's work on satiric form asks us to consider how Enlightenment satires of religion produce a difference between bad forms of "religion" that are violent and not conducive to secular forms of governance and liberal tolerance and good forms of religion that are. Satire would thus help produce religious subjects proper for secular regimes – though it would usually appear to do so under our cognitive radar.

An especially illuminating example of Enlightenment satire working to put in place a good, "buffered" relation to religion by casting out a bad form of it – one that dispossesses its followers of rationality and agency – appears in the Third Earl of Shaftesbury's defence of religious tolerance in his *Letter Concerning Enthusiasm* (1709). He describes how a satirical puppet show can defuse religious sectarianism and violence by criticizing the persecution of some zealous Huguenots who had fled from France. Such persecution, he contends, will only inflame their zealotry.

> Their own mob [i.e., the Huguenot ministers] are willing to bestow kind blows upon them and fairly stone them now and then in the open street. [...] But how barbarous still and more than heathenishly cruel are we tolerating Englishmen! For, not contented to deny these prophesying enthusiasts the honour of a persecution, we have delivered them over to the cruelest contempt in the world. I am told, for certain, that they are at this very time the subject of a choice droll or puppet-show at Bartholomew Fair. There doubtless their strange voices and involuntary agitations are admirably well acted, by the motion of wires and inspiration of pipes. For the bodies of the prophets in their state of prophecy, being not in their own power but (as they say themselves), mere passive organs, actuated by an exterior force, have nothing natural or resembling real life in any of their sounds or motions, so that how awkwardly soever a puppet show may imitate other actions, it must needs represent this passion to the life. And while Bartholomew Fair is in

possession of this privilege, I dare stand security to our national Church that no sect of enthusiasts, no new venders of prophecy or miracles, shall ever get the start or put her to the trouble of trying her strength with them, in any case.[25]

While their fellow French Huguenots – shaped by an absolutist political regime – want to "stone [the enthusiasts] now and then," and while the Anglican Church is also interested in "trying her strength," the satirical puppet show, Shaftesbury claims, enables the public to regulate itself by giving individuals reason and agency. This agency appears, for example, in the way that Shaftesbury opposes the mechanical prophets to the freedom of the spectators. He figures the bodies of the prophets as "mere passive organs [...] hav[ing] nothing natural or resembling real life." Passive, unnatural, lifeless: the puppets' "involuntary" actions produced by "wires" and "pipes" are able to satirically imitate the enthusiasts' "passion to the life." The enthusiasts are "not in their own power" but are dispossessed of themselves. In contrast, Shaftesbury represents the effects of the satirical puppet show as restoring self-possession: the spectators disidentify with and distance themselves from the lifeless, mechanical behaviour of religious enthusiasts. Both the imagined spectators of the puppet show and the readers of Shaftesbury's account of it learn what it means to be human and not mechanical, a distinction that Shaftesbury links to other important differences – such as peace and violence, reason and emotion, and good and bad religion. Shaftesbury's theory and practice of religious satire convey an implicit understanding of a proper religious subject as buffered, peaceful, cheerful, and in possession of itself. In this passage, satire is clearly making many significant differences.

At the same time, however, satire is a sure thing for Shaftesbury: he is willing to "stand security" to the state church that religious satires like the puppet show will quell sectarianism better than religious persecution. This representation of the effects of satire in terms of freedom and self-possession, however, is strangely at odds with how the passage represents the action of satire. First, Shaftesbury's appeal to and description of these entertainments demonstrate his trust in the coercive power of wit and raillery. For if satire is to prove more reliable than state-authorized persecution and violence, these spectators – and Shaftesbury's readers – must also be mechanically moved. In so far as it urges us to reject a painful identification with the satiric object and to indulge the pleasure of identifying with the satirist, the form of satire works upon us prior to self-reflection. In Bogel's words, satire can thus function as "the mechanical application of values that we do not so much hold as are held by."[26] There is thus a tension between Shaftesbury's claims about satire's emancipatory power and the rhetorical action of satirical form, a tension between the autonomy of spectators and readers and Shaftesbury's confidence in the power of satirical puppet shows to put us in possession of ourselves.

For Bogel, the form of satire not only works to make a difference but does so "in the face of a potentially compromising similarity" that is *not alien enough.*"[27] In the above passage from Shaftesbury, both satire and the religious enthusiasm it seeks to reform threaten a self in full possession of itself. If Enlightenment satires of religion seek to construct and protect a "buffered" religious subject, the form of satire itself points to some shared features between bad religion and satire. Both have the power to breach a buffered self. Shaftesbury's text, however, acknowledges such power only in relation to bad religion. As John Modern observes, "Earnest celebrations of the buffer[ed self] make it incredibly difficult to sustain conversations about the ways in which the self is subject to the agencies of the object-world, to history, to strangers and expertly branded institutions, to forces that do not announce themselves as such."[28] Satire is one such force.

It is a commonplace to note the construction of religion in relation to legal discourse in politically liberal regimes (e.g., in order to maintain the separation of church and state, courts must define what is and is not religion).[29] Religious satire, however, can also perform the same function, though more subtly and with powerful affective investments. The construction of such a conception of religion is not just a matter of statecraft, not simply the exercise of legal power in pursuit of the safety and security of the state; it is also a matter of literary practice and disciplinary power. In short, perhaps we should approach Enlightenment satires of religion, in some respect, as rituals of separation through which the felt meaning of "religion" in secular cultures is partly constructed.[30]

Yet if Shaftesbury's satire constructs a particular conception of religion in terms of self-possession, choice, and what he would call "good humour," an analysis of satiric form can make this process visible. As Swift's satire of readers of satires as self-interested reveals, the form can call attention to itself. By doing so, it can provoke us to reflect on the judgments satire asks us to make and the boundaries it attempts to draw. It can push us to "meditate on the problematic intricacies of identification and difference by which we define our own identities and our relation to others."[31] Formal analyses of Enlightenment religious satires, therefore, offer us the possibility of seeing how such works contribute to tacitly organizing the "specific historical schemes" through which "religion" is experienced "prior to any possibility of judgment."[32] By revealing how these "taken-for-granted categorical schemes" shape our "affective and evaluative response" in the dominant, secular Euro-Atlantic context, it becomes possible to recognize the cultural limits of these frameworks and their dependency on formative practices such as satire.[33]

This claim about the relationship between the practice of religious satire and secularism as a discipline finds further support in the ur-text of English Enlightenment religious satires, Samuel Butler's *Hudibras* (1662–78). Perhaps the most-read poem in the second half of the seventeenth century, it resonates with our own historical moment not only because of its concern with religion and violence but also because of the way it contributes to the enduring historical framework within which we understand their relationship. Relying on and extending Protestant efforts to dematerialize religion, the poem helps put in place a modern understanding of religion in terms of interiority and symbolic meanings, and it cultivates a buffered self for both ethical and political ends. At the same time, the poem generates a number of paradoxes through its efforts to limit the proper agency of words to their meanings, paradoxes that highlight the difficulty of fully distinguishing the materiality of words from their meaning.[34]

The poem opens with violence, religion, ignorance, hard words, and various forms of confusion.

> When *civil* Fury first grew high,
> And men fell out they knew not why;
> When hard words, *Jealousies* and *Fears*,
> Set Folks together by the ears,
> And made them fight, like mad or drunk,
> For Dame *Religion* as for Punk,
> Whose honesty they all durst swear for,
> Though not a man of them knew wherefore:
> When *Gospel-trumpeter*, surrounded
> With long-ear'd rout, to Battel sounded,
> And Pulpit, Drum Ecclesiastick,
> Was beat with fist, instead of a stick. (I.i.1–12)[35]

The lines mix low and high diction, incongruously juxtaposing "Folks," "rout," and "Punk" with the elevated diction of "*civil* Fury," "Battel sounded," and "Dame religion" (I.i.1, I.i.4, I.i.6, I.i.10). This confusion is perhaps also played out in the irony of the first line's "high," which could mean both "extreme and violent" and "exalted and honourable" (I.i.1). The key confusions are about "religion," which cannot be distinguished from a prostitute ("Punk") and – when the Gospel and pulpit sound for battle – also exceeds its proper moral and political bounds. For the religion depicted in these lines, sound overtakes the meaning of words and of human agency. It is "hard words" that have agency; they set "Folks together by the ears" (I.i.3–4). These ears are picked up again in "long-ear'd rout," a repetition that connects bad religion to hearing but not understanding (I.i.10). The "rout" hear and are passionately moved to violence through language as mere sound – the word of the Gospel is reduced to the sound of a trumpet; the pulpit delivers not a text or a sermon but a violent "beat" to imitate (I.i.10, I.i.12). The "long-ear'd rout" do not have ears to hear and understand but only to hear and be acted upon (I.i.10). The ambiguity in the literal and figurative meanings of "Battel sounded" drives home the mindlessness of this fury: it is not only a call to arms but in a more literal sense a description of "Battel" caused by sound (I.i.10). These lines claim that instead of understanding, religion offers the irrational spell of "hard words"; instead of liberating, religion dispossesses us of freedom and drives us to violence (I.i.3). Overall, the passage contends for containments: religion should not lead to violence, words should communicate meanings not passions, and the materiality of words should be subordinate to their meaning. We should base our actions on those meanings; otherwise, we act as if "mad or drunk," and true religion cannot be identified (I.i.5). The differences that Butler's satire of religion makes in these lines – differences between the reasonable and the fanatical, meanings and bodies, self-possession and dispossession, and the peaceful and the violent – are perhaps so familiar that we might be tempted to claim, like the editor of the modern scholarly edition of the poem, that the satirical representation of religion in *Hudibras* simply relies on principles of "practical, empirical common sense" (xxix).

But perhaps one might feel this way because we live in a world partly formed by Enlightenment satires and their construction of religion. A more recent analysis of the poem by Blanford Parker gives Butler credit for helping to construct "religion" as a category: "He was in a sense an early anthropologist" because it was his "genius to discover the underlying likeness between all the varieties of religious imagination."[36] Parker, however, does not celebrate Butler's genius. Instead he criticizes it as part of a vicious, impoverishing march towards the secular in which Augustan poetics disenchants the world, destroys the rich poetic practices of the baroque, and establishes a "rhetoric of exclusion" characterized by "portraits of dissenters, Catholics, and even Anglicans as the moral freaks of the Age." Appearing with "the contorted smile of the sober gentleman thrust among the mad," the sane satirist is separated, in Parker's account, from the religious madness he stands above, and the poem invites us to align ourselves with this representation of a rational, self-controlled, and smiling buffered self.[37] If *Hudibras* is making a difference to religion through a rhetoric of exclusion that casts out the poem's satiric objects from "common sense" as mad, stupid, and incapable of debate, then we could see the poem as seeking to manage religion by privatizing it and excluding it from a rational public sphere: it does not "admit the possibility of a rational interlocutor."[38] For Parker, the instrument of this process of secularization is empiricist epistemology. And while he sees this as aesthetically, ethically, and politically impoverishing, it is also the usual way of thinking about the rise of religious toleration: the privatization of religion allows for the eventual separation of church and state that makes possible the practice of religious tolerance.

For both Parker and the modern editor of *Hudibras*, John Wilders, the poem contributes to the process of secularization – whether commonsensical or lamentable – by appealing either to empirical common sense or to the discovery of an "empirical poetics, an original literalism."[39] In both accounts, the rise of modern science is the motor driving secularization. This is a familiar story that primarily treats modernity as a response to epistemological changes. It is also now a very contested story, and one task for eighteenth-century literary studies might be to reorient our understanding of the development of "poetic literalism" from an exclusively epistemological account to one that recognizes the role played by Protestant efforts to disenchant the world and promote a particular kind of ethical and political subject. Such an effort might also do more to help us think about how the practice of Enlightenment satire has shaped modernity in ways that limit how we can imagine religious toleration.

And, after all, Butler's poetics seem motivated not by science but by something else. If the poem opens with the claim that the agents of the civil war did not understand why they were fighting – "When civil Fury first grew high, / And men fell out they knew not why" (I.i.1–2) – the poem links this ignorance to a misunderstanding about the agency of words, a misunderstanding that requires a reformed understanding of religion in order to be corrected. The poem explains religious violence as the result of an incomplete reform of religion.

> For he was of that stubborn Crew
> Of Errant Saints, whom all men grant
> To be the true Church *Militant*;
> Such as do build their Faith upon
> The holy Text of *Pike* and *Gun*;
> Decide all Controversies by
> Infallible *Artillery;*
> And prove their Doctrine Orthodox
> By Apostolic *Blows* and *Knocks*;
> Call *Fire* and *Sword* and *Desolation,*
> *A godly-thorough-reformation,*
> Which always must be carry'd on,
> And still be doing, never done:
> As if Religion were intended
> For nothing else but to be mended. (I.i.187–204)

As in the previous passage, the lines lament and criticize the ubiquitous failure to distinguish between immaterial meanings and bodies: words vs. pike and gun, doctrine orthodox vs. blows and knocks, controversies vs. artillery. This inability to properly police the boundary between words and things, meanings and violent actions, is linked to Roman Catholicism through allusions to saints, infallibility, and apostolic succession.[40]

Yet if an insufficiently reformed understanding of religion is the problem, reform is also represented as its cause, as summed up in the couplet: "Call

Fire and *Sword* and *Desolation*, / *A godly-thorough-reformation*" (I.i.199–200). Reform is a problem in so far as its religious motivation and energy exceed the bounds of religion. If reform leaps the bounds between words and actions, religion and society, Butler seeks to contain and redirect its energies by delimiting "religion." The poem pursues reform by trying to reform reform. It frequently criticizes reform as a ubiquitous and endless project. There is "A strange harmonious inclination / Of all degrees to Reformation" (I.ii.55–4).[41] He claims it is a betrayal of England, since it is pursued "According to the Purest mode / Of Churches, best Reform'd abroad," and describes it in strikingly similar terms to the poem's opening equation of religion and ignorance: "For when we swore to carry on / The present *Reformation* [...] What did we else but make a vow / To doe we know not what, nor how?" (I.ii.641–2, I.ii.644–5). Ultimately, unreformed reform leads to destruction: "Unless the *Work* be carry'd on / In the same way they have begun, / By setting Church and Common-weal / All on a flame bright as their zeal" (I.ii.604–8). The ambiguity between a figurative and literal "flame" in that last line – like the transgressions elsewhere between religion as mental meaning and religion as body – suggests that the real work of reform remains urgent, since reformers still fail to treat religion in terms of signs and meanings and not literal burnings.

As we have seen, the poem's criticisms and investment in religious reform appear in the character of Hudibras himself, who is against reform but is a reformer. His first adventure is to rescue a bear from bear-baiting: "For if *Bear-baiting* we allow, / What good can *Reformation* doe?" (I.ii.518). The irony in this question implies that this particular effort at reform is misdirected. It is Hudibras himself who most needs reform. He is relentlessly satirized for substituting the physical for the spiritual. His carnal appetites appear abundantly, not least in the "Pack / Of his own Buttocks on his back: Which now had almost got the upper- / Hand of his Head" and which balance "A *Paunch* of the same bulk before" (I.i.289–92, I.i.294). Self-interested and hypocritical, Hudibras is interested only in motes in the eyes of others.

But most importantly, the poem carries on the work of iconoclasm by satirizing those who approach words in terms of their materiality and rhetorical force instead of their dematerialized meanings. Butler's poetics seem animated less by empiricist epistemology than by the moral energy and the politics enabled by the semiotic ideology that was part of Protestant religious reform.[42] To give one more example of many lines that depict Hudibras and his followers as dupes of language's materiality, consider Hudibras's mastery of classical languages: "'tis known he could speak Greek, / As naturally as Pigs squeak: / That *Latin* was no more difficile, / Then to a Blackbird 'tis to whistle" (I.i.51–4). Greek and Latin are just so much animal noise, which is produced "naturally" – suggesting both effortlessness and the absence of intention. Like the pigs and the blackbird, Hudibras does not understand what he speaks and is not in control of what he says. Elsewhere we're told that "he could not ope / His mouth, but out there flew a Trope" (I.i.82–3). Like Greek and Latin, tropes come to Hudibras "naturally" without his control or understanding. This passivity before language extends to the crowds he addresses. The spell of words and political oppression are neatly linked, for "when with hasty noise he spoke'em, / The Ignorant for currant took'em" (I.i.113–14). Pronouncing Greek and Latin words is satirized as an empty ritual before such crowds, and the reformer Hudibras appears as a priest who continues to practise his own form of hocus pocus. The poem extends Protestant criticisms of Roman Catholic fetishism by extending iconoclasm to words: Butler criticizes both the Presbyterian Hudibras and his squire Ralpho, an Independent, as enthusiasts who treat words as magical instead of meaningful.

Poetry, however, is enmeshed in and enabled by the nonsemantic elements of language, so how we can we understand *Hudibras*'s embrace of the semiotic ideology of Protestantism? Given the workings of satiric form, the proximity of the poem to what it satirizes is not especially surprising. As Bogel points out, you can't be an apple if you're going to call the kettle black. This is because "the pot earns the right to call the kettle black by being closely enough related to it [...] where as [an] apple is another kind of thing."[43] That is, satiric form begins with a shared connection, a threatening proximity. Perhaps the most obvious example of this – and a typically disturbing feature of satire – is the poem's rather rabid moral certitude. If the poem declares that fanatics believe that "All Piety consists therein / In them, in other men all Sin," we may wonder whether the satire is simply reversing this fanatical judgment by claiming that not in the sane narrator and not in sane readers like you and me but "in other men all Sin" (I.i.221–2).

Such moral discomfort may also put us in mind of other discomforts caused by the poem. Consider, for example, its outrageous rhymes. They are either cheap – "wit / it," "Fowl / Owl," "smatter / matter," "Ass / Hudibras" (39–40) – or absurd – "Ecclesiastic / a stick," "philosopher / gloss over" (I.i.751–2; 73–4; 185–6; 39–40; 11–12; 127–8). They are often conspicuously feminine rhymes. The poem constantly criticizes those who mistake materiality for meaning, and yet the poem foregrounds the materiality of words through its conspicuous rhyming. In fact, the poem hails rhyme as productive: "For Rhyme the Rudder is of verses / With which like ships they stear their courses" (I.i.457–8). As Butler elsewhere explains:

> But those that write in Rhime, still make
> The one *Verse*, for the others sake:
> For, one for *Sense*, and one for *Rhime*,
> I think's sufficient at one time. (II.i.27–30)

The agency of the materiality of words is here acknowledged and celebrated. Through rhyme, the poem seems to rely on the "noise" that it decries. This is also apparent in its endless puns and delight in obscure terminology. Its form and diction are always calling attention to the materiality of language – though not only in ways that highlight loss of agency and duplicity. After all, if Hudibras "could not ope / His mouth, but out there flew a Trope" (I.i.82–3), then what about the poem? Indeed, what would nontropological poetry be? Butler's poem certainly does not eschew the use of figures. In response to a challenge from Hudibras to "prove / *Bear-baiting* equal / With *Synods*," Ralpho eloquently denounces Presbyterianism through a powerful series of figures, a denunciation that the poem doesn't criticize as an abuse of language but instead endorses (I.iii.1085–6).

So one threatening proximity between the poem and what it satirizes appears in the materiality of language, which this satire both decries and relies upon. The poem's efforts to distinguish between good and bad religion based on a distinction between the materiality of language and its immaterial meanings depends upon the materiality of language and the productivity of tropes. It also depends, of course, on the force of satiric form. As Webb Keane observes, the dematerialization of religion in Protestantism requires for its dissemination that it be "embedded in pervasive practical disciplines."[44] The practice of Enlightenment religious satires is one of these disciplines. Keane also highlights the paradoxical relationship that Protestant semiotic ideology has to the material forms and practices through which it is disseminated. However committed it is to a dematerialized religion, even Protestantism circulates "by means of concrete practices such as [...] sermons, prayers, hymns, scripture reading," and published texts. Butler's poem finds in this paradox a wellspring of energies for attacking this same paradox, which necessarily remains unresolved. In this – and perhaps in other Enlightenment satires of religion as well – there is an attempt, in Keane's words, "To master an otherwise unmasterable ambiguity."[45]

What might be some further implications of an approach to Enlightenment satires of religion that attends to the paradoxes of the semiotic ideology of Protestantism and the operations of satiric form? In Mahmood's analysis of the construction of "religion as belief," she highlights how it rejects the ritualistic, community-binding, and affective elements of religion in favour of a more Protestant understanding of religion as choice and symbol. Are Enlightenment satires of religion one site where these elements are displaced? Satire appears to pick up and perhaps in some sense replace and re-enact these aspects of religion that satire distinguishes from true "religion as belief." To what extent can we understand the rise of religious satire in English literature from 1660–1750 as in some ways filling in the gap of what was lost in the course of the Protestant Reformation and Catholic Counter-Reformation? Enlightenment satire would thus be a kind of spilled Catholicism or, more precisely, the negation of the negation of Roman Catholicism.

To put this point somewhat differently, by examining the difference that satire makes between good and bad religion, is it possible to see Enlightenment religious satire as a ritual enactment of European trauma over its wars of religion, a trauma that such satires reinvoke and seek to separate themselves from by casting off past violence as a result of bad religion? Perhaps Enlightenment satires of religion should not be seen as revealing the eternal "truth" of religion but rather as a kind of formative practice, as a tradition or disciplinary discourse that contributes to the construction of a virtuous, buffered, properly religious subject. By carefully attending to satiric form, we can better understand the historical formation of the conceptual and affective frameworks of the "felt meaning" of religion for secular people. Extending the energies of Protestant reform, Enlightenment satire constructs "religion" in ways that enable Christians to tolerate religious difference. It can do so, however, in a universalizing way that disavows its implicit, culturally specific religious understandings and affects. The historical distance of *Hudibras* and a formalist approach make it easier to perceive this cultural specificity.

Finally, such an approach might help us to think about the Danish cartoon controversy and the Hebdo murders in a different framework than that of blasphemy and the right to free speech. If Enlightenment religious satire is a tradition of ethical formation and a form of disciplinary power, what happens when these satires no longer address the conception of religion that has been formed by this tradition?[46] We might perhaps better understand an element of the causes of the Charlie Hebdo attack by considering it as, in part, the result of a combination of the powerful, identity-producing aspects of the tradition of Enlightenment satires of religion in politically liberal societies with a religious tradition that has not been similarly trained into a politicized conception of "religion as belief." Might this not exacerbate public expressions of resentment and violence instead of assuaging and containing them? If the tradition of Enlightenment religious satire has helped to produce and maintain a particular form of religious subject and felt meaning of religion in which an Islamic structure of affect does not fit, then satire restricts the practice of toleration. Accordingly, analysing the extent to which the legal framework of free speech and blasphemy has been historically constructed through the practice of Enlightenment satires of religion (i.e., by helping to produce a subject amenable to such forms of governance) is one way to begin to think about toleration beyond this framework.

If, as Mahmood contends, "the future of the Muslim minority in Europe depends not so much on how secular-liberal protocols of free speech might be expanded to accommodate" the concerns of this minority but "on a larger transformation of the cultural and ethical sensibilities of the Judeo-Christian population that undergird the cultural practices of secular-liberal law," then perhaps one way to a make a small contribution to such a change is through the practice of formalist literary criticism of religious satire.[47] By reflecting on the difference that Enlightenment satire makes to religion, such an approach might improve our historical self-understanding, making it possible for us to see more clearly our own secular, collectively myopic lens of good "religion" and perhaps enabling us to feel differently towards others who do not share it. If, in Bogel's terms, we could read satire to contest the categorical distinction between the religious and the secular, in such a case, perhaps satire could begin to move us towards a reimagining of what "tolerance" could henceforth be.[48]

NOTES

1 Fredric Bogel, *The Difference Satire Makes: Rhetoric and Reading from Jonson to Byron* (Ithaca: Cornell University Press, 2001), 21.

2 Ibid., 42.

3 Saba Mahmood, *Religious Difference in a Secular Age: A Minority Report* (Princeton: Princeton University Press, 2016), 3. Cf. Charles Taylor's critique of accounts of secularization as "subtraction stories" in *A Secular Age* (Cambridge, MA: Belknap Press of Harvard University Press, 2007), 26–9, 570–9.

4 Saba Mahmood, "Secularism, Hermeneutics, and Empire: The Politics of Islamic Reformation," Public Culture 18, no. 2 (2006), 326.

5 Saba Mahmood, "Religious Reason and Secular Affect: An Incommensurable Divide?" in *Is Critique Secular? Blasphemy, Injury, and Free Speech* (Berkeley: University of California Press, 2009), 64.

6 On the distinction between secularization and secularity, see the "Editor's Introduction" in *Varieties of Secularism in a Secular Age*, ed. Michael Warner, Jonathan VanAntwerpen, and Craig Calhoun (Cambridge, MA: Harvard University Press, 2013), 4–5, 9–10.

7 See, for example, the essays by Sharon Achinstein, Humberto Garcia, and Corrinne Harol in this volume. See also Alison Conway and Corrinne Harol, "Toward a Postsecular Eighteenth Century," *Literature Compass* 12, no. 11 (2015): 566. Here Conway and Harol call for more work along these lines: "We argue that because of this deep collaboration between literature and secularity, literature may reveal most clearly how theological and religious formations interact with secular institutions in Enlightenment and post-Enlightenment England." One effect of this work by literary scholars is to bridge the gap between Taylor's interest in secularity as the ground for individual spiritual and ethical concerns and Talal Asad's and Mahmood's focus on how secularity enables forms of political secularism.

8 Mahmood, "Religious Reason," 67.

9 Ibid., 67, 66, 72.

10 Ibid., 68, 81–2, 78.

11 Charles Taylor, *A Secular Age* (Cambridge, MA: Belknap Press of Harvard University Press, 2007), 27; cf. 29–41, 131–42, 300–7.

12 Ibid., 26.

13 Ibid., 38.

14 John Locke, "Essay Concerning Toleration (1689)," in *Essay Concerning Toleration and Other Writings on Law and Politics, 1667–1683*, ed. John R. Milton (Oxford: Oxford University Press, 2010), 34.

15 This is partly to historicize Bogel's claims about satire's capacity to satisfy the desire for an integral self, which he approaches largely through psychoanalytic theory.

16 Misty G. Anderson, "Unholy Laughter," *Eighteenth-Century Fiction* 26, no. 4 (2014): 738.

17 Mahmood, "Religious Reason," 89.

18 Alexander Pope, *Essay on Man*, ed. John Butt (London: Methuen, 1967), 2.217–18.

19 Tim Parks, "The Limits of Satire," *The New York Review of Books Daily*, 6 January 2015.

20 Ibid.

21 Jonathan Swift, *A Tale of a Tub to Which is Added The Battle of the Books and the Mechanical Operation of the Spirit*, 2nd ed., ed. A.C. Guthkelch (Oxford: Clarendon Press, 1958), 215.

22 Ibid., 52.

23 Frederic Bogel, *The Difference Satire Makes*, 65.

24 Ibid., 21, 43, 57.

25 Anthony Ashley Cooper Shaftesbury, *Characteristics of Men, Manners, Opinions, Times*, ed. Lawrence E. Klein (Cambridge: Cambridge University Press, 1999), 15–16.

26 Frederic Bogel, *The Difference Satire Makes*, 81.

27 Ibid., 42, 41.

28 John Lardas Modern, "Confused Parchments, Infinite Socialities," accessed 6 April 2018, https://tif.ssrc.org/2013/03/04/confused-parchments-infinite-socialities/. For other examples of how the process of disenchantment relies on "forces that impinge on subjects and condition them in ways they do not control," see John Modern, *Secularism in Antebellum America: With Reference to Ghosts, Protestant Subcultures, Machines, and Their Metaphors; Featuring Discussions of Mass Media, Moby-Dick, Spirituality, Phrenology, Anthropology, Sing State Penitentiary, and Sex with the New Motive Power* (Chicago: University of Chicago Press, 2015).

29 See, for example, Michael Allan's *In the Shadow of World Literature: Sites of Reading in Colonial Egypt* (Princeton: Princeton University Press, 2016), 10.

30 On satire and ritual see Robert C. Elliott's *The Power of Satire: Magic, Ritual, Art* (Princeton: Princeton University Press, 1960); Bogel, *The Difference Satire Makes*, 29, 43, 73.

31 Bogel, *The Difference Satire Makes*, 47.

32 Judith Butler, "The Sensibility of Critique: Response to Asad and Mahmood," in *Is Critique Secular? Blasphemy, Injury, and Free Speech* (Berkeley: University of California Press, 2009), 115.

33 Ibid.

34 On this, see Webb Keane, *Christian Moderns: Freedom and Fetish in the Mission Encounter* (Berkeley: University of California Press, 2007), 3–6, 59–72.

35 Samuel Butler, *Hudibras*, ed. John Wilders (Oxford: Clarendon Press, 1967).

36 Blanford Parker, *The Triumph of Augustan Poetics* (Cambridge: Cambridge University Press, 1998), 33. It would be more accurate to say that this is the genius of Protestantism. Ashley Marshall also highlights how Butler redefines religion in *Hudibras* by conflating Presbyterians with Independents in order to support Anglican Royalists in *The Practice of Satire in England*, 1658–1770 (Baltimore: Johns Hopkins University Press), 93.

37 Parker, *The Triumph of Augustan Poetics*, 27, 26.

38 Ibid., 45.

39 Ibid., 36.

40 Cf. Parker's discussion of the poem's criticism of Roman Catholicism in *The Triumph of Augustan Poetics*, 37–41.

41 Taylor, in *A Secular Age*, suggests that "what is peculiar to Latin Christendom is a growing concern with Reform, a drive to make over the whole society to higher standards" (63).

42 On the semiotic ideology of Protestantism see Keane, *Christian Moderns*, 16–21.

43 Bogel, *The Difference Satire Makes*, 32.

44 Keane, *Christian Moderns*, 67–8.

45 Ibid., 69. Cf. Anderson's argument that the "Protestant thrust of modernity thus gave visual satires on religious subjects fresh vigour" (742).

46 On the usefulness of thinking about disciplinary power and tradition together, see David Scott, "Appendix: The Trouble of Thinking: An Interview with Talal Asad" in *Powers of the Secular Modern: Talal Asad and His Interlocutors*, ed. David Scott and Charles Hirschkind (Stanford: Stanford University Press, 2006), 286–90.

47 Mahmood, "Religious Reason," 89.

48 Bogel, *The Difference Satire Makes*, 81.

7 Daniel Defoe and the Geopolitics of Islamic Toleration

HUMBERTO GARCIA

They are greatly mistaken, who think the Affairs of the [Ottoman] Port have not their Influence on these Parts of the World where I dwell; they who plac'd me here, who are now shining in the Garden of Beauty, had other Notions, or they would not have obliged me to reside here so many Years.[1]

Daniel Defoe, *A Continuation of Letters Written by a Turkish Spy at Paris*

The Ottoman military incursion into central Europe posed a greater threat to Protestant Britain's pluralist state than Catholic France, so warned Daniel Defoe in *A Continuation of Letters Written by a Turkish Spy at Paris* (1718). In this satire, persecuted Christians who flee to infidel lands for political asylum relive the dreadful memory of Ottoman troops marching to the gates of Vienna in 1683, backed by Protestant Hungarians fighting Catholic-Austrian persecution in their homeland. For Defoe, the failed siege of Vienna epitomizes the geopolitics of Islamic toleration: the Turkish policy of protecting Protestants undermined Hapsburg rule, facilitating France's expansionist agenda. In the cynical voice of a "Turkish Spy" who has lived undercover in Paris for over forty-five years, Defoe attacks Protestant extremists in Hungary and Britain whom he holds responsible for abetting the Turco-French takeover of Europe.

A Continuation ponders British nationality through a Muslim writing letters to Ottoman officials, family, and friends, which resonates with Defoe's interest in Ibn Tufayl's *Hayy ibn Yaqdhan*: a twelfth-century Islamic-Arabic fiction that influenced latter novels – most notably, *Robinson Crusoe*. Because the geopolitical history of religious toleration that motivated the English novelist's initial foray into "Ottoman cosmopolitanism" has yet to be examined,[2] rather than treating *A Continuation* as a precursor to his bestselling novels, in this essay, I locate its roots in Defoe's journalism and Giovanni Paolo Marana's Italian fiction *L'Esploratore Turco e le di lui relazioni segrete alla Porta Ottomana* – both fixated on a resilient Ottoman Empire. Though reflecting British ambivalence towards the "terrible Turks,"[3] *A Continuation* is more prone, I argue, to examining the precarious international relations between Britain and rival European states than positing an orientalist contrast between Eastern and Western civilizations.[4] This satire castigates pro-Hungarian English Dissenters and Whigs for their shortsighted tolerationist politics, while exalting the Ottomans as models for the centralized fiscal-military state Britain aspired to become. This process of differentiation and identification is constitutive of the enemy-friend distinction that, for Carl Schmitt and Giorgio Agamben, predisposes absolutist-monarchal and liberal-constitutional modes of governance to a sovereign power that decides unilaterally to wage war against those whom it deems unfit for toleration – for Defoe, the Protestant Turcophile enemy who threatens the British state internally and externally.[5]

At the core of Defoe's ambivalent treatment of the Ottoman Empire, then, lies an anxiety about the historical significance of the 1688 "Glorious Revolution" for Britain's transformation into a tolerant imperial state, which, paradoxically, monopolized violence against the religious minorities it was supposed to protect. The year 1688 was meant to resolve Britain's religious and political crises with the passage of the Toleration Act in May 1689, halting King James II's plan to remodel the state after France's Catholic absolutism and empowering his Protestant successors, King William III and Queen Mary. Their ascendency to the British throne consolidated Anglo-Dutch overseas trading against a hostile French empire that – in alliance with the Ottomans – threatened the established pattern of trade, finance, and diplomacy in Europe.[6] With William III's remaking of Britain into a powerful fiscal-military empire, the Toleration Act was "bound intimately to matters of statecraft."[7] Broadly designed to forestall a Jacobite counterrevolution backed by the French and appease William III's Catholic allies – namely, the Austrian Hapsburgs – the Act protected, regulated, and partially incorporated Christian dissidents in order to project an international image of a pluralist Britain untainted by Europe's religious wars. The Toleration Act enforced the Corporation (1662) and Test (1673) Acts barring Catholics and Protestant Dissenters from holding public offices, obtaining legal preferment, and earning university degrees from Oxford and Cambridge. Some Dissenters, however, were exempted from statute penalties and allowed to worship privately, conditional on taking a series of oaths meant to strengthen the Anglican regime. Defoe traces this "first modern revolution" to an absolute Ottoman governmentality that Britain should emulate in order to defeat its domestic and foreign enemies. He sees the Islamic state as antithetical to trade and economic development yet astute in disciplining populations and managing territories through the legal regulation of nonconforming faiths.[8]

Aware that the political economies of the Ottoman Levant and the Atlantic states – Britain, France, and the Netherlands – were integrated to facilitate intercultural encounters and exchanges since the early 1600s,[9] Defoe identifies the revolutionary years of 1683–88 as the birth of a fragile European order in which warring sovereigns maintained their territorial integrity by pursuing toleration as, to quote Wendy Brown, "a practice of governmentality" that "fashions, regulates, and positions subjects, citizens, and states."[10] Such was the case in tolerant Muslim empires before the advent of European and U.S. liberal democracies in the nineteenth century.[11] The Ottoman Empire made the Quranic injunction to protect the Peoples of the Book – Jews and Christians – integral to its assimilationist imperial program; *dhimmis* lived in semi-autonomous communities after paying a poll tax that qualified them for civil and administrative positions. Especially by the 1680s, this program served to pacify dissidents, convert them to the sultan's reformed version of Islam, and extend hegemonic rule in Europe.[12] *A Continuation* therefore challenges the myth of the Pax Ottomanica: an exceptional Muslim empire that grants religious minorities more peace and freedom than that provided by intolerant Christian governments. Although this myth has basis in historical fact, Defoe satirizes Protestant contemporaries who treat Islamic toleration as a universal virtue unmoored from the geopolitics that condition its felt meanings. That some historians continue to think about Islamic toleration in this depoliticized sense underscores how Defoe's critical views on international relations are germane to twenty-first-century debates about Islam and the European Enlightenment.[13]

For Defoe, the tolerant Ottoman Empire's perceived exceptionality is the historical source of Protestant Europe's political woes and a rhetorical resource for redrawing social boundaries within a split Christendom. Although the state ultimately decides which religious minorities should be protected, this decision acquires ideological coherence through the imaginative literature produced in this period, particularly satire. By the late seventeenth century, this genre greatly influenced thinking about the Toleration Act's secular politics beyond the Lockean paradigm of privatized religious belief.[14] I argue that Defoe's satire on a beleaguered Protestant Reformation inverts the relationship between inside and outside, us and them, and friend and enemy in order to uphold William III's victorious legacy, normalizing Britain's geopolitical rise in the early 1800s as the new state of exception. My interpretation of *A Continuation* builds on David Alvarez's theorization of Enlightenment satires of religion in this volume, inspired by Fredric Bogel's work – namely, in that the affective logic of the *Turkish Spy* letters, from Marana to Defoe, is to posit a reformed Christian subject amenable to secular forms of tolerant governance, a drastic reconfiguration of sovereign power in which those previously deemed the enemies (Ottoman Muslims) and friends (Protestant Dissenters and Hungarians) of Christendom switch places. The British ambivalence towards the Ottomans – both a threat to and a model for modern imperialism – expressed in Defoe's satiric writings registers rhetorically "the production of difference in the face of potentially compromising similarity."[15] In *A Continuation*, the subject's rational self-possession is ruptured less by its proximity to intolerant others – the militant Turks and their Christian allies – than by a connected history of confessional empire-building wherein a good Christian toleration is differentiated from its bad, if uncannily similar, Muslim counterpart. Hence, *A Continuation* does not satirize pre-existing divisions among religious communities but rather invents these divisions by making imaginable what Schmitt calls the *Jus Publicum Europaeum*: a situation in which contending, European states achieved mutual recognition in the seventeenth and eighteenth centuries by displacing the violence of civil wars onto controlled territorial conflicts among Christian sovereigns, making the question of who should be tolerated and who should be persecuted or killed central to international law.[16] In Defoe's satire, an open-minded Ottoman agent, Mahmut, invests this question with political urgency in regard to his narrow-minded partisans, Hungarian and English Protestants whose anti-Christian rebellions demarcate the external/ internal line of enmity. Defoe thereby distinguishes himself (and his readers) geopolitically from Whig and Dissenting friends-turned-enemies, condemning Ottoman toleration for its violent expulsions yet harnessing its power to transform Britain into an acceptable absolutist monarchy.

To show how Defoe vilifies Protestant Turcophiles while admiring the success of Ottoman toleration as an imperial policy, the first section of this essay considers his source, the Ottoman governmentality fictionalized by Marana, in which disciplinary regimes of rational faith police dissident subjects. The second section analyses Defoe's polemical writings on the pro-Turkish, pro-French politics shared by Hungarian rebels and Whig Dissenters. The last section interprets *A Continuation* as a fusion of Marana's thriller with Defoe's journalism, a counter-intelligence work that cynically ponders a post-1715 Whig-Anglican government torn apart by a homegrown enemy – a rancorous and misguided Dissenting community.

Ottoman Governmentality in *Letters Written by a Turkish Spy*

Geopolitical rivalries among European Christian states vulnerable to Muslim interference constitute the historical backdrop of the original *Turkish Spy*. This fiction is set in Bourbon France from 1637 to 1682, from the regency of Anne of Austria and Cardinal Richelieu to King Louis XIV under Cardinal Mazarin's guidance. The Genoese exile Giovani Paolo Marana published the first Italian volume in 1683 as a gift to his protector, Louis XIV, in the vain hope of becoming his royal historiographer during the year when the Austrians had defeated the Ottomans, a French ally who, for centuries, encroached upon Genoa's economic and political autonomy. The king granted refuge and a pension to Marana, who took part in a conspiracy to overthrow a Genoese republican

Figure 1. "Mahmut The Turkish Spy," engraved frontispiece, *The Eight Volumes of Letters Writ by a Turkish Spy* (London: J. Rhodes, 1723). Courtesy of the William Andrews Clark Memorial Library, University of California, Los Angeles.

government supported by the Spanish Hapsburgs, the king's nemesis. Published with his approval, the volume pays homage to Louis XIV's statecraft in the historical context of Ottoman secret agents who infiltrated European information systems[17] – in this case, an Arab Muslim named Mahmut, alias "Titus the Moldavian," disguised as a Catholic monk and employed as a multilingual translator by the French absolutist state. The frontispiece to *Turkish Spy* depicts him surrounded by letters, books, a globe, and sacks of coins (fig. 1); the names on the book spines – the Qur'an, Tacitus, and St Augustine – hint at an Ottoman sovereignty that had claimed a Roman-Christian classical patrimony.

Subsequent editions and volumes turned this thriller into an international bestseller during the height of Christian intolerance. Government surveillance of dissidents was on the rise in France after the Revocation of the Edict of Nantes and in Britain after the restoration of the Stuart monarchy, when thousands of nonconformists were fined, imprisoned, tortured, and killed.[18] *Turkish Spy* responds to this state-sponsored violence beyond Marana's intention to flatter his patron: he prepared a French translation, *L'Espion du Grand Seigneur*, which appeared in 1684–6 in multiple volumes and 102 letters. An anonymous English translation of the first volume was published in 1687, with six editions to follow. In 1691–4, seven new volumes appeared, totalling 630 letters, probably written by various English authors rather than translated from an Italian or French original. These editions inspired myriad translations and imitations in different European languages.[19] Entertainment, news, and political satire rolled into one, these proliferating texts are composite archives, a sprawling multiauthored compendium of chronicles, periodical essays, broadsides, and diplomatic dispatches. They invite a comparative approach to modern European governments that takes into consideration religious, social, intellectual, economic, and military developments in the Ottoman Empire.[20] As satire, *Turkish Spy* isolates the Muslim imperial vices shared by Christian polities in Europe, a production of difference fraught with uneasiness about cross-cultural similarities.

This satirical function highlights the growth of Turco-French power in the seventeenth century. Marana claims to have discovered the Arabic manuscript of Mahmut's letters in a corner of his Paris lodgings in 1682. According to the landlord, the letter writer had resided there for twenty years until he mysteriously vanished, his dead body later found in a river. The supposed translator of these letters, Marana, asks his readers to have "Respect for the Memory of this *Mahometan*" because the author wrote about "the transactions of *Christians*, with no less truth than eloquence."[21] Displaying his erudition in Greek and Latin classics as well as in European philosophy and history, his letters are not "barbarous"; unlike pretentious Christian scholars, some Turks are "men of great understanding that write the *Annals* of the *Ottoman* Empire."[22] Francophilia blends into Ottomania in the preface, reiterated in Mahmut's snarky remark that the French envy the "formidable" Ottomans. He writes,

> wise Men who have knowledge of our History, speak with more Admiration of the *Ottoman* Empire, than that of the *Romans*; and if these last were restored by the Civil Wars which tore them in Pieces, the other will increase and maintain it self, by the great Pre-cautions used to hinder them, and by the Union of their Forces.[23]

Echoed by Defoe, this positive spin on the Ottoman Empire's unmatched political and religious unity drives Mahmut's secret mission. In route to Paris, he crosses Hungary and then stays 140 days in Vienna, "where [he] observ'd all the Motions of the *Court*, according as I was ordered."[24] Politically astute, his primary objective is to gather intelligence on the Christians' internecine wars in order to stir French-Austrian hostilities and thereby "to facilitate the *Sultan's Conquest in Hungary*."[25]

Ottoman meddling in Catholic-Protestant disputes becomes a flashpoint in volumes 2 to 8. Whereas the first volume presents Mahmut as an open-minded Francophile afflicted by an existential tension between his inner Islamic beliefs and outward Christian practices, the subsequent volumes satirically fold this tension into an Enlightenment assault on French absolutism, the papacy, and biblical revelation, landing *Turkish Spy* in the Vatican's index of banned books in 1705–9.[26] Many European readers were ravished by the outspoken Muslim correspondent, a suave cosmopolitan shapeshifter. Culturally embedded in early modern Europe's international milieu, Mahmut adopts conflicting personas depending on his various addressees, whose letters are not included but whose attitudes and ideas can be inferred from the spy's replies. In these replies, he morphs from a Muslim proselytizer, to a Cartesian sceptic, to a Pythagorean vegetarian, to a believer in Indian reincarnation, to a runaway slave from Sicily, to a pining lover of a Greek wife, to a defender of women's education, to a deist proponent of natural religion, and to a proto-Christian classicist, all the while struggling to keep his cover. He evades Cardinal Richelieu's detection, the Catholic inquisition, and imprisonment in Paris even as he mollifies suspicious government officials and religious leaders in Istanbul. Although these self-transformations obscure his identity, his cross-cultural immersion advances a clear political agenda: to familiarize himself with Catholics and Protestants so as to mediate their conflicts under the auspices of a universal Muslim sovereign, as had been the dream of every sultan since Süleyman I captured Hungary in 1526 and launched the first unsuccessful siege of Vienna in 1529.[27]

To fulfil this dream, Mahmut learns Christian politics, philosophy, science, and theology under orders from his master, Sultan Mehmed IV (r. 1648–87), who aspired to integrate cultural diversity into a reformed state under which Christians, Jews, and heterodox Muslims are converted to a rational Islam free from corrupt superstitions. Imperial rivalry with the Hapsburgs and the Safavids spurred the sultan to assimilate religious dissidents by granting them civic protections, as customary, while persecuting others deemed hostile to the empire's internal Sunnitization from the 1450s to 1690s. State-sanctioned Islamic orthodoxy characterized the Köprülü period from 1652 to 1702, when the call for an international *jihad* (holy war) to purify the empire compelled all subjects to embrace the Kadizadeli teachings of Vani Mehmed Efendi, the sultan's personal preacher. Addicted to hunting and pleasure in his court in Edirne (Adrianople), the sultan legitimized his reign by endorsing these teachings, based on an austere Sunni Islam that was not only opposed to alcohol-drinking, impiety, and Sufi rituals, but was also rationalist, nonceremonial, and faithful to the pristine monotheism practised by the first Muslims. Spread by zealous imams, the Kadizadeli movement sanctified the sultan's attack on Vienna, as officers and viziers were goaded into battle by Mehmed Efendi. The official campaign preacher, he lifted the army's morale with the prospect of converting Christians and Jews.[28] Even after this failed *jihad*, Kadizadeli Islam altered "Ottoman rule from toleration to large-scale conversion and assimilation."[29]

Mahmut's political reporting is therefore tinged with a religious zeal for the "Light and Reason [that] ought to appear in the Actions of the Musselmans" continuous with a long process of Sunni state consolidation culminating in "the Mighty and Invincible *Sultan Mahomet*, whose *Throne* may *God* fortify."[30] In letters to Ottoman administrators and religious leaders, he exhorts Muslims to shun "vice and debauchery" by reforming themselves, the only cure for the imperial malaise that has led to the imprisonment of the previous sultan, Ibrahim, and the enthronement of a new one, Mehmed IV. Accordingly, Mahmut's espionage is twofold: to exploit Christian weaknesses favourable to Muslim rule and to test his comrades' moral integrity by censuring their vices rationally and candidly with legal impunity. As he writes in his 1650 letter to the "Reis Effendi, Principal Secretary of the Ottoman Empire,"

> [O]ne chief End of my being plac'd here is, that being out of the Limits of the *Ottoman Empire*, yet holding a constant Intelligence, I may freely and without Fear, reprove the Vices and encourage the Virtues of the Greatest *Governors* and *Princes* among the *Mussulmans*. Nay, I am threat'ned with Punishment and the *Sultan's* Displeasure, if I neglect any Opportunity of this Nature, or appear Partial and Timorous in my Reprehensions.[31]

In casting himself as an instrument of the sultan's reformist ideology, the Turkish spy justifies his potentially blasphemous criticisms as part of the internal surveillance and social disciplining meant "to reform the Corruptions that are crept into Court, Camp, and City."[32] Assuming this moral high ground affords him protection from government scrutiny, a clever ruse for concealing his own lapsing faith as a practising Christian. Ironically, Kadizadeli teachings help excuse the heretical doubts sprinkled in his letters to Ottoman authorities. After all, his relentless ridicule of idolatrous Christian rites and contradictory beliefs is as much guided by Kadizadeli reformers who levelled similar accusations against infidels as by European deists who espoused the rational ecumenical monotheism taught by the first Christians.

Mahmut blends Christian deism with Islamic rationalism in order to identify the state's internal and external enemies. The tolerant outlook he learned from deist "Philosophers or Lovers of Wisdom" is akin to that of the Ikhwân al-Safâ' or "Brethren of Purity," the tenth-century Arab Muslim philosophers whose interpretation of ancient Greek thought was disseminated in the clandestine literature of the Radical Enlightenment.[33] Open to the cross-cultural transmission of ideas, Mehmed IV's spiritual revitalization program is capacious enough to hide Mahmut's heresy from Ottoman officials ideologically devoted to a "rationality in religion," even as his intellectual curiosity often counters the sultan's political theology.[34]

Torn by this religious quandary, Mahmut's nostalgia for a tolerant past in which "no man was put to Death for Words or Thoughts of Things above his Reach" is both personal and political.[35] His frequent ruminations on this topic dramatize the differentiation and sameness inherent in satire: he ridicules and thus others the Christian dissidents he often identifies with. His mixed feelings as an exiled Ottoman agent allude to an oppressive state that would forbid his heterodoxy, yet these feelings index a split self seeking to subject Christian heretics to Muslim rule. That the "*Nazarenes*," as he calls Euro-Christians, are "a'sham'd that the Followers of *Mahomet* [...] shou'd outstrip them in the Peaceableness of their Temper" makes him feel self-righteous in manipulating their tolerationist cause to convert them to Islam. As he advises an effendi, persecuted Christians in Italy, Spain, France, Poland, and Hungary "would all rise, and fly to the *Mahometan Standard*" if he would grant them asylum.[36] Writing to the sultan's official preacher (possibly Vani Mehmed Efendi), Mahmut quips that Molinist and Quietist heretics in Italy would welcome an Ottoman invasion to escape Catholic persecution.[37] To carry out this mission, he poses as "a Native of *Moldavia* [...] habited like an *Ecclesiastick*," typical of the religious attire worn by Ottoman double agents stationed in European monasteries.[38] This disguise demarcates the state's subdued enemy. On the one hand, the Moldavians were Greek Orthodox Christians colonized by the Ottomans since the fifteenth century, yet also known as fierce freedom fighters who resisted Muslim and Catholic conversion. On the other, the Moldavians were suppressed brutally in 1648–79, when the sultan recruited them as soldiers to fight German forces in the Balkans and reinforce armed rebels in Hungary.[39] Thus, Mahmut's clerical habit communicates to his Catholic French hosts – and to *Turkish Spy*'s readers – that religious liberty is a political tool for subjugating and eventually converting rebellious populations.

This lesson is emphasized in volume 8, in which the plot to encourage "the *Rebels* of *Hungary*, *Croatia*, and Mutinous *Provinces*" thickens. As the anonymous author/translator warns, the Hungarian rebellion is shown to have brought "the *Turks* once more upon us, to our final Ruin and Confusion; since those *Infidels* never take greater Advantage to Invade and Conquer the *Dominions* of *Christians*, than when they find us involv'd in domestick Wars one with another."[40] In a 1667 letter to Vizir Azem, Mahmut details his plan to forge an alliance between Hungarian rebels and "the most Invincible *Osmans*" to weaken an Austria besieged by Louis XIV on its western border.[41] To fulfil this plan, he counts on Imre Thököly (1656–1705), known in England as "Count Teckely," the leader of the Kuruc movement (connoting the word "crusader"). His sweeping military victories in Moravia and upper Hungary in 1680 propelled him to international infamy. He was a champion of an embattled Protestantism but was despised as a Turcophile who had betrayed his faith and people by soliciting Muslim help. His decision to reject Leopold I's armistice, accept the crown of upper Hungary conferred to him by Sultan Mehmed IV in 1682, and join grand vizier Kara Mustafa's army in 1683 sent shockwaves throughout Europe.[42] The opportunistic spy and the French king admire Thököly's patriotic cause, as promoted by Nathan Ben Saddi, a Jewish agent stationed in Vienna and entrusted to run the spy's covert operation.[43] Mahmut instructs him to elicit classified information on Thököly from Viennese officials and stir the anti-Hapsburg "Hungarian faction" without showing partiality to the Protestants or the Jesuits, "for the *Sultan* will gain by the Divisions of the *Nazarenes*, let the Case go how it will between themselves." Nathan's job is to inflame "the Discontents of *Hungary*, by all the Arts of a cunning *Statesman*."[44] Responsible for the civil unrest leading to the siege of Vienna, he is the ultimate scapegoat of a war-torn Christian Europe, insofar as *Turkish Spy* tethers Christian anti-Semitism to the assimilated figure of Ottoman Jewry.[45]

Among the Jews Mahmut unsuccessfully tries to convert, Nathan represents the widespread presence of Jewish communities in the Ottoman Levant that were granted protective status and yet were harassed by Muslim reformers. Indeed, his name alludes to Sabbateanism, the Jewish messianic movement that spread from Egypt to Europe in the late seventeenth century. In 1665, Nathan of Gaza became the prophet of a Kabbalist rabbi from Smyrna, Sabbatai Sevi (1626–76), a self-proclaimed messiah who was to reunite his people in Israel after usurping the sultanate. Jews in Vienna were spreading news and propaganda about the messiah's arrival through letters sent back and forth across Hungary.[46] But these messianic expectations were thrown into doubt after Sevi, having been summoned before Sultan Mehmed IV and ready to take his crown, converted to Islam to avoid a death sentence. Under duress, the apostate became the right-hand man of Vani Mehmed Efendi, who oversaw his conversion. Given a Muslim name, honorary robes, and a pensioned position, Sevi was assimilated according to Kadizadeli state policy, even as Nathan continued to promote a movement Ottoman officials considered heretical and potentially seditious. Before his death in 1680, he prophesized that the sultan would launch the failed siege of Vienna but recover his losses with demonic aid, after which the messiah would reappear.[47] These tidings explain why Mahmut mocks Nathan's "New Messias, that Imposter *Sabbati Sevi*," who represents the loss of "Sense and Reason" the Israelites possessed before falling into theological error and rabbinical corruption.[48] According to the Turkish spy, Sevi's apostasy should compel Nathan to adopt a rational Islam, as many of his disillusioned co-religionists in the Levant had done. Modelled after his historical counterpart, the unconverted Nathan functions as a satiric figure for another lost cause: the Hungarian rebellion. He is the internal state enemy, manipulated by a Muslim spy who considers the Talmud and Torah silly fables.

Nonetheless, Mahmut's epistolary exchanges with Nathan are theologically and politically suspect. Sabbateanism was taken up by millenarian Christians who saw Sevi as part of God's plan to eliminate the Turkish menace that had blocked the long-lost ten tribes of Israel from leading the Jews to the Promised Land, a prerequisite for Christ's Second Coming.[49] Keen on these ideas, Mahmut's anti-Semitic letters are sometimes intermingled with prophecies about Ottoman decline and British ascendency following an apocalyptic "Reformation of Christianity" in 1700, as related to him by Ahasuerus, the legendary Wandering Jew.[50] Should Ottoman officials discover that their spy has indulged these heresies, he could be charged with sedition. Whether or not this occurs, his life is in danger after he learns that Nathan has been murdered by "Order from the *Divan*."[51] Panicked and confused, Mahmut realizes that political machinations beyond his ken are afoot. Ten months before the siege of Vienna begins he suddenly disappears in Paris, leaving readers in suspense. Volume 8 ends with unresolved questions: have Kadizadeli agents in Istanbul assassinated Nathan and Mahmut on suspicion that they were secretly propagating seditious Sabbatean prophecies? Has the Turkish spy's rationalist fascination with Christian and Jewish heterodoxy betrayed his European acculturation, given his apparent role as a double agent who has leaked compromising information to the infidels? Or perhaps he and Nathan have outlived their political usefulness? In pondering these questions, the perplexed reader participates in the symbolic violence latent in all satires: identifying the sacrificial victim (Mahmut and Nathan) from the margins of society, and outside of it, to create a coherent community based on exclusions. From a Bogelian perspective, the reader's imaginary identification with an invisible Ottoman force is what enables the state of exception to be rescued from civil war.[52]

In this case, secrecy and silence are ideologically resonant. By drawing readers into its narrative open-endedness, *Turkish Spy* reveals the vexing power operative in the empty spaces of secular toleration, consistent with what Colin Jager describes as the "common quiet" emerging from the heroic couplet in Restoration England. The novel's truncated ending dramatizes the disturbances surrounding the post-1688 state's creation of loyal subjects, the management of populations, the policing of dissidents, and the monopolization of violence for advancing an exclusive ideology of civility and justice.[53] *Turkish Spy*'s mysterious conclusion, then, signals the silent workings of a governmentality that binds a limited toleration to the violent persecution of subjects whose lives are disposable. Surveilling, manipulating, and subduing friends and foes alike under an all-powerful, all-knowing confessional-like state is what Defoe recommends to his English readers – an Ottomanized Anglican government stealthy enough to outwit the French and their Hungarian allies in order to realize British imperial ambitions.

Defoe, Religious Liberty, and the Siege of Vienna

The plot of *Turkish Spy* displays a heightened awareness that the relatively peaceful coexistence of different faiths in Ottoman territories has rendered the orthodoxy of church and state in seventeenth-century Christian Europe ideologically exhausted.[54] Persistent conflicts within and across intolerant Christian communities triggered what Jonathan Israel has diagnosed as the unravelling of the "old edifice of thought" in Europe, the fragmentation of monarchic and aristocratic rule that erupted into an urgent crisis in the 1680s:[55] Hungarian Protestant noblemen suffering from centuries of Catholic-Hapsburg persecution asked the Ottoman Porte to help them restore their constitutional right to elect their own king, worship as they please under their own appointed clergymen, and protect their kingdom with their own army, free from German interference. These armed Hungarian "malcontents," as they were called, joined Ottoman troops in 1683 in a desperate bid to oust Holy Roman Emperor Leopold I and his Catholic administration from power. Countering the call for a unified Christian coalition to drive the sultan out of Eastern Europe as stipulated in the 1648 Treaty of Westphalia, which ended Germany's Thirty Years' War (c. 1618–48), the Hungarian uprising sparked fierce debates about whether subjects had the legal right to topple a legitimate monarchy and clerical authority in order to secure their liberty, especially if aided by a Muslim empire. Andrew Marvell, John Dryden, Jonathan Swift, and Gottfried Leibniz wrote about this topic, but only Defoe provides a keen analysis of how religious toleration constituted "the reason of state," a rationality intrinsic to the governmental control over disparate populations independent of divine and natural law.[56] Opposed to the Hungarian war of independence that lasted until 1711, he implores his readers not to be fooled by the three political actors who threaten British security: the Hungarian Protestants who used freedom of conscience to justify their illegal usurpation of Austrian royal power, the French who fomented a revolt to weaken and invade a Hapsburg Empire distracted by civil unrest on its eastern border, and the Ottomans who exploited this unrest to conquer and Islamize a religiously fractured Christendom under the sultan's protection.

The Turco-Hungarian alliance deeply informed Defoe's understanding of how the Protestant Dissenting cause resonated with political events across the English Channel. From 1704 to 1714, Defoe was a secret spy and avid propagandist for Robert Harley, Speaker of the House of Commons from 1701 to 1705. Defoe helped publicize Harley's moderate Tory policies under Queen Anne in exchange for his release from Newgate prison, where he was serving a long sentence and humiliation at the pillory for having published *The Short-est Way with the Dissenters*.[57] Persecution under an intolerant government at-tached Defoe to Harley, a Dissenter and ex-Whig leader who headed the Tory ministry in 1710. Loyal to his patron, Defoe claims in *An Appeal to Honour and Justice, tho' it be of his Worst Enemies* (1715) to have written a pamphlet in 1683 (never found) describing "the first time" be broke ranks with Whig "Friends."[58]

> *The First Time* I had the Misfortune to differ with my Friends, was about the Year 1683, when the *Turks* were besieging *Vienna*, and the *Whigs*, in *England*, generally speaking, were for the *Turks* taking it; which I having read the History of the Cruelty and perfidious Dealings of the *Turks* in their Wars, and how they had rooted out the Name of the Christian Religion in above Threescore and Ten Kingdoms, could by no means agree with: And tho' then but a young Man, and a younger Author, I opposed it, and wrote against it; which was taken very unkindly indeed.[59]

This passage is directed at Whig readers who regarded him as a turncoat for having supported a Tory government.[60] Perhaps because of his difficulty in reintegrating within the Whig party after its return to power in 1715 – as well as a desire to avoid another libel charge – Defoe withheld the names of those who supposedly favoured the Turks. Though there are no known Whigs who did so, the idea that they sympathized with the Muslim enemies of Christendom was a common trope in anti-Dissenting Tory propaganda during the lead up to the 1688 Revolution, when "all the Republicans of England, [were] Tooth and Nail for the *Turk*."[61]

Defoe's critique of Whig admiration for the Turks most likely refers to pro-Hungarian English Protestants, many of whom preferred Ottoman toler-ation over Catholic persecution in the context of a repressive Restoration or-der. Between 1661 and 1665, the Cavalier Parliament passed the Clarendon Code confirming pre-existing statute penalties against nonconformists. Their enforcement in pursuit of Anglican uniformity primarily targeted Dissenting Christians, who had been blamed for inciting the country's long civil war. Meanwhile, members of the Protestant Hungarian nobility and clergy were plotting to assassinate King Leopold I in order to end his Jesuit-driven poli-cies of Catholic uniformity in northwestern Royal Hungary. In 1673, Leopold suspended the Hungarian constitution, an act that led to the mass desecration of Lutheran and Calvinist churches in Royal Hungary, the incarceration and execution of over a hundred Protestant magnates, the confiscation of their property, and a populist Hungarian backlash fuelled by Ottoman military aid.[62] According to Schmitt, the anti-Muslim Christian unity mandated in the Treaty of Westphalia codified the legal framework by which territorial states ought to conduct war and peace within a Christocentric global order differentiated from infidel lands west and east.[63] Defoe had arrived at a similar position when faulting the Hungarian rebels who had embraced their Ottoman-Muslim protectors to battle Catholic oppressors, an improper response to the problem of state-sponsored toleration. To his dismay, many Protestants disregarded the Westphalian framework by justifying the Hungarian nobility's alliance with the Porte as unfortunate but necessary, because, as a pro-Hungarian English pamphleteer wrote, the Turk "lets *Christians* live under him, with more ease and freedom than they do."[64]

"The bulwark of Christendom," Hungary had been a battleground for Hapsburg-Ottoman rivalry from the early sixteenth century onward, making Christian unification in Europe impossible to achieve.[65] Spearheading the fight against Austrian authoritarianism was Thököly. Under his leadership the Hungarian Kurucs saw the Ottoman *dar-al-sulh* or "land of peace" as their last hope, preferring to establish a tributary kingdom modelled after Transylvania than to remain in an Austrian colony under religious and military oppression. For some Britons worried about a Stuart monarchy amenable to Louis XIV's Catholic absolutism, Hungarian rebels marching westward with Ottoman troops under the star and crescent ensign offered the only resistance to the popish powers that had taken territories from European Protestant nations.[66] Thököly's fight for Islamic toleration recalled a divinely inspired and militant Oliver Cromwell expunging papal tyranny from the Church of England, given that the brave Hungarian commander "appear[ed] to be no ordinary hero" in battling the Counter-Reformation forces that threatened to engulf Europe and Britain at that time.[67]

But for Defoe, Thököly's Ottoman army of malcontents endangered the delicate balance of power in Europe. In *The Two Great Questions Consider'd* (1700), Defoe writes, "*A just Ballance of Power is the Life of Peace*," for otherwise "Every King in the World would be the Universal Monarch if he might, and nothing restrains but the Power of Neighbours [italics in the original]."[68] On these grounds he vehemently opposed the Hungarian rebels' violation of the Christian "Leagues and Confederacies" that checked ambitious European monarchs in accordance with the Treaty of Westphalia, which he considered essential to British national security.[69] For Defoe (and Schmitt), this treaty formalized the legal terms under which sovereign states declare war against a respected enemy, one who adheres (at least in theory) to the established rules of military engagement in order to maintain political equilibrium in a Christian Europe vulnerable to internal civil wars and external Muslim pressure.[70] By this logic Defoe defended Pope Innocent XI's Holy League alliance among Charles V, Duke of Lorraine, thirty German princes, the prince of Venice, and the King of Poland, whose combined forces routed the Ottoman army, recaptured territories in Hungary and the Balkans, and defeated Thököly's rebels. The crushing Ottoman defeat at Vienna resulted in the restoration of European absolutism and Catholic persecution in Eastern Europe and, by 1690, Transylvania, which Thököly failed to defend from Hapsburg troops.[71] His subsequent exile and death near Istanbul was seen by many Christians as God's will to protect a united Christendom that could curb the overreach of the monarch who now posed the greatest threat to Britain and "the Protestant Interest": the Ottoman ally King Louis XIV, sarcastically known as "the *French* Grand Seignior, the most Christian *Turk*."[72]

That Hungarian rebels have unwittingly promoted Turco-French hegemony in Europe emerges as a dominant theme in Defoe's journalistic publication in support of the Harleian ministry and British foreign policy, aptly titled *A Weekly Review of the Affairs of France: Purged from the Errors and Partiality of News-Writers and Petty-Statesmen of all Sides*. It distils his views on Hungary into a roundabout justification of Britain's war with Bourbon France, which was vying with the Hapsburgs and Bavarians over the vacated Spanish throne between 1701 and 1713 – the same years in which a renewed Hungarian uprising against Leopold I, this time without Ottoman support, gave Louis XIV a political and military edge. In the 1704 September through December issues of the *Review*, Defoe launches into a long exposition on the siege of Vienna to to conflate rhetorically two separate phases of the Hungarian rebellion.[73] This merging of different times and events stresses Hungary's pivotal role in facilitating French designs. The essays are aimed at readers who "had so little Sense of Public Safety, and so much Zeal for the Protestant Religion in *Hungaria*, that they wish'd every day the *Turks* should take *Vienna*."[74] Thököly's "Unhappiest League" with the sultan should convince Britons to support their country's wartime effort to forestall the Bourbon takeover of Spain, rather than siding with the Hungarians' renewed fight against Britain's ally, the Hapsburgs. This was a scare tactic for winning over Whigs and Tories opposed to any prolonged military involvement in continental affairs.[75]

Defoe was not merely parroting government propaganda, but elaborating on his suspicion (in 1683) that diplomats in Paris and Istanbul were working together to weaken England and eradicate Christianity from Europe.[76] The *Review* fuses two prior discourses: Tory broadsides accusing England's "Protestant Mahometans" of conspiring with Hungarian rebels to undo the Restoration settlement, and English tracts accusing Louis XIV of arming and training them in order to defeat Hapsburg Austria, the only buffer zone protecting Protestant countries from an Ottoman invasion. These accusations jointly clinch Defoe's rhetorical case for why Protestant Turcophiles who endanger the balance of power should be considered the prime enemy.[77] Whereas Harley sought to convince the English public that French absolutism in Europe required an aggressive military response, Defoe twisted this polemic to locate the state's enemy in the Whigs and Dissenters who favoured the Hungarian rebels. In this case, toleration defines enmity at home and abroad, an ideological justification for normalizing the British revolution in taxation, finance, and warfare on a permanent basis.

Without political moderation, Defoe fears, extremist English Dissenters are doomed to repeat the "politick madness" that led their Hungarian counterparts to almost subject all Christians to Muslim despotism.[78] Needless to say, this hyperbolic claim would have alienated many of Defoe's English co-religionists, who saw in war-torn Hungary the failure of intolerant Catholic policies. They instead championed the Protestant toleration that the French king had dismantled after the 1685 Revocation of the Edict of Nantes, leading to the persecution and exile of French Protestant Huguenots. Defoe condemned this act as hypocritical, given the king's support of the Hungarian revolt, but he called for a moderate loosening of the Toleration Act's anti-Dissenting strictures under a centralized Anglican Church unwilling to accommodate Catholics, atheists, and antitrinitarians. Even so, he was moved by Hungarians suffering under "the Cruelties and Oppressions of the House of *Austria*" and the Jesuits' "Cruel Ecclesiastick Tyranny," and he would designate the Hapsburgs the new universal monarchy that posed the greatest threat to European stability in 1711.[79] As a persecuted Presbyterian, he sympathized with the Hungarian rebels' noble ends but loathed their selfish means, since handing over their country to Muslim rulers for a spurious protection is a betrayal of Christian Europe. Defoe writes in the *Review*: "If I'm to be Murthered, Rob'd, Plundered and Destroyed, I had rather a *Roman* Catholic was the Butcher, than a *Turk*; I had rather he had the Power over me, that acknowledges Christ, than he that despises him, and defies him." By this comparative logic, he prefers to "be Persecuted by the *Roman* Catholick Power, than Tollerated by the *Turks*."[80] Accordingly, the malcontents have lost their Protestant identity, because, in embracing Islamic toleration, they have become more barbaric than Muslims and Catholics. Lacking humanity, Hungarian backstabbers need to be sacrificed in order to preserve Europe's interstate Christian order.

To prove why these people are to blame for the Dutch and British failure to broker a truce in Austria during the War of the Spanish Succession, the *Review* dwells on Thököly's political sins. That "*Protestant Turk*," as Defoe calls him, exchanged his "*Hungarian* Bonnet" for a "*Turban*" – "Protestant Liberty" for "Turkish Slavery."[81] Islamic toleration masks an unlawful power grab: "Here's Religion and Liberty! Here's the exact Principle of an *Hungarian Malecontent*! – The Crown of *Hungary* is the point," proof that Thököly's stepson, Ferenc Rákóczi II (1676–1735), is Protestant Europe's true unjust enemy. In 1703, he rekindled the rebellion against Hapsburg rule with Louis XIV's support.[82] For Defoe, these two French-subsidized revolts are "an Engine of secret Devices, a Cloak to Villainous Pretences, and a Sham to hide the Devil in the Robes of an Angel of Light."[83] The malcontents have unleashed the fury of the Ottoman

Figure 2. Etching by Romeyn de Hooghe, entitled *Huldiging der Hongaren en Tyrannie der Rebellen Turken Tartaren, Hommage des Hunarois et Tirannie des Rebelles Turcqs et Tartares*, depicting the Siege of Vienna by the Turks. Dutch School, 1683. © Victoria and Albert Museum, London.

army upon fellow Christians, as pictured in Nicolass Visscher II's widely circulating print on the siege of Vienna (fig. 2): Turkish and Tartar "rebels" plunder and beat Catholic monks who have surrendered gold coins and large keys, some kneeling for mercy at the feet of Kara Mustafa and Thököly, who is looking the other way. In this intra-religious treachery, Defoe saw the tolerationist cause hijacked by Thököly's ragtag army of mercenaries, outlaws, and peasants against European international protocols for conducting contained wars between Christian princes.[84]

How toleration works in tandem with persecution, expulsion, intimidation, and the abuse of power is what the *Review* describes as a shameful scandal in modern European history, contrary to the belief of Protestants who idealized the Ottoman Empire as an exception to this rule. Defoe's information on Hungary's revolution derives from a book from which he had in his youth transcribed stories about strong Ottoman militants and treacherous Hungarian Christians: Richard Knolles and Paul Rycaut's *The Turkish History* (1687), which covers up to the years 1676–86.[85] Defoe then turned for inspiration to the Royalist soldier and historian Roger Manley, who updated Knolles and Rycaut's history. A possible author of *Turkish Spy*, Manley justifies the German occupation of Hungary on the grounds that the malcontents had forfeited their rights in 1683 by turning their country into an Ottoman tributary kingdom. He argues that they had formed a hereditary monarchy entailed to Thököly and his progeny, rather than an elective monarchy based on the ancient constitutional prerogative that guaranteed the Hungarian nobility's autonomy.[86] Manley's political cynicism counters the familiar narrative of Christians worshipping freely and peacefully in Ottoman territories, as documented in Rycaut's writings, which Pierre Bayle and John Locke cited in their defences of Islamic toleration.[87] Not only did Defoe ignore Rycaut's views in favour of Manley's, but he also drew on Jean Le Clerc's positive biography on Thököly only to dismiss the author – a persecuted Huguenot who fled to the Netherlands – as a propagandist of Louis XIV's crooked plan to elicit sympathy for Hungarian Protestants. That Defoe smears one of the most influential advocates of religious toleration suggests his strong antipathy towards leading Protestant intellectuals of the 1680s and 1690s.[88] In his mind, they fail to recognize that the Ottoman protection of *dhimmis* is part of a divide-and-conquer tactic for Islamizing post-Reformation Europe.

Since the 1540s, the Lutheran and Calvinist churches had thrived in the Ottoman-controlled areas of Hungary, facilitating the spread of Protestantism after Catholic priests fled Muslim persecution. While many Hungarian subjects stayed in these areas and paid the poll tax expected of *dhimmis*, Ottoman officials exploited their homeland economically but preserved it socially as a bridgehead for expanding westward. Non-interference in Protestant communities was meant to forestall Austrian-Catholic control and incorporate central Europe into a great Muslim Afro-Eurasian empire.[89] To realize this ambitious policy, Sultan Mehmed IV crowned Thököly prince of upper Hungary and besieged the Hapsburg capital in 1683. Though halted in that year, this policy made Defoe envy the Turks. As he writes in the *Review*, "Commend me to the *Turks*, they are the Truest Fighters for Religion, that I know of, in the World; they scorn the Assistance of Christians to Erect *Mahometanism*."[90] The idea that Ottomans do not backstab one other as the Hungarian Protestants and the French Catholics have done to fellow Christians is indicative of Defoe's "imperial envy," an ambivalent feeling that for Gerald MacLean is tied to the performance of an English national identity in a powerful Muslim empire.[91] This feeling permeates Defoe's *A Continuation*, in which the fate of a religiously divided Britain depends on the tolerated Hungarian scapegoat who must be destroyed.

Whig Dissenters as Enemies of the State: Defoe's *A Continuation*

The links between toleration, absolute power, and satire coalesce in Defoe's 1704 private letter to Secretary of State Robert Harley, to whom he recommends a fictional exposé of the Ottoman Empire. British government officials should station spies in European cities modelled after an empire adept in spying on Christian powers since the sixteenth century, the sophisticated espionage network presented in "a Book in Eight Volumes Published in London about 7 or 8 yeares Ago Call'd Letters writ by a Turkish Spye." Defoe calls this book "a Meer Romance" full of good morals worth emulating. It could teach Harley how to outsmart a French empire that has benefited from the "unfortunate Christians of Hungaria."[92] Led by Rákóczi II, these rebels had prevented the Austrian army at the Danube River from reinforcing British troops in the Rhine during the War of the Spanish Succession. As Defoe privately advises, the story of an Ottoman spy living in seventeenth-century Paris shows how Hungarians who have "Little Regard to the Interest of the Protestant Religion in General" will decide whether Europe should have "Liberty Or Universall Monarchy."[93] *Turkish Spy* not only informed Defoe's identity as a paid government mole but also served as a foreign policy guidebook for grooming Harley into a shrewd Turk-like statesman: by duplicating the Ottoman system of international espionage under Queen Anne's reign, he could re-engineer Britain into a strong imperial state closer to the French absolutism perfected by Cardinal Richelieu in the previous century than the balanced constitutionalism theorized by John Locke after 1688.[94] Marana's satire reveals the *raison d'état* of all great empires: know your true enemy. Only the Hungarians can pose a danger from without proportional to the bickering Dissenters who had weakened the British state from within, for, as Defoe tells Harley, "it were Better for all the Rest of Europe That the Protestants of Hungaria were Entyrely Rooted Out and Destroyed, Than That the Turks Should Take the Citty of Vienna."[95]

Having important implications for Britain's struggle to tip the European balance of power in its favour, the "Meer Romance" informed Defoe's journalism. It also formed the crux of an exilic story that predates *Robinson Crusoe*. *A Continuation* features a "banished" Mahmut desperate to return to the orthodox Islamic fold after living forty-eight years in Paris, continuing his letter writing from 1687 to 1693.[96] Alive but homesick, Defoe's Muslim alter ego pleads to quit the secret service and settle in his Arabian homeland to perform the *hajj* as he explains in his first letter, addressed to the Reis Effendi and dated 4 January 1687. This year marks three momentous events connected in the Turkish spy's comeback: the English translation of Marana's volume 1, inciting novelistic innovations imbued with satiric ambiguity; the dethronement of Mehmed IV, who was blamed for the demoralizing Ottoman defeat at Vienna; and the Declaration of Indulgence issued by King James II, suspending penal laws against Catholics and Dissenters and inviting French-papal meddling in Protestant-ruled Britain.[97] In the context of these events, Defoe's sequel is more than "another anti-Jacobite tract, to demonstrate the hypocrisy of Louis XIV and the French in the promises they seemed to hold out to James II and, by implication, his descendants," as Maximillian Novak proposes. Rather, it is a cautionary tale aimed at English Dissenters whose call for universal Protestant toleration (the partial repeal of the Test and Corporation Acts) threatened to subvert the anti-French policy spearheaded by King William III during the Nine Years' War (1688–97), which is the geopolitical backdrop to the sequel.[98] The 1683–6 gap between the original *Turkish Spy* and *A Continuation* gravitates around the Ottoman-Hungarian debacle, used by Defoe to cast his gullible co-religionists as enemies of the state. He lampoons Whig and Presbyterian in-fighting that, in his mind, tragically repeats the Christian weakness culminating in the siege of Vienna.

Stressed in the title, *A Continuation* forges thematic and stylistic continuities with its forerunner by including some previous addressees, readapting the frontispiece, dating the letters according to the Islamic lunar calendar, attacking Jewish religiosity, deriding Catholic traditions, scandalizing the French and the Hungarians for their political recklessness, and praising Muslim harmony over Christian divisiveness. According to the pseudo-translator, Defoe, the letters were obtained from a "Correspondent at *Vienna*" (possibly Nathan).[99] The letter writer mocks those who have betrayed Jesus's "first Institutes" in "daily fighting and shedding Blood about the single Question, of what it was their Prophet did command, and what he did not; and who shall or shall not interpret the Mind and Will of their Prophet." This rancour is more egregious than that of Sunni "*Ottomans*" and Shiite "*Persians*," "for the intestine Broils of these *Nazareen* Nations have always been, and ever will be, the Advancement of the glorious Ensigns of *Mahomet*."[100] Rancorous Christians at fault for hastening the Turks to overrun Europe are fighting wars of imperial expansion in the guise of religious wars. This message constitutes the fulcrum that enables Defoe to continue his political journalism in an epistolary satirical fiction published anonymously, in the manner of a spy applying literary camouflage to evade potential libel charges.

Continuities at the level of form and style integrate discontinuities in the Turkish spy's altered world view. No longer does he treat deism as a viable, tolerant religion, nor does he indulge in Christian and Jewish heterodoxy (Sabbateanism is not referenced). He unequivocally upholds a reformed Sunni Islam, imploring an Ottoman judge to "Put strictly in Execution the Laws of *Mahomet* IV, the just and invincible Lawgiver and Emperor," for the empire to recover militarily.[101] A political throwback, Mahmut remains loyal to a Kadizadeli piety that, although influential among religious leaders, had lost administrative support after Mehmed IV's imprisonment.[102] The spy's situation is thus analogous to the disaffected Defoe struggling to assimilate within the new Whig ministry after the Tory Party's fallout in 1715, when Harley was impeached by Parliament and imprisoned for nearly two years upon King George I's coronation. Defoe merges his prior persona as a Dissenter with a Muslim character for whom "the practical Atheism, so rife in the World in this Age [is] [...] a Sin engrossed among Christians" but unknown "among the Mussulmans," an individual self-delusional in his belief that the Turks alone have averted the "Revolutions common to these *European* kingdoms."[103] Mahmut favours an outdated state orthodoxy tantamount to a moderate Anglicanism, a policy opposed to ministers James Stanhope's and Charles Spencer Sunderland's new Whig program to undo the Occasional Conformity Act, which prevented Dissenters from circumventing the Test Acts by occasionally performing Anglican rites, and the Schism Act, which required Dissenting academies to be licensed by an Anglican bishop. These Tory anti-Dissent laws passed under Queen Anne were repealed in 1719 – to the outrage of orthodox Dissenters who, like Defoe, feared that such an action would dissolve the Anglican church-state. Hence, the sequel rhetorically performs a "continuation" in two respects: first, as a cross-generic hybrid that renews the *Review*'s call for political moderation in order to convince the English public why a universal Protestant toleration would destabilize a nascent British Empire that had made significant gains after the War of the Spanish Succession, and, second, as a self-critical mirror for English Dissenters' setbacks, intra-religious backstabbing, divisive polemics, and party factionalism that had brought Christendom to the brink of ruin in 1683.

Nonetheless, *A Continuation* interrupts the contemporary national focus featured in Defoe's first experimentation with Marana's fictional tour de force. In *The Conduct of Christians made the Sport of Infidels* (1717), Defoe satirizes regime change at home through the letters of a Turkish merchant from Amsterdam (actually, an Armenian-born Christian reared as a Muslim) who relays to a grand mufti in Istanbul the shameful disputes that have overtaken the Church of England. He focuses on the Bangorian controversy initiated by Bishop of Bangor Benjamin Hoadly (1676–1761), who in 1716 delivered a fiery sermon at the Chapel Royal before the new Whig ministry. He indirectly casts anti-Dissenting legislation as antithetical to the Gospels, igniting a pamphlet war that lasted until 1721.[104] Conversely, Defoe's Mahmut makes no allusions to this controversy or present-day signs of internal Anglican degeneration. Instead, he dwells on the late-seventeenth-century plight of persecuted Protestants, especially French Huguenots whom he identifies with and is mistaken for.[105] He also reports on the curtailment of French-Catholic tyranny when Protestants William of Orange – the "resplendent Star" – and Mary ascended the British throne after James II fled to Paris.[106] In *A Continuation*, Williamite England emerges as the idealized bastion of a militant royalist state (William III as the ideal warrior king who has claimed temporal and spiritual authority), built on the ideal of religious liberty rather than the defence of parliamentary rule, since the Anglo-Dutch king's toleration policy is part of a geopolitical expedient for securing British military victory over the French.[107]

The Revolution of 1688 therefore functions as the counterweight to "the grossest Hypocrites in the Universe," who have misused toleration as "a meer Guise of Deceit" for self-aggrandizement: King Louis and his accomplice "Count *Teckeli*."[108] Antithetical to British foreign policy, Mahmut's new mission is to restart the siege of Vienna. He informs Ottoman officials about the exhausted Austrian army fighting the French in the Palatinate, a military boost to the Ottoman troops who reoccupied Nissa and Belgrade in 1690 (taken by the Austrians in 1688). Emboldened by these victories, he advises his masters to advance into Austrian Hungary, an unruly "Kingdom [that] will fall naturally into the Hands of the just Nation [the Ottomans], without fighting, as it did before" thanks to Thököly's military resurgence. This diversion would pave the way for new grand vizier Köprülü Fazil Mustapha Pasha ("a Man who well knows how to rectifie the Mistakes of his Predecessors") to relaunch a counter-offensive against the Hapsburgs, who will be impeded from helping the Dutch and British fight "the King of *France*: who is now esteemed among them as the common Enemy of [...] Christendom."[109] According to this satiric logic, radical Protestants are more menacing than a "common Enemy" allied to the Ottomans, and must therefore be expelled from Christian Europe.

Unlike in *The Conduct of Christians*, this renewed obsession with the Hungarian malcontents is aimed not at an Anglican establishment rocked by religious turmoil but at the Whig politics that precipitated it: the dismantling of High Church Tory restrictions on Dissenters' participation in government, supporting and supported by heterodox churchmen like Hoadly rather than orthodox Presbyterians like Defoe.[110] Hence, the reason why he polemicizes the Whigs' pro-Turkish fervour in the 1680s. Nevertheless, writing a fiction on Ottoman efforts to renew the siege of Vienna during the Nine Years' War proved to be irrelevant to contemporary geopolitics. The Hungarian constitution had been restored in 1711, the country thereafter incorporated into the Hapsburg Empire, and the Ottomans had ceded Belgrade, the Banat of Temesvár, little Wallachia, and parts of Hungary, Bosnia, and Serbia to Austria in 1718 owing to Prince Eugene of Savoy's victory in Petrovaradin the previous year.[111] Of lasting relevance, however, were the British and Hungarian resistances to Catholic absolutism circa 1688, when the viability of a Protestant confessional state was at stake: it remained to be seen whether the Toleration Act would help build a united pluralist Britain or drag the restored island kingdom into a Hungarian-style civil war.

For Defoe, this national dilemma is figured in the Ottoman siege of Belgrade, as satirically enacted in Mahmut's (and the author's) antiquated response to current events. Convinced that the Turkish defeat in 1683 indicated "the Anger of God upon the Mussulmans Empire, for their Sins," Mahmut operates according to the reformist piety of Sultan Mehmed IV and, most problematically, the backdated information acquired from Christians.[112] In a 1691 letter to the Reis Effendi, for example, he reports on months-old news about Thököly's defeat of the Austrian field marshal Count Sigbert Von Heister in September 1690. His account is gleaned from biased European newspapers that the spy relies on for intelligence gathering in lieu of the Divan's terse communication. His reporting is informed by "The Publick Printed Papers handed about among the Infidels; wherein ... the Spirit of Falsehood ... reigns among these Pretenders to Uprightness." Likewise, in a March 1691 letter to the "Aga of the Janizaries," he rejoices at the "good news" about the grand vizier's triumph over Austrian forces in "Hungaria" and Belgrade: "Fainting under the Weight of exuberant Joy, I made good that Saying of the Ancients, (*viz*) *That sudden Joys, like Griefs, confound at first* [italics in the original]."[113] Speaking at a time when Ottoman hopes for retaking Hungary were high, he believes an event that transpired on 3 October 1690 took place recently: the Austrian surrender at Belgrade after a Turkish shell accidently ignited a powder magazine in the fort and the explosion breached the walls, an incident bemoaned in the *Review* as "the strange Retaking of *Belgrade*."[114] Yet the naïve foreigner assumes the information about this victory arrived in Paris by post mail in sixteen days, delivered across the Levant like "the Thunder of the Blast from *Belgrade*."[115] In perceiving this event as almost synonymous with its news, he cannot fathom the slow mediations by which the postal system and newspaper printing convey information over space and time. He thereby instils among his correspondents false hopes in launching another siege of Vienna – too belated, misinformed, and prideful to realize that Köprülü's military inroad into the Balkans could not sustain such an ambitious campaign.

Other temporal-spatial conflations inflect Mahmut's skewed reporting. Set apart in the text, the line "*That sudden Joys, like Griefs, confound at first*" was circulated by the Presbyterian minister and poet Robert Wild (1609–79) in *Dr. Wild's Humble Thanks for His Majesties Gracious Declaration for Liberty of Conscience, March 15, 1672.* This poetry broadside defends King Charles II's suspension of the penal laws against Catholics and Dissenters, imploring him to "keep a Jubilee" and "suspect them [the Dissenters] not [...] nor think the Worse: / For sudden joys, like grief, confound at first." Protestants should rejoice at the heavenly toleration "burst from the Royal Breast, / More Fragrant than the Spices of the East."[116] The orientalist-royalist simile used to express this mixture of joy and grief renders Wild's praise ironic, even more so after the king quickly withdrew his "indulgence" under pressure from an Anglican Parliament wary of the popish cabal in court that supported his Catholic brother James's succession. The king was suspected of having signed a secret treaty with Louis XIV in 1670 for establishing Catholic absolutism in Britain, a strategic alliance they indeed had ratified.[117] Fearful Britons rejected this "indulgence," which in Defoe's text is made doubly ironic by coming from an orthodox Muslim who is disguised as a Moldavian Catholic monk and protected by the French state. The playful ambiguity conveyed in this satiric irony creates a strange doubleness that vexes the reader, forced to interpret the italicized line as a condemnation of Stuart England's pro-French agenda or a celebration of the successful indoctrination of subjects under an executive power. In choosing one meaning over another, the reader of this satire is invited to determine the boundary line between the expeller and the expelled – inside and outside, friend and enemy – an exercise that distances the reader from, or connects the reader to, the people or ideas under scrutiny. This back-and-forth pull indicates a normative social order created through expulsions and exclusions that overturn satire's self-defensive rhetoric; it implies that the object of contempt is not us but somebody else.[118] Generating even greater uneasiness over this self-complicit irony is that Mahmut, the English double, unconsciously spews Restoration discourses consistent with his anachronistic temperament, reciting Wild's verse as if it were the "Ancient" maxim of the Greek and Roman authors he admires.

In placing this verse in Mahmut's mouth, Defoe parodies the Presbyterian rector's afterlife among Whigs who recirculated his broadside to convince Dissenters to embrace King James II's Declaration of Indulgence issued on 4 April 1687.[119] Early on Defoe urged the Dissenters – mainly Quakers and Presbyterians – to reject this underhanded ploy to make "Popery [...] the *Established Religion* of the nation," as about 200 addresses were delivered by Catholics, Dissenters, and Whigs (78 from nonconformists in England and Wales) in thanks for the royal protection of religious minorities.[120] But like Defoe, many Dissenters had misgivings about the king's extra-parliamentary decision to suspend the penal laws as head of the church, and rightly so: his Indulgence not only curtailed Dissenting speech through the use of court spies tasked with monitoring anti-Catholic sentiments in Protestant meetings but also facilitated a French-style state modernization program for Britain, establishing an absolutist Catholic monarchy in which toleration was instrumental for converting Protestant subjects to the king's faith.[121]

Fear of this possibility occasioned Defoe's next disagreements with Whig friends: the first concerning their rooting for the Turks to invade Vienna, the second for their approval of James, who "was wheedling the *Dissenters* to take off the Penal Laws and Tests."[122] These two issues are geopolitically interlinked in Defoe's convoluted analogy.

> And as *in the first* I used to say, I had rather the Popish House of *Austria* should
> ruin the Protestants in *Hungaria*, than the Infidel House of *Ottoman* should ruin

both Protestant and Papist, by over-running *Germany*; so in the other, I told the *Dissenters* I had rather the Church of *England* should pull our Cloaths off by Fines and Forfeitures, than the Papists should fall both upon the *Church*, and the *Dissenters*, and pull our Skins off by Fire and Fagot.[123]

Favouring the lesser of two evils, Defoe establishes a complex set of religious analogues – Catholic Austrians comparable to British Anglicans, Muslim persecutors to Catholic inquisitors – to argue counterintuitively that disfranchised Protestants should submit to penalization by their countrymen and reject the toleration of foreign despots, figured as an absolutist Stuart monarchy allied with a pro-Turkish France ready to catholicize Britain. Rhetorically, this scary analogy should jolt Dissenters duped by James's "wheedling," which is akin to – as Defoe writes in the *Review* –"The *Turkish* Ambassador [who] wheedl'd Count *Teckeley* and the *Hungarian* Nobility, with Hopes of great Things to be done for them."[124] Such parallels are meant to demonize naïve Whigs committed to the kind of misleading libertarian ideology the jubilant Mahmut basks in after the Ottomans had taken Belgrade. After all, the besieged city is emblematic of English national disunity: in *Advice to the People of Great Britain* (1714), Defoe compares the Turk's breaching of the fortress to the sectarian strife and party quarrels that have decayed Dissenting morals and faith, a state of affairs that prompted his own disillusionment with contemporary English Dissent.[125]

Indeed, one year after *A Continuation* was published, English Presbyterians became as divided as the Whigs over the proper criterion for subscribing to the Trinity and the Athanasian Creed. In 1719, Presbyterian ministers met at Salters' Hall to debate, among other topics, what to do about cases in which heterodox ministers were barred from preaching because they had refused to subscribe to these tenets. Non-subscribers outvoted subscribers in mandating that orthodoxy be defined by scripture alone rather than by any specific doctrines, resulting in a heated controversy in which Defoe, who favoured the Trinitarian minority, participated.[126] Mahmut's emotions obliquely allude to the prehistory of the Salters' Hall debate. On 6 March 1691, three days after the date of his letter to the "Aga of the Janizaries," London Presbyterians and Independents rejoiced over their union, instituting a common fund for the relief of ministers, support for the education of lay preachers, and training of students in biblical studies.[127] But this joyous occasion was premature and fleeting. Theological differences over the scope of rationality in religion and the apostolic legitimacy of the Anglican Church remained unaddressed, exacerbating old animosities between the denominations. By the Turkish spy's last letter, dated October 1693, joy was turning into grief as the rupture among these Dissenters precipitated the permanent breakup of nonconformity in 1719.[128] At the level of affect and rhetoric, Mahmut's "exuberant Joy" registers the compounded misfortunes that have kept (and will keep) Protestants from forming a strong coalition to liberate European Christendom from tyrannical regimes, Christian and Islamic.

Taking my cue from Alvarez's formalist analysis of Samuel Butler's *Hudibras*, I am arguing that Mahmut, in trying to posit a distinctive religion of secular reason, ends up losing control over his words, thoughts, and actions; he becomes a "punctured self" (as opposed to Charles Taylor's "buffered self"), whose enthusiasm has exposed him unwittingly to the bigotry and blind faith he ascribes to others.[129] The materiality of the italicized verse, "*That Sudden Joys, like Griefs, confound at first*," a quotation aloof from the text, renders the subject of toleration an enemy of the state, because the spy's Protestant-like claim to personal autonomy is, ironically, the essential means by which powers like Stuart Britain, Bourbon France, and the Ottoman sultanate have inflicted tyranny, that is, through the enlistment of religious dissidents as pawns for advancing rival imperial claims over their conscience, wealth, and land.

Conversely, the resilient Ottoman Empire portrayed in *A Continuation* characterizes the durable, religiously unified state Defoe wished Britain would flourish into in order to fulfil its imperial destiny. However deluded and archaic, Mahmut's Ottoman cosmopolitanism metaphorically represents the worst and the best of Georgian Britain: the pitfalls of a Dissenting community fraught with religio-political tensions juxtaposed with the promises of an Anglican state surging triumphantly after a century of internal and external warfare. Vainly awaiting the day when "*Lewis* XIV and the bright Scepter of the invincible Race of *Ottoman* the glorious [...] will meet on the Banks of *Danubius*" to "make the walls of *Vienna* tremble" once more, the Ottoman spy revived from Marana's fiction portends a mighty English Empire whose future survival and expansion necessitates an enemy to be sacrificed: extremist Protestants who have willingly and foolishly subjected themselves to an Islamic toleration that haunts Englishness itself.[130] As a satirist, Defoe wants to imagine a cohesive national community different from the one codified into law by the current Whig administration, undermining while assuming the tolerant state's violent exclusions similar to those at play in the ending of volume 8 of *Turkish Spy*.

Unresolved in this satire, the problem of regulating dissident faiths under one sovereign is taken up in Defoe's next novel about another adventurous expatriate, Robinson Crusoe, who coexists with pagan cannibals and Catholic Spaniards on a remote Atlantic island. Ingrid Creppell has argued that this story presents "an indispensable tool for the process of reflection that is necessary for securing toleration," but, I would add, as a corollary to absolute monarchic rule.[131] Uncannily, Crusoe behaves like a naïve Mahmut in quoting the line "*That sudden Joys, like Griefs, confound at first*," unaware of its ironic import.[132] The Protestant Englishman autocratically governs a multireligious society in his tolerant island kingdom after escaping Moorish slavery and – tinged with satiric irony – growing "a large pair of *Mahometan* whiskers" like those "worn by some *Turks*, who I saw at Sallee [italics in the original]."[133] Whether this novel resolves the issues raised in *A Continuation* must be the subject of another essay.

Ultimately, Defoe's satirical critique of the Islamic toleration admired by late-seventeenth-century Protestants fleeing Catholic persecution speaks directly to this volume in terms of how the literary registers the forms of lived experience, mental habits, and affective self-conceptions. The *Turkish Spy* satires reveal how the tolerant state's rhetoric of peaceful coexistence can mask an imperial agenda. A fiction about the Ottoman Empire's negative effects on European Christendom counters the theorization of toleration as an intrinsic virtue detached from its geopolitical context. In the spirit of the English *Turkish Spy*, Defoe's sequel demystifies the state-sponsored pluralism that Protestant Turcophiles mistook for a benevolent good rooted in Quranic-biblical teachings. Not coincidentally, *A Continuation* was published in the same year as John Toland's *Nazarenus*, which incorporated the heterodox thought of Baruch Spinoza and Henry Stubbe to argue that the original uncorrupted Gospel is based on a rational antitrinitarian monotheism preserved in the Qur'an and practised only by Muslims who mostly live in the sultan's accommodating empire. Perhaps because this deism was aimed against Tory efforts to enforce anti-Dissenting legislation, Defoe wrote a satiric rejoinder that, as Katherine Clark has argued, "sought to undermine Toland's use of Islam as a vehicle for attacking orthodox Christianity" as radical freethinkers were gaining political traction in the post-1715 Whig administration.[134] In effect, Defoe rewrote the deist sections of *Turkish Spy* in orthodox Christian terms in order to condemn the heterodox excesses of a Whig Hanoverian state more inclined to befriend Muslim empires than Catholic ones. He published counter-intelligence propaganda to stem the deist tide that imperilled Christian orthodoxy and scandalized Dissenters – namely, the Presbyterians – who were seeking limited comprehension within the Church of England.

Defoe's fiction offers a warning to admirers of influential Protestant thinkers like John Locke, Pierre Jurieu, and Pierre Bayle, who, for various purposes, used Islam rhetorically to argue for government concessions to Protestant heretics during a time when the Ottoman sultanate grew increasingly belligerent and chauvinistic. They regarded tolerant Muslims favourably in comparison with persecutory Christians without taking into account the imperial rivalries that Defoe saw as the historical catalyst for confessional state-building, international warfare, and religious violence across the emerging East-West divide.[135] He is one of the few writers to examine deftly how Christians fought one another while Muslims had appropriated their tolerationist politics in 1683, eager to conquer and convert a fragmentary Christendom that could not properly distinguish friends from enemies as its political theologies degenerated into irreligion, hypocrisy, and bigotry.

NOTES

1 Daniel Defoe, "A Continuation of Letters Written by a Turkish Spy at Paris (1718)," in *Satire, Fantasy and Writings on the Supernatural by Daniel Defoe*, ed. David Blewett (London: Pickering & Chatto, 2005), 4:143.

2 "Ottoman cosmopolitanism" is briefly mentioned but never explained in Srinivas Aravamudan's *Enlightenment Orientalism: Resisting the Rise of the Novel* (Chicago: University of Chicago Press, 2012), 44. On the influence of *Hayy ibn Yaqzan* on European fiction, including Defoe's novels, see Aravamudan, "East-West Fiction as World Literature: The Hayy Problem Reconfigured," *Eighteenth-Century Studies* 47, no. 2 (2014): 195–231, esp. 213–23; Mahmoud Baroud, *The Shipwrecked Sailor in Arabic and Western Literature: Ibn Tufayl and His Influence on European Writers* (London: I.B. Tauris, 2012); Shelly Ekhtiar, "Hayy Ibn Yaqzan: The Eighteenth-Century Reception of A Self-Taught Oriental Philosopher," *Studies on Voltaire and the Eighteenth-Century* 302 (1992): 217–45; and Nawal Muhammad Hassan, *Hayy bin Yaqzan and Robinson Crusoe: A Study of An Early Arabic Impact on English Literature* (Baghdad: Al Rashid House for Publication, 1980).

3 See Daniel O'Quinn, *Engaging the Ottoman Empire: Vexed Mediations, 1690–1815* (Philadelphia: University of Pennsylvania Press, 2019); Christine Laidlaw, *The British in the Levant: Trade and Perceptions of the Ottoman Empire in the Eighteenth Century* (London: I.B. Tauris, 2015), esp. 82–91; Hasan Baktir, *The Representation of the Ottoman Empire in Eighteenth Century English Literature: Ottoman Society and Culture in Pseudo-Oriental Letters, Oriental Tales and Travel Literature* (Stuttgart: Ibidem-Verlag, 2010), esp. 37–94, on Marana's Turkish Spy letters; Gerald Maclean, *Looking East: English Writing and the Ottoman Empire before 1800* (Basingstoke: Palgrave Macmillan, 2007); Brandon H. Beck, *From the Rising of the Sun: English Images of the Ottoman Empire to 1715* (New York: Peter Lang, 1987), esp. 67–90; and Ezel Kural Shaw and C.J. Heywood, *English and Continental Views of the Ottoman Empire, 1500–1800* (Los Angeles: William Andrews Clark Memorial Library, 1972).

4 The following studies analyse *A Continuation* within the postcolonial paradigm of orientalism as defined by Edward Said and his disciples, underestimating the geopolitical significance of the Ottoman Empire in the late seventeenth and early eighteenth centuries: Jacob Crane, "The Long Transatlantic Career of the Turkish Spy," *Atlantic Studies* 10, no. 2 (2013): 228–46, esp. 234–6; Gönül Bakay, "Occidental Time, Oriental Space: Daniel Defoe's *Continuation of Letters Writ by a Turkish Spy*," *Interactions: Ege University Journal of British and American Studies* 21, nos. 1–2 (2012): 15–24; and Beyazit H. Akman, "The Turk's Encounter with Defoe," *Digital Defoe: Studies in Defoe and His Contemporaries* 1, no. 1 (2009): 76–85. On the figure of the Turks and Islam in Defoe's writings, excluding *A Continuation*, see Emily M.N. Kugler, *Sway of the Ottoman Empire on English Identity in the Long Eighteenth Century* (Leiden: Brill, 2012), 55–81, and Robert

Merrett, "Daniel Defoe and Islam," *Lumen: Selected Proceedings from the Canadian Society for Eighteenth-Century Studies* 24 (2005): 19–34.

5 I consider the friend-enemy distinction as inherently political in demanding an absolute decision by the sovereign state. See Carl Schmitt, *The Concept of the Political*, trans. George Schwab (Chicago: University of Chicago Press, 1996 [rpt. 2007]), and Giorgio Agamben, *Homo Sacer: Sovereign Power and Bare Life*, trans. Daniel Heller-Roazen (Stanford: Stanford University Press, 1998).

6 Challenging the triumphant story of secular Whig constitutionalism, scholars have interpreted 1688 as the modern culmination of an authoritarian, militarized, and bureaucratic government shaped as much by internal disputes about confessional affiliation – whether Britain should be a Catholic or Protestant nation – as by state-building and peace-making in a post-Reformation European order ravaged by centuries-long sectarian wars. See Colin Jager, "Common Quiet: Tolerance around 1688," *ELH* 79, no. 3 (2012): 569–96; Steven Pincus, *1688: The First Modern Revolution* (New Haven: Yale University Press, 2009); and Tim Harris, *Revolution: The Great Crisis of the British Monarchy, 1685–1720* (New York: Penguin, 2006).

7 Jager, "Common Quiet," 572.

8 "First modern revolution" is the phrase Pincus uses to describe 1688. On governmentality as an apparatus of security, territorial acquisition, and population management that emerged in the early eighteenth century, see the essays in *The Foucault Effect: Studies in Governmentality*, ed. Graham Burchell, Colin Gordon, and Peter Miller (Chicago: University of Chicago Press, 1991). In *A Plan of the English Commerce* (1728), Defoe defines the Ottoman economy as follows: "The *Turks*, who are enemies of trade, and who discourage Industry and Improvement, 'tis plain they dispeople the World, rather than improve and cultivate it [italics in the original]." See *Political and Economic Writings of Daniel Defoe*, ed. John McVeagh (London: Pickering & Chatto, 2000), 7:115–341, at 7:133. Yet Defoe also admires the executive actions of Muslim warrior kings from the Ottoman Empire, kings free from parliamentary-constitutional constraints and the consent of the governed. See Manuel Schonhorn, *Defoe's Politics: Parliament, Power, Kingship, and "Robinson Crusoe"* (Cambridge: Cambridge University Press, 1991), 16.

9 Mehmet Bulut, "The Role of the Ottomans and Dutch in the Commercial Integration between the Levant and the Atlantic in the Seventeenth Century," *Journal of the Economic and Social History of the Orient* 45, no. 2 (2002): 197–230.

10 Wendy Brown, *Regulating Aversion: Tolerance in the Age of Identity and Empire* (Princeton: Princeton University Press, 2006), 4, 7, 10.

11 Brown notes that toleration emerged as a political expedient in the early modern period, before it became unique to Western cosmopolitanism (ibid., 37).

12 On Ottoman toleration as an imperial strategy, see Tijana Krstić, *Contested Conversions to Islam: Narratives of Religious Change in the Early Modern Ottoman Empire* (Stanford: Stanford University Press, 2011); Stefan Winter, *The Shiites of*

Lebanon under Ottoman Rule, 1516–1788 (Cambridge: Cambridge University Press, 2010); Marc David Baer, Ussama Makdisi, and Andrew Shryock, "Tolerance and Conversion in the Ottoman Empire: A Conversation," *Comparative Studies in Society and History* 51, no. 4 (2009): 927–40, esp. 929; Marc David Baer, *Honored by the Glory of Islam: Conversion and Conquest in Ottoman Europe* (Oxford: Oxford University Press, 2008); Karen Barkey, *Empire of Difference: The Ottomans in Comparative Perspective* (Cambridge: Cambridge University Press, 2008); and "Islam and Toleration: Studying the Ottoman Imperial Model," *International Journal of Politics, Culture, and Society* 19.½ (2005): 5–19; and Aron Rodrigue, "Difference and Toleration in the Ottoman Empire: Interview by Nancy Reynolds," *Stanford Humanities Review* 5, no. 1 (1995): 81–90.

13 The Ottoman historians cited above have corrected this depoliticized interpretation, yet other scholars argue for an idealistic Islamic toleration (versus an inherently intolerant Christianity) grounded solely in the Qur'an's spirituality rather than in the Muslim empires that codified these teachings into law in order to regulate, assimilate, and possibly convert religious dissidents. For a notable example of this scholarship, see Reza Shah-Kazemi, *The Spirit of Tolerance in Islam* (London : I.B. Tauris, 2012), in which the author asserts that "tolerance of the Other is in fact integral to the practice of Islam" (15).

14 On the complex linkages between the Whig narrative of liberty, individual rights, and secularity in 1688, and the co-dominant rise of innovative literary methods, genres, and styles, especially satire, see the essays in the special issue of *Restoration* 39, nos. 1–2 (2015).

15 Fredric V. Bogel, *The Difference Satire Makes: Rhetoric and Reading from Johnson to Byron* (Ithaca: Cornell University Press, 2001), 42.

16 Carl Schmitt, *Nomos of the Earth in the International Law of Jus Publicum Europaeum*, trans. G.L. Ulmen (New York: Telos Press, 2003).

17 On Marana's life and his connection to the French court, see W. McBurney, "The Authorship of the Turkish Spy," *PMLA* 72, no. 5 (1957): 915–35, esp. 917, 926–7, 931, and Joseph Tucker, "*The Turkish Spy* and Its French Background," *Revue de la littérature comprée* 32 (1958): 74–91. On the success of Ottoman spying in early modern Europe, see Emrah Safa Gürkan, "The Efficacy of Ottoman Counter-Intelligence in the 16th Century," *Acta Orientalia Academiae Scientiarum Hungaricae*, 65, no. 1 (2012): 1–38.

18 John Marshall, *John Locke, Toleration and Early Enlightenment Culture: Religious Intolerance in Early Modern and "Early Enlightenment" Europe* (Cambridge: Cambridge University Press, 2006), 94, 112–13.

19 On the complex publication history of *The Turkish Spy* volumes, see McBurney, "The Authorship"; Tucker, "On the Authorship"; Virginia H. Aksan, "Is there a Turk in the *Turkish Spy*?" *Eighteenth-Century Fiction* 6, no. 3 (1994): 201–14, at 202; and Arthur J. Weitzman, "Introduction," in *Letters Writ by a Turkish Spy* (New York: Columbia University Press, 1970), vii–xix.

20 Aksan, "Is there a Turk," 209–10, 213–14; Baktir, *The Representation*, 38–51; Ahmad Gunny, *Images of Islam in Eighteenth-Century Writings* (London: Grey Seal, 1996), 106–7.

21 "To the Reader," in *The Eight Volumes of Letters Writ by a Turkish Spy* (London: Joseph Dindmarth, 1694), vol. 1.

22 Ibid.

23 *The Eight Volumes*, 1:16.

24 Ibid., 1:1.

25 Ibid., 1:45.

26 Tucker, "On the Authorship," 35.

27 Krstić, *Contested Conversions*, 87.

28 For an informed discussion of the Kadizadeli movement's contribution to Ottoman state-building during Sultan Mehmed IV's reign, see Krstić, *Contested Conversions*, 13–14, and Baer, *Honored*, 6–7, 209–10.

29 Barkey, *Empire of Difference*, 190.

30 *The Eight Volumes*, 4:238, 4:140.

31 Ibid., 4:150–1.

32 Ibid., 4:151.

33 Ibid., 5:169–71. On deist influences in *Turkish Spy*, see Richard H. Popkin, "The Deist Challenge," in *From Persecution to Toleration: The Glorious Revolution and Religion in England* (Oxford: Clarendon Press, 1991), 195–215, at 207–8. On European Enlightenment thinkers' positive recuperation of a medieval Islamic rationalism equated with heterodox Christianity, see Jonathan I. Israel, *Enlightenment Contested: Philosophy, Modernity, and the Emancipation of Man, 1670–1752* (Oxford: Oxford University Press, 2006), 615–39.

34 Baer, *Honored*, 7.

35 *The Eight Volumes*, 2:117.

36 Ibid., 8:30, 8.96.

37 Ibid., 8:92–6.

38 "To the Reader," in *The Eight Volumes*, vol. 1. On Ottoman spies disguised as Christian priests and monks, see Gürkan, "The Efficacy," 6.

39 On Ottoman-Moldavian relations in the fifteenth through seventeenth centuries, see Jonathan Eagles, *Stephen the Great and Balkan Nationalism: Moldova and Eastern European History* (New York: I.B. Tauris, 2014), 11–12, 44, 47, 53–4, 57, 71; Thomas Barker, *Double Eagle and Crescent: Vienna's Second Turkish Siege and Its Historical Setting* (Albany: State University of New York Press, 1967), 64; and Beck, *From the Rising of the Sun*, 97.

40 "To the Reader," in *The Eight Volumes*, vol. 7.

41 *The Eight Volumes*, 8:47.

42 On Thököly's political actions, military prowess, and international reputation, see László Kontler, *A History of Hungary: Millennium in Central Europe* (New York: Palgrave MacMillan, 2002), 178–80; Barker, *Double Eagle and Crescent*, 33–6;

Ian Almond, *Two Faiths, One Banner: When Muslims Marched with Christians across Europe's Battlegrounds* (London: I.B. Tauris, 2009), 165, 168–9, 173; and Humberto Garcia, *Islam and the English Enlightenment, 1670–1840* (Baltimore: Johns Hopkins University Press, 2012), 33–4, 39.

43 Mahmut says of Thököly, "The *Count* has a good Character among the *French*, who are no Friends to the House of *Austria*, or Enemies to the *Grand Signior*." See *The Eight Volumes*, 8:349.

44 *The Eight Volumes*, 8:349, 7:135, and 7:42.

45 Although Jews suffered less persecution in the Ottoman Empire than in Christian Europe, they were tolerated and assimilated within a Muslim polity and society that reduced them to the status of second-class subjects. See Bruce Masters, *Christians and Jews in the Ottoman Arab World: The Roots of Sectarianism* (Cambridge: Cambridge University Press, 2001), 16; Mark R. Cohen, *Under Crescent and Cross: The Jews in the Middle Ages* (Princeton: Princeton University Press, 1994); and "Persecution, Response, and Collective Memory: The Jews of Islam in the Classical Period," in *The Jews of Medieval Islam: Community, Society, and Identity; Proceedings of an International Conference Held by the Institute of Jewish Studies, University College London, 1992*, ed. Daniel Frank (Leiden: E.J. Brill, 1995), 145–64.

46 See Gershom Scholem, *Sabbati Sevi: The Mystical Messiah, 1626–1676* (Princeton: Princeton University Press, 1973), 559.

47 On Sevi's conversion to Kadizadeli Islam, see Scholem, *Sabbati Sevi*, 673–86; Krstić, *Contested Conversions*, 115–16; Barkey, *Empire of Difference*, 189–90; Cengiz Sisman, *The Burden of Silence: Sabbatai Sevi and the Evolution of the Ottoman-Turkish Dönnes* (New York: Oxford University Press, 2015), 61–3, 78–9; and John Freely, *The Lost Messiah: In Search of Sabbatai Sevi* (London: Penguin Books, 2001), 133–4. Nathan's prophetic anticipation of the siege of Vienna is discussed in Scholem, *Sabbati Seni*, 925–6, and Freely, *The Lost Messiah*, 212–14. On Ottoman officials who viewed the Sabbatean movement as a seditious menace, see Sisman, *The Burden of Silence*, 45, 51–7.

48 *The Eight Volumes*, 7:76.

49 On Christian appropriations of Sabbatian prophecies in England, see Freely, *The Lost Messiah*, 70–4, 79; Sisman, *The Burden of Silence*, 61–3; Arthur H. Williamson, *Apocalypse Then: Prophecy and the Making of the Modern World* (London: Praeger, 2008), 210–17; Richard H. Popkin, "Jewish Messianism and Christian Millenarianism," in *Culture and Politics from Puritanism to the Enlightenment*, ed. Perez Zagorin (Berkeley: University of California Press, 1980), 79–83; Richard H. Popkin, "Jewish-Christian Relations in the Sixteenth and Seventeenth Centuries: The Concept of the Messiah," *Jewish History* 6.½ (1992): 163–77, at 166, 169–70; Michael McKeon, "Sabbatai Sevi in England," *Association for Jewish Studies Review* 2 (1977), 131–69; Bernard Capp, *The Fifth Monarchy Men: A Study in Seventeenth-Century English Millenarianism* (London: Faber and Faber, 1972), 213–14;

and Michael Fixler, *Milton and the Kingdom of God* (London: Faber and Faber, 1964), 237–48.

50 *The Eight Volumes*, 7:307.

51 Ibid., 8:355.

52 Bogel, *The Difference Satire Makes*, 44–5.

53 Jager, "Common Quiet," 590.

54 On tolerance/intolerance as coextensive with sixteenth- and seventeenth-century religious wars in Europe, see Benjamin J. Kaplan, *Divided by Faith: Religious Conflict and the Practice of Toleration in Early Modern Europe* (Cambridge, MA: Harvard University Press, 2010); Hans-Erich Bödeker, Clorinda Donato, and Peter Hanns Reill, *Discourses of Tolerance and Intolerance in the European Enlightenment* (Toronto: University of Toronto Press, 2009); Marshall, *John Locke*; Perez Zagorin, *How the Idea of Religious Toleration Came to the West* (Princeton: Princeton University Press, 2003); and *Toleration in Enlightenment Europe*, ed. Ole Peter Grell and Roy Porter (New York: Cambridge University Press, 2000). On early modern European travellers who noted and sometimes praised Ottoman toleration, see Barkey, "Islam and Toleration"; Gerald MacLean and Nabil Matar, *Britain and the Islamic World, 1558–1713* (Oxford: Oxford University Press, 2011), 15–16, 165–7; and Nabil Matar, "The Toleration of Muslims in Renaissance England: Practice and Theory," in *Religious Toleration: "The Variety of Rites" from Cyrus to Defoe*, ed. John Christian Laursen (New York: St Martin's Press, 1999), 127–46, esp. 129–32, 139.

55 Jonathan Israel, *Radical Enlightenment: Philosophy and the Making of Modernity 1650–1750* (Oxford: Oxford University Press, 2001), 17–18.

56 On Swift's and Leibniz's interest in the Hungarian rebellion, see Almond, *Two Faiths*, 168; Almond, *History of Islam in German Thought: From Leibniz to Nietzsche* (New York and London: Routledge, 2010), 13; and Béla Köpeczi, "The Hungarian War of Independence," in *From Hunyadi to Rakóczi: War and Society in Late Medieval and Early Modern Hungary*, ed. János M. Bak and Béla K. Király (New York: Brooklyn College Press, 1982), 445–53, at 452. Also see Jonathan Swift, *On the Conduct of the Allies and of the Late Ministry, in bringing and carrying on the War* (London, 1712). Thököly and his army of Hungarian malcontents are referenced in Marvell's *The Third part of advice to the painter concerning the great Turk, Count Teckley, and the forces against them, the French, the Spaniards, the Dutch, and the English* (London: Printed for Walter Davis, 1684) and Dryden's *A true coppy of the Epilogue to Constantine the Great that which was first published being false and surreptitious* (London, 1684).

57 In May 1703, Defoe was arrested on libel charges for anonymously publishing this tract, which impersonates a bigoted high churchmen. It was interpreted by some Anglicans and Dissenters as a seditious assault on the British church-state. See W.R. Owens, "Introduction," in *Political and Economic Writings of Daniel Defoe*, ed. W.R. Owens and P.N. Furbank (London: Pickering & Chatto, 2000), 3:17–18.

Biographer Paula R. Backscheider claims that Defoe, by the summer of 1704, was working as a spy for Robert Harley, setting up an espionage network modelled after that of the Whigs in the 1680s. See Backscheider, *Daniel Defoe: His Life* (Baltimore: Johns Hopkins University Press, 1989), 160.

58 Defoe, *An Appeal to Honour and Justice, tho' it be of his Worst Enemies* (London: J. Baker, 1715), 51.

59 Ibid.

60 On Defoe's shifting and complex political affiliations after the Tory ministry's fallout and the return to power of a divided Whig party in 1715, see P.N. Furbank and W.R. Owens, *A Political Biography of Daniel Defoe* (New York: Routledge, 2006), 136, 174.

61 Although Defoe insists that his criticisms of the Hungarian rebellion are not guided by Tory partisanship, his rhetorical choices do reflect earlier anti-Whig satires like those by Marvell and Dryden, cited above. See Daniel Defoe, *A Review of the Affairs of France*, ed. John McVeagh (London: Pickering & Chatto, 2003), 1.2: 455, 1.2:462. On Tory polemics linking Hungarian rebels to radical Whigs and Dissenters during the 1680s and 1690s, see Garcia, *Islam and the English Enlightenment*, 41–51. The quotation comes from the anonymous anti-Dissent, anti-Whig satire *Great News from Count Teckely, or, An Account of Some Passages 'Twixt a True Protestant English Volunteer and a Teckelytish Mahumetan in the Turkish Camp sent over by the Counts secretary to a brother in London* (London: George Croom, 1684), 2.

62 On the extreme Austrian intolerance that precipitated the Hungarian rebellion, see Miklós Molnár, *A Concise History of Hungary*, trans. Anna Magyar (Cambridge: Cambridge University Press, 2001), 129; and Barker, *Double Eagle and Crescent*, 27–8, 31–2.

63 Schmitt, *Nomos of the Earth*.

64 *A Short Memorial of the Most Grievous Sufferings of the Ministers of the Protestant Churches in Hungary by the Instigation of the Popish Clergy There* (London: William Nott, 1676), 2. Another anonymous writer claims that the tolerant Ottoman Empire is more rational and civilized than Catholic countries that outlaw Protestant churches, making the pope more tyrannical than the sultan. See *Weekly Pacquet of Advice from Rome; or, the History of Popery*, ed. Henry Crane (London: Langley Curtis, 1680–81), 3:254. The following late-seventeenth-century works justify persecuted Hungarians' desperate decision to seek Ottoman protection: Paul Rycaut, *The History of the Turks beginning with the Year 1679, Being a Full Relation of the Last Troubles in Hungary, with the Siege of Vienna, and Buda* (London: Robert Clavell and Abel Roper, 1700), 18–21, 27; Jean Le Clerc, *Memoirs of Emeric Count Teckely in Four Books, wherein are related all the most considerable transactions in Hungary and the Ottoman Empire*, trans. unknown (London: Tim Goodwin, 1693); and Edward Littleton, *Observations upon the Warre of Hungary* (London: Randell Taylor, 1689), 3.

65 Sixteenth- and seventeenth-century Hungary's status as a contested space between Christendom and Islamic domains is discussed in Palmira Brummett, "Mapping Trans-Imperial Ottoman Space: Alterity and Attraction," in *Representing Imperial Rivalry in the Early Modern Mediterranean*, ed. Barbara Fuchs and Emily Weissbourd (Toronto: University of Toronto Press, 2015), 33–57; and Carina L. Johnson, "Imperial Succession and Mirrors of Tyranny in the Houses of Habsburg and Osman," in the same volume, 80–100. The country's precarious situation as "the bulwark of Christendom" is often referenced in English and European writings published in Defoe's lifetime, as in the following anti-Hungarian, anti-French polemic: *An Account of the Secret Services of the Monsieur de Vernay, the French Minister at Ratisbonne to Count Teckeley* (Ratisbonne [Amsterdam]: 1683), 41.

66 On the multi-religious and multi-ethnic make-up of the Ottoman armies that besieged Vienna in 1683, see Almond, *Two Faiths*, 174, 176. For an informed analysis of how English anti-popery sentiments were partly a response to increasing Catholic conquests of Protestant lands in Europe, see Jonathan Scott, *England's Troubles: Seventeenth-Century English Political Instability in European Context* (Cambridge: Cambridge University Press, 2000).

67 Littleton, *Observations*, 24.

68 Defoe, "The Two Great Questions Consider'd (1700)," in *Political and Economic Writings of Daniel Defoe*, ed. P.N. Furbank (London: Pickering & Chatto, 2000), 5:26–55, 34. On Defoe's writings on Hungary's centrality to the European balance of power, see Furbank, "Introduction," in *Political and Economic Writings*, 9–10.

69 Defoe, "The Two Great Questions," 34.

70 Schmitt, *Nomos of the Earth*, 13, 66, 145, 148, 168–71, 189.

71 Kontler, 183; Almond, *Two Faiths*, 177–8.

72 Daniel Defoe, *A Review of the Affairs of France*, ed. John McVeagh (London: Pickering & Chatto, 2003), 1.1:380. Louis XIV's notorious nickname, "the Christian Turk," was pervasive in Defoe's lifetime as France, especially after 1700, replaced the Ottoman menace in Europe. See Beck, *From the Rising of the Sun*, 95.

73 John McVeagh, "Introduction," *A Review*, 1.1:xxix, xxxiii; Furbank and Owens, *A Political Biography*, 35; and Köpeczi, "The Hungarian War," 452.

74 Defoe, *A Review*, 1.1:356.

75 Ibid., 1.2:426. *A Review*'s anti-Hungarian stance fed into Harleian propaganda for justifying Britain's involvement in the War of the Spanish Succession, geared primarily toward anti-war Tories. See Béla Köpeczi, "Defoe and Hungary [including an abridgment of Defoe's "A Review of the Affairs of France"], *The New Hungarian Quarterly* 3, no. 8 (1962): 217–35, at 219–20; and J.A. Downie, *Robert Harley and the Press: Propaganda and Public Opinion in the Age of Swift and Defoe* (Cambridge: Cambridge University Press, 1979), 58–9, 65, 723. Hence, Defoe's propaganda is part of a vibrant print culture that sought to convince Britons that France was the hegemonic power that threatened Protestant Europe, an idea that

was not taken for granted but had to be sustained through polemic. See Tony Claydon, "The Revolution in Foreign Policy, 1688–1713," in *The Final Crisis of the Stuart Monarchy: The Revolutions of 1688–91 in Their British, Atlantic and European Contexts*, ed. Tim Harris and Stephen Taylor (Woodbridge: Boydell Press, 2013), 219–41, esp. 222–3.

76 Defoe entertains fears of Franco-Ottoman collusion during the siege of Vienna in one of his earliest publications, a translation of a French work: *An Account of Monsieur De Quesne's Late Expedition at Chio Together with the Negotiation of Monsieur Guilleragues, the French Ambassador at the Port / in a Letter Written by an Officer of the Grand Vizir's to a Pacha; translated into English* (London: 1683).

77 On Tory propaganda linking Whigs to "Protestant Mahametans," see note 61 above. On late-seventeenth-century conspiracy theories about France's strategic meddling in the Hungarian uprising, see Rycaut, *The History of the Turks*, 15; *Mercurius Reformatus or the New Observator*, issue 1 (1689); *An Account of the Secret Services*, 2–6, 18, 27–8, 53–4, 66–8; *Journals of the House of Commons* (19 April 1689); and *The Intrigues of the French King at Constantinople, to Embroil Christendom: Discovered in Several Dispatches past betwixt Him and the Late Grand Seignior, Grand Vizier, and Count Teckily* (London: Dorman Newman, 1689). These tracts falsely insinuate that France caused the Hungarian uprising. Although Louis XIV had secretly sided with Thököly, formed an alliance with the Ottomans, and approved their 1683 Siege of Vienna, his financial and military assistance of armed Hungarian rebels was not reliable and substantial enough to validate such allegations. The king provided limited aid to them in 1688, but he did not actively solicit their co-operation in weakening the Austrian Empire's eastern front, even as he welcomed this favourable outcome. The rebels were keenest on pursuing a French alliance. However, the French king did partly subsidize the subsequent Hungarian rebellion in the early 1700s, when his diplomats in Istanbul tried to convince the sultan to launch another assault on Vienna. See Köpeczi, "The Hungarian Wars," 447; Almond, *Two Faiths*, 170–1; Barker, *Double Eagle and Crescent*, 66–8; and Linda Frey and Marsha L. Frey, *Societies in Upheaval: Insurrections in France, Hungary, and Spain in the Early Eighteenth Century* (New York: Greenwood Press, 1987), 61, 72.

78 Defoe, *A Review*, 1.1:361.

79 Ibid., 1.1:336 and 1.2:468. On Defoe's later journalistic focus on the dangerous overreach of Hapsburg Austria in seeking to control Spain and Hungary, see Claydon, "The Revolution in Foreign Policy," 228.

80 Defoe, *A Review*, 1.1:360, 1.1:356.

81 Ibid., 1.2:422, 1.2:452.

82 Ibid., 1.2:451. Defoe is writing on behalf of English and Dutch efforts to negotiate peace between Leopold I and Rákóczi II for redirecting the Austrian army against the French, a peace that fell through owing to Austrian officials' unwillingness to meet Hungarian demands. Nevertheless, Defoe blames Rákóczi for this diplomatic failure, demonizing him as an "enemy [...] to the Protestant powers of

Europe." Like his stepfather before him, he is allegedly fighting "a War of Ambition" rather than a war for religious toleration (*A Review*, 1.1:336, 1.1:349). Defoe's political views on Hungary's strategic importance for Britain winning the War of the Spanish Succession are discussed in Köpeczi's "Defoe and Hungary," 218–20, 222–3.

83 Defoe, *A Review*, 1.2:433–4.

84 Almond, *Two Faiths*, 172.

85 Richard Knolles and Paul Rycaut, *The Turkish History, from the Original of that Nation, to the Growth of the Ottoman Empire: with the Lives and Conquests of Their Princes and Emperors; with a continuation to this present year, MDCLXXXVII, whereunto is Added the Present State of the Ottoman Empire* (London: T. Basset, 1967). Defoe transcribed a dozen stories about brave yet brutal warrior kings from Knolles's *General History of the Turks* in his early manuscript (never published) entitled *Historical Collections: or, Memoirs of Passages [and Stories] Collected from Several Authors* (1683), now housed in the William Andrews Clark Memorial Library in Los Angeles, California. Among these stories, one pertains to Hungarian Christians who betray their German rulers to the Turks for economic gain and another to their unlawful breach of a peace treaty with Muslims for political reasons antithetical to Christian morals. See Maximillian E. Novak, "Lost Defoe Manuscript Discovered," *The Clark Newsletter* 1 (1980): 1–3.

86 The paragraphs in *A Review*, 1.2:451–2, matches, almost verbatim, Roger Manley's rhetoric in "The History of the Turkish Empire Continued," included in *The Turkish History, Beginning from Mahomet III and Continued to this Present Year 1687*, 6th ed. (London: Tho. Basset, 1687), 2:277–338, esp. 279, 282, 285. In the *Review*, Defoe cites Manley's account of the siege of Vienna as an authoritative source. See Defoe, *A Review*, 1.1:366–7, 1.2:438, 1.2:516. Literary critics speculate that Manley may have written one or more of the seven English volumes of *Turkish Spy* that appeared after Marana's first volume. See Baktir, *The Representation*, 39; Tucker, "On the Authorship," 40; McBurney, "The Authorship," 921–2; and Gustave Leopold Van Roosbroeck, *"Persian Letters" before Montesquieu* (New York: Publications of the Institute of French Studies, 1932), 45.

87 Paul Rycat's *The Present State of the Greek and Armenian Churches* (1678) and *The Present State of the Ottoman Empire* (1668) provide evidence of Muslim toleration of Christians, often cited by Locke, Bayle, and other advocates of religious toleration. See Marshall, *John Locke*, 395, and Nabil Matar, "John Locke and the 'Turbanned Nations,'" *Journal of Islamic Studies* 2, no. 1 (1991): 67–77.

88 Defoe, *A Review*, 1.2:525–6. On Le Clerc as a major Protestant proponent of a comprehensive religious toleration in the 1680s and 1690s, see Marshall, *John Locke*, 477–501.

89 Nándor Dreisziger, *Church and Society in Hungary and in the Hungarian Diaspora* (Toronto: University of Toronto Press, 2016), 64–73; Molnár, *A Concise History*, 103; and Almond, *Two Faiths*, 158–9, 160–1.

90   Defoe, *A Review*, 1.2:546.

91   MacLean, *Looking East*, 97.

92   Defoe, *The Letters of Daniel Defoe*, ed. George Harris Healey (Oxford: Clarendon Press, 1955), 38, 46. On the Ottomans' use of effective espionage networks to undermine Hapsburg and Safavid military and diplomatic missions, see Emrah Safa Gürkan, "Espionage in the 16th Century Mediterranean: Secret Diplomacy, Mediterranean Go-betweens and the Ottoman-Habsburg Rivalry" (PhD diss., Georgetown University, 2012), and Gürkan, "The Efficacy."

93   Defoe, *The Letters*, 45.

94   On Defoe's private advocacy for restructuring Britain into an absolute executive power in his correspondences with Harley, see Schonhorn, *Defoe's Politics*, 101–8.

95   Defoe, *The Letters*, 46.

96   Defoe, *A Continuation*, 60. According to Maximillian E. Novak, Defoe first developed Crusoe's story of exile in the character of Mahmut. See "'The Sum of Humane Misery'? Defoe's Ambiguity toward Exile," *Studies in English Literature* 50, no. 3 (2010): 601–23, 612–15.

97   On Mehmed IV's dethronement, see Baer, *Honored*, 235–6.

98   Maximillian E. Novak, *Daniel Defoe: Master of Fictions: His Life and Ideas* (Oxford: Oxford University Press, 2001), 529.

99   Defoe, *A Continuation*, 47. On Mahmut's anti-Semitic attacks on rabbinical knowledge, see ibid., 93–6, 130, 132, 155.

100   Ibid., 70, 74.

101   Ibid., 104.

102   Krstić, *Contested Conversions*, 171.

103   Defoe, *A Continuation*, 47, 97. On the diverse authorial voices Defoe adopted to explore tensions within the nonconformist community, especially in his orientalist fiction, see Penny Pritchard, "Voices of Dissent: Rhetorical Strategies in Defoe's Writings before 1719," in *Positioning Daniel Defoe's Non-Fiction: Form, Function, Genre*, ed. Aino Mäkikalli and Andreas K.E. Mueller (Newcastle: Cambridge Scholars Publishing, 2011), 17–37, esp. 18.

104   On Defoe's *The Conduct of Christians* as responding to the Bangorian controversy, see Furbank and Owens, *A Political Biography*, 158–9; David Blewett, "Introduction," in *Satire, Fantasy and Writings on the Supernatural by Daniel Defoe*, ed. David Blewett (London: Pickering & Chatto, 2005), 4:1–22, esp. 2–7; and Katherine Clark, *Daniel Defoe: The Whole Frame of Nature, Time and Providence* (New York: Palgrave Macmillan, 2007), 117.

105   Defoe, *A Continuation*, 70, 80–2, 119–20, 216.

106   Ibid., 212.

107   On Defoe's defence of William III's royal prerogative over Whig-parliamentary opposition, see Schonhorn, *Defoe's Politics*, 43–88, 99. On the geopolitics of William III's toleration policy, see Jager, "Common Quiet."

108   Defoe, *A Continuation*, 139, 136, 112.

109 Ibid., 144, 101, 143.

110 Clark, *Daniel Defoe*, 115–22.

111 The Treaty of Szatmár (30 April 1711) established a peace between the Hapsburg emperor and the Hungarian rebels. It recognized Hungary's constitutional status, granted a general amnesty to the rebels, and secured freedom of conscious while forcing the country to accept the hereditary succession of the Hapsburg monarchy. The treaty therefore curtailed Hungary's sovereign independence, resulting in its subsequent absorption into the empire. See Frey and Frey, *Societies in Upheaval*, 76, and Harold W.V. Temperley, "Introductory Essay," in *Hungary in the Eighteenth Century*, ed. Henry Marczali (Cambridge: Cambridge University Press, 1910), lviii–lxii.

112 Defoe, *A Continuation*, 101.

113 Ibid., 112, 113, 115.

114 Defoe, *A Review*, 1.2:457.

115 Defoe, *A Continuation*, 115.

116 Robert Wild, *Dr. Wild's Humble Thanks for His Majesties Gracious Declaration for Liberty of Conscience, March 15, 1672* (London, 1672), 1.

117 Marshall, *John Locke*, 29. On Defoe's allusion to Wild as a subtle critique of Dissenters duped by Charles II's indulgence, see Geoffrey Sill, "The Source of Robinson Crusoe's 'Sudden Joys,'" *Notes and Queries* 45 (243).1 (1998): 67–8.

118 On the interrelationship among irony, ambiguity, and violence in satire, see Bogel, *The Difference Satire Makes*, 66–9.

119 See George Southcombe, "'A Prophet and a Poet Both!': Nonconformist Culture and the Literary Afterlives of Robert Wild," *Huntington Library Quarterly* 73, no. 2 (2010): 249–62, esp. 253, 255–60.

120 Defoe, *A Letter to a Dissenter from his Friend at the Hague concerning the Penal Laws and the Test* (Tot de Hague: Gedruckt door Hans Verdraeght, 1688), 4. On the complex political rationale for King James II's indulgence and Dissenters' ambivalent response to it, see Marshall, *John Locke*, 69–71, and Harris, *Revolution*, 216–18.

121 Defoe, *A Letter*, 268, 337; Pincus, 137–8, 167–8, 199–201.

122 Defoe, *An Appeal*, 51.

123 Ibid., 51–2.

124 Defoe, *A Review*, 1.1:386.

125 Defoe, *Advice to the People of Great Britain* (London: J. Baker, 1714), 39. In another pamphlet, *Charles Nice Davies The present state of the parties in Great Britain: particularly An Enquiry into the State of the Dissenters in England, and the Presbyterians in Scotland* (London: J. Baker, 1712), Defoe writes: "the *Decay* and *Declining* of the *Dissenters* lies in the *Decay* of their *Interest*; their *Friends*, their *Ministry*; their *General Practice*, whether Religious or Politick; their *Union* and *Unanimity* among themselves; their *Knowledge* and *Pursuit* of their own *Cause*; [...] a *decay* of their *Sanctity* of *Life*, end even of their *Morals* [italics in the original]" (286).

126 See Roger Thomas, "The Non-Subscription Controversy amongst Dissenters in 1719: The Salters' Hall Debate," *The Journal of Ecclesiastical History* 4, no. 2 (1953): 162–86. Maximillian Novak and Paula Backscheider have argued that Defoe's *A Letter to the Dissenters* (1719) and *Some Remarks upon the Late Differences among the Dissenting Ministers and Preachers* (1719) were written in response to the Salters' Hall debate. See Novak, *Daniel Defoe*, 524, and Backscheider, *Daniel Defoe*, 402, 417–18.

127 This union was codified in John Howe's *Heads of Agreement asserted to the United Ministers in and about London, Formerly called Presbyterian and Congregational* (London: R.R., 1691).

128 See Roger Thomas, "The Break-up of Nonconformity," *The Beginnings of Nonconformity* (Bedford: Foundry Press, 1964), 33–60, esp. 36–9, 45, 47–8, 51–9. On this earlier controversy as the backdrop to the Salters' Hall debate, see Thomas, "The Non-Subscription," 183–4.

129 On David Alvarez's interpretation of Butler's influential satiric poem, see the essay in this volume. On the buffered self as predicated on a "new ethics of rational control [that] supposes disenchantment" and the exclusion of irrational passions, see Charles Taylor, *A Secular Age* (Cambridge, MA: Harvard University Press, 2007), 134.

130 Defoe, *A Continuation*, 238, 240.

131 Ingrid Creppell, *Toleration and Identity: Foundations in Early Modern Thought* (London: Routledge, 2003), 126, 152. On the political fantasy of absolute royal power in *Robinson Crusoe*, see Schonhorn, *Defoe's Politics*, 141–64.

132 Defoe, *Robinson Crusoe*, 2nd ed., ed. Michael Shinagel (New York and London: Norton, 1994), 35.

133 Ibid., 109.

134 Clark, *Daniel Defoe*, 119. On Defoe writing against early eighteenth-century deist ideas that were partly ignited by the publication of Toland's *Nazarenus*, see Maximillian E. Novak, "Defoe, the Occult, and the Deist Offensive during the Reign of George I," in *Deism, Masonry, and the Enlightenment: Essays Honoring Alfred Owen Aldridge*, ed. J.A. Leo Lemay (Newark: University of Delaware Press, 1987), 93–108, esp. 94 and 98. On Toland's publication as furthering a Whig polemic against Tory attempts to limit the Toleration Act, see Garcia, *Islam and the English Enlightenment*, 51–8.

135 On these thinkers' rhetorical appeal to Islamic toleration, see Marshall, *John Locke*, 393–5; Matar, "John Locke"; Nabil Matar, "Introduction: The 'Copernican Revolution' of Henry Stubbe," in *Henry Stubbe and the Beginnings of Islam: The Originall & Progress of Mahometanism*, ed. Nabil Matar (New York: Columbia University Press, 2014), 1–48; and Justin A.I. Champion, *Pillars of Priestcraft Shaken: The Church of England and Its Enemies, 1660–1730* (Cambridge: Cambridge University Press, 1992), 99–132.

8 The Toleration of Enthusiasts

JOANNA PICCIOTTO

In 1742, responding to widespread suspicion of the movement associated with him, John Wesley published *The Character of a Methodist*. Wesley's contribution to the popular "character" genre stretched its conventions to the breaking point.[1] Identifying the very name "Methodist" as one "fixt upon them, by way of Reproach, without their Approbation or Consent," he went on to deny the people thus "fixt" any particular confessional identity at all.[2]

> The *Distinguishing Marks* of a *Methodist* are not, His *Opinions* of any sort. His assenting to This or That Scheme of Religion, his embracing any Particular Set of Notions, his espousing the Judgment of one Man or of another, are all quite wide of the Point. [...] [A]s to all Opinions which do not strike at the Root of Christianity, we *think and let think*.[3]

This was intended less to reassure than to disarm. The readers Wesley was targeting were not prepared to make any distinction between religious zeal and sectarian intolerance. For the most part, scholars of the period aren't either. Lawrence Stone's portrayal of toleration as the "child of indifference," resulting from a decline in "religious enthusiasm" after extended religious warfare, has survived decades of criticism largely intact.[4] Enthusiasm and toleration are still imagined as two buckets: as one goes up, the other goes down. And so the Methodist revival, the movement most associated with enthusiasm in the period, is generally understood as a response to – a reaction against – the historical developments that favoured the emergence of a secular sphere of toleration (whose arrival we continue to await). This essay suggests that it might be better analysed as one of these developments. I'm interested in early Methodism as it fostered an acceptance of religious pluralism under the sign of Christian perfection. It's an example that puts useful pressure on our image of what the secular sphere of toleration might be.

Rejecting the logic of escalation that governed polemical exchange in print, Wesley's strategy was to focus attention on the terms that organized it. Rather than deny the charge of enthusiasm, he equivocally embraced it, as his followers made do with the name Methodist. These imperfect accommodations, like his adaptation of the "character" genre, had usefully estranging effects. Sometimes he achieved these effects directly through verbal analysis. When a contemporary accused George Whitefield's *Journal* of being "damned cant, enthusiasm from end to end," Wesley observed that, judging from common usage, "enthusiasm" seemed to refer to "the inward workings of the Spirit of God" by "those who have not felt them": an admirably dispassionate account of how a slur comes into existence (according to this analysis, a third-person description without the modifying influence of a first-person account is not likely to generate much else).[5] As it was deployed in the eighteenth century, the label "enthusiast" might well be considered hate speech today: an expression of motivated ignorance, vacuous in content but potent in use, placing entire groups of people (Quakers, Methodists) outside the bounds of reasonable discourse. As an object of experience or aspiration, enthusiasm was indeed the core of Methodism. But this was enthusiasm of a provocatively tolerant sort.

Methodist experiments in holy living were also experiments in toleration, and not just because they challenged the Church of England to tolerate deviations from its order. It's well known that Methodist innovations put the tolerance of the Anglican Church and English society as a whole to the test, a test they spectacularly failed. The history of early Methodism is largely one of violent attacks on Methodist buildings and their persons, attacks undertaken with the active or passive support of local authorities, and of the tactics Methodists developed to cope with this onslaught. These constitute an important chapter in the history of non-violent resistance. If loving one's enemies under such conditions was a challenge, the day-to-day lives of Methodists were shaped by the no less arduous trial of tolerating one another. To become a Methodist was to join a mixed association with members from widely diverse backgrounds, in many different states of spiritual development, and possessed of a variety of theological intuitions, some well beyond the margin of respectable opinion. When challenged to defend examples of the latter, Wesley responded serenely: "*Right Opinions* is, at best, but a very slender *Part* of Religion, if it can be allowed to be any Part of it at all."[6] As always, he had empirical support for the claim. Having "made diligent inquiry into the experience of many," he had found that clarity regarding such doctrines as the trinity did not seem to be a prerequisite for "Christian perfection": the ability to love God and one's neighbour.[7]

These priorities explain Wesley's commitment to publishing "exemplary models of Christian experience" across the spectrum of belief, from French Roman Catholics to Scottish Presbyterians.[8] Methodists themselves contributed to the treasury, producing testimonials that were circulated in manuscript, published in Wesley's *Journal* (appearing in twenty-one parts from 1739 to 1791), and printed as pamphlets for distribution by itinerant preachers. The Christian Library put polite literature of all kinds within the reach of the working poor, but lives of eminent Christians enjoyed a privileged place in this series.[9] Through regular exposure to such literature, readers became habituated to the practice of abstracting themselves from their own theological commitments and the particulars of their own lives, thinking their way into different historical and personal circumstances, in order to focus on certain recurring features of Christian experience and the habits and behaviours associated with it. The sympathetic credit they became accustomed to extending had limits, but those limits were continually being stretched.

In defence of his expensive publishing projects, Wesley insisted that "it cannot be that the people should grow in grace unless they give themselves to reading: a reading people will always be a knowing people."[10] His use of the participle rather than the noun is tendentious: a knowing person is not a reader possessed of any particular knowledge, doctrinal or otherwise. A knowing person is a practised person, expert not in a body of doctrine but in a sort of activity, like John Milton's "knowing reader" (as he put it, "any knowing reader") with whom he made his general covenant in *The Reason of Church Government*.[11] The sacramental language Milton consistently used to describe the activities of writing, publishing, and reading expresses a conviction that these activities could accomplish what communication in the Eucharist so often did not. Both kinds of communication were "exercises in perception, recognition, and acknowledgement" that ideally fostered charity, the former providing preparation and even a kind of training for the latter.[12] Similarly, in "giv[ing] themselves to reading," early Methodists grew in grace by training in the rigours of intersubjectivity, across a field more expansive than their immediate neighbourhoods or parishes could provide.[13]

The challenge of articulating the value of such expertise is familiar to any teacher of literature. Literary scholars can't help acquiring a great deal of propositional knowledge, but this isn't the knowledge that distinguishes them, and it's not the knowledge whose value perpetually needs defending. What does it mean to be expert in knowledge that resists propositional expression? How is it possible to measure progress in such knowledge? To administer a multiple-choice test is to use not just a blunt instrument but an inappropriate one. What one wants to measure are increasingly differentiated sensitivities, greater endurance in acts of attention, an enlarged capacity for restricted focus on one hand and progressively unrestricted awareness on the other. In contexts where what you learn is what you train yourself to become, "knowing" describes not the possession of an object but a fitness for tasks. Methodists were tireless producers of questionnaires and study aids, and such fitness is what these materials sought to measure and promote. These documents constitute an archive of literary as well as religious instruction, what we might call, if current circumstances didn't make it sound so plaintive, an education in the humanities.

Such training resulted in something like T.S. Eliot's "historical sense," an achievement of perception rather than memorization, and an aesthetic accomplishment by virtue of being a practical one.[14] Methodist literary pedagogy offers a powerful demonstration of the continuity of aesthetic experience with everyday practice: "the normal processes of living," which, as John Dewey argued long ago, may be the only premise on which aesthetic theory – and aesthetic education – can securely build.[15] The capacity of literature to reimagine the shape and scope of lived communities was exhaustively tested by early Methodists through the circulation of life-narratives. Scholarship on such writing (under the label of spiritual autobiography) has tended to stress its status as a "feeder-genre" to the novel rather than tracking their ongoing continuity.[16] While much work on the novel has focused on its relationship to subject-formation, my interest here is in the lack of fixity of the subject at the heart of life-writing, offering a continual object lesson in the fluidity of religious experience and thus of confessional identity itself.

Wesley's "reading people" were being inducted into a highly diversified tradition whose knowledge was for the most part not teachable through "articulated assertions," but rather acquired through "intimate association and empathy with the acts of exemplification in the persons who perform[ed] them."[17] What mattered was to get examples into circulation, examples revealing the workings of the spirit under the greatest possible diversity of circumstances. A Roman Catholic French nobleman, a hermit in Mexico, a Church father: the experiences of all these people were authoritative not because their subjects were exemplars of doctrinal purity, but because they were witnesses to an experience of intense interest, whatever heresies they professed. To take seriously the devotional experiences of a papist was an exercise in charity – one that enabled something like an anthropological perspective on one's own devotional experience. To exercise such charity made it possible to dramatically reconstitute one's assumptions of what a properly religious self might be. Once such reconstitution became a habit, certain conclusions would be hard to resist: the conclusion, for example, that the thoughts one might entertain in the course of a Christian life, in any of the versions history had made available, was an unsystematic subset drawn from a vastly larger set of thoughts that one could have entertained had an occasion for them arisen. This was to grasp Christian doctrine itself as an open-ended family of possible statements, brought out according to occasion. This understanding, in turn, invited fairly exotic reflections that an earlier tradition had handled through the doctrine of implicit faith.[18] For example: is one responsible for all the logical consequences of a belief one has taken on in faith, even if one has never had occasion to ponder them? If so, might one believe something that one doesn't think is true? To entertain such questions, even beneath the level of conscious articulation, is already to be working within an understanding of the Christian subject as a self splayed across many possible histories: a bundle of processes so delicately responsive to external circumstance that they might unfold in any number of directions. Of course, a self thus exposed to outside influences could be – indeed, from a Methodist perspective, had to be – actively shaped towards certain ends, but such a self would at the same time be learning to understand these very ends as mutable.

The continuity of spiritual self-cultivation with attention to historically diverse exempla was a given for Wesley: accordingly, he instructed his lay preachers to read for no less than five hours each morning. To the objection, "But I read only the Bible," he had a ready answer: "If you need no book but the Bible, you are got above St. Paul. He wanted others too."[19] Wesley's challenge to *sola scriptura* anticipates Cardinal Newman's: "When it is declared that 'the Word became flesh,' three questions immediately present themselves: What is meant by 'the Word,' what by 'flesh,' what by 'became'?"[20] The syntax is perfectly straightforward, the sentence anything but. One can't simply accept what it says because what it would mean to accept it isn't obvious. One can only manipulate the statement in various ways and manipulate oneself in relation to it, triangulating one's response using coordinates that the tradition has provided; cognitive and mimetic practices that have accumulated around the statement may make available the forms of thought and life to which it points. More modestly, such practices may refresh one's perception of (or sustain minimally transformative acts of attention to) the familiar statement of truth that can never be entirely accepted or known, and that, given the vagrancy of thought, can often barely be attended to.[21] With a sense that the strength of one's grasp of such a sentence comes and goes, making nonsense of any hard division between believer and non-believer, Methodists encountered scattered parts of themselves, historically and geographically distant selves, and one another on the continually evolving grounds of practice, developing habits and routines thought to be conducive to experiences they very much wanted to have. The multiform nature of this task ensured its permanence.

There are many reasons why the early Methodists did not constitute a sect, but this systematic flexibility is one.[22] If they hadn't insisted on their intention to remain conforming members of the Church of England – had they been content to proclaim themselves a sect from the beginning – they would have been easier for eighteenth-century society, and our own accounts of it, to cope with. As Voltaire declared, "This is the country of sects. An Englishman, as a free man, goes to Heaven by whatever road he pleases."[23] His famous remarks about the Exchange, "where the Presbyterian trusts the Anabaptist and the Anglican accepts a promise from the Quaker," rest on a by now familiar interpretation of

England's history.[24] On this understanding, what Voltaire calls "the fury of the sects" released during the civil wars made inevitable what it could not survive: a severely voluntarist and contractual marketplace of worship, whose smooth operation would ultimately require most forms of religious speech to be exiled from the category of public discussion.[25] In the interactions taking place at the Exchange, Voltaire believes he sees the future, and he encourages us to imagine him reporting on this withdrawal as it occurs. The remaining space held in common is a purely transactional one, populated by individuals with vastly different, even incommensurable, constitutive commitments, engaged in a variety of mutually beneficial exchanges, often, we are to imagine, through gritted teeth or averted eyes – but at least not with "fury."

To cull evidence from educated eighteenth-century opinion for our standard narratives of toleration is no great challenge, since such accounts are paraphrases of those very sources, even reproducing their silences. In recent decades, a host of critics have filled this silence, taking aim at the hollow model of public reason with which the secular public sphere is ostensibly identified. It is blamed for the erosion of shared substantive commitments, the weakening of bonds of reciprocal concern, and the market control of domains once controlled by norms.[26] On this understanding, a society can't be built on toleration not only because its demands are too minimal (no one wants merely to be tolerated), but because toleration simply describes a special variety of rejection – a "rejection without practical consequences."[27] A society built on toleration has effectively given up on being a society.

Such critiques depend for their force on an impoverished idea of their object, considered either as a historical phenomenon or a useful object of fantasy. Accounts like Voltaire's and Stone's present us with a paradox: the very enthusiasm they identify as a menace to the civil society under construction in the eighteenth century was, in fact, enormously influential within it (despite being under constant attack), helping to keep open possibilities for exchange on matters of ultimate concern while sheltering those exchanges from dogmatically – much less legally – enforced conclusions, or "opinions," as Wesley liked to call them. An arsenal of eighteenth-century opinion identifies enthusiasm as a threat to civility, reasonable conversation, and public peace, but there is little evidence to suggest that this opinion was right. As members of the fastest-growing religious movement in the period daily demonstrated, enthusiasm did not inevitably express itself as fury when it entered public space, despite the fury it aroused in others.

Before elaborating this claim, it might be helpful to clarify the normative ideal at the heart of my argument, as imagined by its strongest modern defender. Critics of Habermas often imagine that his model of public speech is constricted by the limits of what he calls postmetaphysical thinking, thinking whose ethical modesty obligates it to resist any generally binding concept of the good. He has insisted otherwise. His reflections on the predicament of liberal society – which depends for its flourishing on conditions it can't legally enforce – emphasizes the crucial role of "pre-political sources" in particular religious traditions.

> Holy scriptures and religious traditions [...] have articulated intuitions concerning transgression and salvation and the redemption of lives experienced as hopeless, keeping them hermeneutically vibrant by skillfully working out their implications over centuries. This is why religious communities [...] can preserve intact something that [...] cannot be [provided] by the professional knowledge of experts alone. I have in mind sufficiently differentiated expressions of and sensitivity to squandered lives, social pathologies, failed existences, and deformed and distorted social relations.[28]

If "religious speech" – like aesthetic productions – must be treated as "a serious vehicle for possible truth contents" by the public at large, acts of translation into "publicly intelligent" language are clearly needed. Since it serves the interest of "the constitutional state to conserve all cultural sources that nurture citizens' solidarity and their normative awareness," Habermas insists that such translation "must be conceived as a cooperative task," rather than remaining the responsibility of believers alone. (In this connection, it's worth stressing again that early Methodists were keenly attentive to the fragility of the line separating believers from non-believers, since most moved back and forth across this line many times in a life, and often in a week, as their archive of life-writing amply demonstrates.) Habermas's discussion of "political virtue" emphasizes habituation into "demanding" forms of communication that require participants to progressively "decenter their cognitive perspectives," imaginatively adopting the perspectives of distant others, however provisional these efforts may be.[29] The trials of intersubjectivity permit an approach towards a consensus that can assume the authority accorded to an impersonal (or transpersonal) objective truth, were such a thing available to us. Such a consensus must be approached in the short run – in the long short run of the *saeculum* – by frequently idiosyncratic means.

This would not be news to early Methodists tasked with reading the lives of people they had been taught from birth to despise, and to read them not only as historical specimens but as potentially reliable witnesses to the operations of the Holy Spirit. For such readers, working through the Christian Library was an ongoing process of "translating" enigmatic, even repugnant, revelations into language from which something essential might be learned (usually about an experience or a technique for shaping one). If this hermeneutic exercise was an ongoing exercise in charity, it was also an exercise of Christian liberty, a version of the "free writing and free speaking" that Milton had opposed to mere licence by linking it to discipline.[30]

Methodist "freedom" was likewise a discipline, joined to an improvisatory ethos whose radicalism still shocks. As I've suggested, this radicalism had little to do with heretical speculation; for the most part, it had nothing to do with doctrine at all. As the Wesleys continually insisted, they intended to "live and die in the Church of England."[31] Understood by Methodists as the freedom to experiment, and indeed as an imperative to experiment, Christian liberty was exerted not on doctrine but discipline in the largest sense. This, I think, is the context in which to understand early Methodism's commitment to the empirical study of emotion, its highly sophisticated theorizations of habit, and its innovations in intellectual organization and communicative practice. All were expressions of "experimental religion."[32] One might say much more here about what this term meant to English Protestants, but for Wesley and the early Methodists, experimental religion was at least two things: improvisatory (responsive to providential occasion), and, like experimental philosophy, evidence-based. The improvisatory ethos expressed itself in continual innovation: open-air preaching; the use of itinerant lay preachers; the organization of bands and classes that often relied on female leadership; and the notorious system of tickets, intended to make participation in collectives continuous with accountability to them. To these we might add less central experiments in "divine amusement," from holy playing-cards to strategic participation in debate societies.[33] We might even adduce Wesley's work with electricity, resulting in an early version of ECT that he administered as a spiritual therapy.[34] Each of these projects built on the pastimes and preoccupations of the culture at large, offering a possible medium for the "translations" Habermas defends, and substantiating Sir Leslie Stephen's judgment of Wesleyan Methodism as "in many respects by far the most important phenomenon of the century."[35]

In his ruthlessly experimental approach to holy living, Wesley was as hostile to mere dogmatizing as any Royal Society Fellow; his interest in results bred a scientistic interest in psychological evidence. Enthusiasm, the direct experience of the Holy Spirit, was the very channel through which early Methodists participated in the culture of sensibility, the messy assemblage of medical, scientific, literary, and aesthetic discourses that shaped common opinion and practice in the period. Experimental religion had a large research component in attempts to discover the effect of the spirit, whatever it was, on individuals and groups – emotionally, physiologically, behaviourally.[36] In his work with electricity, for example, Wesley was probing into the secrets of the nerve: the site where the body and the soul seemed to meet, the very place where the spirit might be thought to enter.[37] The challenge was to catch the spirit before it precipitated into divisively categorical statements of "opinion," and to cultivate habits and practices that kept its potentials in circulation. Wesley was promoting a full-blown culture of enthusiasm, one in which sectarian or fundamentalist zeal could find no purchase.

Wesley's subordination of doctrine to other forms of knowing was no modern innovation. As scholars of Christianity often emphasize, what linked ancient philosophical projects like Stoicism to early Christian askesis in the first place was a shared understanding of divine philosophy as an exercise. For early Christians, theology was construed above all as the habitus of the Christian believer. It was the relocation of theology from the monastery to the university that encouraged its identification with a system of doctrines.[38] The Oxford "Holy Club" which served as the incubator for the Methodist movement enacted a reversal of this history, it seems quite deliberately: the experimental practices of the club were largely modelled after the spiritual athleticism of the desert fathers, whom Wesley and his companions were studying.[39] Not satisfied with extending this tradition, they worked to open it. Within a decade, their experimental askesis had become a popular undertaking, fuelled by the Augustinian conviction that "the gospel of Christ knows of no religion, but social; no holiness, but social holiness."[40] Their commitment to refining spiritual technique would be pursued not in the cloister of the university but through the "common life."[41]

Literary forms provided a medium for that translation. If early Methodism accelerated and intensified the process that Max Weber identified long ago with the spread of ascetic discipline beyond the cloister, Wesley's mobilization of literary modes of knowing had much to do with this rapid growth. The conference of 1744 finds him urgently asking "What shall I write next? What abridge?"[42] Getting people writing was just as important. Methodists wrote continually. Wesley found it hard to send a letter to one of his followers without including a writing prompt: we find him advising young correspondents to read and imitate the verse of poets like James Thomson, taking God's creation as their theme; to write about their dreams; to keep in touch with distant brethren by correspondence; and, most importantly, to recount their life stories. As Wesley travelled around the country, he sought out, collected, and published writings produced by his followers either individually – as in the case of "An Extract from the Journal of Mrs Elizabeth Harper," the uneducated wife of a shopkeeper – or for inclusion in *The Journal*. The printed material is just the tip of a very large iceberg. First- and third-person narratives were in constant manuscript circulation within Methodist communities: narratives of sin and redemption; relations of dreams, fantasies, and deathbed experiences; and pseudo-journalistic circumstantial relations, with titles like "An Account of the Lords Dealing with the Children at Latonstone [i.e., Leytonstone] July 14 1766."[43]

In promoting ordinary people as agents of discourse as well as its objects, Wesley was following the lead of his father, Samuel Wesley, who had been responsible for the religious content of John Dunton's periodical, *The Athenian Mercury*. The *Mercury*'s innovative question-and-answer format introduced a give-and-take between authors and a popular readership that was unprecedented in print. The place of the *Athenian Mercury* in what Lennard Davis called "the novel-news matrix" was illuminated long ago by J. Paul Hunter and George Starr.[44] Wesleyan Methodism folded this mode back into a circuit of practice, providing the "matrix" for an experimental way of life.

The novelistic mode structured Methodist experiments in holy living by enhancing a "sense of self as a person with potential for development" and of Christian perfection as a process, a state consistent with a growth in grace (like the Jesus of Luke 2:52: though always pure, "increasing in wisdom and stature, and favour with God and man").[45] As scholars of spiritual autobiography and the novel have always emphasized, producers and consumers of life-writing believed that this process unfolded on the grounds of the most apparently contingent circumstances of everyday life, rendering strict fealty to any pre-existing model positively dangerous. In light of this conviction, it's not surprising that what distinguishes Methodist narrative from earlier exemplary Christian lives is largely what distinguishes eighteenth-century prose fiction: its relentlessly circumstantial character. However strong the links that connect formal realism to Lockean epistemology and providentialist doctrine, they were cultivated and strengthened through practice: the exercise of life-writing that shaped the lives of the godly for generations before the Wesley brothers were born. Their grandfather Samuel Annesley, whose "morning exercises" at Cripplegate were attended by thousands (including Daniel Defoe), had urged writing as spiritual therapy: "Write down your case as *nakedly* as you can. [...] *perplexed* thoughts have another *aspect* when *written*, than when *floating*."[46] This conviction informed Methodist discipline from the very beginning. Thirty years after the Holy Club, anti-Methodist writers were still ridiculing the obsessive facticity of its records: a Reverend Doctor Free attacked the members as having been "so methodical, as to keep a diary of the most trivial actions of their lives, as how many slices of bread and butter they ate, how many country dances they danced at their dancing club, or after a fast, how many pounds of mutton they devoured."[47] This was Watt's "formal realism" as practice.[48]

In the years of early Methodism, novels constituted an increasingly large share of published material, enabling feedback loops that shaped Methodist style. As Vicky Tolar Burton has observed, we can see the impact of this fiction on Wesley's approach to defending the movement – and himself. His publication of the first volume of *The Journal* was prompted by public attacks on his character and beliefs after his disastrous stint as a missionary in Georgia. In response to this assault, he came out with "An Extract of the Rev Mr John Wesley's Journals from His Embarking for Georgia to his Return to London." Wesley chose to defend himself not with a statement of doctrine or an explanation of his beliefs, but through an account of someone going through a process: a narrative spun out of a travelogue and diary excerpts, like so much eighteenth-century fiction. Prefixed to the journal is a letter dated Oxon, 18 October 1732, which begins with these words: "Sir: The occasion of my giving you this trouble is of a very extraordinary nature. On Sunday last I was informed (as no doubt you will be e'er long) that my brother and I had killed your son" (as Burton remarks, "No eighteenth-century novel begins with more outrageous lines. John and Charles Wesley accused of murder!").[49] The letter continues: "that the rigorous fasting which he had imposed upon himself, by our advice, had increased his illness and hastened his death."[50] Information that exonerates the Wesleys is of course swiftly provided, but by this time, enough interest in this controversial regimen has been raised to keep the reader going. It's often observed that the circumstantial details of Crusoe's existence on the island are of disproportionate interest since they bear directly on his survival; the presence or absence of a handful of seeds might literally be a matter of life or death. But the formal argument of the circumstantial mode is that it always is.

The autobiography of Sarah Ryan, housekeeper of John Wesley and later the companion of Mary Fletcher, became a canonical text for Methodists because of the extremity of her self-transformation after conversion, but it could not have hurt its reception that for long stretches it reads like an Eliza Haywood novel. As Phyllis Mack observes, the adventure-prone Ryan read romances as a girl and told her story in their language, presenting herself as a beautiful young woman set loose in the world: "since my person [was] rather agreeable ["She was remarkable hansom," Fletcher adds], snares surrounded [me] on all sides."[51] Abandoned by a corkcutter husband who tried to whore her out and turned out to be a bigamist, she falls into relationships with an Irish merchant and then a Jewish merchant: while engaged to the second, she ends up in bed with the first. "Mr Ryan had not only an agreeable Person; but good Sense, and a very well Pollished tongue. His words stole as Oil into my bones ..."[52] From here, things escalate as expected: "This night Proved the womb of sorrowful Years to come. – He was bent on my Ruin – and affection joined with force made me that Night wholly his own!"[53] The events that follow bring us up to the present: she befriends other disgraced women in a hospital, goes to hear Wesley preach, starts attending Methodist meetings, and finally becomes a stalwart member of the movement.

Ryan's life story had a long afterlife, not just through a written sequel but through numberless oral retellings as well. As Fletcher wrote in the "Further Account of Sarah Ryan," Ryan worried that she could never speak enough about her life story to other Methodists, and she made it her constant practice to rehearse "all the Remarkable Periods of her Life" in meetings, "leaving out nothing that could Blacken or aggravate her Crimes – and this she found a kind of holy delight."[54] As she put it in her diary (excerpts of which are included in the account), "I am willing to have all Wretchedness wrote on my forehead if that can be for thine Honour" (47). She even left her diary in common areas to be combed through by others.

> [O]ne day a certain Person saying to her – "Sister Ryan – I met with your Diary – (being in a Room where she had left It) and have made free to read it – but I cannot Receive you as a sanctified soul – for though I believe such may be Tempted I can never believe there can be *suffering* without *sin* being in the Heart." – She answered little but carried it to the Lord. (50)

As related in Fletcher's sequel, this small chapter in the reception history of Ryan's text invites our indignation, not because the theological basis of the reader's objection is examined and found wanting but because, as in Wesley's "Extract," we are given a narrative episode to work with. Taking up imaginative residence in Ryan's position as she absorbs the insult and resists striking back tells us all we need to know about her spiritual state. Nothing encourages us to find fault with the *occasion* of the conflict. Lest we imagine that the person who "made free to read" the diary abused her Christian liberty in doing so, another entry three pages later records Ryan's own feelings upon reading the diary of someone else (50).

> O how was I ashamed of my Weakness and short comings before the Lord. It seemed as if Every lively Believer brought more Glory to GOD than me [...] At night heard some Letters Read – and was delighted to see my Lord had some Children who could Glorify him much more than me – but O My Father let me not be behind – for none has more Cause to praise and love thee than myself. (53)

To read or hear such a narrative was to want to be the subject, perhaps the author, of another. And one life story was never enough, even for a single person.

For even in the absence of such adventures as Ryan enjoyed, the subjects of life-narrative were not just potentially multiple in light of their vulnerability to external influence but inevitably so. The self's discontinuity across a whole life was to be assumed, but even when considered in a single instant, the seat of mental agency had a tendency to disperse. William Spurstowe, a member of the authorial collective Smectymnuus famously defended by Milton and a formative influence on the Oxford group, declared it "a work of inexpressible difficulty" to "bring the subtil and volatile acts of the mind to a fixation."[55] Thomas Halyburton's *Memoirs*, first published in 1715 and released in abridged form by Wesley in 1739, testified to the persistence of such volatility even after sanctification, documenting occasions when he fell out of "Compliance with the Design of the Gospel," when he was not completely "emptied of my self, subjected to GOD, and careful to have him alone exalted."[56] As it turned out, these were precisely the moments when he was preoccupied with worries about the condition of his soul. Reflecting on his susceptibility to these worries bred a further worry – that he was again, as he had been before his conversion, "altogether selfish," so quickly did piety seem to fluctuate into its opposite (35).

> But GOD at length clear'd up this Case to me. Our Minds have many Concerns, but through their limited Nature cannot be intent about several of them at once; therefore when any one, even the least of them, is in danger, their Care must be about that chiefly, and, as it were, only. (35)

Even for the sanctified, the mere act of attending to anything in this life inevitably made one inattentive to everything else.[57] If life-narratives offered readers a means to incorporate the experiences of others into what Wesley conceived as a common treasury or "magazine," they offered their writers the further opportunity to trace connections between far-flung versions of themselves. Since there was no question of achieving what is now optimistically called an integrated self, either on the page or beyond it, this pursuit was a permanent one.

Wesley made extravagant claims for Halyburton's text: "I cannot but value it next to the Holy Scriptures, above any other Human Composition, excepting only the Christian Pattern [i.e., Thomas à Kempis's *De Imitatione Christi*], and the small Remains of *Clemens Romanus, Polycarp* and *Ignatius*."[58] Some readers may have found this praise puzzling, since the text is almost comically uneventful. The ratio of incident and elaboration is so lopsided that in the text's first London edition, its first recommender, Isaac Watts, felt a duty to anticipate the objection that the author "multiplies Particulars beyond all Necessity" (ix). He acknowledged that Halyburton's tendency, when relating an experience, to provide an enumerated list of its constituent features rather than a summary description of the whole would try the patience of most readers when they found the "Heads" running up to "Nineteenthly, and *Six-and-Twentiethly*" (x). Given the meagerness of the action, this subtle parsing seems crazy. To the degree that Halyburton's text emphasizes any activity, it is the action of reading, and the most eventful passages are those that document its consequences. At a crucial turn in his spiritual development, "*Clark's Martyrology* was cast in to my Hand [...] The Patience, Joy, and Courage of the Martyrs, perswaded me that there was Power, a Reality in Religion" (32). This is a major change, enabling God's work "to be carried on" in him, but a fallow period follows, when "[f]or near a Year and half I read scarce any Thing; and this slothful Posture laid me open to Fresh Temptations, and made my Corruptions grow stronger still" (60). It is reading and reading alone that makes the difference between spiritual sloth and activity.

Although Wesley's "Extract" of the life feels long enough, it's less than half the size of the original. What Wesley decided to omit can tell us much about what he considered the essential function of such texts. To the extent that he can do so without rendering the narrative unintelligible, he trims away references to political allegiances and conflicts likely to activate partisan reflexes. While the original text explains that Halyburton and his mother moved abroad to escape "the Heat of the Persecution" faced by Scottish Presbyterians, Wesley's version neglects to offer any reason at all for the move (needless to say, expressions of outrage on behalf of other persecuted covenanters are deleted as well).[59] As a result, before contemporary readers had the chance to identify Halyburton as an ideological enemy, they had a chance to identify *with* him. But the political panic that marked the end of James's reign is too critical to Halyburton's spiritual development for Wesley to avoid altogether. It's in this period that "Fears of a Massacre or some sudden Stroke from the Papists gave an Edge to [his] Convictions," confronting him with the prospect of a sudden death (*Memoirs*, 23). The "continual Fears we were in of being suddenly destroy'd by the Papists: This kept Death in its most terrible Shape, ever in mine Eyes and Thoughts: And to my great Terror, I saw Wrath and Judgment following it" (24). He continues,

> I set Imagination a work, and did sometimes strongly impress my self with the Fancy of an *Irish* Cut-throat holding a Dagger to my Breast, and offering me these Terms, *Quit your Religion, turn Papist, and you shall live: Hold it, and you are dead.* The Imagination was sometimes so strong, that I have fainted almost with it, and still I was dreadfully unresolved what to do: Sometimes I would let him give the fatal Stroke: But hereon my Spirits shrunk, and my Heart fail'd at the Apprehensions of Death. (24)

Compare Wesley's version:

> There was often imprest on my Fancy, One holding a Dagger to my Breast, with, "Quit your Religion, or die": And that so strongly, that I have almost fainted under it, being still terribly unresolved what to do. Sometimes I would let him give the fatal Stroke; but then my Spirits failed, and my Heart sunk within me. (Wesley, *An Abstract*, 8)

The removal of explicit ethnic and religious identity-markers makes all the difference. The imagined conflict now seems quite unrelated to the political and territorial hatreds that occasioned it, of a piece with John Bunyan's struggle in *Grace Abounding* to suppress the intrusive thought of "selling Christ," an episode seemingly abstracted from the political (and indeed the interpersonal) sphere altogether.[60]

It is not that Wesley shies away from controversy in this text. He picks a fight with the reader on the very title page by replacing the original epigraph, the unexceptionable "Come and hear, all ye that fear God, and I will declare what he hath done for my Soul" (Psalm 66:16), with the fighting words of Acts 13:41: "Behold ye Despisers, and wonder and perish. For I work a work in your Days, a work which you shall in no wise believe, tho' a Man declare it unto you." The truculent epigraph declares the text's value as a testimonial, urging readers to overcome their resistance to the evidence it contains. It's in order to shelter readers' responsiveness to this evidence that Wesley shields them from material liable to trap them in polemical reactivity. Of course, actual information is not finally withheld (readers can't help but learn who and what Halyburton was), but it comes in diminutive increments, as if through a drip feed, and finally ceases to feel material.

Wesley's aims justify other omissions as well. Material that displays Halyburton's consciousness of generic convention – e.g., the requisite episode of fruit-stealing that proclaims the text's Augustinian lineage – has to go, since its very conventionality threatens the text's standing as a repository of evidence.[61] As far as Wesley was concerned, a good life-narrative was functionally equivalent to what a Royal Society Fellow would call an experimental relation. For this very reason, it might be objected that this survey of Methodist literature has led us a long way from aesthetic education. Halyburton observed that "where Scripture and Experience join, there we have the fullest Confirmation of the Truths that are *established in the mouth of two such witnesses*; the last not only confirming, but illustrating the Testimony of the former" (*Memoirs*, 47). Life-writing delivered that experience. But this describes the horizon of the early novel itself, its ambitions and the readerly expectations those ambitions seeded. As Robert Mayer argues in *History and the Early English Novel: Matters of Fact from Bacon to Defoe*, the novel at this juncture understood itself as a genre that could do the work of history; its aesthetics of verisimilitude was a promise, authenticating its power to deliver matters of fact or at least likely patterns of fact. Defoe took serious offence at suggestions that his narratives were fictions; this label directly threatened their proper use as carriers of virtual experience, experience readers might consult in managing their lives.[62]

Of course, in the cases of experimental relations and life-writing alike, one could only make such experience one's own through an imaginative exercise of self-projection. In recent years, the usefulness of the category of identification for understanding eighteenth-century narrative has been questioned by a number of critics, most influentially Deidre Lynch.[63] But her objections are easily handled by the simple acknowledgment that identification need not be individuating and is more likely to be emphatically non-exclusive. (Indeed, in the absence of so fundamental a mechanism it isn't clear how culture would be possible.) It would be hard to maintain, for example, that the fifteenth-century Everyman was not intended as a general identificatory object. And for post-Reformation readers, the emphasis placed on "application to the self" in scriptural study made identification a habitual cognitive exercise.[64]

That the technique of self-application inflected Methodist approaches to Bible study is demonstrated by Mary Fletcher's class-meeting preparation notes, containing prompts for discussion and hopeful scripts which any teacher will recognize. Here are some for two successive meetings: "Q. We have here an account of the prophet Elijah and his servant walking together in a very peculiar & delicate situation. What may we suppose to be the feeling of Elijahs soul at this season?" Then a follow-up question: "Q. But why doth he desire Elisha his servant and beloved Companion to leave him at such a time[?]" Fletcher sketches out possible answers and the directions they might open up for further conversation: "A. [...] that he might Listen to the inward voice of God & be able to speak what the Lord should inspire him with. But what is the most needful posture of mind for waiting on God[?]" The explication concludes with a prompt to identification, inviting pupils to imagine the protagonist's "peculiar & delicate situation" for themselves: "A. *Solemn Stillness* & yes there requires an *outward* in order to have an inward stillness."[65] Here was an opening for students to compare versions of this experience, now on the grounds of their own circumstances.

Something like identification would seem inevitably to condition our responses to the works of human authors and makers. Here, again, Dewey proves useful. In contemplating an aesthetic work, he argues, a beholder must create his own experience, and that creation "must include relations comparable to those which the original producer underwent." The identificatory effort to reprise the work's making describes the relation between art as production and art as perceptive appreciation. This relation, in turn, reprises the more basic relation between doing and undergoing that structures all human experience. We can describe the act of thinking as either a doing or a suffering: a thought occurs or comes to us, or we arrive at or entertain a thought. Because aesthetic experience, on both the productive and receptive ends, shares with other experience a perceived relation between "doing and undergoing," it is impossible not to relate the one to the other, and it is by means of such mapping that identification thrives.[66] The familiar paradoxes of agency associated with all mental life – and with grace itself – shaped the reading and writing of life narratives in a uniquely powerful way, since the relation between undergoing and doing describes the relation between experience and its shaping through technique. Put simply, narratives documenting efforts to shape a life were read by people engaged in the same effort. These narratives mediated a general collective experiment with feeling like, and being like, another – sometimes an earlier or better version of oneself. Because the subject at the centre of life-writing resolved into processes to be analysed, reflected on, and tinkered with, this mass of subjective testimony was common property.

Life-writing was material through which one could exercise toleration remotely or at close range. The journal of Charles Wesley abounds with such instances of forbearance. Consider the entry for 25 April 1738, when he and his brother visit Blendon Hall.

> [W]e were met in the little chapel, Mrs Delamotte came to us. Sang, fell into a dispute whether conversion was gradual or instantaneous. My brother was very positive for the latter, and very shocking – mentioned some later instances of gross sinners believing in a moment. I was much offended at his worse than unedifying discourse. Mrs Delamotte left abruptly. I stayed, and insisted a man need not know when first he had faith. His obstinacy in favouring the contrary drove me at last out of the room. Mr Broughton was only not so much scandalized as myself. After dinner, he and my brother returned to town. I stayed behind, and read them the *Life of Mr Halyburton* – one instance, but only one, of instantaneous conversion.[67]

Charles is furious, but he responds by reading out loud a life that provides hard evidence for his brother's position (and, as it happens, it is a position he comes to find increasingly less outrageous). As we would expect, these instances of forbearance alternate with efforts to grapple with his own weaknesses: his luke-warmness, "deadness," and misdirected zeal (*The Manuscript*, 1:114). Indeed, one regularly finds his irritation with others turn, via a perspectival shift, into self-directed criticism. To forgive the enemy of the moment is first to identify with him: "At Mr Stonehouse's, with Mrs Vaughan and others. I urged him to throw away his mystics; but he adhered to them with the greater obstinacy. Saw myself in him" (1:157). The challenge of putting up with himself, however, is often almost too much to bear. Consider these successive entries in the summer of 1738: "Was troubled today that I could not pray; utterly dead at the Sacrament"; "Still unable to pray; still dead in communicating; full of a cowardly desire of death"; "My deadness continued. [...] could not help asking myself, 'Where is the difference between what I am now and what I was before believing?'" (1:114). The trials of intersubjectivity did not stop where the self began. The day after his fight with his brother finds him passing the day "in singing and reading and mutual encouragement. In the evening we finished *Halyburton*. The meltingness it occasioned in me (like those before) soon passed away as a morning cloud" (1:100). Halyburton's own text is replete with similar experiences of ephemerality: it was the predictability of such inconstancy that made reading and writing necessary.

The reading and writing practices of early Methodism, and its understanding of the volatility of religious experience – an understanding that these practices reinforced as a condition of the temporary remedies they offered – might have worked to hasten rather than to retard the widespread acceptance of religious pluralism, since it continually exposed multitudes inside of every Christian subject, many of whom were rank unbelievers. Or it could have done so, had Methodists been tolerated. But they were responded to as sectarians, and were at last driven to become a sect. One could think of worse models for public discussion than a mass movement that unleashed multiple processes for genuinely popular learning, that engaged the main currents of their culture to bend them towards matters of ultimate concern, and that cultivated intense normative awareness while retaining remarkably large frames of reference and resisting the temptation of sectarianism. That this movement remains so marginal to our histories of toleration suggests an interesting opportunity for aesthetic as well as historical education. If the Methodist movement offered contemporaries a distinctly modern model of tolerant society, this model relied on forms of literary training that sustained and were themselves practices of charity, the most traditional virtue of all.[68] To give the Methodist example its due is thus to underscore the role of religion – and, as I have argued, of enthusiasm itself – in the creation of a secular sphere. The Methodist example also suggests that the enabling conditions of toleration may be associated less with particular conceptual innovations than with innovations in practice: communicative practice above all. Finally, the Methodist example challenges the limits of our aesthetic vocabulary. A more incisive aesthetic discourse would emphasize not superficial and revisable divisions of labour, like that between maker and audience, but more fundamental shared practices that shape common life.

NOTES

1 Characters offered broad depictions of social types, usually with a partisan slant, and were quick sellers in the market for cheap print. Typical examples include *The Character of a Modern Tory* (1713) and *The Character of a Quaker* (1704), which, like most early representations of Methodists, leaned heavily on the stock figure of the enthusiast. See Misty G. Anderson, *Imagining Methodism in Eighteenth-Century Britain: Enthusiasm, Belief, and the Borders of the Self* (Baltimore: Johns Hopkins University Press, 2012).

2 John Wesley, *The Character of a Methodist*, 2nd ed. (Bristol: F. Farley, 1742).

3 Ibid. His later assertion that "from Real Christians, of whatsoever Denomination they be, we earnestly desire not to be distinguish'd at all," makes the text almost an anti-character (sig. 1v, 1, 16–17). The epigraph from Philippians 3:12 ("not as tho' I had already attained") muddies the waters from the beginning, implying that "the character of a Methodist" had not even been achieved by its most famous representative and defender.

4 Lawrence Stone, *The Causes of the English Revolution, 1529–1642* (London: Routledge Classics Edition, 2017), 83. This despite an equally venerable historiographical tradition, extending from Hugh Trevor-Roper through J.G.A. Pocock and beyond, that stresses the centrality of religion to the Enlightenment in Britain. See, for example, Trevor-Roper's *The Crisis of the Seventeenth Century: Religion,*

the Reformation, and Social Change (Indianapolis: Liberty Fund, 2001), especially chapter 4 ("The Religious Origins of the Enlightenment"), and J.G.A Pocock, "Post-Puritan England the Problem of the Enlightenment," in *Culture and Politics: From Puritanism to the Enlightenment*, ed. Perez Zagorin (Berkeley: University of California Press, 1980), 91–112.

5 Journal entry for 12 November 1739, in *The Bicentennial Edition of the Works of John Wesley*, ed. Richard P. Heitzenrater (Nashville: Abingdon Press, 1975–), 19 vols., 19:121–2. Hereafter *BEW*. Wesley was responding to a "young gentleman" he met on the road after preaching. Wesley had an equally vivid understanding of how names could become slurs by the same process. His pamphlet, *The Question, What is an Arminian? Answered* (Bristol: 1770) began with the observation: "To say, 'This man is an Arminian,' has the same effect on many Hearers, as to say, 'This is a mad dog'" (*The Question*, 2).

6 John Wesley, *A Plain Account of the People Called Methodists* (Bristol: 1749), 4.

7 Letter of 11 June 1777, quoted in Isabel Rivers, *Reason, Grace, and Sentiment: A Study of the Language of Religion and Ethics in England, 1660–1780*, vol. 1 (Cambridge: Cambridge University Press, 1991), 220.

8 Rivers, *Reason, Grace, and Sentiment*, 221.

9 It's largely because of this narrative outpouring that, as Brian Young has observed, it can be difficult "to make any ready separation between the world of fiction and that of theological books in this period" ("Theological Books from *The Naked Gospel* to *Nemesis of Faith*," in *Books and Their Readers in Eighteenth-Century England: New Essays*, ed. Isabel Rivers [London: Continuum, 2003], 84, esp. 79–104).

10 Letter of 8 November 1790 to George Holder, quoted in Isabel Rivers, "John Wesley as Editor and Publisher," in *The Cambridge Companion to John Wesley*, ed. Randy L. Maddox and Jason E. Vickers (Cambridge: Cambridge University Press, 2009), 144–59, esp. 150. Holder was one of Wesley's preachers. To the objection that most of Wesley's followers could not afford to buy books, he responded, "It is true, most of the Methodists are poor; but what then? Nine in ten of them would be no poorer, if they were to lay out a whole penny in buying a book every other week in the year. By this means, the work of God is both Widened and Deepened in every place" (*BEW*, 12:309–10).

11 *Collected Prose Works of John Milton*, ed. Don M. Wolfe, 8 vols. (New Haven: Yale University Press, 1953–1982), 1:820. Hereafter *CPW*.

12 See Christopher Mead, "Mass Communication: The Eucharist and Authorship in Early Modern England" (PhD diss., UC Berkeley, 2015). Thanks to David Marno for this formulation.

13 Letter to George Holder, quoted in Rivers, "John Wesley as Editor and Publisher," 150.

14 "Tradition and the Individual Talent," in *Selected Prose of T.S. Eliot*, ed. Frank Kermode (New York: Harcourt Brace Jovanovich and Farrar Strauss Giroux, 1975), 37–44, esp. 38.

15 John Dewey, *Art as Experience* (New York: Minton, Balch, 1934), 10, 46. Dewey is more categorical on this point. Vicky Tolar Burton's exploration of Methodism as a literacy movement has also been an important influence on my argument (*Spiritual Literacy in John Wesley's Methodism: Reading, Writing, and Speaking to Believe* [Waco, TX: Baylor University Press, 2008]).

16 Sarah Mangin, "Skeptical Pilgrims of Spiritual Autobiography" (working diss., UC–Berkeley, 2018).

17 Edward Shils, *Tradition* (Chicago: University of Chicago Press, 1981), 22.

18 See John Henry Newman, *An Essay in Aid of a Grammar of Assent* (London: Longmans Green, 1917), 153, and my discussion in "Implicit Faith and Reformations of Habit," *Journal of Medieval and Early Modern Studies* 46, no. 3 (2016): 513–43.

19 To the objection, "But I have no taste for reading," he had the answer, "Contract a taste for it by use, or return to your trade" (*BEW*, 8:315).

20 John Henry Cardinal Newman, *An Essay on the Development of Christian Doctrine* (Notre Dame: University of Notre Dame Press, 1989), 59. See also John Norris, *An Account of Reason and Faith in Relation to the Mysteries of Christianity* (London: 1697), 77, 93–4, whose influence on Wesley ran through his mother. See John A. Newton, *Susanna Wesley and the Puritan Tradition in Methodism* (London: Epworth Press, 2003).

21 See David Marno, *Death Be Not Proud: The Art of Holy Attention* (Chicago: University of Chicago Press, 2016).

22 There is a large literature on the application of "church-sect theory" to Methodism and earlier Protestant movements in England; see C. John Sommerville's useful overview in "Interpreting Seventeenth-Century English Religion as Movements," *Church History* 69, no. 4 (2000): 749–69. David Hempton comments on the irony that Wesley, "who pioneered the formation of a non-sectarian religious association, should have been instrumental in heightening sectarian rivalries at the end of the eighteenth century"; see his *Methodism and Politics in British Society, 1750–1850* (London: Hutchinson University Library, 2013), 42.

23 Voltaire, *Letters on England*, trans. Leonard Tancock (Harmondsworth: Penguin, 1980), 41. See Richard H. Dees's excellent discussion in "Establishing Toleration," *Political Theory* 27, no. 5 (1999): 667–93.

24 Ibid., 41.

25 Ibid.

26 Brad Gregory's screed *The Unintended Reformation* (Cambridge, MA: Harvard University Press) exemplifies one version of this trend, but see also the essays in *Toleration and Its Limits*, ed. Melissa S. Williams and Jeremy Waldron (New York: New York University Press, 2008), especially the nuanced contribution of Lawrence A. Alexander, "Is There Logical Space on the Moral Map for Toleration?" 300–12, as well as Bernard Williams, "Toleration: An Impossible Virtue," in *Toleration: An Elusive Virtue*, ed. David Heyd (Princeton: Princeton University Press, 1998), 18–27.

27 Ali Rizvi, "Tolerance Makes Great Demands. Jürgen Habermas Shows What Is Involved," *Habermasian Reflections* (blog), 29 August 2005, http://habermasians. blogspot.com/2005/08/tolerance-makes-great-demands-jrgen.html. See also George P. Fletcher's "The Instability of Tolerance," in Heyd, *Toleration: An Elusive Virtue*, 158–72.

28 Habermas, *Between Naturalism and Religion: Philosophical Essays*, trans. Ciarin Conin (Cambridge: Polity, 2008), 110.

29 Ibid., 105, 131, 111, 84, 5.

30 *CPW*, 2:559.

31 Luke Tyerman, *The Life and Times of the Rev. John Wesley*, 3 vols. (London: Hodder and Stoughton, 1876), 2:245, 2:252.

32 In the introduction to his first published volume of sermons Wesley declared, "I have endeavoured to describe the true, the scriptural, experimental religion, so as to omit nothing which is a real part thereof, and to add nothing thereto which is not" (*BEW*, 1:106). The literature on experimental religion is vast, but see Peter Harrison, "Experimental Religion and Experimental Science in Early Modern England," *Intellectual History Review* 21, no. 4 (2011): 413–33 and, more broadly, Henry D. Rack, *Reasonable Enthusiast: John Wesley and the Rise of Methodism* (London: Epworth Press, 1989).

33 Methodist playing cards can be seen at the Museum of Methodism in the house of John Wesley in London. See Mary Thale's suggestive "Deists, Papists, and Methodists at London Debating Societies, 1749–1799," *History* 86, no. 283 (2001): 328–47.

34 See Paola Bertucci, "Revealing Sparks: John Wesley and the Religious Utility of Electrical Healing," *British Journal for the History of Science* 39, no. 3 (2006): 341–62; Linda S. Schwab, "'This Curious and Important Subject': John Wesley and *The Desideratum*," in *"Inward and Outward Health": John Wesley's Holistic Concept of Medical Science, the Environment, and Holy Living*, ed. Deborah Madden (Eugene, OR: Wipf and Stock, 2012), 169–212; and, more generally, Randy L. Maddox, "John Wesley's Precedent for Theological Engagement with the Natural Sciences," *Wesleyan Theological Journal* 44, no. 1 (2009).

35 Sir Leslie Stephen, quoted in Sommerville, "Interpreting Seventeenth-Century English Religion as Movements," 765.

36 On Wesley's recuperation of the language of the Holy Spirit for the Arminian tradition, see Jason E. Vickers, "Wesley's Theological Emphases" in the *Cambridge Companion*.

37 See note 32 and G.S. Rousseau, "Towards a Semiotics of the Nerve: The Social History of Language in a New Key," in *Language, Self, and Society: A Social History of Language*, ed. Peter Burke and Roy Porter (Cambridge: Polity, 1991), 213–75.

38 See Randy L. Maddox, "The Recovery of Theology as a Practical Discipline," *Theological Studies* 51 (1990): 650–72; Pierre Hadot, *Philosophy as a Way of Life: Spiritual Exercises from Socrates to Foucault*, ed. Arnold I. Davidson, trans. Michael Chase (Oxford: Blackwell, 1995); Constant Mews, "St. Anselm and the Development of Philosophical Theology in Twelfth-Century Paris," in *Anselm and Abelard:*

Investigations and Juxtapositions, ed. Giles E.M. Gasper and Helmut Kohlenberger (Toronto: Pontifical Institute of Mediaeval Studies, 2006), 196–222; and, for a popular treatment, Peter Sloterdijk, *You Must Change Your Life: On Anthropotechnics*, trans. Wieland Hoban (Cambridge: Polity, 2013).

39 See A.C. Outler, *John Wesley* (Oxford: Oxford University Press, 1980), 17–18.

40 *BEW*, 14:321. See George Lawless, "Augustine's Decentering of Asceticism," in *Augustine and His Critics: Essays in Honour of Gerald Bonner*, ed. Robert Dodaro and George Lawless (London: Routledge, 2000), 141–62.

41 Dewey, *Art as Experience*, 81.

42 Minutes for 1744, quoted in Rivers, "John Wesley as Editor and Publisher," 152.

43 Rylands Library Fletcher-Tooth Collection, box 33, folder 2, "Biographical and Autobiographical Account."

44 Lennard J. Davis, *Factual Fictions: The Origins of the English Novel* (New York: Columbia University Press, 1983), 67, passim; J. Paul Hunter, *Before Novels: The Cultural Contexts of English Fiction* (New York: Norton, 1990); G.A. Starr, "From Casuistry to Fiction: The Importance of the *Athenian Mercury*," *Journal of the History of Ideas* 28, no. 1 (1967): 17–32; G.A. Starr, *Defoe and Casuistry* (Princeton: Princeton University Press, 1971).

45 Burton, *Spiritual Literacy*, 103.

46 *The Morning-Exercise at Cripple-Gate* (1661), 16.

47 *BEW*, 8:506–7. See discussion in Burton, *Spiritual Literacy*, 102.

48 Ian P. Watt, *The Rise of the Novel: Studies in Defoe, Richardson, and Fielding* (Berkeley: University of California Press, 1957, 2001).

49 *BEW*, 1:123; Burton, *Spiritual Literacy*, 79.

50 *BEW*, 1:123.

51 Fletcher-Tooth Collection, box 24, folder 1, "Account of Sarah Ryan," 10.

52 Ibid.

53 Ibid., 14.

54 Fletcher-Tooth Collection, box 24, folder 1, "Some Further Account of Mrs Ryan," 34.

55 *The Spiritual Chymist, or, Six Decades of Divine Meditations on Several Subjects* (1666), sig. A4. See *BEW*, 2:138.

56 Thomas Halyburton, *Memoirs* (London: 1718), 34.

57 On distraction and attention as versions of one another, see Marno, "Easy Attention: Ignatius of Loyola and Robert Boyle," *Journal of Medieval and Early Modern Studies* 44, no. 1 (2014): 135–61.

58 John Wesley, "Preface," in *An Abstract of the Life and Death of the Reverend Learned and Pious Mr. Tho. Halyburton*, ed. with preface by John Wesley (London: 1741), vi.

59 Halyburton, *Memoirs*, 47.

60 Passim, but see esp. par. 139, 141, and 171. Also see Brooke Conti, *Confessions of Faith in Early Modern England* (Philadelphia: University of Pennsylvania Press, 2014), 140–3.

61 Compare Halyburton, *Memoirs*, 22, and Halyburton, *Abstract*, 8.

62 Robert Mayer, *History and the Early English Novel: Matters of Fact from Bacon to Defoe* (Cambridge: Cambridge University Press, 1997).

63 *The Economy of Character: Novels, Market Culture, and the Business of Inner Meaning* (Chicago: University of Chicago Press, 1998).

64 See Kate Narveson, *Bible Readers and Lay Writers in Early Modern England: Gender and Self-Definition in an Emergent Writing Culture* (Farnham, UK: Ashgate, 2012), esp. chap. 3 ("Application to the Self: Reading and the Restructuring of Identity").

65 Fletcher-Tooth Collection, Box 27, Folder 6, Bundles for Nights 160 and 161, on 2 Kings 2–3.

66 Dewey, *Art as Experience*, 56, 54, 46–7.

67 *The Manuscript Journal of the Reverend Charles Wesley*, ed. S.T. Kimbrough, Jr, and Kenneth G.C. Newport, 2 vols. (Nashville: Kingswood), 1:100.

68 See Alexandra Walsham's *Charitable Hatred: Tolerance and Intolerance in England, 1500–1700* (Manchester: Manchester University Press, 2006), and Istvan Bejczy, "*Tolerantia*: A Medieval Concept," *Journal of the History of Ideas* 58, no. 3 (1997): 365–84.

9 Joseph Priestley's Romantic Progressivism

MARK CANUEL

The work of Joseph Priestley has often been acknowledged for its importance and influence in the long eighteenth century. The sheer volume of his writing makes him difficult to ignore: he was author of nearly two hundred books and pamphlets on a wide range of subjects – education, chemistry, theology, and politics, to name a few. But it was surely the intellectual rigour and inventiveness of his work that produced such an indelible imprint across this range of fields: he was revered by poets like Samuel Taylor Coleridge and Anna Barbauld; he was a friend to luminaries like Benjamin Franklin, whose pioneering work on electricity Priestley popularized; and his political thinking inspired Jeremy Bentham and the entire course of utilitarianism throughout the nineteenth century. This leaves us with little reason to quarrel with Isaac Kramnick's claim that Priestley was "the central figure in political, educational, and religious radicalism" of his era.[1] Kramnick's description of Priestley's "scientific worldview," however, exemplifies how Priestley is perhaps one of the most consistently misunderstood figures in eighteenth-century letters.[2] In scholarly accounts of his scientific investigations, his "empiricist" account of rhetoric, and his "rational" religious Dissent, Priestley's writing is frequently oversimplified in order to make his work as a whole conform to Enlightenment scientific and rationalist paradigms that it often complicated and subtly resisted.[3]

In this essay, I attend to Priestley's writing for different reasons – for its far more eccentric and adventurous mode of progressivist political thinking, which teaches us to reflect with a renewed and modified attention on the substantial influence he had on writers of his day and on generations to follow. I ultimately argue that Priestley contributes to what I understand as a thoroughly "Romantic" form of tolerant political progressivism. What this means is that his imaginative rendering of a reformed political system borrows a range of tropes from the Enlightenment, but it drastically reorients their significance. In particular, his call for political and civil institutions to tolerate Dissenters and Catholics (among other believers) incessantly draws on notions of history as an improvement in understanding and refinement in manners. But he also challenges narratives of uniform political advancement with daring visions of new institutional forms that cultivate contention and disagreement from within. I close my argument by discussing the relation between Priestley's work and the interconnected histories of prose fiction and political theory, both of which display investments in enlightened institutional apparatuses that manage the energies of political and religious dissent.

Priestley's Enlightenment

Throughout his work, Priestley explicitly opposes a range of repressive measures that restricted institutional participation for religious nonconformists. These date back to the early modern period, as analysed by Paul Yachnin in this volume. Further legislation – especially the Corporation Act of 1661 and the Test Act of 1673 – imposed the Church of England sacraments on political, civil, and military office holders; the restrictions were eventually extended to teachers and students at Oxford and Cambridge. To some degree, Priestley's argument against these and other exclusionary policies at the heart of the confessional state focuses on touting the virtues of reason over barbarism and tyranny; he undermines damaging stereotypes of Protestant Dissenters in particular as "canting hypocrites" and enemies of "liberal taste or disposition."[4] In contrast to that view, he insists on the intellectual advancements of the Dissenting community: that community, he declares, rejects church rituals reminiscent of "barbarous and superstitious ages"; they share in a general "increasing light of the age," and "politeness of the times."[5] At one point in his *View of the Principles and Conduct of the Protestant Dissenters*, he even suggests that the children of Dissenting families, because of frequent challenges levelled at their faith, have ended up with "more [...] knowledge than [Anglican] church men of the same class and rank in life."[6] The strategy is clearly designed to provoke some shame or envy among his audience: he urges the institutions of the state to further their own analogously progressive impulses. And thus, the goal would be to align social institutions with the most intellectually advanced of their members.

This aspect of Priestley's argument makes toleration look like a uniform cultural progressivism, and it is therefore possible for him to review a series of legislative enactments to make it seem as if history demonstrated a corresponding enlightened loosening of restrictions: he contrasts the violent suppression of nonconformists under Elizabeth I to the limited but insufficient concessions under William III and Mary's 1689 Toleration Act. That entire trend can seem like the outgrowth of scientific inquiry in that it coincides with an ability to see religious believers as they really are – not as dangerous but as supremely rational. Priestley repeatedly made use of the term "rational Dissent" to describe members of this religious community. It is only rational, the argument goes, to allow political participation and civil liberty from other rational beings. Conversely, practices of religious persecution, he occasionally suggests, could be written off as an inadequate understanding of "the true principles of religious liberty."[7] At still other moments – more or less consistent with this way of thinking – he concocts elaborate metaphors suggesting that the social body is a natural one with improper parasites or growths upon it which need to be "extirpate[d]" to ensure national health.[8] The idea of the political body as a biological one is, of course, a time-honoured idea, and Priestley knows that Milton had used it effectively in *Areopagitica*,[9] but increasing professionalization and experimentation in medicine expanded and refined the implications of the connection. Both Voltaire in France and Barbauld's younger brother, John Aikin, in England saw liberal political change as medical advancement; thus toleration could be seen on analogy with smallpox vaccination.[10] Whether viewing the nation as a medicalized body in need of curing, or as a deluded mind in need of rational correction, Priestley makes political reform over time follow a logic of scientific advancement.

The expansion of civil and political liberty and participation for nonconformists, however, was less easily assimilated to the progressivist model than some of these expressions might make us think. Acquired taste, learning, propriety, and even "politeness," as we have seen, occasionally seem to be positive attributes of Dissenters and of the tolerant society that would accommodate them, but the progressive acquisition of knowledge can just as often appear to be negative traits in Anglicanism, conventional institutions, and those who defend them. When Priestley recounts that a friend of his, an "excellent scholar, and a person of philosophical taste," espouses an idea of Dissenters shaped by Samuel Butler's *Hudibras*, he links prejudice (against Presbyterians, in Butler) not with a primitive form of belief but rather with literary and scholarly refinement, as if literature and literary taste progress in order to harden into inflexible conceptual categories.[11] As shown in David Alvarez's essay in this volume, eighteenth-century satire's coercive appeals to common sense are thoroughly consistent with Priestley's judgments on Butler and with eighteenth-century literary taste in general.

Indeed, for Priestley, the cultivation of polite learning, and even of a literary canon itself, perniciously dictates a "common conversation," a term that he uses to refer to a repetitive and confining political norm for all subjects.[12] Even scientific inquiry can tend in the same direction, as Priestley makes abundantly clear when texts like his *Letters to a Philosophical Unbeliever* spoke of a sceptical and scientific empiricism as "received rules of philosophizing" that shut down inquiry as much as they expanded them.[13] A common conversation with commonly held rules may not seem like the worst way of thinking about political interaction, and it may even resemble the way that Jürgen Habermas famously describes the public sphere.[14] But, for Priestley, that common conversation coincides with an emphasis on cultured "moderation" in intellect and sentiment; this, in turn, prevents an active exchange of potentially offensive views, and a consequent "sinking" in the quality of intellectual exchange.[15] This is a point of view that he had firmly developed long before the French Revolution, but we can see him mobilizing the argument consistently still later, in his *Letters to the Right Honourable Edmund Burke*, in response to Burke's *Reflections on the Revolution in France*. There, Priestley associates Burke's sophisticated taste with a "heated" imagination resulting in extravagant aesthetic sensibilities.[16] Absent from Burke's impassioned defence of a "splendid church establishment," Priestley says, is any religious discussion or debate that would ruffle the elegant surfaces of Burke's political aesthetic.[17] The criticism of Burke's rhetorical skill was more or less a staple of the Revolution controversy, and we find similar arguments in Thomas Paine's *Rights of Man* and Mary Wollstonecraft's *A Vindication of the Rights of Men*, among other texts of the moment.

Priestley's writing, then, appears to endorse a politics of scientific and cultural advancement over time, but that advancement poses a threat to the very political agents it supposedly benefits. To some extent, he reaches for a resolution to this impasse by making value judgments about the character of knowledge itself. On the one hand, there is the kind of progressive acquisition of knowledge that only serves hypocritically to cover up empirical truths: this is the problem with Burke. On the other hand, there is the kind of progressive acquisition of knowledge that exposes those empirical truths: this is what Priestley upholds. A version of this distinction is at work when Priestley regards Anglicanism in *Letters to ... Burke* as a mere "superstition," a devotion to outward rituals at the expense of an "inward temper of mind"; likening his own scientific knowledge to a natural light source, Priestley writes that "prejudice and error is only a *mist*, which the sun, which has now risen, will effectually disperse." This kind of argument has a significant amount of traction – in these letters and indeed throughout his theological writings – when he likens Anglicanism to popery, in that both are instances of "error and false religion."[18]

Priestley's strange way of aligning himself with a blazing sun even while he has just criticized Burke's heated imagination only begins to indicate the inconsistencies in this line of attack. But the apparent contradiction can be traced to the fact that the truth revealed by his own work could be described as the truth of the political, for the truth that the established church covers up is most accurately seen as a truth of contentious religious beliefs; the church is a beautiful unity that hides a more complex and unharmonious underside. Within the same letter in *Letters to ... Burke*, Priestley looks around him and notes the rise of agrarian "White Boys" in Ireland, Methodists in England, in addition to a "great number of Dissenters" of multiple denominations throughout the kingdom. He closely monitors the rapidly advancing construction of physical buildings in Birmingham to house the increasing numbers of Methodist and Dissenting congregations. Furthermore, he notes that "the increase of the dissenters and Methodists in Sheffield, in Leeds, and, [that he has] no doubt, in other manufacturing towns [...] has been nearly in the same proportion."[19] Priestley is noting the spread of new and varied religious congregations in a publication printed by Thomas Pearson, who had also published the work of other nonconformists like John Wesley, and, therefore, is exploiting the medium of an expanding Dissenting print culture to reinforce his point about Dissent's general public visibility. The accommodations in print and the built environment, which the text describes in detail, reinforce each other. Although it is not the purpose of my argument to discuss print culture at any length, it is still worth mentioning here that the vast amount of recent work on print culture – because it has tended to limit itself to an argument about print as sympathetic identification – has not quite come to terms with the central position of Dissenting cultures as a driving force behind literacy and print. Far from a common conversation, both the physical and discursive landscapes of Great Britain were characterized in Priestley's work by political and religious contention.

Public Dissent and Public Good

Priestley's point in accounting for these varied beliefs within the British political landscape is not merely to show that an established religion is a false view of actual religious belief and conduct. His point is rather to suggest that there could be an alternative mode of constructing a more tolerant form of government. The question is, of course, what is the alternative to this false or hypocritical mode of unity? If it's true, as Priestley insists throughout his political and theological writing, that belief takes many forms, how can political subjects be governed? Such questions relate to debates up into our own day about toleration and its limits, and I want to touch on them just for a moment. Political theorists ranging from Michael Sandel to Wendy Brown routinely find the logic of toleration to be flawed because toleration always implies a position of power from which persons and groups can be tolerated. The irony of the position is that the complaint often lands theorists squarely back in the camp of toleration: a critique of unjust assertions of power often implies that institutions should somehow tolerantly refrain from wielding it.[20] But the irony is virtually inevitable simply because talking about government necessarily requires talking about power. Debates about toleration from early modernity to the present can never really be about the mere existence of power but rather about how power is shaped and mobilized in relation to political subjects. It is this particular configuration that I want to discuss in regard to Priestley.

Any discussion of Priestley's account of tolerant government must be distinguished from a classical liberal view, which it superficially resembles. At first glance, that is, Priestley's response appears to be a call for freedom from Anglican "imposition" – a call, in other words, to consider religion as a private matter. Occasionally there are areas in his writing that appear to involve a merely laissez-faire logic with respect to adherents of different faiths. In *Letters to ... Burke*, he repeatedly criticizes his opponent for "confounding religion with the civil establishment of it"; in his earlier *View ... of the Protestant Dissenters*, he similarly criticizes the "tools of court policy" which impinge upon the "independence of mind" regarding matters of faith.[21] This falls more or less easily into a defence of "negative liberty" – a freedom from external influence and imposition.[22]

Protecting "independence of mind" also requires limiting the influence of the Anglican Church. Priestley is not always entirely clear on the degree to which he favours complete disestablishment versus a more generous accommodation within Anglicanism. Although his early writing argues for a modification of establishment so that it would become more inclusive, the success of the American model of disestablishment becomes an important example for him, one which he cites with some regularity.[23] Virulent defences of Anglicanism in the wake of the French Revolution, combined with equally virulent attacks on Priestley and his fellow Birmingham parishioners in 1791, only seem to have hardened rather than weakened his resolve after the 1790s to seek full disestablishment, which, of course, was not ever to happen. At the very same time, he insisted that questioning the church's political authority did not – as his detractors insisted – align Dissenters with the French or with "republican" sympathies; he remained staunchly in support of constitutional monarchy.[24] But the various iterations of Priestley's position are somewhat less important than some very consistent and complex arguments, ones that go beyond seeing secular toleration as a privatization of belief. He was obviously well aware of the fact that such an argument would simply amount to what he regarded as a "popish" version of secular government: one that confined religion to privacy and levied requirements with little to no influence or complaint from religious subjects. Privatizing religion, in other words, clearly seemed to reproduce the problem of religious establishment while calling it by another name.

Instead of enforcing this public/private split, Priestley argues for expanding the tolerant inclusiveness of religious beliefs, while insisting on that inclusiveness as a maximization of public contact points between believing subjects and institutions. Even in *Letters to ... Burke*, where Priestley most passionately argues against the "civil establishment" of religion, his point is not to say that religion should be private but that its public value should not result in a uniform public expression. When he declares in the argument against establishment that "religion [...] is useful to all men [...] as it furnishes an additional motive to good behavior in every situation," he exposes some of the complexity and tension within his position.[25] Religion gets to be included among a range of other beliefs and practices and evaluated for its usefulness – even though the motives that would lead to useful conduct are not themselves imposed by a legislative authority. They are analysed and measured, but they are not preordained.

The word "useful" is crucial in his formulation. In all of his writings – regardless of their particular stance vis-à-vis establishment – he thinks of the institutions of an ideal government as capacious facilitators of public good. As Peter Miller has convincingly argued, the notion of "public good" is hardly an invention of the eighteenth century, and it may go back at least as far as Cicero; it re-emerges in full force with Francis Bacon's understanding of knowledge as "*commodis humanis inservire*," or "the relief of human suffering."[26] But there are peculiar features of its direction in Priestley's work which would have significant ramifications for later political writing and for the development of a range of literary genres like the novel, which also became interested in the maximization of utility.

The emphasis on public good does indeed depend upon a discourse of progressive maximization, and this in turn makes government into both a subject and means of analysis: a mechanism for subjecting actions for assessment even as it could be analysed for its effectiveness in furthering and fostering useful actions. The distinction between Priestley and a thinker like Pierre Bayle may be obvious enough: Bayle spoke of surprisingly wide tolerance for adherents of many faiths (as Elena Russo points out in this volume), but he was not quite committed to a comprehensive theory of government. But when Priestley accuses Burke of neglecting the subject of "government," the claim sounds downright perverse: isn't Burke's uneasiness about abstract liberty's threat to ancient laws and institutions inspired by an admiration for government? Not quite, Priestley says. His point (one that so clearly influenced Bentham and others following him) is that by confusing religion with its establishment, Burke makes government appear to be identical to the beliefs, intentions, and affects of political subjects, and Priestley's contrasting emphasis on government as its own framework for analysis departs from what he sees as Burke's error. "Government," Priestley writes, "not only in theory, and in books, but in actual practice [is] calculated for the general good."[27] Notice Priestley's tactic of calculating government's calculations. This is more or less an extension of an argument that he consistently makes elsewhere in more elaborate and theoretical terms, particularly in his *Essay on the First Principles of Government*, where the "good and happiness" and "mutual happiness" of society is the object of government and the standard by which governing institutions and policies can themselves be measured.[28] Government, in order to maximize utility, is continually engaged in the "management of public affairs," and this management consists of reducing the possibility for injury and increasing – indeed perfecting – the amount of happiness among the governed.[29]

But as much as Priestley thinks of government, and even of "human nature," as capable of "perfection," that perfection is most often detached from any standard version of virtue ethics or political theology.[30] Indeed, the emphasis on government as an artifice capable of standing both apart from yet entangled with contentious and unruly political subjects takes centre stage in his account. This is because utility-advancing technologies of affiliation bridge over differences in religious orientation, to such an extent that the *Principles* goes so far as to admire Turkish government in its ability to tolerate Christians and Muslims at the same time.[31] Humberto Garcia's essay in this volume provides a relevant context for understanding Priestley here: it is clear that Priestley's assessment of Ottoman political practices is far more abstract than Defoe's. Political systems, for him, are to some extent flexible enough to be transported from one place to another. And thus he imagines secular government in Britain itself as capable of permissively embracing Catholics as well as Dissenters. This was an unusual move for the time, considering that other rational Dissenters like Richard Price refused to do so. Priestley was not entirely alone in his views (Joseph Berington's *Rights of Dissenters* [1790] was another notable exception that Priestley cites approvingly).[32] But he was certainly the era's lightning rod for outraged Anglicans like Spencer Madan, who accused him of improper affiliations with "apostate [...] Jews" and "deceived Mahometans."[33] Priestley's Romantic version of enlightenment – one that imaginatively envisions capacious new institutional forms – requires the embrace of what he considered, from a theological point of view, the unenlightened. I do not mean to imply by this that Priestley was a doctrinal relativist. Indeed, he was anything but that: he was firm in his belief in Unitarian doctrines and in the errors in belief among adherents of other religions. (I will have more to say about this in a moment.) But he thought of the felicitous operations of government as perfectible in their ability to accommodate believers that, from any standpoint within the polis, might regard others as imperfect (and perhaps even verging on dangerous).

To an extent, the mere admission of nonconformists under the auspices of secular government could itself be considered a social good. Priestley argues that "improvement" in government can be assured by making "concessions" to nonconformists.[34] And against Burke's view that an established church contributes to the "general advantage," he insists on Burke's miscalculation of that advantage precisely because he notes that Burke confuses advantage with conventional accounts of dignity and greatness in monarchy and religious establishment.[35] His retort is that the church's exclusionary policies – once submitted to any calculation of harms and benefits – produces far too many injuries to be considered a true "advantage": "the people of this country will at length discover," on the contrary, "that [the church] is really a *nuisance*."[36] Merely removing the church establishment, according to this logic, would contribute to general utility.[37]

But there is more to Priestley's vision of tolerant government than mere inclusion, making institutions an indifferent container for religious affiliations. He endorses a more intimate connection between political subjects and the infrastructure of public environments, and this works in two key directions. First, when Priestley discusses tolerant institutions of government, he is thinking of frameworks of association that enhance collective utility while providing protection. The notion of "protection" against injury is central to this aspect of Priestley's argument; by the same token, government should encourage practices (like Methodism, for instance) that contribute to beneficial conduct.[38] Again, the point to be made here is not that Priestley approves of the religious or ideological sources of this good conduct from a personal point of view; he didn't actually agree with the enthusiasm and sympathy-generated ethics of Methodists, a topic explored in Joanna Picciotto's essay in this volume. It is rather that he endorses a form of government that would employ sanctions in order to enable and direct those sources of favourable conduct. When Priestley defends the "natural rights" of religious believers without interference from tyrannical powers, this is not because religion has become private in relation to public action, but exactly the opposite: rights are held because they have been subjected to a public assessment in terms of their contribution to the social whole.[39] Both interference and non-interference are *actions* subject to a felicific calculation according to whether one or the other can be done to "good purpose."[40]

The incentives and sanctions that lead to enhanced utility and security (which is itself a form of utility) always depend upon what I have already pointed out as Priestley's dedication to government itself and to its organizing features. One of the most prominent recurring claims throughout his works is that these increasingly frequent contact points between governing institutions and political subjects induce a new kind of affiliation. Rather than attending merely to her own interests, a political subject will turn her attention to the "different classes and sects of [...] fellow subjects"; she will "be a friend to equal laws, and regular government."[41] Rather than driving a wedge between government and political subjects, as established religion tends to do, a tolerant form of government would allow society to "benefit" from the "talents" of subjects, and this would, in turn, allow those subjects to be increasingly "attached" to the facilitating structures of government that protect and solicit their energies.[42] They would be as "zealous" for the laws of their country as they would be for their own beliefs, if not more.[43]

The specification and proliferation of these contact points leads to the second, inverse, direction in which Priestley envisions the closely knit relation between individuals and political architecture that I am describing. This is the right of individuals and groups to petition and to seek redress for wrong and injury: it is a cornerstone of Priestley's thinking that is present in all of his works of political theory. Exercising this right opens utilitarian governance to a repeated series of judgments that contest overly narrow or constraining definitions of pleasure or pain. The entire purpose of making government into a distinct object of analysis is to enable its possible correction over time by even the "lowest people" of society, who can curb the will of "tyrants" and "friends of arbitrary power."[44] When he reviews the history of the Puritans from Elizabeth I to the English Revolution, he associates Puritanism only with complaint against injury from the court and the church establishment. Puritans, he argues, "did nothing that could be called seditious"; they adhered to laws but "petition[ed] [...] the legislature for the redress of their grievances."[45] The account contradicts the notion of Puritan opposition as an instance of resistance theory – the notion that opposition for religious reasons justifies revolution. But the argument is taken yet further to apply to numerous political contexts: every citizen, he concludes more broadly, has an "equal voice" in declaring an "injury," and in "bravely redress[ing] public wrongs."[46] A review of history across Europe reveals to him that even when "force of arms" has been used against a government, it is most likely a justified form of complaint: "in all cases of dissatisfaction with government," he concludes, somewhat surprisingly, "it is most probable, that the people are injured."[47]

Such claims understandably reinforced his opponents' suspicions that he supported revolutionary violence; this led to mob attacks on his home and church in Birmingham and to attacks on numerous Dissenting churches and homes in 1791. But his comments also need to be appreciated for their strenuous effort to re-describe revolutionary conflict as legitimate reform. His *Familiar Letters Addressed to the Inhabitants of Birmingham* responds directly to Spencer Madan's virulent and frequently ad hominem attacks precisely by levelling the distinction between dangerous innovation and incremental change. He insists that "innovation" in government – so often the subject of fear among conservative defenders of the church like Madan himself – amounts to nothing other than an "amendment" to it.[48] This coincides with Priestley's larger attempts to insist that – despite his reputation for stirring controversy – his own innovative thinking was only a recommendation for change rather than revolution. And he reaches for a still larger point when he insists that a broad swath of legislative actions – such as the Test and Corporation Acts and the Toleration Act – are all innovations/amendments that require redress and further innovations/amendments. We might easily ask: when does change overturn the "constitution" itself?[49] The ontological question of when change becomes truly revolutionary – one of the key questions that tends to separate liberals from radicals – holds little or no interest for Priestley. He is far more focused on expanding the degree to which divisive alliances might jockey for obtaining redress within the existing laws and institutions of a utilitarian form of government.

Priestley's Disciplines and the Problem of Divine Government

By framing political and religious struggle as tolerable demands for institutional accommodation, Priestley constructs a higher plane of vision that clearly connects to his theological writing where he repeatedly views historical events as products of divine inspiration. The point to be made here is not that political arguments for toleration were identical to theological arguments, but rather that the two kinds of argument in Priestley's writings engaged in a productive tension. In his *Institutes of Natural and Revealed Religion*, Priestley defends the idea of Christianity as a form of "divine government," and spends much of that work pointing to the way that both New and Old Testaments support the view of a divine government that is distinctively, indeed perfectly, benevolent. This was not unusual, by any means: utilitarian legislators, for example, frequently looked to the story of Cain and Abel as evidence of how God favoured milder forms of punishment even for crimes of murder.[50] As one can easily imagine, this requires highly selective and debatable readings of scripture, and Priestley is not an exception here. At one particularly telling moment, he follows Paul's typological reading of Christian faith in Hebrews, suggesting that Abraham was willing to sacrifice Isaac precisely because he knew that God "would not permit him to put his son to death, or that he would raise him from the dead," and thus a sacrifice was never intended or interpreted as a sacrifice at all.[51] It is interesting here that Priestley concentrates on only one dimension of Paul's reading of the narrative of Abraham: that is, he omits the argument from Galatians 4:21–31 about the distinction between Ishmael and Isaac, one son born through the "flesh" and the other from the "promise," which – with its implication that a "promise" is more about bloodlines than belief – endorses an unyielding sense of exclusion rather than any sense of divine benevolence. Priestley conveniently leaves this dimension of Paul's interpretation out, presumably because the discrimination between Ishmael and Isaac is difficult to explain on utilitarian grounds.

The echo of Paul's interpretation of the Old Testament has a deeper significance, I think, in that it points to the real stress and strain that Priestley produces in order to make scripture say what he wants it to say. He doesn't entirely attempt to cover this up, however. He fully acknowledges how easily a sceptical critic could point to pain, violence, and death within and beyond scripture as a way of contradicting the suggestion that God has an interest in furthering the general good. And thus, one of the broader claims of the *Institutes* is that, even if it is true that human history involves a great deal of pain and evil, and even though this may not look like a government for the good at any particular moment, the longer view of history endorses the truth that "the great object of divine government is the production of happiness."[52] By this, Priestley does not even mean that happiness is achieved after temporal existence (as St Augustine had argued) but that greater happiness is achieved when history is considered as a whole rather than in isolated parts.

These theological arguments, and their connections with problems of secular government, alert us to the fact that Priestley's diverse interests as a writer need to be considered as interconnected rather than in terms of individual texts. Two arguments are frequently made about Priestley's massive output in the fields of theology, science, aesthetics, hermeneutics, and politics. One argument is that some modes of thought are more prominent than others; Martin Fitzpatrick thus claims that politics is secondary to theology.[53] Another argument seeks to graft one field to another; I have already mentioned Kramnick's argument about Priestley's rational dissent; we could add to this Simon Schaffer's suggestion that science and politics in Priestley are both revolutionary.[54] These two perspectives err by either over-distinguishing or under-distinguishing the various discourses which Priestley not only participates in but also actively shapes. On the one hand, we must acknowledge that Priestley did indeed think of his works as targeting specific audiences, as even the framing apparatuses of titles and prefaces suggest: the *Letters to Edmund Burke* is very much part of a political pamphlet war, for instance; the *Institutes* is addressed to societies of Christian worshippers. These are implicit acknowledgments that the communities of worshippers, politicians, and scientists cannot simply be superimposed on each other or addressed in precisely the same way with the same arguments.

On the other hand, we must simultaneously appreciate the way that Priestley struggles to make the connections anyway, fraught as they may be. The full set of interconnections requires a rehearsal of a perspective that Priestley himself does not lay out, but I believe that it works as follows: the advance of toleration bears a certain limited resemblance to the advance of scientific inquiry, but the progress of tolerant government is ultimately dependent upon the progressively elaborated artificial structures of felicitous social cooperation. Those structures advance insofar as they advance the greatest good for the greatest number. Such structures, in turn, appear to be a version of Priestley's notion of divine government itself. While very much pitched as a theological, antitrinitarian argument, the most impassioned Unitarian account of divine government simultaneously appears like an entirely tolerant form of social cooperation. Thus, the very errors that seem mistaken from a theological point of view (and this theological point of view often coincided with a scientific perspective) turned out to be politically felicitous from the point of view of utilitarian governance. To put it another way, errors in constituting power are consistent with perfectibility in constituted power. To imagine Unitarianism merely as a yardstick or requirement for political participation would be to repeat the errors of all religious establishments.[55]

The relation between religion and government begins to look homeomorphic rather than isomorphic: distinguishable but related in shape. Government as a "science" can be honed and perfected precisely in order to accommodate substantive interior imperfection, contention, and changeability; the commitment to Christianity and to divine government looks like a recommendation for a model of perfect secular government precisely insofar as it permissively allows for the inclusion and active voicing of radically discrepant, and even unchristian, views (Priestley even sounds surprising notes of tolerance towards atheists).[56] Depending on where you stand, utilitarian inclusiveness looks Christian, or Christianity imitates utilitarian inclusiveness. A correct reading of the relationship would not simply end by congratulating ourselves with the discovery that toleration was Christian all along. It would, however, concede that a certain mode of theological, political, and scientific imagining arises amid intriguing tensions, overlaps, and tentative resolutions.

Postscript

I want to close with two observations, one about the history of literature – in particular, the novel – and one about the history of political theory. I turn to the novel as only one of many literary instances that can be illuminated by this line of inquiry. When Priestley remarks in passing that different theological opinions that engage with and pressure others constitute our "proper character," I think this can be taken as an invitation to reflect on the tensions and struggles that appear throughout the history of the genre utterly devoted to character and its properties and propriety – that is, the history of the novel.[57] Consider, just as an example, the development of the Gothic novel in England. The Gothic was the pre-eminent genre in which the authority of religious institutions was subject to an intertwined political and literary pressure. Imbued with archaic political and religious norms and beliefs, the Gothic conspicuously advertised itself as the knowing ally of enlightened epistemology and social cultivation. But even more important was its attention (as in Priestley's work) to innovative approaches to tolerant governance. A perfect example can be found in Ann Radcliffe's famous novel *The Italian or the Confessional of the Black Penitents: A Romance*, which depicts monastic environments as threats to the movement and visibility of persons who stood at the centre of novelistic narrative. The implicit target of criticism in her fiction is not only Catholicism but also the apparatus of the confessional state more generally, a version of which could be found in Britain. This is why Radcliffe's novels as a whole deploy prefatory matter and plot devices in order to distance the narration and the formal/material support for that narration – as a printed book – from the discursive and political enclosures of churches, monasteries, and convents. All of these enclosures are presumed to disguise rather than disclose action, and to protect rather than reveal offences.[58]

From its very opening pages, *The Italian* analogizes the written medium of the novel itself to a protected confession that must be given a public airing. The manuscript – according to the apparatus of the preface in which a monk hands a written text to a travelling Englishman – is being protected in a church and its adjoining convent. And the manuscript, therefore, turns out to be much like a confessed but protected murderer whose shadowy form is glimpsed by the

Englishman, identified by a monk, and, yet, protected insofar as the particulars of his identity are kept secret. The Englishman supposedly conveys the narrative – now in printed form – to Radcliffe's reader.[59] Reinforcing the point of this frame (a frame that distances the novel from a reading of scripture for doctrinal purposes), the plot of the novel depends upon analogous technologies of exposure. The crimes of the evil monk Schedoni are revealed and punished, and the central characters – Ellena and Vivaldi – are joined in marriage despite sustained and terrifying opposition from Vivaldi's family and the church. The resistance to oppressive and hypocritical religious authority, however, can emerge only from within the mechanisms of ecclesiastical power. Nothing other than the Inquisition itself resolves abuses of confessional power; the marriage between Ellena and Vivaldi occurs under the aegis of a reformed church (which is itself attached to a reformed convent).[60] This is where the subtitle of Radcliffe's work becomes particularly relevant: *The Italian* is a "romance," not because it is unrealistic but because the demands of realism – a telling of the truth outside the hypocritical uniformity of church authority – still depend upon a spiritualized source of authority, reformed though it may be.

Biographical work on Radcliffe has now exposed (as much as possible in the case of an author about which so little is known) the degree to which the novelist's upbringing and early education took place in an intellectual milieu – primarily through her uncle John Jebb – connected to Priestley and other Unitarians.[61] The interwoven intellectual histories of Priestley and Radcliffe invite careful comparison: they demonstrate the degree to which Radcliffe, like Priestley, views "proper character" as the result of tolerant institutional and narrative strategies. This is, to be sure, visible in the aesthetic richness of her novels, which easily move from contemplations of natural scenery to contemplations of divinity. But the Unitarian legacy is also visible in terms of *The Italian*'s politics. On the one hand, the observations of landscape appear to contemplate and endorse an all-embracing "enchantment" of spiritualized nature. On the other hand, the benevolent embrace contains, and indeed requires, a critique of religious uniformity. The alliance between political and ecclesiastical power in furthering the "abundant happiness" and "general gaiety" of political subjects at the novel's end comes only as a consequence of opposing the imposition of religious and political norms. It comes only as a consequence, that is, of a consistent opposition to Inquisitorial violence and cruelty.[62]

For Radcliffe, as for Priestley, a tolerant government is justified by a providential authority that exercises a utilitarian form of divine government even while that divine government is tolerant of dissension and conflict emerging from within. Although Priestley apparently demotes the importance of novels when he calls them products of "ingenuity," Radcliffe's narrative ingenuity is a discursive support for Priestley's equally inventive accounts of tolerant institutional membership.[63] This brings us to a point about political theory more generally.

This is a political theory that, as in Priestley, develops alongside – influencing, and being influenced by – the history of the novel. More particularly, Priestley's thinking most obviously influenced the writing of Jeremy Bentham and the intellectual legacy of utilitarianism. Bentham credited both Cesare Beccaria and Priestley for having developed the idea of government as the greatest happiness for the greatest number.[64] But this legacy became so drastically reduced in its significance that it became virtually synonymous – particularly through the enormously influential work of Michel Foucault – with social engineering and biopolitics. The reason why Priestley has never quite risen to the level of a canonical figure in political history or in literary studies (despite specialized academic appreciation for his accomplishments) is quite possibly that political theorists have never quite known what to do with his dissenting position. Priestley was an institution builder who was resistant to the enforcement of institutional norms: it has been difficult for his interpreters to know what to make of the paradox.

If we examine Priestley's work closely – and by "closely," I mean accepting its tensions rather than resolving or eliminating them – a new and even more theoretically interesting set of connections comes into view. Albert O. Hirschman's distinctions between differing responses to social organization in *Exit, Voice, and Loyalty* are particularly germane to the account I trace out. We can exit organizations, Hirschman says, we can attain voice within them, or we can be loyal to them.[65] Loyalty can be activated, he claims, by encouraging voice: analogously, we could say that Priestley's perspective seeks to augment or amplify the voice permissible within any constellation of institutional and legal loyalties.[66] Another way of looking at the same issue is to see how Priestley strives to open up the policing of common good to what Jacques Rancière (truly the most English of all French political theorists in terms of his influences and sympathies) understands to be the "politics" of disagreement or dissensus.[67] To deny contention is to deny politics.

To trace a line from Priestley to Rancière may at first seem improbable. Although it is true that Rancière is almost as distant from a theory of government as Burke is – at least by Priestley's standard – Priestley may still be closer to Rancière than accounts of the Dissenting tradition might make us think. The Dissenting legacy (just like utilitarianism itself) has too often been smoothed out into a flat, unemotional, and unvaried rationalism. Connecting Priestley to a range of recent theorists and the issues they urgently explore turns out to be far from improbable and indeed truly necessary. The connections, not to mention the truly complex legacy of Dissenting utilitarianism, are clarified once we see how Priestley and others of his age understood the achievement of commonality, the common, the common good, and community to be fractured by contention and debate.

NOTES

1 Isaac Kramnick, "Eighteenth-Century Science and Radical Social Theory: The Case of Joseph Priestley's Scientific Liberalism," in *Motion toward Perfection: The Achievement of Joseph Priestley* (Boston: Skinner House, 1990), 59.
2 Ibid., 73.
3 See, for instance, Kathryn Ready, "Dissenting Heads and Hearts: Joseph Priestley, Anna Barbauld, and Contending Attitudes toward Devotion in Rational Dissent," *Journal of Religious History* 34, no. 2 (2010): 174–90.
4 Joseph Priestley, *A View of the Principles and Conduct of the Protestant Dissenters*, 2nd ed. (London: Joseph Johnson, 1769), 3.
5 Ibid., 14, 52, 87.
6 Ibid., 84.
7 Ibid., 71.
8 Priestley, *Letters to the Right Honorable Edmund Burke, Occasioned by his Reflections on the Revolution in France* (Birmingham: Thomas Pearson, 1791), 82–3.
9 John Milton, *Areopagitica*, in *Complete Poems and Major Prose*, ed. Merritt Y. Hughes (New York: Macmillan, 1985), 745.
10 Voltaire, *A Treatise on Toleration and Other Essays*, trans. Joseph McCabe (Amherst, NY: Prometheus Books, 1994), 186; J. Aikin, MD, *Letters From a Father to His Son* (London: J. Johnson. 1793), 212.
11 Priestley, *View*, 3.
12 Ibid., 85.
13 Priestley, *Letters to a Philosophical Unbeliever*, 2nd ed. (Birmingham: Pearson and Rollason, 1797), 190.
14 Jürgen Habermas, *The Structural Transformation of the Public Sphere: An Inquiry into a Category of Bourgeois Society*, trans. Thomas Burger (Cambridge, MA: MIT Press, 1991), 89–140.
15 Priestley, *View*, 87.
16 Priestley, *Letters to ... Burke*, 2, 19.
17 Ibid., 68, 80.
18 Ibid., 105, 111, 112.
19 Ibid., 86, 87, 72, 127.
20 Michael Sandel, *Liberalism and the Limits of Justice* (Cambridge: Cambridge University Press, 1982); Wendy Brown, *Regulating Aversion: Tolerance in the Age of Identity and Empire* (Princeton: Princeton University Press), 2006.
21 Priestley, *Letters to ... Burke*, 92; Priestley, *View*, 10.
22 On "negative liberty" as freedom from coercion, see Isaiah Berlin, *Four Essays on Liberty* (Oxford: Oxford University Press, 1963), 118–72.
23 Priestley, *Political Writings*, ed. Peter Miller (Cambridge: Cambridge University Press, 1993), 87; Priestley, *Letters to ... Burke*, 143.

24 Priestley, *Familiar Letters, Addressed to the Inhabitants of Birmingham* (Birmingham: J. Thompson, 1790), 12.

25 Priestley, *Letters to ... Burke*, 92.

26 Peter Miller, *Defining the Common Good: Empire, Religion, and Philosophy in Eighteenth-Century Britain* (Cambridge: Cambridge University Press, 1994); J.B. Bury, *The Idea of Progress* (London: Macmillan, 1920), 52.

27 Priestley, *Letters to ... Burke*, 142.

28 Priestley, *Political Writings*, 13.

29 Ibid., 25.

30 I have reservations about Margaret Canovan's account of Priestley's endorsement of a "natural moral hierarchy" as the basis for utilitarian government in "The Un-Benthamite Utilitarianism of Joseph Priestley," *Journal of the History of Ideas* 45, no. 3 (1984): 437. She is not able to make sense of Priestley's position on toleration.

31 Priestley, *Political Writings*, 54.

32 Priestley, *Letters to ... Burke*, 138; Joseph Berington, *The Rights of Dissenters from the Established Church* (Dublin: P. Byrne, 1790).

33 Spencer Madan, *Letters to Joseph Priestley, Occasioned by his Late Controversial Writings* (London: J. Dodsley, 1787), 5.

34 Priestley, *View*, 50.

35 Priestley, *Letters to ... Burke*, 24.

36 Ibid., 126.

37 See also Priestley's argument against Blackstone's claim that "the practices of the sectaries are not calculated to make them good subjects," Priestley, *View*, 1.

38 Priestley, *Letters to ... Burke*, 28, 87.

39 Priestley, *Political Writings*, 46.

40 Ibid., 56.

41 Priestley, *View*, 36.

42 Priestley, *Political Writings*, 88.

43 Priestley, *Familiar Letters*, 30.

44 Priestley, *Lectures on History and General Policy* (London: Thomas Tegg, 1826), 24. It would be up to Bentham, in his account of public opinion as a utilitarian watchdog, to develop the precise mechanisms of political action and correction further.

45 Priestley, *View*, 70.

46 Priestley, *Political Writings*, 25.

47 Ibid., 21, 25.

48 Priestley, *Famliar Letters*, 56.

49 Ibid., 56.

50 Mark Canuel, *The Shadow of Death: Romanticism, Literature, and the Subject of Punishment* (Princeton: Princeton University Press, 2007), 1–3.

51 Joseph Priestley, *Institutes of Natural and Revealed Religion*, 2 vols. (London: Joseph Johnson, 1794), 2:24.

52 Priestley, *Institutes*, 2:16.

53 Martin Fitzpatrick, "Joseph Priestley and the Millennium," in *Science, Medicine, and Dissent: Joseph Priestley*, ed. R.G.W. Anderson and Christopher Laurence (London: Wellcome Trust, 1987), 29–37.

54 Simon Schaffer, "Priestley and the Politics of Spirit," in *Science, Medicine, and Dissent*, ed. Anderson and Laurence, 39–53.

55 Although Priestley argued that there should be a "rational and intelligible" religious establishment, this consisted primarily in removing the tithe and other burdensome restrictions. Robert E. Schofield, *The Enlightened Joseph Priestley: A Study of His Life and Work from 1773 to 1804* (University Park: Penn State University Press, 2004), 169. For a contrasting view of the importance of rationality as a limit on toleration in Priestley, see Stephen Bygrave, "'I Predict a Riot: Joseph Priestley and Languages of Enlightenment in Birmingham in 1791," *Romanticism* 18 (2012): 70–88.

56 Priestley, *Letters to a Philosophical Unbeliever*, 231.

57 Ibid., 179.

58 This reading traces out further implications of my argument in *Religion, Toleration, and British Writing, 1790-1830* (Cambridge: Cambridge University Press, 2002), 55–85.

59 Ann Radcliffe, *The Italian or The Confessional of the Black Penitents: A Romance*, ed. Frederick Garber (Oxford: Oxford University Press, 1968), 1–4.

60 Radcliffe, *The Italian*, 411.

61 Rictor Morton, *Mistress of Udolpho: The Life of Ann Radcliffe* (London: Leicester University Press, 1999), 33.

62 Radcliffe, *The Italian*, 413.

63 Priestley, *Lectures on History*, 30.

64 While Canovan notes Bentham's account of his source for this principle ("The Un-Benthamite Utilitarianism," 436), she points out that the formulation did not appear anywhere in Priestley's work.

65 Albert O. Hirschman, *Exit, Voice, and Loyalty: Responses to Decline in Firms, Organization, and States* (Cambridge, MA: Harvard University Press, 1970), 30.

66 Ibid., 30.

67 Jacques Rancière, *Dissensus: On Politics and Aesthetics* (London: Bloomsbury, 2010), 70–83.

10 Translating Love in *Prometheus Unbound*

COLIN JAGER

So faith, hope, love abide, these three; but the greatest of these is love.

1 Corinthians 13:7

In any event, our philological home is the earth: it can no longer be the nation.

Erich Auerbach, "Philology and *Weltliteratur*" (1952)

Like several other dominant thought-patterns of the eighteenth century, religious toleration found its terminus in the French Revolution. It would be too easy to criticize Enlightenment toleration simply by pointing to the Terror. But it is nonetheless true that the enthusiastic secularization and dechristianization that marked the years 1789–92 was both a culmination of distinct eighteenth-century trends and a harbinger of subsequent developments: the surprising tenacity of the conservative counter-revolution, Robespierre's deistic Cult of the Supreme Being and, eventually, the Concordat of 1801, which established an official state secularism that remained in effect throughout the nineteenth century.

Unevenly and fitfully, the French had arrived at what Charles Taylor terms an "independent ethic" theory of secularism. Citing Spinoza and Grotius, among others, Taylor describes this as a largely continental effort to construct a society "as if" there were no God. He contrasts this kind of secularism with what he calls a "common ground" approach, developed by Locke and other English thinkers, who endeavoured to construct a model of a minimalist state adjudicating among a variety of metaphysical orientations.[1] Both approaches, as Taylor notes, have their limitations. The common ground model assumes a basically religious anthropology, no matter how minimal. It is patterned after Protestant denominationalism and thus struggles to accommodate a wider range of beliefs and practices; even though toleration is its professed goal, there are limits to how far the model can be stretched. The independent ethic, by contrast, is methodologically atheist but depends upon an activist state to police the bounds of religious and secular; because it sees secularism as a good in itself and toleration as merely a fortunate by-product, the independent ethic can produce conflict between the state and "religious" expressions.

These models are ideal-types, of course; in practice, we experience the benefits and limitations of both, in domains as varied as immigration, school prayer, war, statecraft, the teaching of science, voting rights, and modern capitalism. Nonetheless, these ideal-types allow us to see something clearly: the common ground model is a specifically religious (indeed, Christian) model of toleration, while the independent ethic is not. And this means that efforts, like those of the French Revolution, to build a culture around the independent ethic will tend to see *religion itself*, rather than denominational conflict, as a threat to order and stability.

The literary and cultural movement that we call "Romanticism" was born in the aftermath of the Revolution, in the awareness of its uneven success and in the consciousness of its cost. This is a conventional observation, to be sure, but its importance for understanding the possibilities and limitations of modern religious toleration has not yet been fully developed. The common ground model is metaphysically constrained and fully invested in a liberal individualism that had come to seem inadequate by the end of the eighteenth century. The independent ethic model, by contrast, is volatile: prone to conflict between state and religion and given to acrimonious debate about what counts as a religion in the first place. The only other option on offer at the beginning of the nineteenth century was a presumably inevitable process of secularization linked to progress, civilization, and empire – that would be the dominant model of the nineteenth century, of course, though it has yet to produce robust religious toleration, and perhaps cannot.[2] So what else might have happened? This must be the question motivating any account of Romanticism and religious toleration: given the Revolution's rupture of historical continuity and its mixed success, we can ask whether a different imagining of toleration might have led to a different outcome. Here we are, of course, in the realm of the counter-factual. But counter-factuals are Romanticism's *raison d'être*, and imagining religious toleration one of its underappreciated possibilities.

Romanticism's presumed belatedness relative to Enlightenment toleration would seem to limit its usefulness for a reimagining of toleration's terms. But that belatedness may also be turned to advantage, for the results of Enlightenment progressivism do not become fully manifest until the early years of the nineteenth century, as writers and artists struggled to come to terms with the radical break in historical continuity that they saw in the French Revolution. In the present volume, Mark Canuel's essay on Joseph Priestley comes nearest to this line of argument. Canuel's account of a thoroughly Romantic form of tolerant political progressivism as "a maximization of public contact points between believing subjects and institutions" is certainly an advance on more familiar accounts of the eighteenth-century privatization of belief within the framework of a non-interventionist state. But even Priestley's progressivism is a modification of an Enlightenment paradigm, and his description of a contentious public sphere driven by the norms and tradition of Dissent is in fundamental *continuity* with the previous century. Those who lived through the Revolutionary era, however, frequently gave voice to their sense that individual experience no longer coordinated with a history (progressive or otherwise) that seemed to be happening *somewhere else*. His dramatic rhetorical flourishes notwithstanding, Priestley rarely confronts what Christopher Bundock has recently described as Romantic historicism's ironic recognition of its own "ultimate failure ... to dictate history." Drawing on Reinhart Koselleck and E.P. Thompson, Bundock depicts a Romantic period of awkward transitions: from linear time to one marked by sudden leaps, and from additive historical progress that could look to the past as a guide to a widespread sense that there were no historical parallels for what was happening.[3] The futures of the past, as Koselleck memorably put it, are not those of the present. Within this context, Priestley's faith in institutional "contact points" as a means for toleration is not, I think, entirely borne out by the actual history of Revolutionary secularism, which forged new and not always liberatory relations between institutions and their subjects.

It would take another generation before English writers could view this break with a measure of analytical detachment. Thus Romanticism's historical belatedness vis-à-vis Enlightenment discourses of toleration is the first reason why its inclusion in a volume like this one is both important and anomalous.

The second reason is more philosophical. Romanticism has long been associated with conceptual and cultural relativism. Though the standard textbook description of a shift from Enlightenment universalism to Romantic particularism is obviously oversimplified, it does nevertheless capture something true about a broad swath of advanced thinking and writing in the late eighteenth and early nineteenth centuries. This Romantic trend towards stronger theorizations of cultural and linguistic *difference* makes the project of religious toleration more complicated. This development relates closely to the first matter discussed above: universal or convergent theories of history can deal with cultural difference, up to a point, by plotting different temporalities along a single line: India or America may be "behind" England, but they are heading in the same direction – just at a different pace. We owe these accounts of "uneven development" especially to Scottish Enlightenment historiography. But this is very different from saying that cultures or nations or peoples actually develop *differently* – that is to say, towards different endpoints, and according to their own unfolding logics. It is one thing to talk about toleration if we are speaking of differences that go only so far down before coming to rest upon a shared bedrock (even if there is disagreement over what that bedrock is). It is another thing to talk of toleration if those differences go all the way down. In the latter case, conflict becomes an existential matter: as Los declares in Blake's *Jerusalem*: "I must Create a System, or be enslav'd by another Man's; / I will not Reason and Compare: my business is to Create" (f. 10, lines 20–1). Here and elsewhere in works of the period, the choices are often posed starkly: either radical resistance or submission to what Blake elsewhere calls the "one law" that is the same for everybody.

Linear historical time as secularized Christian eschatology is fairly easy to map onto universalism; by contrast, multiple time scales moving simultaneously towards different ends tend towards relativism and particularism. This is why conceptual relativism of Blake's sort (my system versus someone else's) often accompanies the account of time and belatedness described above. Hegel's development of the dialectic is an explicit attempt to move past this impasse while acknowledging its intransigence.

Within this historical and philosophical context of post-Revolutionary belatedness and conceptual relativism, the present paper argues that *translation* provides a specifically Romantic model of religious toleration, and thus a method for handling assertions of incommensurable conceptual schemes. I turn to translation because the Romantic-period discovery of the importance of language tends to accompany a turn towards a strong reading of cultural incommensurability. And yet one crucial characteristic of a language is that it is *translatable*. That simple fact points towards a model of toleration appropriate to the discovery of radical difference.

During the eighteenth century, two prominent theories of language competed for prominence: either language was a gift from God, as the orthodox insisted, or language was an arbitrary invention of human beings, as Condillac argued. It would not be entirely wrong to say that "Romanticism" began in 1772, when Johann Gottfried Herder published *Treatise on the Origin of Language* and overturned this apparent opposition. Herder pointed out that both theories took it for granted that humans existed apart from language. And he proposed instead that language was essential to the human as such. There were no human beings around to invent language or to receive it because language and the human arrived at the same time: to invent a language simply *was* to invent a human being as we understand the category. The influence of this Herderian turn was profound: it offered a theory of language to the next generation of writers and critics and inspired a widespread revival of folklore and folktales; it also marked the origin of the "critical turn" that inaugurated continental philosophy and thus the modern interpretive and hermeneutic disciplines, from anthropology to literary theory. And this Romantic turn towards the constitutive power of language provided the opening for a new understanding of how literature (broadly conceived as *poiesis*) could shed new light on the problem of toleration – or, perhaps better, how literary language could actually advance the project of toleration.

The thesis that language constitutes the essence of humanity can have some rather divergent consequences. Herder offered a picture of humanity as deeply culture-bound: we are determined, he sometimes seems to be saying, by the communities, histories, and places into which we are born, and these things are carried most forcefully by language itself. Hence the nineteenth-century revival of interest in the German language (and, down the road, the ugly histories of nationalism and modern racism). Yet as a historian and theologian, Herder was concerned above all with connection: "[G]o into the age, into the clime, the whole history, feel yourself into everything," he instructed in *This Too a Philosophy of History for the Formation of Humanity* (1774).[4] It was the nature of language itself, he claimed, and especially of literary language like poetry, to carry "the very breath of the soul" of a people.[5] Even though historical and cultural distance was central to Herder's thought, his ideal historian nonetheless presupposed that languages and the concepts they expressed could be translated (if always imperfectly) into other languages. Even an utterly alien metaphysics (say, the metaphysics of those who live on Saturn) can be described in a language used on earth. A language that is untranslatable is not a *language* at all.[6] And so Herder's linguistic turn points in two directions simultaneously: towards a conceptual and cultural relativism, and towards an account of translation that presupposes universal translatability. This is the tension that Romanticism inherits.[7]

All this is a way of insisting on Romanticism's crucial role in discussions of religious toleration, and of justifying both the account of the Revolution and the reading of Percy Bysshe Shelley's *Prometheus Unbound* that follows. The first section of this paper begins with a description of Enlightenment-style translation, toleration, and secularization drawn from Jürgen Habermas. It evaluates that model against several efforts of Revolutionary translation in 1790s France, then turns to Shelley's astute, retrospective critique of those efforts in *Prometheus Unbound*. In this section I focus especially on the Revolutionary translation of Christian love into nationalist fraternity, and the violence that attends that translation. The second section begins with a romantic account of translation, toleration, and secularization drawn from M.H. Abrams. It then turns back to *Prometheus Unbound*, interpreting the role of love in the poem as an effort to transcend the nationalist paradigm of fraternity. As an extension of Abrams's Romantic paradigm, I develop an interpretation of an "untranslated love" with global aspirations.

By using the French Revolution to think about the possibilities of a predominantly British Romantic account of toleration, I follow Shelley in disrupting the conflation of secularization with Romantic post-Enlightenment critique. As Alison Conway writes in her introduction to this volume, it has long been too easy to see Romanticism as an aestheticist critique of eighteenth-century Anglican individualism. Part of my effort here is to develop a strand of post-Enlightenment thinking that aims to neither complete nor supplement a story of secularization but to point to an alternative story best captured by the concept of translation.

This is not an historical account of translation in the Romantic era. That work has been well done by others.[8] I am interested less in actual translations than in *translatability*, especially the translation (or not) of concepts, and in the kinds of thinking that the possibility of translation makes available. The thinking runs like this: concepts and thoughts are structured by language; at the heart of what makes something a language is translatability; therefore, tolerance does not have to be *added on top* of deep metaphysical or cultural commitments because it is *built in at the ground level*: tolerance is actually part and parcel of our cultural commitments – just as, for Herder, language is not added on top of humanity but makes the human what it is. Of course, this does not mean that all translations are exercises in tolerance: one needs to distinguish among types and models of translation, and indeed, the first part of this paper is a criticism of attempts to translate Christian love into Revolutionary fraternity. But it does mean that translation, with its twin commitments to original and to target language, and with its presupposition of mutual comprehensibility (not sameness), offers a model for what tolerance might look like in the age of revolution. In the third and final section of this paper, then, I consider *gratitude* as a possible translation of what I call Shelley's "untranslatable Love." I do this by turning back to history, and to the role of the humble country curates who played such an important part in the early days of the Revolution.

Revolution as Translation

In 2006, Jürgen Habermas published an essay called "Religion in the Public Sphere," an important rethinking of the relation of religion and politics on the part of this renowned philosopher and public intellectual. In this essay, Habermas moved away from his earlier enlightened and secular treatment of religion; the turn of the century and its related events (9/11, the Bush presidency, the increasingly public manifestations of religion throughout Western Europe) forced a different and more complicated reckoning. Far from withering away, religion seemed to be a fact of life that normative political theory would have to account for, and the desire of religious citizens to articulate their deepest convictions in the exclusive language of their traditions posed a difficult challenge for the liberal state.

Habermas thought that older models of tolerance were not up to this new task: "It is not enough," he wrote, "to rely on the condescending benevolence of a secularized authority that comes to tolerate minorities hitherto discriminated against. The parties themselves must reach agreement on the always-contested delimitations between a positive liberty to practise a religion of one's own and the negative liberty to remain spared from the religious practices of the others."[9] But how to bring all parties to the table in order to reach such an agreement? Here, Habermas introduced what he called a "translation proviso," a modification of an idea found in John Rawls's *Political Liberalism*. According to this proviso, religious citizens were free to express religious convictions in the public sphere, and to offer exclusively religious reasons for policy proposals. However, Habermas insisted that there was an institutional threshold that could not be crossed. Here is the crucial paragraph:

> Religious traditions have a special power to articulate moral intuitions, especially with regard to vulnerable forms of communal life. [...] [T]his potential [...] can then be *translated* from the vocabulary of a particular religious community into a generally accessible language. However, the institutional thresholds between the "wild life" of the political public sphere and the formal proceedings within political bodies are also a *filter* that from the Babel of voices in the informal flows of public communication allows only secular contributions to pass through. [...] The truth content of religious contributions can only enter into the institutionalized practice of deliberation and decision-making if the necessary *translation* already occurs in the pre-parliamentarian domain, i.e., in the political public sphere itself.[10] (italics added)

"Translation" is the dominant figure of the paragraph and indeed of the essay as a whole, but Habermas uses it in several senses. First, he writes that religious intuitions can be translated into a "generally accessible language." Here, the vector runs from particular to general; content is transformed (but also, ideally, preserved) by the process of translation. Second, Habermas writes of an institutional threshold beyond which religious reasons do not pass. He calls this a "filter" that "allows only secular contributions to pass through." Third, when he returns to the idea of translation, he seems to carry with him the figure of the filter, so that now translation *itself* becomes a kind of filter, something that takes place among the "Babel of voices" in the public sphere and strains out the exclusive content before it arrives at a legislative body, much as a coffee filter strains out the grounds.

It is to Habermas's credit that he recognizes an "asymmetrical cognitive burden" in this proposal. In his scheme, it is incumbent on religious citizens to undertake the work of translation, while it is incumbent on nonreligious citizens simply to listen with an open mind. Still, he seems to think that doing the work of translation is not an especially heavy burden: "all that is required here," he declares, "is the epistemic ability to consider one's faith reflexively from the outside."[11] This casual "all" points to the rather thin conception of personhood operating in the essay. Habermas may mean simply that one requirement of liberal democracy is that we acknowledge the fact of pluralism. This is uncontroversial. But he also seems to be assuming that acknowledging the mere *fact* of pluralism is tantamount to the kind of reflexivity that will encourage individual actors to engage in the translation for which he is calling. This seems a tougher sell, given that Habermas's model of translation is in every sense post-metaphysical. It may even involve the entire procedure in a performative conundrum: translation might filter out the very kinds of deep motivations that provide the normative basis for undertaking an act of translation in the first place.

Despite the rhetoric of open-mindedness, then, Habermas tends to conceive of religious and secular subjectivities as self-enclosed entities that need to be opened up through the kind of reflexivity that characterizes the liberal democratic state. He gives little attention to the possibility that individual actors might themselves be motivated by mixtures (even incoherent combinations) of religious and secular reasons – or indeed that there may not even *be* such things as "religious" or "secular" reasons in any pure form. His model, rather, is one of self-estrangement – of stepping outside oneself, as it were.

How is Habermas thinking about translation? Not, it seems, along Platonic lines of original and copy, where the ideal is faithfulness to the original. Rather, secular translation here improves upon and replaces the religious original, at least in an institutional context. The underlying figures are familiar: domestic and foreign, familiar and strange. Intellectually, this accords nicely with eighteenth-century norms of translation, wherein the original was rendered in language familiar to its readers – Homer in heroic couplets, for example. Politically, these are the categories that underlie the form we know as the nation-state. This is hardly a surprise, for Habermas's explicit concern is with the institutional mechanisms of the state. Within that imaginative frame, secular translation domesticates an otherwise unknowable religious otherness, making something familiar out of something strange. Translation also works the other way, turning the provincial into the universal, estranging the comforting intuitions of religion in order to make them relevant within a pluralist polity.

The early years of the Revolution offer a historical analogue to Habermas's theorization. On 14 July 1790, on the one-year anniversary of the fall of the Bastille, France celebrated the Festival of the Federation. Talleyrand said mass in a specially constructed amphitheatre, calling down God's blessing on the Revolution. Newly arrived from England, Helen Maria Williams called the festival "the most sublime spectacle which, perhaps, was ever represented on the theatre of this earth."[12] This was the beginning of the Revolutionary pageantry discussed by historians: public spectacles, patriotic symbolism, hymn sings, Voltaire's bones carried to the Panthéon (itself a sort of secular cathedral) – in short, the origins of a "revolutionary religion," complete with a new calendar and a list of martyrs.[13]

Celebrations were carried to towns and villages throughout the nation. Students of Romanticism will think immediately of Wordsworth's account in *The Prelude*, book 6.

> ... The Supper done,
> With flowing cups elate, and happy thoughts,
> We rose at signal given, and form'd a ring
> And, hand in hand, danced round and round the Board;
> All hearts were open, every tongue was loud
> With amity and glee; we bore a name
> Honour'd in France, the name of Englishmen,
> And hospitably did they give us Hail,
> As their forerunners in a glorious course;
> And round, and round the board they danced again.[14]

Wordsworth's "All hearts were open" quotes the Book of Common Prayer, translated now into a celebration of national belonging. Similar translations were also clear to Williams, who witnessed a *Te Deum* at Notre Dame followed by a lengthy musical drama of the events of Bastille Day. She described the music as, by turns, "electrifying," "melancholy," and "exciting ideas of trouble and inquietude." At a particularly stirring moment, "the audience appeared to breathe with difficulty."[15] She asked rhetorically, "How am I to paint the impetuous feelings of that immense, that exulting multitude? [...] Half a million of people assembled at a spectacle, which furnished every image that can elevate the mind of man; which connected the enthusiasm of moral sentiment with the solemn pomp of religious ceremonies; which addressed itself at once to the imagination, the understanding, and the heart!"[16] The Revolution, at least in those early, heady days, was an effort of translation – of monarchy into republicanism, of Christianity into nationalism, of love into fraternity – and never more so than at such affective moments as these, whose aim was to attach the emotions and passions of citizens to the new idea of France.

Institutionally, too, France undertook various acts of translation-as-filtering. In keeping with the radical Enlightenment tradition of secularism as an independent ethic, the Declaration of the Rights of Man had outlined a policy of religious toleration that privatized religion and located it within a free conscience. In theory, this would keep religious feelings from interfering with the new, public, displays of feeling for the nation: "No one can be disturbed for his opinions, even religious ones," as the Declaration put it, "provided that their expression does not infringe the public order declared by the law."[17] But who determines when an expression has infringed on the public order? As with Habermas's translation proviso, the metaphysically neutral language of filtering and "not infringing" marks out religion as a distinct problem to be managed by the state.

Indeed, the tendency of the Declaration's live-and-let-live model became clear first with the confiscation of church property in November 1789 and then with the declaration, in February of 1790, that members of the religious orders could be released from their vows without the consent of the church. Both are potent images of a certain kind of translation: land and vows each considered now as secular facts, subject to the laws of the reorganized nation rather than to their own particular histories of calling, labour, gift, and caretaking.[18]

Then, in July of 1790, the Civil Constitution of the Clergy reduced the number of bishops and fixed their salaries, streamlined clerical appointments, and generally rationalized ecclesiastical governance so that it became amenable to the oversight of a state moving quickly to reorganize the church along democratic and administrative lines.[19] New departments and governing bodies were created, new committees formed, redundancy eliminated, boundaries redrawn, and new organizations proposed.[20] Specifying the exact number of vicars in a given cathedral might seem needlessly finicky, but these bland and bureaucratic details were precisely the point, for they signalled the power of the state to reach into the inner workings of a heretofore autonomous institution. Just as the sale of church lands required that government surveyors and accountants enter the monasteries to assess their value, so, too, the Civil Constitution of the Clergy threw open the organization of the church to the state's all-seeing eye.

From one perspective, these activities remained very much in line with the minimalism of the Declaration of the Rights of Man: religion was fine so long as it didn't disturb the peace. But as scholars of secularism have helped us to see, this kind of minimalism may stoke rather than dampen the flames. When fraternal loyalty to the state is made to outrank other emotions, it can produce those very forms of strong religion that the state is then called upon to manage through the mechanism of tolerance.[21]

In an intriguingly offbeat essay, the Belgian art theorist Thierry de Duve has proposed that the revolutionary motto "Liberty, Equality, Fraternity" is a translation of St Paul's famous triumvirate of "faith, hope, and love" in Corinthians 13. De Duve thinks that this translation was a mistake. Because they insisted on filtering out the specifically theological resonances of faith, hope, and love, he argues, the theorists of the Revolution left behind a residue that curdled into a legacy of betrayal and violence.[22] His counterintuitive thought is that Revolutionary secularization actually made violence *more* likely because it failed to attend to the motivational force of the translated terms. We can see this, he argues, particularly in the case of a Revolutionary fraternity that refused to acknowledge hierarchy because it had secularized hope as equality. He casts this in psychoanalytic language: Revolutionary fraternity declares that now is the moment to do away with the symbolic father altogether so that all might at last be equal. But the Revolutionary "fantasy of a society of fatherless brothers" is naïve about the way that power will always be unequally distributed.

When faith, hope, and love became liberty, equality, and fraternity, they relied on the nation as their guarantor. Fatherland replaced church, and this was not an advance.

In a remarkable group of scenes in act 1 of *Prometheus Unbound*, Percy Shelley offers a similar analysis of the effects of revolutionary tolerance. The passage begins with Jesus, "of gentle worth, / Smiling on the sanguine earth" (1.546–7). His message is soon perverted by the institutional church, however, and so in the next scene Prometheus imagines himself in the place of the crucified Jesus, with his "pillow of thorns."

> Drops of bloody agony flow
> From his white and quivering brow.
> Grant a little respite now – (1.564–6)

Shelley then inserts the first of the three dashes that mark a series of abrupt changes – first, from Prometheus's agony to revolutionary fraternal brotherhood ...

> See! A disenchanted nation
> Springs like day from desolation;
> To truth its state, is dedicate,
> And Freedom leads it forth, her mate;
> A legioned band of linked brothers
> Whom Love calls children – (1.567–72)

... and then from fraternity to fratricide.

>   'Tis another's –
> See how kindred murder kin!
> 'Tis the vintage-time for Death and Sin:
> Blood, like new wine, bubbles within
> Till Despair smothers
> The struggling World – which slaves and tyrants win. (1.572–7)

The Terror, in other words, is the latest dialectical turn in a process that had begun with a translation of the suffering Christ into the suffering Prometheus. This is a surprising argument from a poet generally associated with Enlightenment atheism: that the translation of Christ into Prometheus – and, by extension, the revolutionary substitution of classical for Christian figures, perhaps indeed the entire classically inspired secularization campaign – sets off a chain reaction ending in violent nationalism.[23] Feeling for the nation, in other words, is less a secularizing or a filtering translation of Christianity than a bid to capture its affective repertoire for worldly ends.

Since the groundbreaking work of Joan Landes and Lynn Hunt thirty years ago, we have become attuned to the gender politics of these Revolutionary fraternal bonds and to the ways in which the Revolution was also a revolution in male virility and in the symbols and rituals of law and public reason. In the Revolutionary years, the feminine became associated either with a counter-revolutionary *ancien regime* of mistresses and intrigues (embodied in Marie Antoinette) or with the compensatory female quasi-deities – Nature, Reason, and Liberty – who helped constitute and validate the Revolutionary band of brothers trailing along in their wake.[24] Delacroix's *Liberty Leading the People* (1830) is simply the best known and most visually striking example of the new alliance of masculinity, secularity, and nationalism blind to its own capacity for bloodshed. As great art does, that painting asks some searching questions about the violence that attends this partnership.

Saint-Just dreamed of a "Temple of Friendship" where citizens would record the names of their friends every year and explain to the authorities why any had dropped off the list. That dystopian dream captures the truth that "fraternity" was always the most malleable of the Revolutionary triumvirate, which meant that it brought to fruition both sides of its radical Enlightenment heritage: on the one hand, free (erotic) love as an expression of liberation from the bonds of organized religion; on the other, a model of state sovereignty that rarely hesitated to impose its vision of the good, both on its own citizens and, as events would soon indicate, on those of other nations.[25] The need to transfer passionate attachment from church to nation was very real, but because fraternity (unlike love) was always *subject to* the nation, to a bounded and administered space, it became possible to do violence *in the name of* fraternity. In this way fraternity territorializes love, ties it to a specific place or mode of life. It says: *this* is the way to be French, by loving these things in this way.

Love Untranslated

In a well-known passage from *Natural Supernaturalism* (1971), M.H. Abrams proposed that Romanticism was best understood as a "secularization of inherited theological ideas and ways of thinking."[26] "In England and Germany," he continued, "Biblical culture fostered collateral developments of response to what Shelley called 'the great events of the age,' by which he meant above all the French Revolution, its unbounded promise and its failure, and the revolutionary and counter-revolutionary shock waves it had set up in that era of the turbulent emergence of the modern, political, social, and industrial world." Elsewhere, I have been critical of Abrams's assertion that secularization takes place mostly in the mind – "the assimilation and reinterpretation of religious ideas," as he put it a page later.[27] But here I am interested in Abrams's juxtaposition of ideas and politics in reference to the French Revolution. It is hard to parse the causal vectors in his somewhat gestural overview, but apparently the suggestion is that a political event and its disappointing aftermath produced a desire among certain writers to "reconstitute the grounds of hope" for their own cultural moment,[28] and that the traditions of Protestant Christianity enabled that imaginative reaction to take on a certain shape and texture that we know as Romanticism. The denominational model of the common ground approach to secularism can be glimpsed here, in which Romanticism is a translation of Christianity that is also, and incidentally, a secularization. Or, to put it another way, translation assimilates Christianity to its new historical reality.

Later in the book, Abrams uses the word "translation" in just this way, describing Herder as "translat[ing] the Biblical account of Eden, the fall, and the restoration into his version of universal history." This particular kind of translation from particular to universal was ubiquitous among German thinkers of the period, and Abrams brilliantly demonstrates its influence on English poetry as well as German aesthetic theory. He is less clear, however, on its motivations, falling back on generalizations about what he called the "modern malaise,"[29] a sense of alienation accelerated by the Revolution that motivated translations of the Genesis story especially. Indeed, Abrams's is a story of secularization by accident – as if it were the by-product of these various kinds of translation, languages (Hebrew, Latin, German, and English), and levels (particular and universal). No one set out to secularize Christianity because of its provincialism or political exclusivity; rather, they sought to make it relevant in a new moment and wound up secularizing it accidentally. In this way, Christianity's denominational structure provided the theory of toleration that would eventually secularize it. This makes Abrams's Romantic account markedly different from Habermas's. For Habermas, translation is a reaction to the political dilemma of pluralism; its imaginative frame is the nation-state; and the stability of that state its announced goal. For Abrams, by contrast, translation is a reaction to the ethical dilemma of modernity; its imaginative frame is the globe; and the preservation of a particular sensibility its announced goal.

If one is trying to *imagine* religious toleration, Abrams's account of translation is more useful than Habermas's precisely because of its historical belatedness and attention to cultural depth that I outlined at the beginning of this essay. Rather than translating religious insights by filtering out their particular motivations, it seeks to preserve the strangeness of those motivations even in radically changed circumstances. In terms of translation theory, then, it attempts to balance the needs of the target language with the enlightening strangeness and difference of the original.

I turn again to *Prometheus Unbound* in order to test out this possibility, focusing on Shelley's description of a love that is not translated into fraternity (and thereby linked to the nation) but rather translated into a universal action directed at what Shelley terms the "whole world."

As embodied in the figure of Asia, love is the prime agent and mover in *Prometheus Unbound*. When the drama opens, Prometheus and Jupiter are locked in a heroic contest of masculine egos that renders them indifferent to the suffering their conflict visits upon the rest of the earth. In act 2, Asia breaks into this frozen, static world, undertakes the journey to Demogorgon that initiates Jupiter's defeat, and eventually drags Prometheus off-stage at the end of act 3.

When she arrives at Demogorgon's cave in act 2, Asia asks him what principle or power rules the universe; Demogorgon famously replies that there is no certain answer because "the deep truth is imageless." "For what would it avail," he goes on, "to bid thee gaze / On the revolving world? What to bid speak / Fate, Time, Occasion, Chance, and Change?" (2.iv.116–19). Shelley developed this notion of infinite process from his wide reading in Lucretius, Spinoza, and various authors of the French Enlightenment. And though he generally endorses the metaphysics of a revolving, changing world as more palatable than the metaphysics associated with the Christian God, in *Prometheus Unbound*, he has Demogorgon add a proviso: "To these / All things are subject but eternal Love."

That love is an escape from Lucretian process would seem to be both the most clichéd of notions and a barrier to thinking love's political force. Such a love would be entirely interpersonal, limited to the couple form and dedicated to sameness rather than multiplicity: we look for our better selves, our other halves, our soul mates. This is the theory of love sketched by the early speeches of Plato's *Symposium*, which Shelley translated in 1818. It is the same theory of love that leads Hannah Arendt in *The Human Condition* to declare confidently that love is unworldly, "not only apolitical but antipolitical, perhaps the most powerful of all antipolitical human forces."[30] Yet the notion of love finally endorsed in *The Symposium*, philo-sophia, also amounts to an escape from the world. Socrates argues that love is lack and desire rather than something that exists in itself – not a thing but a relation *to* things, an idea Shelley would recommend a few years later in *A Defense of Poetry*.[31] But this leads Socrates to turn away from individual examples of beauty and towards an ascetic contemplation of eternal Beauty: he refuses sex with Alcibiades, drinks without getting drunk, survives the cold without a coat, and so on. Love like this is an escape from the body and from the world, too, despite its relational focus.

Neither of these conceptions of love seem adequate to Demogorgon's difficult statement. Indeed, if either interpersonal erotic escape or contemplative eternity had sufficed, the play could have ended with act 3. And, indeed, Shelley originally planned *Prometheus Unbound* as a three-act drama. One explanation for the added fourth act, then, is that Shelley realized that the politics of the play required a different kind of love from the two on offer – a love *in* and *of* the world, untranslated and unfiltered. What would such a love be?

In fact, it is already present in the figure of Asia, who, over the course of act 2, undergoes a remarkable transfiguration from passive mirror of Prometheus to something else entirely.[32] It almost blinds her sister Panthea: "How thou art changed! I dare not look on thee; / I feel, but see thee not," she says (2.v.16–17). Felt rather than seen, a "working in the elements," as Panthea calls it, "love, like the atmosphere," ranges everywhere:

> nor is it I alone,
> Thy sister, thy companion, thine own chosen one,
> But the whole world which seeks thy sympathy.
> Hearest thou not sounds i' the air which speak the love
> Of all articulate beings? Feelest thou not
> The inanimate winds enamoured of thee? (2.v.32–7)

Panthea is startled because the love now pouring forth from Asia is multidirectional, a mutual interchange with the world that is dazzling and elemental. Asia herself will soon declare that "common as light is love" (2.v.40), and, turning to the politics of this idea, that "[i]t makes the reptile equal to the God" (2.v.43). Love's role is not to close lovers off from the world but, on the contrary, to multiply points of contact in a series of exchanges, infusions, and "interpenetrations" (4.370), that, as act 4 demonstrates, go on forever.[33] With Asia's experience of love in mind, Shelley's excitable account of interconnection at the end of the play appears as a de-territorialized version of the fraternal fête described by Wordsworth in *The Prelude* and a postinstitutional version of the "maximization of public contact points" described in Mark Canuel's essay on Priestley. Here is Shelley's rendering:

> The joy, the triumph, the delight, the madness,
> The boundless, overflowing bursting gladness,
> The vaporous exultation, not to be confined!
> Ha! Ha! The animation of delight
> Which wraps me, like an atmosphere of light,
> And bears me as a cloud is borne by its own wind! (4.319–24)

"Ha! Ha!" may seem rather silly, but it points to the way that Shelley's drama approaches a non-representational sense experience of pure sound and the animation of all things (4.322). Such experiences are "not to be confined" by the fraternal state and its institutions. This is not fraternity, after all, but love itself – a love of the world manifested as a radical multiplication of social bonds.[34]

Such worldliness and generality bring us to Abrams's assimilationist model of translation, and to the Christian universalism that motivates it. Indeed, Shelley's infinitive-ridden conclusion to act 4 ("to suffer, to forgive, to love, and bear, to hope") echoes Paul's famous first letter to the Corinthians: "Love bears all things, believes all things, hopes all things, endures all things [...] So faith, hope, love abide, these three; but the greatest of these is love" (1 Corinthians

13:7, 13:13). When Paul turns to the politics of that love, he emphasizes not endurance but radical equality. All should pay their taxes, he writes in the Book of Romans, so that the way is cleared for more important obligations: "Owe no one anything, except to love one another" (13:8). Love, that is to say, is the thing people owe one another, the device that brings them into communal solidarity. And, unlike taxes or other institutional points of contact, the obligation to love is endless, for it no longer stops at the boundaries of nations or people: there is no telling whom one might be called upon to love in the future.[35]

Love in *Prometheus Unbound* thus points in two directions. It interrupts the secularizing translation of love into fraternity (and fraternity into fratricide); its universalism, pulling on Paul's radical theorization of universal love, is a trenchant critique of nationalism and of the way that feeling for a nation replaces feeling for humanity so as to produce violence in the name of toleration. If a too-easy translation limits love to the nation, then love untranslated points beyond it. At the same time, though, Shelley's lyrical drama attempts to write world literature in an orientalizing vein. It mixes classical and Christian imagery; one of its main characters is named Asia, and much of its action takes place in the Caucasus; it zooms up into the heavens and down into caves under the earth, and its speakers are disembodied voices, moons, and oceans, spirits, and echoes – even the earth itself. Even the ecstatic dance at the end of *Prometheus Unbound* is described at such length that one begins to suspect that Shelley doesn't quite know what the point is. There are moments when a redeemed humanity seems triumphant, moments that feel like examples of deep ecology, moments of Lucretian swerving and moments where individuality seems to be swallowed up entirely.

Is this kind of romantic orientalism the price that must be paid for escaping the boundaries of the nation? Those who find Romanticism to be either hopelessly complacent or wildly idealistic will have plenty to point to in *Prometheus Unbound*: it seems to substitute assimilation for tolerance and to trade a careful treatment of actual differences in the real world for metaphysical speculation. It is reticent about its lingering debt to Christian imagination. Shelley, like Paul, seems so intent on changing his reader's notion of what politics even *means* that it is not clear what one might *do* after reading such words. Does being children of love rather than children of the nation change anything?

In her recent critique of the idea of world literature, Emily Apter describes what she calls the "untranslatable," a moment when dissonance and misunderstanding raise questions about the nature of translation itself. Even if a translation is eventually undertaken, she argues, untranslatable moments should be celebrated rather than rushed past, since they trouble an institutional and literary endorsement of "cultural equivalence and substitutability" amenable to neoliberal globalization.[36] Apter's is not, of course, an argument for radical incommensurability. It is simply a reminder of one of the dangers of any translation: the assumption that one object is equivalent to another, that things (languages, people, traditions) are all ultimately exchangeable.

That reminder resonates with many of the Romantic-era writers who watched the French Revolution unfold. Some, like Blake, resisted what they experienced as a single standard applied across the board. Others felt that they were encountering "several parallel but discordant times" all at once.[37] Walter Scott's historical novels narrate this feeling again and again. This experience of discord collides with the sense of radical newness brought on by the Revolution itself, what Koselleck describes as "the start of a future that had never yet existed" and for which the past could offer little guidance.[38]

In this way, the difficulty of Apter's "untranslatable" offers an important corrective to the enthusiasm of act 4 of *Prometheus Unbound*. It is a romantic reminder that the original language is strange, and that even as one undertakes a translation into the target language, such strangeness – conceptual, historical, and linguistic – must be preserved. This marks an important departure both from Habermas's filtering and Abrams's assimilationist models of translation, which in their different ways tend to treat untranslatability as a problem to be overcome. As Koselleck has noted, the Revolution produced a crisis of historiography in part because of the uneven and uncertain progress of what we now call "secularization." Secular time seemed to accelerate in a fashion previously associated with Christian eschatology – but now without the guide of either past actions or overarching *telos* to guide interpretation.[39] In this context, smooth translation – of past to future, of sacred to secular – became impossible. And the revolutionary violence that attends efforts to accelerate the transition suggests that it might be a good idea to slow down and attend to the untranslatable.

Shelley, too, may have recognized that he was getting carried away. Here is Demogorgon's final speech in act 4, which is something of a benediction after the universal celebratory dance that occupies most of the final act. "This is the Day," Demogorgon says, when

> Love from its awful throne of patient power
> In the wise heart, from the last giddy hour
> Of dread endurance, from the slippery, steep,
> And narrow verge of crag-like Agony, springs
> And folds over the world its healing wings. (4.557.61)

Earl Wasserman claims that for Shelley, "The Hour of Love must succeed the Hour of Revolution with [...] unrelenting haste."[40] This is because the vacancy created by political revolution, if not filled with love, will be filled with something else: terror or war. That is why Asia ascends so rapidly after Demogorgon. Yet consider the syntactical difficulty of this passage. Hesitation is built into its grammar. The space between subject and verb is packed with problems, and it stretches out long enough for the syntax to bend, if not break entirely. Even amid the renewal of all things, love's triumph is a tentative, late-springing one. Such grammatical manipulation is Shelley's great contribution to a political account of love. It is an acknowledgment of the difficulty of the task, perhaps even a recognition of love's impossibility or at any rate the obstacles that stand in its way. Love, even when translated, may be untranslatable.

Love Translated; or, Gratitude

In the final section of this essay, I will, however, propose a translation of love – into gratitude. I turn to that word, and that affect, as a model of a kind of translation aligned with the goals of toleration. This will require leaving Shelley behind, and returning to some of the political machinations of the early revolutionary years. And it will also (as promised) require entering the realm of the counterfactual, rewriting the Revolution not, with Shelley, as an exercise in unbounded Love but as a practice of attending to the efforts that others make in the name of a larger good.

I focus here on a group of low-status parish priests, many of them from poor backgrounds, during the earliest days of the Revolution. These *curés* were part of the church, but their sympathies lay with ordinary people, not privileged bishops. They made up an important anti-aristocratic, proto-revolutionary, pro-church bloc positioned within a secularizing state. We get a sense of their power from Edmund Burke's stinging dismissal in the *Reflections* of "mere country curates" who are charged with the "great and arduous work of new-modelling a state," and again from the chapter of Notre-Dame, who protested that "when the inferior class of ministers of religion puts itself on the same level as the superior class [...] the submission which is a special characteristic of the government of the Church will be entirely annihilated."[41] This is the voice of the *ancien régime*.

These maligned parish priests, however, refused to submit. Instead, they undertook a different kind of translation. This is a good time to remind ourselves that *translation* means "to remove from one place to another." For the stalemate of the fateful Estates General of 1789 was broken only when the *curés* removed themselves from the meeting of the First Estate, where the bishops had been horrified by their presence anyway, and joined the Third Estate (the Commons): three one day, six the next, and eight in the next two days – until, on 17 June, the Commons had both the numbers and the moral authority to declare itself the National Assembly. By 21 June, most of the First Estate had joined them, the Revolution had started, and the rest, as they say, is history.

Or, perhaps, not quite. It is worth contrasting Alphonse Aulard's enthusiastic account of these translated *curés* with a more recent and dyspeptic observation. "Without the parish priests the Revolution would have come to pass," wrote

Aulard in 1927, "but it would have come more slowly and in a different way. The revolutionists long cherished ardent gratitude to the priests, and the Catholic religion itself profited by this gratitude."[42] Here, by contrast, is John McManners, writing in 1998: "Already the *curés* were spoken of as the mediators [...] they served the nation well, and for a few months they were able to bask in the illusion that it would show its gratitude."[43] Gratitude: what Aulard, the founder of modern French revolutionary history, regarded as a settled, that is to say historical, fact, McManners regards as an illusion. As Catherine Morland says in Austen's *Northanger Abbey*, Aulard is "describing what never happened."[44]

McManners has a claim to make about why this history "never happened."[45] He argues that the cause was the Civil Constitution of the Clergy: as we have already seen, a bland and bureaucratic document that nonetheless irrevocably divided the church along class and regional lines and gave a shape and focus to what had until then only been an inchoate counter-revolutionary impulse. When in November of 1790 the National Assembly demanded that all clergy swear an oath to the Constitution (which included the Civil Constitution of the Clergy), about half did so. The division generally followed class lines: only 7 out of 160 bishops took the oath; but many more *curés*, who stood to gain by the dismantling of the *ancien régime* and had long resented the extreme wealth of their superiors, signed on. Priests from the poorest families took the oath in the highest numbers, though there was substantial regional variation.[46] Those who took the oath threw in their lot with the Revolution; for those who didn't, what might have been simply an emotional attachment to inherited wealth and privilege or an inclination to defend tradition became a noble matter of conscience, and the counter-revolution was born. The choice was a stark one. McManners develops this thought as a counter-factual: "had the zeal for national sovereignty," he writes, "not inspired the deputies of the National Assembly to enforce a Church settlement without respect for the canonical means by which ecclesiastical decisions are made, the chances are that the political leaders of the episcopate would have steered the Gallican Church united and peacefully into the new revolutionary order."[47] By aligning church with *ancien régime* and then forcing a choice between church and nation, the revolutionaries set the table for the violent recriminations that were to come. Here we have a more concrete example of de Duve's description of the revolutionary translation of love into fraternity.

In gradually leaving their ecclesiastical associates and joining the Third Estate, the *curés* enacted a form of translation that might have become a model for the Revolution as a whole. Unlike Habermas's model, there was no filtering involved, and unlike Abrams's the goal was not assimilation. The *curés* entered the Third Estate as *curés*, members of an ecclesiastical body with loyalties beyond the nation. But they entered it, too, as members of a nascent state committed (at least in theory) to tolerance. What doomed this particular act of translation, or what consigned it to the realm of the counterfactual, was a collective inability to imagine selves who could be loyal to more than one of these things. And the name of that imaginative ability, in both Aulard and McManners, is *gratitude* – a word that preserves the affective weight of *love* while also opening up its potential range. A translation, in other words.

Since the topic of this volume is the way that literature helps to imagine alternative models of toleration, I want to end this essay by insisting on the *literary* quality of the actors and attitudes that I have been exploring. This is obviously true in Shelley's imaginative rewriting of the French Revolution, of course. But it is also true of the Revolution itself, its manifold representations and the various possibilities and missed opportunities that it generated. Literature in its broadest sense – not just *Prometheus Unbound* but historical writing, too – is one way to rescue those opportunities for a more tolerant future.

Gratitude, in fact, may be the affect most nearly allied to tolerance precisely because it is directed outward. In an essay called "The Politics of Secularism and the Recovery of Religious Tolerance," Ashis Nandy has written of the "somewhat fluid definitions of the self with which many South Asian cultures live [and] which can be conceptually viewed as configurations of selves."[48] Nandy's point is that fluid notions of the self (which he contrasts with Western/colonial notions of a bounded self) contain an implicit theory of toleration largely foreign to the missionary and colonial Westerners who arrived in South Asia, bringing with them both Christianity and political secularism. The meddling of secular and colonial powers tended to harden identities and prevent the kind of fluid identities that might, under the right conditions, have become the place where conflict could be worked out.

What are those conditions? Translation offers a good model, since it depends upon a formal acknowledgment of difference and the plurality of lifeworlds but also presumes, as an act of faith, that languages are translatable – in other words, that something can be put another way, and that although there are always losses there are also gains in this. Strong tolerance, Nandy goes on to say, does not merely tolerate others; it also imputes tolerance to them. It assumes there is something to be gained, *on both sides*, by tolerance. On this reading, toleration is not something that must be *brought to* religion by an outside force like the state but something developed internally – *within* religious traditions themselves. Like the Herderian theory of language, it is there from the beginning.

Is this what Shelley had in mind when he turned to Asia as a representative of boundary-dissolving Love? We need to be careful here: as already noted, the tradition of romantic orientalism runs deeply through Shelley's lyrical drama, as through so much writing of the period. "We must seek the supreme romanticism in the Orient," wrote Friedrich Schlegel in 1800 in the grip of his initial enthusiasm for India.[49] But it is also the case that Schlegel's modelling of subjectivity on the literary fragment that seeks out a reader, just as Shelley's interactive description of metaphor in *A Defense of Poetry*, and, in a quieter way, Coleridge's development of "conversation" in the handful of great poems he wrote in 1797–8 – that, in all these cases, Romantic writers turned to literary modes of incompletion and partiality as a way to name the possibility of a formal relation to otherness. This strategy is substantially different both from an idea of toleration modelled on the nation-state, and from one modelled on a borderless, globalized world literature. It points instead towards translation as an implicit theory of tolerance – as a characteristic of the self and a quality imputed to others. Which is why *gratitude* hovers as a literary possibility over the work of the *curés* – if not as historical truth, then as counterfactual hope.

NOTES

1   Charles Taylor, "Modes of Secularism," in *Secularism and Its Critics*, ed. Rajeev Bharghava (Delhi: Oxford University Press, 1998), 31–53. For a discussion of the relation of the continental radical Enlightenment to toleration and the French Revolution, see Jonathan Israel, "Spinoza, Locke, and the Enlightenment Battle for Toleration," in *Toleration in Enlightenment Europe*, ed. Ole Peter Grell and Roy Porter (Cambridge: Cambridge University Press, 2006), 102–13.

2   For a critique of secularization theory as dependent on a "subtraction story," see Taylor, *A Secular Age* (Cambridge: Harvard University Press, 2007). For a discussion of secularism and tolerance as it relates to free speech, see Talal Asad et al., *Is Critique Secular? Blasphemy, Injury, and Free Speech* (Berkeley: Townsend Center for the Humanities, 2009). For some recent complications of the secularization thesis itself, see the latest Pew study of Christianity in Europe: http://www.pewforum.org/2018/05/29/being-christian-in-western-europe/; and for the difficulty of sorting out secular from religious, the recent Beyoncé Mass: https://www.youtube.com/watch?v=PXci-sRayAQ [accessed 31 May 2018].

3   See Christopher M. Bundock, *Romantic Prophesy and the Resistance to Historicism* (Toronto: University of Toronto Press, 2016), 32 and 10–11. Whether this feeling actually matches the reality is of course another matter; the point is that the Romantic era is characterized by the widespread *perception* that something dramatic has changed.

4   Johann Gottfried Herder, *Philosophical Writings*, trans. and ed. Michael N. Forster (Cambridge: Cambridge University Press, 2002), 292.

5   Herder, *The Spirit of Hebrew Poetry* [1782], trans. James Marsh (Burlington, VT: Edward Smith, 1833), 35.

6   This argument is worked out, in more technical detail than I have space for here, in an influential 1974 paper by Donald Davidson, which argues that the notion of incommensurable belief systems is, like the notion of an untranslatable language, incoherent. See Davidson, "On the Very Idea of a Conceptual Scheme," *Proceedings and Addresses of the American Philosophical Association* 47 (1973–4): 5–20.

7 See, for instance, Schleiermacher's *On the Different Methods of Translation* (1813). The most famous English Romantic meditation on translation is doubtless Keats's "On First Looking into Chapman's Homer" (1816). In general during the period we can observe an increased interest in translation as an experience of otherness.

8 See Antoine Berman, *The Experience of the Foreign: Culture and Translation in Romantic Germany*, trans. S. Heyvaert (Albany: SUNY Press, 1992), and Frederick Burwick, "Romantic Theories of Translation," *Wordsworth Circle* 39, no. 3 (2008): 68–74.

9 Jürgen Habermas, "Religion in the Public Sphere," *European Journal of Philosophy* 14, no.1 (2006): 1–25, esp. 4.

10 Habermas, "Religion in the Public Sphere," 10.

11 Ibid., 6, 11, 9–10.

12 Helen Maria Williams, *Letters Written in France*, ed. Neil Fraistat and Susan S. Lanser (London, ON: Broadview, 2001), 63.

13 Suzanne Desan, *Reclaiming the Sacred: Lay Religion and Popular Politics in Revolutionary France* (Ithaca: Cornell University Press, 1990), 2. "By 1795 [...] the Revolution had created a whole cultural system of revolutionary rituals, symbols, and language, which aimed to replace Christianity and reeducate people according to the political ideals of the Revolution."

14 William Wordsworth, 1805 *Prelude*, book 6, lines 404–13. The 1850 version is substantially unrevised.

15 Williams, *Letters Written from France*, 63–4.

16 Ibid., 64–5.

17 This is the translation in Michael Burleigh, *Earthly Powers: The Clash of Religion and Politics in Europe, from the French Revolution to the Great War* (New York: Harper, 2006), 52.

18 In 1790, Helen Maria Williams described encountering three nuns, "the decree of the National Assembly giving them liberty," walking to visit some friends (*Letters Written in France*, 113). See the lovely analysis of this scene in Anahid Nersessian, *Utopia, Limited: Romanticism and Adjustment* (Cambridge, MA: Harvard University Press, 2015), 64–7. On the confiscation of church property, see Desan, *Reclaiming the Sacred*, 5, and Byrnes, *Priests of the Revolution*, 5.

19 For example, rather than clergy being appointed "in-house," any citizen – including Protestants, *philosophes*, and so on – could vote for clergy provided they attended the mass which preceded the vote. See John McManners, *The French Revolution and the Church* (London: SPCK, 1969), 40; Desan, *Reclaiming the Sacred*, 5–6; W.R. Ward, *Christianity under the Ancien Régime, 1648–1789* (Cambridge: Cambridge University Press, 1999), 236; A. Aulard, *Christianity and the French Revolution*, trans. Frazer (Boston: Little, Brown, and Co., 1927), 60. For details on the electoral colleges and voting, see Malcolm Crook, "Citizen Bishops: Episcopal Elections in the French Revolution," *The Historical Journal* 43, no. 4 (2000): 955–76, esp. 956–9 and 972.

20 For details, see Aulard, *Christianity and the French Revolution*, 59–61.

21 Here I mark my allegiance with one, by no means dominant, thesis about secularism: that, far from a principle of neutrality, it tends in practice to manufacture the forms of "religion" that it is then tasked with overseeing. Versions of this argument can be found in Talal Asad, *Formations of the Secular* (Stanford: Stanford University Press, 2003); Charles Taylor, *A Secular Age* (Cambridge: Harvard University Press, 2007); and my own *Unquiet Things: Secularism in the Romantic Age* (Philadelphia: University of Pennsylvania Press, 2015). For a version specific to the eighteenth century and the toleration debates, see my "Common Quiet: Tolerance around 1688," *ELH* 79 (2012): 569–96.

22 Thierry de Duve, "Come on Humans, one more effort if you want to be post-Christian," in *Political Theologies: Public Religions in a Post-Secular World*, ed. Hent de Vries and Lawrence E. Sullivan (New York: Fordham University Press, 2006). De Duve's title echoes Sade's 1795 pamphlet "Frenchman, one more effort if you want to be Republicans."

23 For Target, see Aulard, *Christianity and the French Revolution*, 48.

24 Joan B. Landes, *Women and the Public Sphere in the Age of the French Revolution* (Ithaca: Cornell University Press, 1988); Lynn Hunt, *The Family Romance of the French Revolution* (Berkeley: University of California Press, 1992). Shelley himself deployed such imagery in the feminized figure of Hope in *Mask of Anarchy* and more ambivalently in Cythna's revolutionary leadership in *Laon and Cythna*. The sexual energy in Wordsworth's description of the revolutionary fête is also not hard to discern: "the great Spousals newly solemniz'd" (*Prelude*, book 6, line 396) – the poet "upon the bosom of the gentle Soane" (386). Historians have remarked on the Revolution's enthusiasm for sex; unmentioned in the *Prelude* – or mentioned only elliptically, in the "Vandracour and Julia" episode – is that, on his next trip to France, Wordsworth himself had a love affair with Annette Vallon.

25 These twin aspects of the Radical Enlightenment and their legacy for the Revolution are laid out in great detail in Jonathan I. Israel's *Radical Enlightenment: Philosophy and the Making of Modernity, 1650–1750* (Oxford: Oxford University Press, 2001), albeit without a shred of self-consciousness that a tradition jointly culminating in Robespierre and Sade might not look to everyone like an unalloyed triumph. See especially Israel's chapter on "Women, Philosophy, and Sexuality," in *Radical Enlightenment*, 82–96. As manifested in the Shelley circle, unfortunately, free love largely recapitulated the gendered categories and the naïveté of the Revolution itself. Shelley's poetry is, in this case, more ethically insightful than its author.

26 M.H. Abrams, *Natural Supernaturalism: Tradition and Revolution in Romantic Literature* (New York: Norton, 1971), 12.

27 Ibid., 12, 13. For a critique, see my *The Book of God: Secularization and Design in the Romantic Era* (Philadelphia: University of Pennsylvania Press, 2007), 1.

28 Abrams, *Natural Supernaturalism*, 12.

29 Ibid., 202, 199.

30 Hannah Arendt, *The Human Condition*, 2nd ed. (Chicago: University of Chicago Press, 1998), 242.

31 Love, Shelley writes in *A Defense*, is "a going out of our own nature, and an identification of ourselves with the beautiful which exists in thought, action, or person, not our own." *Shelley's Poetry and Prose*, 2nd ed., ed. Donald H. Reiman and Neil Fraistat (New York: Norton, 2002), 517. For a helpful account of Shelley's shifting ideas of love, including in *Prometheus Unbound*, see Richard Isomaki, "Love as Cause in *Prometheus Unbound*," *Studies in English Literature, 1500–1900* 29, no. 4 (1989): 655–73. Isomaki is committed to an idealist reading of *Prometheus Unbound* in which its events happen simultaneously, whereas my interpretation of the poem depends upon a temporal sequencing. In any case, even if act 1 and act 2 "happen," in some sense, simultaneously, as Stuart Curran, for example, argues, the reader experiences them sequentially – that is to say, within time. See Curran, *Shelley's Annus Mirabilis*, 103.

32 Shelley wrote his prose fragment "On Love" in 1818, just before beginning work on act 2. In that fragment, we read of the quasi-Platonic search of the Self for an Other: "we are born into the world and there is something within us that from the instant that we live and move thirsts after its likeness" (*Shelley's Poetry and Prose*, 504). So conceived, Asia is merely a projection of Prometheus, his mirror or ego-ideal much as Jupiter had been, and, indeed, her passivity as she wakes from sleep at the beginning of act 2 suggests as much. But, as the play develops, it becomes clear that Asia is neither Love personified (though she does recall Venus in some respects) nor merely the emotional, feminine counterpart to Prometheus's rational masculinity. It is Asia, after all, who engages in philosophical debate with Demogorgon and who initiates the chief events of the drama.

33 Here, I follow the account in Jerrold E. Hogle, *Shelley's Process: Radical Transference and the Development of His Major Works* (New York and Oxford: Oxford University Press, 1988), 183–5.

34 The ease with which love can be co-opted by nationalism is presumably why Arendt insisted in *The Human Condition* that love was "antipolitical": all political forms of love seemed dangerous to her.

35 This is what Talal Asad nicely terms "the freedom and bondage that comes from *being in love*." Asad, "Trying to Understand French Secularism," in De Vries and Sullivan, *Political Theologies*, 517.

36 Emily Apter, *Against World Literature: On the Politics of Untranslatability* (London: Verso Books, 2014), 2.

37 Bundock, *Romantic Prophesy and the Resistance to Historicism*, 8. On uneven development, see James Chandler, *England in 1819: The Politics of Literary Culture and the Case of Romantic Historicism* (Chicago: University of Chicago Press, 1998).

38 Reinhart Koselleck, *Futures Past: On the Semantics of Historical Time*, trans. Keith Tribe (New York: Columbia University Press, 2004), 56.

39 Ibid., 18.

40 Earl Wasserman, *Shelley: A Critical Reading*, 325.

41 Edmund Burke, *Reflections on the Revolution in France*, ed. L.G. Mitchell (Oxford: Oxford University Press, 1993), 46; McManners, *Church and Society*, 743.

42 Aulard, *Christianity and the French Revolution*, 49.

43 McManners, *Church and Society*, 744. See also Aulard, *Christianity and the French Revolution*: "They were received with a unanimous burst of gratitude, with an enthusiasm which became contagious" (47–8).

44 This is Catherine Morland's response when confronted with the claim that she has given encouragement to a suitor for whom she claims to feel no interest. For an elaboration of this idea in the context of Romanticism more generally, see William H. Galperin, *The History of Missed Opportunities: British Romanticism and the Emergence of the Everyday* (Stanford: Stanford University Press, 2017), esp. 73–99.

45 Ibid.

46 See McManners, *The French Revolution and the Church*: "This marked the end of national unity, and the beginning of civil war" (38). See also Joseph F. Byrnes, *Priests of the French Revolution: Saints and Renegades in a New Political Era* (University Park: Penn State University Press, 2014), 42–3; Burleigh, *Earthly Powers*; and Edward A. Allen, "The 'Patriot' *Curés* of 1789 and the 'Constitutional' *Curés* of 1791: A Comparison," *Church History* 54 (1985): 473–81. The schism created by this decree, writes Michael Burleigh, "lasted for nearly two hundred years" (57). Edward A. Allen writes: "The class of ministering curés were exploited and maligned from all sides, by a great assortment of church people – titheowners, cathedral canons, abbots, priors, and bishops. Their protest, coming as it did amidst the campaign for increased representation of the Third, was a plea for more just representation within the first order as well" (475). Even so, Allen argues, the numbers of patriot *curés* in at least some dioceses were smaller than might be expected, given their historical ill-usage. See also the famously reactionary account of Abbé Barruel: *The History of the Clergy during the French Revolution. A Work Dedicated to the English Nation: By the Abbé Barruel, Almoner to Her Serene Highness the Princess of Conti*, vol. 1 (Dublin: 1794).

47 McManners, *Church and Society*, 744. See, for example, Robespierre's apparently common-sense proclamation that "since ecclesiastical officials have been instituted for the good of mankind and the well-being of the people, it naturally follows that the people should choose them"; quoted in Crook, "Citizen Bishops," 956.

48 Ashis Nandy, "The Politics of Secularism and the Recovery of Religious Tolerance," in *Secularism and Its Critics*, ed. Rajeev Bhargava (New York: Oxford University Press, 2005), 321–44, esp. 324–5.

49 See Raymond Schwab, *The Oriental Renaissance: Europe's Rediscovery of India and the East, 1680–1880* (New York: Columbia University Press, 1984), 13. For a critical account, see Aamir R. Mufti, "Orientalism and the Institution of World Literatures," *Critical Inquiry* 36 (Spring 2010): 458–93.

Contributors

Sharon Achinstein is the Sir William Osler Professor of English at Johns Hopkins University. She is the author of *Milton and the Revolutionary Reader* (1994, winner of the 1995 James Holly Hanford Award for Best Book, Milton Society of America) and *Literature and Dissent in Milton's England* (2003), and co-editor of *Milton and Toleration* (winner of the 2008 Irene M. Samuel Award, Milton Society of America). She is currently working on an edition of Milton's writings on divorce.

David Alvarez is Associate Professor and Chair of the Department of English at DePauw University. Recent publications include "Reading Locke after Shaftesbury: Feeling Our Way towards a Postsecular Genealogy of Religious Tolerance," in *Mind, Body, Motion, Matter: Eighteenth Century British and French Literary Perspectives* (2016). He has also published essays on religious toleration in Mary Astell and Daniel Defoe, and is working on a book project titled "The Passions and Politics of Religious Tolerance in the English Enlightenment."

Mark Canuel is Professor of English at the University of Illinois, Chicago. His 2002 monograph, *Religion, Toleration, and British Writing*, maps a transformation in the relation between ideas of government, secularism, and the literary during the Romantic period through a broad range of texts ranging from the Gothic novel to Byron's drama. He is currently working on a project titled "British Romanticism and the Fate of Progress."

Alison Conway is Professor of English and Gender and Women's Studies at the University of British Columbia, Okanagan. She is the author of *Private Interests: Women, Portraiture, and the Visual Culture of the English Novel, 1709–1791* (2001) and *The Protestant Whore: Courtesan Narrative and Religious Controversy in England, 1680–1750* (2010), and co-editor, with Mary Helen McMurran, of *Mind, Body, Motion, Matter: Eighteenth-Century British and French*

Literary Perspectives (2016). Her current book project investigates interfaith marriage and the British eighteenth-century novel.

Humberto Garcia is Associate Professor of English at the University of California, Merced. His work investigates the close ties between British Romanticism and Islam, most comprehensively in his *Islam and the English Enlightenment, 1670–1840* (2012). His current book project is titled "England Re-Oriented: Indian Occidentalism in English Literary Culture, 1770–1830."

Corrinne Harol is Associate Professor of English and Film Studies at the University of Alberta. She is the author of *Enlightened Virginity in Eighteenth-Century Literature* (2006), and editor of a special edition of *Restoration* titled, *1688: Literature, Politics, and the Long Restoration* (2015). Her current book project is titled "1688: The Fiction of Politics and the Politics of Fiction."

Colin Jager is Professor of English and Director of the Center for Cultural Analysis at Rutgers University. His two books, *The Book of God: Secularization and Design in the Romantic Era* (2007) and *Unquiet Things: Secularism in the Romantic Age* (2015), rethink secular modernity in relation to the presence of persistent religious ideas – such as the idea of design – and to Romantic literature's "mood" as an outcome of secular-religious negotiations in the period.

Andrew McKendry is Associate Professor of English at Nord University. His most recent work has appeared in *Eighteenth-Century Studies* and *Studies in Romanticism,* and he has also published essays on Dissent and education. His current book project examines the conceptual history of toleration, in particular how seventeenth-century attitudes towards religious difference were inflected by shifting paradigms of disability.

Joanna Picciotto is Associate Professor of English at the University of California, Berkeley. She is the editor of a special issue of *The Journal of Medieval and Early Modern Studies* titled "Devotion and Intellectual Labor" (2014), as well as a monograph, *Labors of Innocence in Early Modern England* (2010). Her current book project, "Union without End: The Physico-Theological Vision," moves beyond the seventeenth century, tracing engagements with natural theology into the present.

Elena Russo is Professor of French at Johns Hopkins University. Her monographs include *Styles of Enlightenment: Taste, Politics and Authorship in Eighteenth-Century France* (2007) and *Skeptical Selves: Empiricism and Modernity in the French Novel* (1996). She has also published extensively on authors such as Diderot, Montesquieu, and Marivaux. She recently presented a paper,

"On Giving Offence," at the American Society for Eighteenth-Century Studies as part of a session titled "Tolerance, Free Speech, and Civility from Voltaire to Charlie Hebdo – II: On Incivility and Enlightenment." Her current book project explores the relationship between aesthetics, culture, and theology.

Paul Yachnin is the Tomlinson Professor of Shakespeare Studies at McGill University. His publications include *Shakespeare's World of Words* (2014), *Making Publics in Early Modern Europe: People, Things, Forms of Knowledge* (2010), and *Stage-wrights: Shakespeare, Jonson, Middleton and the Making of Theatrical Value* (1997). He is the director of the "Early Modern Conversions: Religions, Cultures, Cognitive Ecologies" project, funded by a SSHRC Partnership Grant, 2013–18.

Index